MW01709065

Wiley Study Guide for 2015 Level I CFA Exam

Volume 1: Ethics & Quantitative Methods

Thousands of candidates from more than 100 countries have relied on these Study Guides to pass the CFA® Exam. Covering every Learning Outcome Statement (LOS) on the exam, these review materials are an invaluable tool for anyone who wants a deep-dive review of all the concepts, formulas and topics required to pass.

Originally published by Elan Guides, this study material was produced by CFA® Charterholders, CFA® Institute members, and investment professionals. In 2014 John Wiley & Sons, Inc. purchased the rights to Elan Guides content, and now this material is part of the Wiley Efficient Learning suite of exam review products. For more information, contact us at info@efficientlearning.com.

Wiley Study Guide for 2015 Level I CFA Exam

Volume 1: Ethics & Quantitative Methods

WILEY

Copyright © 2015 by John Wiley & Sons, Inc. All rights reserved.

Published by John Wiley & Sons, Inc., Hoboken, New Jersey.

The material was previously published by Elan Guides.

Published simultaneously in Canada.

No part of this publication may be reproduced, stored in a retrieval system, or transmitted in any form or by any means, electronic, mechanical, photocopying, recording, scanning, or otherwise, except as permitted under Section 107 or 108 of the 1976 United States Copyright Act, without either the prior written permission of the Publisher, or authorization through payment of the appropriate per-copy fee to the Copyright Clearance Center, Inc., 222 Rosewood Drive, Danvers, MA 01923, (978) 750-8400, fax (978) 646-8600, or on the Web at www.copyright.com. Requests to the Publisher for permission should be addressed to the Permissions Department, John Wiley & Sons, Inc., 111 River Street, Hoboken, NJ 07030, (201) 748-6011, fax (201) 748-6008, or online at http://www.wiley.com/go/permissions.

Limit of Liability/Disclaimer of Warranty: While the publisher and author have used their best efforts in preparing this book, they make no representations or warranties with respect to the accuracy or completeness of the contents of this book and specifically disclaim any implied warranties of merchantability or fitness for a particular purpose. No warranty may be created or extended by sales representatives or written sales materials. The advice and strategies contained herein may not be suitable for your situation. You should consult with a professional where appropriate. Neither the publisher nor author shall be liable for any loss of profit or any other commercial damages, including but not limited to special, incidental, consequential, or other damages.

For general information on our other products and services or for technical support, please contact our Customer Care Department within the United States at (800) 762-2974, outside the United States at (317) 572-3993 or fax (317) 572-4002.

Wiley publishes in a variety of print and electronic formats and by print-on-demand. Some material included with standard print versions of this book may not be included in e-books or in print-on-demand. If this book refers to media such as a CD or DVD that is not included in the version you purchased, you may download this material at http://booksupport.wiley.com. For more information about Wiley products, visit www.wiley.com.

Required CFA Institute ® disclaimer:

"CFA® and Chartered Financial Analyst® are trademarks owned by CFA Institute. CFA Institute (formerly the Association for Investment Management and Research) does not endorse, promote, review or warrant the accuracy of the products or services offered by John Wiley & Sons, Inc.

Certain materials contained within this text are the copyrighted property of CFA Institute. The following is the copyright disclosure for these materials:

"Copyright 2014, CFA Institute. Reproduced and republished with permission from CFA Institute. All rights reserved."

These materials may not be copied without written permission from the author. The unauthorized duplication of these notes is a violation of global copyright laws and the CFA Institute Code of Ethics. Your assistance in pursuing potential violators of this law is greatly appreciated. "Copyright (year), CFA Institute. Reproduced and republished with permission from CFA Institute. All rights reserved."

Disclaimer: John Wiley & Sons, Inc.'s study materials should be used in conjunction with the original readings as set forth by CFA Institute in the 2014 CFA Level 1 Curriculum. The information contained in this book covers topics contained in the readings referenced by CFA Institute and is believed to be accurate. However, their accuracy cannot be guaranteed.

ISBN 978-1-119-03255-7

Contents

© 2015 Wiley

© 2015 Wiley

Study Session 1: Ethical and Professional Standards

© 2015 Wiley

Reading 1: Code of Ethics and Standards of Professional Conduct

LESSON 1: CODE OF ETHICS AND STANDARDS OF PROFESSIONAL CONDUCT

LOS 1a: Describe the structure of the CFA Institute Professional Conduct Program and the process for the enforcement of the Code and Standards.

Vol 1, pp 9–10

CFA Institute Professional Conduct Program

All CFA Institute members and candidates enrolled in the CFA Program are required to comply with the Code and Standards. The CFA Institute Board of Governors maintains oversight and responsibility for the Professional Conduct Program (PCP), which, in conjunction with the Disciplinary Review Committee (DRC), is responsible for enforcement of the Code and Standards. The DRC is a volunteer committee of CFA charterholders who serve on panels to review conduct and partner with Professional Conduct staff to establish and review professional conduct policies. The CFA Institute Bylaws and Rules of Procedure for Professional Conduct (Rules of Procedure) form the basic structure for enforcing the Code and Standards. The Professional Conduct division is also responsible for enforcing testing policies of other CFA Institute education programs as well as the professional conduct of Certificate in Investment Performance Measurement (CIPM) certificates.

Professional Conduct inquiries come from a number of sources.

- Members and candidates must self-disclose on the annual Professional Conduct Statement all matters that question their professional conduct, such as involvement in civil litigation or a criminal investigation or being the subject of a written complaint.
- Written complaints received by Professional Conduct staff can bring about an investigation.
- CFA Institute staff may become aware of questionable conduct by a member or candidate through the media, regulatory notices, or another public source.
- Candidate conduct is monitored by proctors, who complete reports on candidates suspected to have violated testing rules on exam day.
- CFA Institute may also conduct analyses of scores and exam materials after the exam, as well as monitor online and social media to detect disclosure of confidential exam information.

When an inquiry is initiated, the Professional Conduct staff conducts an investigation that may include:

- Requesting a written explanation from the member or candidate.
- Interviewing the member or candidate, complaining parties, and third parties.
- Collecting documents and records relevant to the investigation.

Upon reviewing the material obtained during the investigation, the Professional Conduct staff may:

- Take no disciplinary action.
- Issue a cautionary letter.
- Continue proceedings to discipline the member or candidate.

© 2015 Wiley

If the Professional Conduct staff believes a violation of the Code and Standards or testing policies has occurred, the member or candidate has the opportunity to reject or accept any charges and the proposed sanctions. If the member or candidate does not accept the charges and proposed sanction, the matter is referred to a panel composed of DRC members. Panels review materials and presentations from Professional Conduct staff and from the member or candidate. The panel's task is to determine whether a violation of the Code and Standards or testing policies occurred and, if so, what sanction should be imposed.

Sanctions imposed by CFA Institute may have significant consequences; they include public censure, suspension of membership and use of the CFA designation, and revocation of the CFA charter. Candidates enrolled in the CFA Program who have violated the Code and Standards or testing policies may be suspended or prohibited from further participation in the CFA Program.

Adoption of the Code and Standards

The Code and Standards apply to individual members of CFA Institute and candidates in the CFA Program. CFA Institute does encourage firms to adopt the Code and Standards, however, as part of their code of ethics. Those who claim compliance should fully understand the requirements of each of the principles of the Code and Standards.

Once a party—nonmember or firm—ensures its code of ethics meets the principles of the Code and Standards, that party should make the following statement whenever claiming compliance:

"[Insert name of party] claims compliance with the CFA Institute Code of Ethics and Standards of Professional Conduct. This claim has not been verified by CFA Institute."

CFA Institute welcomes public acknowledgment, when appropriate, that firms are complying with the CFA Institute Code of Ethics and Standards of Professional Conduct and encourages firms to notify it of the adoption plans.

CFA Institute has also published the Asset Manager Code of Professional Conduct, which is designed, in part, to help asset managers comply with the regulations mandating codes of ethics for investment advisers. Whereas the Code and Standards are aimed at individual investment professionals who are members of CFA Institute or candidates in the CFA Program, the Asset Manager Code was drafted specifically for firms. The Asset Manager Code provides specific, practical guidelines for asset managers in the following areas:

- Loyalty to clients.
- The investment process.
- Trading.
- Compliance.
- Performance evaluation.
- Disclosure.

Why Ethics Matters

Ethics can be defined as a set of moral principles or rules of conduct that provide guidance for our behavior when it affects others. Widely acknowledged fundamental ethical principles include honesty, fairness, diligence, and care and respect for others. Ethical

© 2015 Wiley

conduct follows those principles and balances self-interest with both the direct and the indirect consequences of that behavior for other people.

Not only does unethical behavior by individuals have serious personal consequences—ranging from job loss and reputational damage to fines and even jail—but unethical conduct from market participants, investment professionals, and those who service investors can damage investor trust and thereby impair the sustainability of the global capital markets as a whole. Unfortunately, there seems to be an unending parade of stories bringing to light accounting frauds and manipulations, Ponzi schemes, insider-trading scandals, and other misdeeds. Not surprisingly, this has led to erosion in public confidence in investment professionals. Empirical evidence from numerous surveys documents the low standing in the eyes of the investing public of banks and financial services firms—the very institutions that are entrusted with the economic well-being and retirement security of society.

Governments and regulators have historically tried to combat misconduct in the industry through regulatory reform, with various levels of success. Global capital markets are highly regulated to protect investors and other market participants. However, compliance with regulation alone is insufficient to fully earn investor trust. Individuals and firms must develop a "culture of integrity" that permeates all levels of operations and promotes the ethical principles of stewardship of investor assets and working in the best interests of clients, above and beyond strict compliance with the law. A strong ethical culture that helps honest, ethical people engage in ethical behavior will foster the trust of investors, lead to robust global capital markets, and ultimately benefit society.

LOS 1b: State the six components of the Code of Ethics and the seven Standards of Professional Conduct. **Vol 1, pp 15–19**

CFA INSTITUTE CODE OF ETHICS AND STANDARDS OF PROFESSIONAL CONDUCT

Preamble

The CFA Institute Code of Ethics and Standards of Professional Conduct are fundamental to the values of CFA Institute and essential to achieving its mission to lead the investment profession globally by promoting the highest standards of ethics, education, and professional excellence for the ultimate benefit of society. High ethical standards are critical to maintaining the public's trust in financial markets and in the investment profession. Since their creation in the 1960s, the Code and Standards have promoted the integrity of CFA Institute members and served as a model for measuring the ethics of investment professionals globally, regardless of job function, cultural differences, or local laws and regulations. All CFA Institute members (including holders of the Chartered Financial Analyst [CFA] designation) and CFA candidates have the personal responsibility to embrace and uphold the provisions of the Code and Standards and are encouraged to notify their employer of this responsibility. Violations may result in disciplinary sanctions by CFA Institute. Sanctions can include revocation of membership, revocation of candidacy in the CFA Program, and revocation of the right to use the CFA designation.

The Code of Ethics

Members of CFA Institute (including CFA charterholders) and candidates for the CFA designation ("Members and Candidates") must:

- Act with integrity, competence, diligence, and respect and in an ethical manner with the public, clients, prospective clients, employers, employees, colleagues in the investment profession, and other participants in the global capital markets.
- Place the integrity of the investment profession and the interests of clients above their own personal interests.
- Use reasonable care and exercise independent professional judgment when conducting investment analysis, making investment recommendations, taking investment actions, and engaging in other professional activities.
- Practice and encourage others to practice in a professional and ethical manner that will reflect credit on themselves and the profession.
- Promote the integrity and viability of the global capital markets for the ultimate benefit of society.
- Maintain and improve their professional competence and strive to maintain and improve the competence of other investment professionals.

Standards of Professional Conduct

I. Professionalism

A. Knowledge of the Law
B. Independence and Objectivity
C. Misrepresentation
D. Misconduct

II. Integrity of Capital Markets

A. Material Nonpublic Information
B. Market Manipulation

III. Duties to Clients

A. Loyalty, Prudence, and Care
B. Fair Dealing
C. Suitability
D. Performance Presentation
E. Preservation of Confidentiality

IV. Duties to Employers

A. Loyalty
B. Additional Compensation Arrangements
C. Responsibilities of Supervisors

V. Investment Analysis, Recommendations and Actions

A. Diligence and Reasonable Basis
B. Communication with Clients and Prospective Clients
C. Record Retention

VI. Conflicts of Interest

A. Disclosure of Conflicts
B. Priority of Transactions
C. Referral Fees

© 2015 Wiley

VII. Responsibilities as a CFA Institute Member or CFA Candidate

A. Conduct as members and candidates in the CFA program

B. Reference to CFA Institute, the CFA Designation, and the CFA Program

We discuss the next four LOS together to make for easier reading and understanding. They are covered in Volume 1, pages 22–176 of the Level I curriculum. The Code of Ethics and the Standards of Practice apply to *all* candidates in the CFA program and members of CFA Institute. All examples and other extracts from the Standards of Practice Handbook that are included in this Reading are reprinted with permission of CFA Institute.

LOS 1c: Explain the ethical responsibilities required by the Code and Standards, including the subsections of each Standard. **Vol 1, pp 15–19**

© 2015 Wiley

Reading 2: Guidance for Standards I-VII

LESSON 1: STANDARD I: PROFESSIONALISM

A. Knowledge of the Law
B. Independence and Objectivity
C. Misrepresentation
D. Misconduct

LOS 2a: Demonstrate the application of the Code of Ethics and Standards of Professional Conduct to situations involving issues of professional integrity. **Vol 1, pp 21–176**

LOS 2b: Distinguish between conduct that conforms to the Code and Standards and conduct that violates the Code and Standards. **Vol 1, pp 21–176**

LOS 2c: Recommend practices and procedures designed to prevent violations of the Code of Ethics and Standards of Professional Conduct. **Vol 1, pp 21–176**

Standard I(A): Knowledge of the Law

The Standard

Members and candidates must understand and comply with all applicable laws, rules, and regulations (including the CFA Institute Code of Ethics and Standards of Professional Conduct) of any government, regulatory organization, licensing agency, or professional association governing their professional activities. In the event of conflict, members and candidates must comply with the more strict law, rule, or regulation. Members and candidates must not knowingly participate or assist in and must dissociate from any violation of such laws, rules, or regulations.

Guidance

- Members and candidates must understand the applicable laws and regulations of the countries and jurisdictions where they engage in professional activities.
- On the basis of their reasonable and good faith understanding, members and candidates must comply with the laws and regulations that directly govern their professional activities and resulting outcomes and that protect the interests of the clients.
- When questions arise, members and candidates should know their firm's policies and procedures for accessing compliance guidance.
- During times of changing regulations, members and candidates must remain vigilant in maintaining their knowledge of the requirements for their professional activities.

Relationship between the Code and Standards and Applicable Law

- When applicable law and the Code and Standards require different conduct, members and candidates must follow the stricter of the applicable law or the Code and Standards.
    - "Applicable law" is the law that governs the member's or candidate's conduct. Which law applies will depend on the particular facts and circumstances of each case.
    - The "more strict" law or regulation is the law or regulation that imposes greater restrictions on the action of the member or candidate, or calls for the member or candidate to exert a greater degree of action that protects the interests of investors.

© 2015 Wiley

NS: country with no securities laws or regulations

LS: country with ***less*** strict securities laws and regulations than the Code and Standards

MS: country with ***more*** strict securities laws and regulations than the Code and Standards

Global Application of the Code and Standards

Members and candidates who practice in multiple jurisdictions may be subject to varied securities laws and regulations. The following chart provides illustrations involving a member who may be subject to the securities laws and regulations of three different types of countries:

Applicable Law	Duties	Explanation
Member resides in NS country, does business in LS country; LS law applies.	Member must adhere to the Code and Standards.	Because applicable law is less strict than the Code and Standards, the member must adhere to the Code and Standards.
Member resides in NS country, does business in MS country; MS law applies.	Member must adhere to the law of MS country.	Because applicable law is stricter than the Code and Standards, member must adhere to the more strict applicable law.
Member resides in LS country, does business in NS country; LS law applies.	Member must adhere to the Code and Standards.	Because applicable law is less strict than the Code and Standards, member must adhere to the Code and Standards.
Member resides in LS country, does business in MS country; MS law applies.	Member must adhere to the law of MS country.	Because applicable law is stricter than the Code and Standards, member must adhere to the more strict applicable law.
Member resides in LS country, does business in NS country; LS law applies, but it states that law of locality where business is conducted governs.	Member must adhere to the Code and Standards.	Because applicable law states that the law of the locality where the business is conducted governs and there is no local law, the member must adhere to the Code and Standards.
Member resides in LS country, does business in MS country; LS law applies, but it states that law of locality where business is conducted governs.	Member must adhere to the law of MS country.	Because applicable law of the locality where the business is conducted governs and local law is stricter than the Code and Standards, member must adhere to the more strict applicable law.
Member resides in MS country, does business in LS country; MS law applies.	Member must adhere to the law of MS country.	Because applicable law is stricter than the Code and Standards, member must adhere to the more strict applicable law.

© 2015 Wiley

Applicable Law	Duties	Explanation
Member resides in MS country, does business in LS country; MS law applies, but it states that law of locality where business is conducted governs.	Member must adhere to the Code and Standards.	Because applicable law states that the law of the locality where the business is conducted governs and local law is less strict than the Code and Standards, member must adhere to the Code and Standards.
Member resides in MS country, does business in LS country with a client who is a citizen of LS country; MS law applies, but it states that the law of the client's home country governs.	Member must adhere to the Code and Standards.	Because applicable law states that the law of the client's home country governs (which is less strict than the Code and Standards), member must adhere to the Code and Standards.
Member resides in MS country, does business in LS country with a client who is a citizen of MS country; MS law applies, but it states that the law of the client's home country governs.	Member must adhere to the law of MS country.	Because applicable law states that the law of the client's home country governs and the law of the client's home country is stricter than the Code and Standards, the member must adhere to the more strict applicable law.

Participation in or Association with Violations by Others

- Members and candidates are responsible for violations in which they *knowingly* participate or assist. Standard I(A) applies when members and candidates know or should know that their conduct may contribute to a violation of applicable laws, rules, or regulations or the Code and Standards.
- If a member or candidate has reasonable grounds to believe that imminent or ongoing client or employer activities are illegal or unethical, the member or candidate must dissociate, or separate, from the activity.
- In extreme cases, dissociation may require a member or candidate to leave his or her employment.
- Members and candidates may take the following intermediate steps to dissociate from ethical violations of others when direct discussions with the person or persons committing the violation are unsuccessful.
    - Attempt to stop the behavior by bringing it to the attention of the employer through a supervisor or the firm's compliance department.
    - If this attempt is unsuccessful, then members and candidates have a responsibility to step away and dissociate from the activity. Inaction combined with continuing association with those involved in illegal or unethical conduct may be construed as participation or assistance in the illegal or unethical conduct.

© 2015 Wiley

- CFA Institute strongly encourages members and candidates to report potential violations of the Code and Standards committed by fellow members and candidates, although a failure to report is less likely to be construed as a violation than a failure to dissociate from unethical conduct.

Investment Products and Applicable Laws

- Members and candidates involved in creating or maintaining investment services or investment products or packages of securities and/or derivatives should be mindful of where these products or packages will be sold as well as their places of origination.
- They should understand the applicable laws and regulations of the countries or regions of origination and expected sale, and should make reasonable efforts to review whether associated firms that are distributing products or services developed by their employing firms also abide by the laws and regulations of the countries and regions of distribution.
- Finally, they should undertake the necessary due diligence when transacting cross-border business to understand the multiple applicable laws and regulations in order to protect the reputation of their firms and themselves.

Recommended Procedures for Compliance

Members and Candidates

Suggested methods by which members and candidates can acquire and maintain understanding of applicable laws, rules, and regulations include the following:

- Stay informed: Members and candidates should establish or encourage their employers to establish a procedure by which employees are regularly informed about changes in applicable laws, rules, regulations, and case law.
- Review procedures: Members and candidates should review, or encourage their employers to review, the firm's written compliance procedures on a regular basis to ensure that the procedures reflect current law and provide adequate guidance to employees about what is permissible conduct under the law and/or the Code and Standards.
- Maintain current files: Members and candidates should maintain or encourage their employers to maintain readily accessible current reference copies of applicable statutes, rules, regulations, and important cases.

Distribution Area Laws

- Members and candidates should make reasonable efforts to understand the applicable laws—both country and regional—for the countries and regions where their investment products are developed and are most likely to be distributed to clients.

Legal Counsel

- When in doubt about the appropriate action to undertake, it is recommended that a member or candidate seek the advice of compliance personnel or legal counsel concerning legal requirements.

© 2015 Wiley

- If a potential violation is being committed by a fellow employee, it may also be prudent for the member or candidate to seek the advice of the firm's compliance department or legal counsel.

Dissociation

- When dissociating from an activity that violates the Code and Standards, members and candidates should document the violation and urge their firms to attempt to persuade the perpetrator(s) to cease such conduct. Note that in order to dissociate from the conduct, a member or candidate may have to resign his or her employment.

Firms

Members and candidates should encourage their firms to consider the following policies and procedures to support the principles of Standard I(A):

- Develop and/or adopt a code of ethics.
- Provide information on applicable laws.
- Establish procedures for reporting violations.

Application of the Standard

Example 1 (Notification of Known Violations)

Michael Allen works for a brokerage firm and is responsible for an underwriting of securities. A company official gives Allen information indicating that the financial statements Allen filed with the regulator overstate the issuer's earnings. Allen seeks the advice of the brokerage firm's general counsel, who states that it would be difficult for the regulator to prove that Allen has been involved in any wrongdoing.

Comment: Although it is recommended that members and candidates seek the advice of legal counsel, the reliance on such advice does not absolve a member or candidate from the requirement to comply with the law or regulation. Allen should report this situation to his supervisor, seek an independent legal opinion, and determine whether the regulator should be notified of the error.

Example 2 (Dissociating from a Violation)

Lawrence Brown's employer, an investment banking firm, is the principal underwriter for an issue of convertible debentures by the Courtney Company. Brown discovers that the Courtney Company has concealed severe third-quarter losses in its foreign operations. The preliminary prospectus has already been distributed.

Comment: Knowing that the preliminary prospectus is misleading, Brown should report his findings to the appropriate supervisory persons in his firm. If the matter is not remedied and Brown's employer does not dissociate from the underwriting, Brown should sever all his connections with the underwriting. Brown should also seek legal advice to determine whether additional reporting or other action should be taken.

Example 3 (Following the Highest Requirements)

Laura Jameson works for a multinational investment adviser based in the United States. Jameson lives and works as a registered investment adviser in the tiny, but wealthy, island nation of Karramba. Karramba's securities laws state that no investment adviser registered and working in that country can participate in initial public offerings (IPOs) for the adviser's personal account. Jameson, believing that, as a U.S. citizen working for a U.S.–based company, she should comply only with U.S. law, has ignored this Karrambian law. In addition, Jameson believes that as a charterholder, as long as she adheres to the Code and Standards requirement that she disclose her participation in any IPO to her employer and clients when such ownership creates a conflict of interest, she is meeting the highest ethical requirements.

Comment: Jameson is in violation of Standard I(A). As a registered investment adviser in Karramba, Jameson is prevented by Karrambian securities law from participating in IPOs regardless of the law of her home country. In addition, because the law of the country where she is working is stricter than the Code and Standards, she must follow the stricter requirements of the local law rather than the requirements of the Code and Standards.

Example 4 (Reporting Potential Unethical Actions)

Krista Blume is a junior portfolio manager for high-net-worth portfolios at a large global investment manager. She observes a number of new portfolios and relationships coming from a country in Europe where the firm did not have previous business and is told that a broker in that country is responsible for this new business. At a meeting on allocation of research resources to third-party research firms, Blume notes that this broker has been added to the list and is allocated payments for research. However, she knows the portfolios do not invest in securities in the broker's country, and she has not seen any research come from this broker. Blume asks her supervisor about the name being on the list and is told that someone in marketing is receiving the research and that the name being on the list is OK. She believes that what may be going on is that the broker is being paid for new business through the inappropriate research payments, and she wishes to dissociate from the misconduct.

Comment: Blume should follow the firm's policies and procedures for reporting potential unethical activity, which may include discussions with her supervisor or someone in a designated compliance department. She should communicate her concerns appropriately while advocating for disclosure between the new broker relationship and the research payments.

Example 5 (Failure to Maintain Knowledge of the Law)

Colleen White is excited to use new technology to communicate with clients and potential clients. She recently began posting investment information, including performance reports and investment opinions and recommendations, to her Facebook page. In addition, she sends out brief announcements, opinions, and thoughts via her Twitter account (for example, "Prospects for future growth of XYZ company look good! #makingmoney4U"). Prior to White's use of these social media platforms, the

© 2015 Wiley

local regulator had issued new requirements and guidance governing online electronic communication. White's communications appear to conflict with the recent regulatory announcements.

Comment: White is in violation of Standard I(A) because her communications do not comply with the existing guidance and regulation governing use of social media. White must be aware of the evolving legal requirements pertaining to new and dynamic areas of the financial services industry that are applicable to her. She should seek guidance from appropriate, knowledgeable, and reliable sources, such as her firm's compliance department, external service providers, or outside counsel, unless she diligently follows legal and regulatory trends affecting her professional responsibilities.

Standard I(B) Independence and Objectivity

The Standard
Members and candidates must use reasonable care and judgment to achieve and maintain independence and objectivity in their professional activities. Members and candidates must not offer, solicit, or accept any gift, benefit, compensation, or consideration that reasonably could be expected to compromise their own or another's independence and objectivity.

Guidance

- Members and candidates should endeavor to avoid situations that could cause or be perceived to cause a loss of independence or objectivity in recommending investments or taking investment action.
- Modest gifts and entertainment are acceptable, but special care must be taken by members and candidates to resist subtle and not-so-subtle pressures to act in conflict with the interests of their clients. Best practice dictates that members and candidates reject any offer of gift or entertainment that could be expected to threaten their independence and objectivity.
- Receiving a gift, benefit, or consideration from a *client* can be distinguished from gifts given by entities seeking to influence a member or candidate to the detriment of other clients.
- When possible, prior to accepting "bonuses" or gifts from clients, members and candidates should disclose to their employers such benefits offered by clients. If notification is not possible prior to acceptance, members and candidates must disclose to their employer benefits previously accepted from clients.
- Members and candidates are personally responsible for maintaining independence and objectivity when preparing research reports, making investment recommendations, and taking investment action on behalf of clients. Recommendations must convey the member's or candidate's true opinions, free of bias from internal or external pressures, and be stated in clear and unambiguous language.
- When seeking corporate financial support for conventions, seminars, or even weekly society luncheons, the members or candidates responsible for the activities should evaluate both the actual effect of such solicitations on their independence and whether their objectivity might be perceived to be compromised in the eyes of their clients.

© 2015 Wiley

Investment Banking Relationships

- Some sell-side firms may exert pressure on their analysts to issue favorable research reports on current or prospective investment banking clients. Members and candidates must not succumb to such pressures.
- Allowing analysts to work with investment bankers is appropriate only when the conflicts are adequately and effectively managed and disclosed. Firm managers have a responsibility to provide an environment in which analysts are neither coerced nor enticed into issuing research that does not reflect their true opinions. Firms should require public disclosure of actual conflicts of interest to investors.
- Any "firewalls" between the investment banking and research functions must be managed to minimize conflicts of interest. Key elements of enhanced firewalls include:
    - Separate reporting structures for personnel on the research side and personnel on the investment banking side.
    - Compensation arrangements that minimize pressures on research analysts and reward objectivity and accuracy.

Public Companies

- Analysts may be pressured to issue favorable reports and recommendations by the companies they follow. In making an investment recommendation, the analyst is responsible for anticipating, interpreting, and assessing a company's prospects and stock price performance in a factual manner.
- Due diligence in financial research and analysis involves gathering information from a wide variety of sources, including public disclosure documents (such as proxy statements, annual reports, and other regulatory filings) and also company management and investor-relations personnel, suppliers, customers, competitors, and other relevant sources. Research analysts may justifiably fear that companies will limit their ability to conduct thorough research by denying analysts who have "negative" views direct access to company managers and/or barring them from conference calls and other communication venues. This concern may make it difficult for them to conduct the comprehensive research needed to make objective recommendations.

Buy-Side Clients

- Portfolio managers may have significant positions in the security of a company under review. A rating downgrade may adversely affect the portfolio's performance, particularly in the short term, because the sensitivity of stock prices to ratings changes has increased in recent years. A downgrade may also affect the manager's compensation, which is usually tied to portfolio performance. Moreover, portfolio performance is subject to media and public scrutiny, which may affect the manager's professional reputation. Consequently, some portfolio managers implicitly or explicitly support sell-side ratings inflation.
- Portfolio managers have a responsibility to respect and foster the intellectual honesty of sell-side research. Therefore, it is improper for portfolio managers to threaten or engage in retaliatory practices, such as reporting sell-side analysts to the covered company in order to instigate negative corporate reactions.

© 2015 Wiley

Fund Manager and Custodial Relationships

- Research analysts are not the only people who must be concerned with maintaining their independence. Members and candidates who are responsible for hiring and retaining outside managers and third-party custodians should not accepts gifts, entertainment, or travel funding that may be perceived as impairing their decisions.

Credit Rating Agency Opinions

- Members and candidates employed at rating agencies should ensure that procedures and processes at the agencies prevent undue influences from a sponsoring company during the analysis. Members and candidates should abide by their agencies' and the industry's standards of conduct regarding the analytical process and the distribution of their reports.
- When using information provided by credit rating agencies, members and candidates should be mindful of the potential conflicts of interest. And because of the potential conflicts, members and candidates may need to independently validate the rating granted.

Issuer-Paid Research

- Some companies hire analysts to produce research reports in case of lack of coverage from sell-side research, or to increase the company's visibility in financial markets.
- Analysts must engage in thorough, independent, and unbiased analysis and must fully disclose potential conflicts, including the nature of their compensation. It should also be clearly mentioned in the report that the research has been paid for by the subject company. At a minimum, research should include a thorough analysis of the company's financial statements based on publicly disclosed information, benchmarking within a peer group, and industry analysis.
- Analysts must try to limit the type of compensation they accept for conducting research. This compensation can be direct, such as payment based on the conclusions of the report, or more indirect, such as stock warrants or other equity instruments that could increase in value based on positive coverage in the report. In those instances, analysts would have an incentive to avoid negative information or conclusions that would diminish their potential compensation.
- Best practice is for analysts to accept only a flat fee for their work prior to writing the report, without regard to their conclusions or the report's recommendations.

Travel Funding

- The benefits related to accepting paid travel extend beyond the cost savings to the member or candidate and his firm, such as the chance to talk exclusively with the executives of a company or learning more about the investment options provided by an investment organization. Acceptance also comes with potential concerns; for example, members and candidates may be influenced by these discussions when flying on a corporate or chartered jet, or attending sponsored conferences where many expenses, including airfare and lodging, are covered.
- To avoid the appearance of compromising their independence and objectivity, best practice dictates that analysts always use commercial transportation at their expense or at the expense of their firm rather than accept paid travel arrangements from an outside company.

© 2015 Wiley

- In case of unavailability of commercial travel, they may accept modestly arranged travel to participate in appropriate information gathering events, such as a property tour.

Performance Measurement and Attribution

- Members and candidates working within a firm's investment performance measurement department may also be presented with situations that challenge their independence and objectivity. As performance analysts, their analyses may reveal instances where managers may appear to have strayed from their mandate. Additionally, the performance analyst may receive requests to alter the construction of composite indices owing to negative results for a selected account or fund. Members or candidates must not allow internal or external influences to affect their independence and objectivity as they faithfully complete their performance calculation and analysis-related responsibilities.

Influence during the Manager Selection/Procurement Process

- When serving in a hiring capacity, members and candidates should not solicit gifts, contributions, or other compensation that may affect their independence and objectivity. Solicitations do not have to benefit members and candidates personally to conflict with Standard I(B). Requesting contributions to a favorite charity or political organization may also be perceived as an attempt to influence the decision-making process. Additionally, members and candidates serving in a hiring capacity should refuse gifts, donations, and other offered compensation that may be perceived to influence their decision-making process.
- When working to earn a new investment allocation, members and candidates should not offer gifts, contributions, or other compensation to influence the decision of the hiring representative. The offering of these items with the intent to impair the independence and objectivity of another person would not comply with Standard I(B). Such prohibited actions may include offering donations to a charitable organization or political candidate referred by the hiring representative.

Recommended Procedures for Compliance

Members and candidates should adhere to the following practices and should encourage their firms to establish procedures to avoid violations of Standard I(B):

- Protect the integrity of opinions: Members, candidates, and their firms should establish policies stating that every research report concerning the securities of a corporate client should reflect the unbiased opinion of the analyst.
- Create a restricted list: If the firm is unwilling to permit dissemination of adverse opinions about a corporate client, members and candidates should encourage the firm to remove the controversial company from the research universe and put it on a restricted list so that the firm disseminates only factual information about the company.
- Restrict special cost arrangements: When attending meetings at an issuer's headquarters, members and candidates should pay for commercial transportation and hotel charges. No corporate issuer should reimburse members or candidates for air transportation. Members and candidates should encourage issuers to limit the use of corporate aircraft to situations in which commercial transportation is not available or in which efficient movement could not otherwise be arranged.
- Limit gifts: Members and candidates must limit the acceptance of gratuities and/or gifts to token items. Standard I(B) does not preclude customary, ordinary business-related entertainment as long as its purpose is not to influence or reward

© 2015 Wiley

members or candidates. Firms should consider a strict value limit for acceptable gifts that is based on the local or regional customs and should address whether the limit is per gift or an aggregate annual value.

- Restrict investments: Members and candidates should encourage their investment firms to develop formal polices related to employee purchases of equity or equity-related IPOs. Firms should require prior approval for employee participation in IPOs, with prompt disclosure of investment actions taken following the offering. Strict limits should be imposed on investment personnel acquiring securities in private placements.
- Review procedures: Members and candidates should encourage their firms to implement effective supervisory and review procedures to ensure that analysts and portfolio managers comply with policies relating to their personal investment activities.
- Independence policy: Members, candidates, and their firms should establish a formal written policy on the independence and objectivity of research and implement reporting structures and review procedures to ensure that research analysts do not report to and are not supervised or controlled by any department of the firm that could compromise the independence of the analyst.
- Appointed officer: Firms should appoint a senior officer with oversight responsibilities for compliance with the firm's code of ethics and all regulations concerning its business.

Application of the Standard

Example 1 (Research Independence and Intrafirm Pressure)

Walter Fritz is an equity analyst with Hilton Brokerage who covers the mining industry. He has concluded that the stock of Metals & Mining is overpriced at its current level, but he is concerned that a negative research report will hurt the good relationship between Metals & Mining and the investment banking division of his firm. In fact, a senior manager of Hilton Brokerage has just sent him a copy of a proposal his firm has made to Metals & Mining to underwrite a debt offering. Fritz needs to produce a report right away and is concerned about issuing a less-than-favorable rating.

Comment: Fritz's analysis of Metals & Mining must be objective and based solely on consideration of company fundamentals. Any pressure from other divisions of his firm is inappropriate. This conflict could have been eliminated if, in anticipation of the offering, Hilton Brokerage had placed Metals & Mining on a restricted list for its sales force.

Example 2 (Research Independence and Issuer Relationship Pressure)

As in Example 1, Walter Fritz has concluded that Metals & Mining stock is overvalued at its current level, but he is concerned that a negative research report might jeopardize a close rapport that he has nurtured over the years with Metals & Mining's CEO, chief finance officer, and investment relations officer. Fritz is concerned that a negative report might result also in management retaliation—for instance, cutting him off from participating in conference calls when a quarterly earnings release is made, denying him the ability to ask questions on such calls, and/or denying him access to top management for arranging group meetings between Hilton Brokerage clients and top Metals & Mining managers.

© 2015 Wiley

Comment: As in Example 1, Fritz's analysis must be objective and based solely on consideration of company fundamentals. Any pressure from Metals & Mining is inappropriate. Fritz should reinforce the integrity of his conclusions by stressing that his investment recommendation is based on relative valuation, which may include qualitative issues with respect to Metals & Mining's management.

Example 3 (Gifts and Entertainment from Related Party)

Edward Grant directs a large amount of his commission business to a New York–based brokerage house. In appreciation for all the business, the brokerage house gives Grant two tickets to the World Cup in South Africa, two nights at a nearby resort, several meals, and transportation via limousine to the game. Grant fails to disclose receiving this package to his supervisor.

Comment: Grant has violated Standard I(B) because accepting these substantial gifts may impede his independence and objectivity. Every member and candidate should endeavor to avoid situations that might cause or be perceived to cause a loss of independence or objectivity in recommending investments or taking investment action. By accepting the trip, Grant has opened himself up to the accusation that he may give the broker favored treatment in return.

Example 4 (Gifts and Entertainment from Client)

Theresa Green manages the portfolio of Ian Knowlden, a client of Tisbury Investments. Green achieves an annual return for Knowlden that is consistently better than that of the benchmark she and the client previously agreed to. As a reward, Knowlden offers Green two tickets to Wimbledon and the use of Knowlden's flat in London for a week. Green discloses this gift to her supervisor at Tisbury.

Comment: Green is in compliance with Standard I(B) because she disclosed the gift from one of her clients in accordance with the firm's policies. Members and candidates may accept bonuses or gifts from clients as long as they disclose them to their employer because gifts in a client relationship are deemed less likely to affect a member's or candidate's objectivity and independence than gifts in other situations. Disclosure is required, however, so that supervisors can monitor such situations to guard against employees favoring a gift-giving client to the detriment of other fee-paying clients (such as by allocating a greater proportion of IPO stock to the gift-giving client's portfolio).

Best practices for monitoring include comparing the transaction costs of the Knowlden account with the costs of other accounts managed by Green and other similar accounts within Tisbury. The supervisor could also compare the performance returns with the returns of other clients with the same mandate. This comparison will assist in determining whether a pattern of favoritism by Green is disadvantaging other Tisbury clients or the possibility that this favoritism could affect her future behavior.

© 2015 Wiley

Example 5 (Research Independence and Compensation Arrangements)

Javier Herrero recently left his job as a research analyst for a large investment adviser. While looking for a new position, he was hired by an investor-relations firm to write a research report on one of its clients, a small educational software company. The investor-relations firm hopes to generate investor interest in the technology company. The firm will pay Herrero a flat fee plus a bonus if any new investors buy stock in the company as a result of Herrero's report.

Comment: If Herrero accepts this payment arrangement, he will be in violation of Standard I(B) because the compensation arrangement can reasonably be expected to compromise his independence and objectivity. Herrero will receive a bonus for attracting investors, which provides an incentive to draft a positive report regardless of the facts and to ignore or play down any negative information about the company. Herrero should accept only a flat fee that is not tied to the conclusions or recommendations of the report. Issuer-paid research that is objective and unbiased can be done under the right circumstances as long as the analyst takes steps to maintain his or her objectivity and includes in the report proper disclosures regarding potential conflicts of interest.

Example 6 (Influencing Manager Selection Decisions)

Adrian Mandel, CFA, is a senior portfolio manager for ZZYY Capital Management who oversees a team of investment professionals who manage labor union pension funds. A few years ago, ZZYY sought to win a competitive asset manager search to manage a significant allocation of the pension fund of the United Doughnut and Pretzel Bakers Union (UDPBU). UDPBU's investment board is chaired by a recognized key decision maker and long-time leader of the union, Ernesto Gomez. To improve ZZYY's chances of winning the competition, Mandel made significant monetary contributions to Gomez's union reelection campaign fund. Even after ZZYY was hired as a primary manager of the pension, Mandel believed that his firm's position was not secure. Mandel continued to contribute to Gomez's reelection campaign chest as well as to entertain lavishly the union leader and his family at top restaurants on a regular basis. All of Mandel's outlays were routinely handled as marketing expenses reimbursed by ZZYY's expense accounts and were disclosed to his senior management as being instrumental in maintaining a strong close relationship with an important client.

Comment: Mandel not only offered but actually gave monetary gifts, benefits, and other considerations that reasonably could be expected to compromise Gomez's objectivity. Therefore, Mandel was in violation of Standard I(B).

Example 7 (Influencing Manager Selection Decisions)

Adrian Mandel, CFA, had heard about the manager search competition for the UDPBU Pension Fund through a broker/dealer contact. The contact told him that a well-known retired professional golfer, Bobby "The Bear" Finlay, who had become a licensed broker/dealer serving as a pension consultant, was orchestrating the UDPBU manager search. Finlay had gained celebrity status with several labor union pension fund boards by entertaining their respective board members and regaling them with colorful stories

© 2015 Wiley

of fellow pro golfers' antics in clubhouses around the world. Mandel decided to improve ZZYY's chances of being invited to participate in the search competition by befriending Finlay to curry his favor. Knowing Finlay's love of entertainment, Mandel wined and dined Finlay at high-profile bistros where Finlay could glow in the fan recognition lavished on him by all the other patrons. Mandel's endeavors paid off handsomely when Finlay recommended to the UDPBU board that ZZYY be entered as one of three finalist asset management firms in its search.

Comment: Mandel lavished gifts, benefits, and other considerations in the form of expensive entertainment that could reasonably be expected to influence the consultant to recommend the hiring of his firm. Therefore, Mandel was in violation of Standard I(B).

Example 8 (Fund Manager Relationships)

Amie Scott is a performance analyst within her firm with responsibilities for analyzing the performance of external managers. While completing her quarterly analysis, Scott notices a change in one manager's reported composite construction. The change concealed the bad performance of a particularly large account by placing that account into a new residual composite. This change allowed the manager to remain at the top of the list of manager performance. Scott knows her firm has a large allocation to this manager, and the fund's manager is a close personal friend of the CEO. She needs to deliver her final report but is concerned with pointing out the composite change.

Comment: Scott would be in violation of Standard I(B) if she did not disclose the change in her final report. The analysis of managers' performance should not be influenced by personal relationships or the size of the allocation to the outside managers. By not including the change, Scott would not be providing an independent analysis of the performance metrics for her firm.

Example 9 (Intrafirm Pressure)

Jill Stein is head of performance measurement for her firm. During the last quarter, many members of the organization's research department were removed because of the poor quality of their recommendations. The subpar research caused one larger account holder to experience significant underperformance, which resulted in the client withdrawing his money after the end of the quarter. The head of sales requests that Stein remove this account from the firm's performance composite because the performance decline can be attributed to the departed research team and not the client's adviser.

Comment: Pressure from other internal departments can create situations that cause a member or candidate to violate the Code and Standards. Stein must maintain her independence and objectivity and refuse to exclude specific accounts from the firm's performance composites to which they belong. As long as the client invested under a strategy similar to that of the defined composite, it cannot be excluded because of the poor stock selections that led to the underperformance and asset withdrawal.

© 2015 Wiley

Example 10 (Travel Expenses)

Steven Taylor, a mining analyst with Bronson Brokers, is invited by Precision Metals to join a group of his peers in a tour of mining facilities in several western U.S. states. The company arranges for chartered group flights from site to site and for accommodations in Spartan Motels, the only chain with accommodations near the mines, for three nights. Taylor allows Precision Metals to pick up his tab, as do the other analysts, with one exception—John Adams, an employee of a large trust company, who insists on following his company's policy and paying for his hotel room himself.

Comment: The policy of the company where Adams works complies closely with Standard I(B) by avoiding even the appearance of a conflict of interest, but Taylor and the other analysts were not necessarily violating Standard I(B). In general, when allowing companies to pay for travel and/or accommodations in these circumstances, members and candidates must use their judgment. They must be on guard that such arrangements not impinge on a member's or candidate's independence and objectivity. In this example, the trip was strictly for business and Taylor was not accepting irrelevant or lavish hospitality. The itinerary required chartered flights, for which analysts were not expected to pay. The accommodations were modest. These arrangements are not unusual and did not violate Standard I(B) as long as Taylor's independence and objectivity were not compromised. In the final analysis, members and candidates should consider both whether they can remain objective and whether their integrity might be perceived by their clients to have been compromised.

Example 11 (Travel Expenses from External Manager)

Tom Wayne is the investment manager of the Franklin City Employees Pension Plan. He recently completed a successful search for a firm to manage the foreign equity allocation of the plan's diversified portfolio. He followed the plan's standard procedure of seeking presentations from a number of qualified firms and recommended that his board select Penguin Advisors because of its experience, well-defined investment strategy, and performance record. The firm claims compliance with the Global Investment Performance Standards (GIPS) and has been verified. Following the selection of Penguin, a reporter from the *Franklin City Record* calls to ask if there was any connection between this action and the fact that Penguin was one of the sponsors of an "investment fact-finding trip to Asia" that Wayne made earlier in the year. The trip was one of several conducted by the Pension Investment Academy, which had arranged the itinerary of meetings with economic, government, and corporate officials in major cities in several Asian countries. The Pension Investment Academy obtains support for the cost of these trips from a number of investment managers, including Penguin Advisors; the Academy then pays the travel expenses of the various pension plan managers on the trip and provides all meals and accommodations. The president of Penguin Advisors was also one of the travelers on the trip.

Comment: Although Wayne can probably put to good use the knowledge he gained from the trip in selecting portfolio managers and in other areas of managing the pension plan, his recommendation of Penguin Advisors may be tainted by the possible conflict incurred when he participated in a trip partly paid for by Penguin Advisors and when he was in the daily company of the president of Penguin Advisors. To avoid violating Standard I(B), Wayne's basic expenses for travel and accommodations should have been paid by his employer or the pension plan; contact with the president of Penguin Advisors

© 2015 Wiley

should have been limited to informational or educational events only; and the trip, the organizer, and the sponsor should have been made a matter of public record. Even if his actions were not in violation of Standard I(B), Wayne should have been sensitive to the public perception of the trip when reported in the newspaper and the extent to which the subjective elements of his decision might have been affected by the familiarity that the daily contact of such a trip would encourage. This advantage would probably not be shared by firms competing with Penguin Advisors.

Example 12 (Recommendation Objectivity)

Bob Thompson has been doing research for the portfolio manager of the fixed-income department. His assignment is to do sensitivity analysis on securitized subprime mortgages. He has discussed with the manager possible scenarios to use to calculate expected returns. A key assumption in such calculations is housing price appreciation (HPA) because it drives "prepays" (prepayments of mortgages) and losses. Thompson is concerned with the significant appreciation experienced over the previous five years as a result of the increased availability of funds from subprime mortgages. Thompson insists that the analysis should include a scenario run with –10% for Year 1, –5% for Year 2, and then (to project a worst-case scenario) 0% for Years 3 through 5. The manager replies that these assumptions are too dire because there has never been a time in their available database when HPA was negative.

Thompson conducts his research to better understand the risks inherent in these securities and evaluates these securities in the worst-case scenario, an unlikely but possible environment. Based on the results of the enhanced scenarios, Thompson does not recommend the purchase of the securitization. Against the general market trends, the manager follows Thompson's recommendation and does not invest. The following year, the housing market collapses. In avoiding the subprime investments, the manager's portfolio outperforms its peer group that year.

Comment: Thompson's actions in running the worst-case scenario against the protests of the portfolio manager are in alignment with the principles of Standard I(B). Thompson did not allow his research to be pressured by the general trends of the market or the manager's desire to limit the research to historical norms.

Example 13 (Research Independence and Prior Coverage)

Jill Jorund is a securities analyst following airline stocks and a rising star at her firm. Her boss has been carrying a "buy" recommendation on International Airlines and asks Jorund to take over coverage of that airline. He tells Jorund that under no circumstances should the prevailing buy recommendation be changed.

Comment: Jorund must be independent and objective in her analysis of International Airlines. If she believes that her boss's instructions have compromised her, she has two options: She can tell her boss that she cannot cover the company under these constraints, or she can take over coverage of the company, reach her own independent conclusions, and if they conflict with her boss's opinion, share the conclusions with her boss or other supervisors in the firm so that they can make appropriate recommendations. Jorund must issue only recommendations that reflect her independent and objective opinion.

© 2015 Wiley

Standard I(C) Misrepresentation

The Standard

Members and candidates must not knowingly make any misrepresentations relating to investment analysis, recommendations, actions, or other professional activities.

Guidance

- A misrepresentation is any untrue statement or omission of a fact or any statement that is otherwise false or misleading.
- A member or candidate must not knowingly omit or misrepresent information or give a false impression of a firm, organization, or security in the member's or candidate's oral representations, advertising (whether in the press or through brochures), electronic communications, or written materials (whether publicly disseminated or not).
    - In this context, "knowingly" means that the member or candidate either knows or should have known that the misrepresentation was being made or that omitted information could alter the investment decision-making process.
- Members and candidates who use webpages should regularly monitor materials posted on these sites to ensure that they contain current information. Members and candidates should also ensure that all reasonable precautions have been taken to protect the site's integrity and security and that the site does not misrepresent any information and does provide full disclosure.
- Members and candidates should not guarantee clients any specific return on volatile investments. Most investments contain some element of risk that makes their return inherently unpredictable. For such investments, guaranteeing either a particular rate of return or a guaranteed preservation of investment capital (e.g., "I can guarantee that you will earn 8% on equities this year" or "I can guarantee that you will not lose money on this investment") is misleading to investors.
- Note that Standard I(C) does not prohibit members and candidates from providing clients with information on investment products that have guarantees built into the structure of the products themselves or for which an institution has agreed to cover any losses.

Impact on Investment Practice

- Members and candidates must not misrepresent any aspect of their practice, including (but not limited to) their qualifications or credentials, the qualifications or services provided by their firm, their performance record and the record of their firm, and the characteristics of an investment.
- Members and candidates should exercise care and diligence when incorporating third-party information. Misrepresentations resulting from the use of the credit ratings, research, testimonials, or marketing materials of outside parties become the responsibility of the investment professional when it affects that professional's business practices.
- Members and candidates must disclose their intended use of external managers and must not represent those managers' investment practices as their own.

© 2015 Wiley

Performance Reporting

- Members and candidates should not misrepresent the success of their performance record by presenting benchmarks that are not comparable to their strategies. The benchmark's results should be reported on a basis comparable to that of the fund's or client's results.
- Note that Standard I(C) does not require that a benchmark always be provided in order to comply. Some investment strategies may not lend themselves to displaying an appropriate benchmark because of the complexity or diversity of the investments included.
- Members and candidates should discuss with clients on a continuous basis the appropriate benchmark to be used for performance evaluations and related fee calculations.
- Members and candidates should take reasonable steps to provide accurate and reliable security pricing information to clients on a consistent basis. Changing pricing providers should not be based solely on the justification that the new provider reports a higher current value of a security.

Social Media

- When communicating through social media channels, members and candidates should provide only the same information they are allowed to distribute to clients and potential clients through other traditional forms of communication.
- Along with understanding and following existing and newly developing rules and regulations regarding the allowed use of social media, members and candidates should also ensure that all communications in this format adhere to the requirements of the Code and Standards.
- The perceived anonymity granted through these platforms may entice individuals to misrepresent their qualifications or abilities or those of their employer. Actions undertaken through social media that knowingly misrepresent investment recommendations or professional activities are considered a violation of Standard I(C).

Omissions

- Members and candidates should not knowingly omit inputs used in any models and processes they use to scan for new investment opportunities, to develop investment vehicles, and to produce investment recommendations and ratings as resulting outcomes may provide misleading information. Further, members and candidates should not present outcomes from their models as facts because they only represent expected results.
- Members and candidates should encourage their firms to develop strict policies for composite development to prevent cherry picking—situations in which selected accounts are presented as representative of the firm's abilities. The omission of any accounts appropriate for the defined composite may misrepresent to clients the success of the manager's implementation of its strategy.

Plagiarism

- Plagiarism refers to the practice of copying, or using in substantially the same form, materials prepared by others without acknowledging the source of the

© 2015 Wiley

material or identifying the author and publisher of the material. Plagiarism includes:
  - Taking a research report or study performed by another firm or person, changing the names, and releasing the material as one's own original analysis.
  - Using excerpts from articles or reports prepared by others either verbatim or with only slight changes in wording without acknowledgment.
  - Citing specific quotations supposedly attributable to "leading analysts" and "investment experts" without specific reference.
  - Presenting statistical estimates of forecasts prepared by others with the source identified but without qualifying statements or caveats that may have been used.
  - Using charts and graphs without stating their sources.
  - Copying proprietary computerized spreadsheets or algorithms without seeking the cooperation or authorization of their creators.
- In the case of distributing third-party, outsourced research, members and candidates can use and distribute these reports as long as they do not represent themselves as the author of the report. They may add value to clients by sifting through research and repackaging it for them, but should disclose that the research being presented to clients comes from an outside source.
- The standard also applies to plagiarism in oral communications, such as through group meetings; visits with associates, clients, and customers; use of audio/video media (which is rapidly increasing); and telecommunications, such as through electronic data transfer and the outright copying of electronic media. One of the most egregious practices in violation of this standard is the preparation of research reports based on multiple sources of information without acknowledging the sources. Such information would include, for example, ideas, statistical compilations, and forecasts combined to give the appearance of original work.

Work Completed for Employer

- Members and candidates may use research conducted by other analysts within their firm. Any research reports prepared by the analysts are the property of the firm and may be issued by it even if the original analysts are no longer with the firm.
- Therefore, members and candidates are allowed to use the research conducted by analysts who were previously employed at their firms. However, they cannot reissue a previously released report solely under their own name.

Recommended Procedures for Compliance

Factual presentations: Firms should provide guidance for employees who make written or oral presentations to clients or potential clients by providing a written list of the firm's available services and a description of the firm's qualifications. Firms can also help prevent misrepresentation by specifically designating which employees are authorized to speak on behalf of the firm.

Qualification summary: In order to ensure accurate presentations to clients, the member or candidate should prepare a summary of her own qualifications and experience, as well as a list of the services she is capable of performing.

Verify outside information: When providing information to clients from third parties, members and candidates should ensure the accuracy of the marketing and distribution

© 2015 Wiley

materials that pertain to the third party's capabilities, services, and products. This is because inaccurate information can damage their individual and their firm's reputations as well as the integrity of the capital markets.

Maintain webpages: If they publish a webpage, members and candidates should regularly monitor materials posted to the site to ensure the site maintains current information.

Plagiarism policy: To avoid plagiarism in preparing research reports or conclusions of analysis, members and candidates should take the following steps:

- *Maintain copies:* Keep copies of all research reports, articles containing research ideas, material with new statistical methodology, and other materials that were relied on in preparing the research report.
- *Attribute quotations:* Attribute to their sources any direct quotations, including projections, tables, statistics, model/product ideas, and new methodologies prepared by persons other than recognized financial and statistical reporting services or similar sources.
- *Attribute summaries:* Attribute to their sources paraphrases or summaries of material prepared by others.

Application of the Standard

Example 1 (Disclosure of Issuer-Paid Research)

Anthony McGuire is an issuer-paid analyst hired by publicly traded companies to electronically promote their stocks. McGuire creates a website that promotes his research efforts as a seemingly independent analyst. McGuire posts a profile and a strong buy recommendation for each company on the website indicating that the stock is expected to increase in value. He does not disclose the contractual relationships with the companies he covers on his website, in the research reports he issues, or in the statements he makes about the companies in Internet chat rooms.

Comment: McGuire has violated Standard I(C) because the website is misleading to potential investors. Even if the recommendations are valid and supported with thorough research, his omissions regarding the true relationship between himself and the companies he covers constitute a misrepresentation. McGuire has also violated Standard VI(A)—Disclosure of Conflicts by not disclosing the existence of an arrangement with the companies through which he receives compensation in exchange for his services.

Example 2 (Correction of Unintentional Errors)

Hijan Yao is responsible for the creation and distribution of the marketing materials for his firm, which claims compliance with the GIPS standards. Yao creates and distributes a presentation of performance by the firm's Asian equity composite that states the composite has ¥350 billion in assets. In fact, the composite has only ¥35 billion in assets, and the higher figure on the presentation is a result of a typographical error. Nevertheless, the erroneous material is distributed to a number of clients before Yao catches the mistake.

Comment: Once the error is discovered, Yao must take steps to cease distribution of the incorrect material and correct the error by informing those who have received the

© 2015 Wiley

erroneous information. Because Yao did not knowingly make the misrepresentation, however, he did not violate Standard I(C). Because his firm claims compliance with the GIPS standards, it must also comply with the GIPS Guidance Statement on Error Correction in relation to the error.

Example 3 (Noncorrection of Known Errors)

Syed Muhammad is the president of an investment management firm. The promotional material for the firm, created by the firm's marketing department, incorrectly claims that Muhammad has an advanced degree in finance from a prestigious business school in addition to the CFA designation. Although Muhammad attended the school for a short period of time, he did not receive a degree. Over the years, Muhammad and others in the firm have distributed this material to numerous prospective clients and consultants.

Comment: Even though Muhammad may not have been directly responsible for the misrepresentation of his credentials in the firm's promotional material, he used this material numerous times over an extended period and should have known of the misrepresentation. Thus, Muhammad has violated Standard I(C).

Example 4 (Misrepresentation of Information)

When Ricki Marks sells mortgage-backed derivatives called "interest-only strips" (IOs) to public pension plan clients, she describes them as "guaranteed by the U.S. government." Purchasers of the IOs are entitled only to the interest stream generated by the mortgages, however, not the notional principal itself. One particular municipality's investment policies and local law require that securities purchased by its public pension plans be guaranteed by the U.S. government. Although the underlying mortgages are guaranteed, neither the investor's investment nor the interest stream on the IOs is guaranteed. When interest rates decline, causing an increase in prepayment of mortgages, interest payments to the IOs' investors decline, and these investors lose a portion of their investment.

Comment: Marks violated Standard I(C) by misrepresenting the terms and character of the investment.

Example 5 (Potential Information Misrepresentation)

Khalouck Abdrabbo manages the investments of several high-net-worth individuals in the United States who are approaching retirement. Abdrabbo advises these individuals that a portion of their investments should be moved from equity to bank-sponsored certificates of deposit and money market accounts so that the principal will be "guaranteed" up to a certain amount. The interest is not guaranteed.

Comment: Although there is risk that the institution offering the certificates of deposit and money market accounts could go bankrupt, in the United States, these accounts are insured by the U.S. government through the Federal Deposit Insurance Corporation. Therefore, using the term "guaranteed" in this context is not inappropriate as long as the amount is within the government-insured limit. Abdrabbo should explain these facts to the clients.

© 2015 Wiley

Example 6 (Plagiarism)

Steve Swanson is a senior analyst in the investment research department of Ballard and Company. Apex Corporation has asked Ballard to assist in acquiring the majority ownership of stock in the Campbell Company, a financial consulting firm, and to prepare a report recommending that stockholders of Campbell agree to the acquisition. Another investment firm, Davis and Company, had already prepared a report for Apex analyzing both Apex and Campbell and recommending an exchange ratio. Apex has given the Davis report to Ballard officers, who have passed it on to Swanson. Swanson reviews the Davis report and other available material on Apex and Campbell. From his analysis, he concludes that the common stocks of Campbell and Apex represent good value at their current prices; he believes, however, that the Davis report does not consider all the factors a Campbell stockholder would need to know to make a decision. Swanson reports his conclusions to the partner in charge, who tells him to "use the Davis report, change a few words, sign your name, and get it out."

Comment: If Swanson does as requested, he will violate Standard I(C). He could refer to those portions of the Davis report that he agrees with if he identifies Davis as the source; he could then add his own analysis and conclusions to the report before signing and distributing it.

Example 7 (Plagiarism)

Claude Browning, a quantitative analyst for Double Alpha, Inc., returns from a seminar in great excitement. At that seminar, Jack Jorrely, a well-known quantitative analyst at a national brokerage firm, discussed one of his new models in great detail, and Browning is intrigued by the new concepts. He proceeds to test the model, making some minor mechanical changes but retaining the concepts, until he produces some very positive results. Browning quickly announces to his supervisors at Double Alpha that he has discovered a new model and that clients and prospective clients should be informed of this positive finding as ongoing proof of Double Alpha's continuing innovation and ability to add value.

Comment: Although Browning tested Jorrely's model on his own and even slightly modified it, he must still acknowledge the original source of the idea. Browning can certainly take credit for the final, practical results; he can also support his conclusions with his own test. The credit for the innovative thinking, however, must be awarded to Jorrely.

Example 8 (Plagiarism)

Fernando Zubia would like to include in his firm's marketing materials some "plain-language" descriptions of various concepts, such as the price-to-earnings (P/E) multiple and why standard deviation is used as a measure of risk. The descriptions come from other sources, but Zubia wishes to use them without reference to the original authors. Would this use of material be a violation of Standard I(C)?

Comment: Copying verbatim any material without acknowledgment, including plain-language descriptions of the P/E multiple and standard deviation, violates Standard I(C). Even though these concepts are general, best practice would be for Zubia to describe them in his own words or cite the sources from which the descriptions are quoted. Members and candidates would be violating Standard I(C) if they either were responsible for creating marketing materials without attribution or knowingly use plagiarized materials.

© 2015 Wiley

Example 9 (Plagiarism)

Through a mainstream media outlet, Erika Schneider learns about a study that she would like to cite in her research. Should she cite both the mainstream intermediary source as well as the author of the study itself when using that information?

Comment: In all instances, a member or candidate must cite the actual source of the information. Best practice for Schneider would be to obtain the information directly from the author and review it before citing it in a report. In that case, Schneider would not need to report how she found out about the information. For example, suppose Schneider read in the *Financial Times* about a study issued by CFA Institute; best practice for Schneider would be to obtain a copy of the study from CFA Institute, review it, and then cite it in her report. If she does not use any interpretation of the report from the *Financial Times* and the newspaper does not add value to the report itself, the newspaper is merely a conduit of the original information and does not need to be cited. If she does not obtain the report and review the information, Schneider runs the risk of relying on secondhand information that may misstate facts. If, for example, the *Financial Times* erroneously reported some information from the original CFA Institute study and Schneider copied that erroneous information without acknowledging CFA Institute, she could be the object of complaints. Best practice would be either to obtain the complete study from its original author and cite only that author or to use the information provided by the intermediary and cite both sources.

Example 10 (Misrepresentation of Information)

Tom Stafford is part of a team within Appleton Investment Management responsible for managing a pool of assets for Open Air Bank, which distributes structured securities to offshore clients. He becomes aware that Open Air is promoting the structured securities as a much less risky investment than the investment management policy followed by him and the team to manage the original pool of assets. Also, Open Air has procured an independent rating for the pool that significantly overstates the quality of the investments. Stafford communicates his concerns to his supervisor, who responds that Open Air owns the product and is responsible for all marketing and distribution. Stafford's supervisor goes on to say that the product is outside of the U.S. regulatory regime that Appleton follows and that all risks of the product are disclosed at the bottom of page 184 of the prospectus.

Comment: As a member of the investment team, Stafford is qualified to recognize the degree of accuracy of the materials that characterize the portfolio, and he is correct to be worried about Appleton's responsibility for a misrepresentation of the risks. Thus, he should continue to pursue the issue of Open Air's inaccurate promotion of the portfolio according to the firm's policies and procedures. The Code and Standards stress protecting the reputation of the firm and the sustainability and integrity of the capital markets. Misrepresenting the quality and risks associated with the investment pool may lead to negative consequences for others well beyond the direct investors.

Example 11 (Misrepresenting Composite Construction)

Robert Palmer is head of performance for a fund manager. When asked to provide performance numbers to fund rating agencies, he avoids mentioning that the fund manager is quite liberal in composite construction. The reason accounts are included/excluded is not fully explained. The performance values reported to the rating agencies

© 2015 Wiley

for the composites, although accurate for the accounts shown each period, may not present a true representation of the fund manager's ability.

Comment: "Cherry picking" accounts to include in either published reports or information provided to rating agencies conflicts with Standard I(C). Moving accounts into or out of a composite to influence the overall performance results materially misrepresents the reported values over time. Palmer should work with his firm to strengthen its reporting practices concerning composite construction to avoid misrepresenting the firm's track record or the quality of the information being provided.

Example 12 (Overemphasis of Firm Results)

Bob Anderson is chief compliance officer for Optima Asset Management Company, a firm currently offering eight funds to clients. Seven of the eight had 10-year returns below the median for their respective sectors. Anderson approves a recent advertisement, which includes this statement: "Optima Asset Management is achieving excellent returns for its investors. The Optima Emerging Markets Equity fund, for example, has 10-year returns that exceed the sector median by more than 10%."

Comment: From the information provided it is difficult to determine whether a violation has occurred as long as the sector outperformance is correct. Anderson may be attempting to mislead potential clients by citing the performance of the sole fund that achieved such results. Past performance is often used to demonstrate a firm's skill and abilities in comparison to funds in the same sectors.

However, if all the funds outperformed their respective benchmarks, then Anderson's assertion that the company "is achieving excellent returns" may be factual. Funds may exhibit positive returns for investors, exceed benchmarks, and yet have returns below the median in their sectors.

Members and candidates need to ensure that their marketing efforts do not include statements that misrepresent their skills and abilities to remain compliant with Standard I(C). Unless the returns of a single fund reflect the performance of a firm as a whole, the use of a singular fund for performance comparisons should be avoided.

Standard I(D) Misconduct

The Standard

Members and candidates must not engage in any professional conduct involving dishonesty, fraud, or deceit, or commit any act that reflects adversely on their professional reputation, integrity, or competence.

Guidance

- While Standard I(A) addresses the obligation of members and candidates to comply with applicable law that governs their professional activities, Standard I(D) addresses *all* conduct that reflects poorly on the professional integrity, good reputation, or competence of members and candidates. Any act that involves lying, cheating, stealing, or other dishonest conduct is a violation of this standard if the offense reflects adversely on a member's or candidate's professional activities.

© 2015 Wiley

- Conduct that damages trustworthiness or competence may include behavior that, although not illegal, nevertheless negatively affects a member's or candidate's ability to perform his or her responsibilities. For example:
    - Abusing alcohol during business hours might constitute a violation of this standard because it could have a detrimental effect on the member's or candidate's ability to fulfill his or her professional responsibilities.
    - Personal bankruptcy may not reflect on the integrity or trustworthiness of the person declaring bankruptcy, but if the circumstances of the bankruptcy involve fraudulent or deceitful business conduct, the bankruptcy may be a violation of this standard.
- In some cases, the absence of appropriate conduct or the lack of sufficient effort may be a violation of Standard I(D). The integrity of the investment profession is built on trust. A member or candidate—whether an investment banker, rating or research analyst, or portfolio manager—is expected to conduct the necessary due diligence to properly understand the nature and risks of an investment before making an investment recommendation. By not taking these steps and, instead, relying on someone else in the process to perform them, members or candidates may violate the trust their clients have placed in them. This loss of trust may have a significant impact on the reputation of the member or candidate and the operations of the financial market as a whole.
- Note that Standard I(D) or any other standard should not be used to settle personal, political, or other disputes unrelated to professional ethics.

Recommended Procedures for Compliance

Members and candidates should encourage their firms to adopt the following policies and procedures to support the principles of Standard I(D):

- Code of ethics: Develop and/or adopt a code of ethics to which every employee must subscribe, and make clear that any personal behavior that reflects poorly on the individual involved, the institution as a whole, or the investment industry will not be tolerated.
- List of violations: Disseminate to all employees a list of potential violations and associated disciplinary sanctions, up to and including dismissal from the firm.
- Employee references: Check references of potential employees to ensure that they are of good character and not ineligible to work in the investment industry because of past infractions of the law.

Application of the Standard

Example 1 (Professionalism and Competence)

Simon Sasserman is a trust investment officer at a bank in a small affluent town. He enjoys lunching every day with friends at the country club, where his clients have observed him having numerous drinks. Back at work after lunch, he clearly is intoxicated while making investment decisions. His colleagues make a point of handling any business with Sasserman in the morning because they distrust his judgment after lunch.

Comment: Sasserman's excessive drinking at lunch and subsequent intoxication at work constitute a violation of Standard I(D) because this conduct has raised questions about his professionalism and competence. His behavior reflects poorly on him, his employer, and the investment industry.

© 2015 Wiley

Example 2 (Fraud and Deceit)

Howard Hoffman, a security analyst at ATZ Brothers, Inc., a large brokerage house, submits reimbursement forms over a two-year period to ATZ's self-funded health insurance program for more than two dozen bills, most of which have been altered to increase the amount due. An investigation by the firm's director of employee benefits uncovers the inappropriate conduct. ATZ subsequently terminates Hoffman's employment and notifies CFA Institute.

Comment: Hoffman violated Standard I(D) because he engaged in intentional conduct involving fraud and deceit in the workplace that adversely reflected on his integrity.

Example 3 (Personal Actions and Integrity)

Carmen Garcia manages a mutual fund dedicated to socially responsible investing. She is also an environmental activist. As the result of her participation in nonviolent protests, Garcia has been arrested on numerous occasions for trespassing on the property of a large petrochemical plant that is accused of damaging the environment.

Comment: Generally, Standard I(D) is not meant to cover legal transgressions resulting from acts of civil disobedience in support of personal beliefs because such conduct does not reflect poorly on the member's or candidate's professional reputation, integrity, or competence.

Example 4 (Professional Misconduct)

Meredith Rasmussen works on a buy-side trading desk of an investment management firm and concentrates on in-house trades for a hedge fund subsidiary managed by a team at the investment management firm. The hedge fund has been very successful and is marketed globally by the firm. From her experience as the trader for much of the activity of the fund, Rasmussen has become quite knowledgeable about the hedge fund's strategy, tactics, and performance. When a distinct break in the market occurs and many of the securities involved in the hedge fund's strategy decline markedly in value, Rasmussen observes that the reported performance of the hedge fund does not reflect this decline. In her experience, the lack of effect is a very unlikely occurrence. She approaches the head of trading about her concern and is told that she should not ask any questions and that the fund is big and successful and is not her concern. She is fairly sure something is not right, so she contacts the compliance officer, who also tells her to stay away from the issue of the hedge fund's reporting.

Comment: Rasmussen has clearly come across an error in policies, procedures, and compliance practices within the firm's operations. According to the firm's procedures for reporting potentially unethical activity, she should pursue the issue by gathering some proof of her reason for doubt. Should all internal communications within the firm not satisfy her concerns, Rasmussen should consider reporting the potential unethical activity to the appropriate regulator.

See also Standard IV(A) for guidance on whistleblowing and Standard IV(C) for the duties of a supervisor.

© 2015 Wiley

LESSON 2: STANDARD II: INTEGRITY OF CAPITAL MARKETS

A. Material Nonpublic Information
B. Market Manipulation

Standard II(A) Material Nonpublic Information

The Standard

Members and candidates who possess material nonpublic information that could affect the value of an investment must not act or cause others to act on the information.

Guidance

- Standard II(A) is related to information that is material and is nonpublic. Such information must not be used for direct buying and selling of individual securities or bonds, nor to influence investment actions related to derivatives, mutual funds, or other alternative investments.

Material Information

Information is "material" if its disclosure would likely have an impact on the price of a security, or if reasonable investors would want to know the information before making an investment decision. Material information may include, but is not limited to, information relating to the following:

- Earnings.
- Mergers, acquisitions, tender offers, or joint ventures.
- Changes in assets.
- Innovative products, processes, or discoveries.
- New licenses, patents, registered trademarks, or regulatory approval/rejection of a product.
- Developments regarding customers or suppliers (e.g., the acquisition or loss of a contract).
- Changes in management.
- Change in auditor notification or the fact that the issuer may no longer rely on an auditor's report or qualified opinion.
- Events regarding the issuer's securities (e.g., defaults on senior securities, calls of securities for redemption, repurchase plans, stock splits, changes in dividends, changes to the rights of security holders, public or private sales of additional securities, and changes in credit ratings).
- Bankruptcies.
- Significant legal disputes.
- Government reports of economic trends (employment, housing starts, currency information, etc.).
- Orders for large trades before they are executed.
- New or changing equity or debt ratings issued by a third party (e.g., sell-side recommendations and credit ratings).
- To determine if information is material, members and candidates should consider the source of information and the information's likely effect on the relevant stock price.
    - The less reliable a source, the less likely the information provided would be considered material.

© 2015 Wiley

  - The more ambiguous the effect on price, the less material the information becomes.
  - If it is unclear whether the information will affect the price of a security and to what extent, information may not be considered material.

Nonpublic Information

- Information is "nonpublic" until it has been disseminated or is available to the marketplace in general (as opposed to a select group of investors). "Disseminated" can be defined as "made known."
  - For example, a company report of profits that is posted on the Internet and distributed widely through a press release or accompanied by a filing has been effectively disseminated to the marketplace.
- Members and candidates must be particularly aware of information that is selectively disclosed by corporations to a small group of investors, analysts, or other market participants. Information that is made available to analysts remains nonpublic until it is made available to investors in general.
- Analysts should also be alert to the possibility that they are selectively receiving material nonpublic information when a company provides them with guidance or interpretation of such publicly available information as financial statements or regulatory filings.
- A member or candidate may use insider information provided legitimately by the source company for the specific purpose of conducting due diligence according to the business agreement between the parties for such activities as mergers, loan underwriting, credit ratings, and offering engagements. However, the use of insider information provided by the source company for other purposes, especially to trade or entice others to trade the securities of the firm, conflicts with this standard.

Mosaic Theory

- A financial analyst may use significant conclusions derived from the analysis of public information and nonmaterial nonpublic information as the basis for investment recommendations and decisions. Under the "mosaic theory," financial analysts are free to act on this collection, or mosaic, of information without risking violation, even when the conclusion they reach would have been material inside information had the company communicated the same.
- Investment professionals should note, however, that although analysts are free to use mosaic information in their research reports, they should save and document all their research [see Standard V(C)].

Social Media

- Members and candidates participating in online discussion forums/groups with membership limitations should verify that material information obtained from these sources can also be accessed from a source that would be considered available to the public (e.g., company filings, webpages, and press releases).
- Members and candidates may use social media platforms to communicate with clients or investors without conflicting with this standard.
- Members and candidates, as required by Standard I(A), should also complete all appropriate regulatory filings related to information distributed through social media platforms.

© 2015 Wiley

Using Industry Experts

- The increased demand for insights for understanding the complexities of some industries has led to an expansion of engagement with outside experts. Members and candidates may provide compensation to individuals for their insights without violating this standard.
- However, members and candidates are ultimately responsible for ensuring that they are not requesting or acting on confidential information received from external experts, which is in violation of security regulations and laws or duties to others.

Investment Research Reports

- It might often be the case that reports prepared by well-known analysts may have an effect on the market and thus may be considered material information. Theoretically, such a report might have to be made public before it was distributed to clients. However, since the analyst is not a company insider, and presumably prepared the report based on publicly available information, the report does not need to be made public just because its conclusions are material. Investors who want to use that report must become clients of the analyst.

Recommended Procedures for Compliance

Achieve public dissemination: If a member or candidate determines that some nonpublic information is material, she should encourage the issuer to make the information public. If public dissemination is not possible, she must communicate the information only to the designated supervisory and compliance personnel in her firm and must not take investment action on the basis of the information.

Adopt compliance procedures: Members and candidates should encourage their firms to adopt compliance procedures to prevent the misuse of material nonpublic information. Particularly important is improving compliance in areas such as review of employee and proprietary trading, documentation of firm procedures, and the supervision of interdepartmental communications in multiservice firms.

Adopt disclosure procedures: Members and candidates should encourage their firms to develop and follow disclosure policies designed to ensure that information is disseminated in the marketplace in an equitable manner. An issuing company should not discriminate among analysts in the provision of information or blackball particular analysts who have given negative reports on the company in the past.

Issue press releases: Companies should consider issuing press releases prior to analyst meetings and conference calls and scripting those meetings and calls to decrease the chance that further information will be disclosed.

Firewall elements: An information barrier commonly referred to as a "firewall" is the most widely used approach to prevent communication of material nonpublic information within firms. The minimum elements of such a system include, but are not limited to, the following:

- Substantial control of relevant interdepartmental communications, preferably through a clearance area within the firm in either the compliance or legal department.
- Review of employee trading through the maintenance of "watch," "restricted," and "rumor" lists.

© 2015 Wiley

- Documentation of the procedures designed to limit the flow of information between departments and of the enforcement actions taken pursuant to those procedures.
- Heightened review or restriction of proprietary trading while a firm is in possession of material nonpublic information.

Appropriate interdepartmental communications: Based on the size of the firm, procedures concerning interdepartmental communication, the review of trading activity, and the investigation of possible violations should be compiled and formalized.

Physical separation of departments: As a practical matter, to the extent possible, firms should consider the physical separation of departments and files to prevent the communication of sensitive information.

Prevention of personnel overlap: There should be no overlap of personnel between the investment banking and corporate finance areas of a brokerage firm and the sales and research departments or between a bank's commercial lending department and its trust and research departments. For a firewall to be effective in a multiservice firm, an employee can be allowed to be on only one side of the wall at any given time.

A reporting system: The least a firm should do to protect itself from liability is have an information barrier in place. It should authorize people to review and approve communications between departments. A single supervisor or compliance officer should have the specific authority and responsibility of deciding whether or not information is material and whether it is sufficiently public to be used as the basis for investment decisions.

Personal trading limitations: Firms should also consider restrictions or prohibitions on personal trading by employees and should carefully monitor both proprietary trading and personal trading by employees. Further, they should require employees to make periodic reports (to the extent that such reporting is not already required by securities laws) of their own transactions and transactions made for the benefit of family members.

Securities should be placed on a restricted list when a firm has or may have material nonpublic information. Further, the watch list should be shown to only the few people responsible for compliance to monitor transactions in specified securities. The use of a watch list in combination with a restricted list has become a common means of ensuring an effective procedure.

Record maintenance: Multiservice firms should maintain written records of communications among various departments. Firms should place a high priority on training and should consider instituting comprehensive training programs, to enable employees to make informed decisions.

Proprietary trading procedures: Procedures concerning the restriction or review of a firm's proprietary trading while it possesses material nonpublic information will necessarily depend on the types of proprietary trading in which a firm may engage. For example, when a firm acts as a market maker, a prohibition on proprietary trading may be counterproductive to the goals of maintaining the confidentiality of information and market liquidity. However, in the case of risk-arbitrage trading, a firm should suspend arbitrage activity when a security is placed on the watch list.

© 2015 Wiley

Communication to all employees: Written compliance policies and guidelines should be circulated to all employees of a firm. Further, they must be given sufficient training to either be able to make an informed decision or to realize that they need to consult a compliance officer before engaging in questionable transactions.

Application of the Standard

Example 1 (Acting on Nonpublic Information)

Frank Barnes, the president and controlling shareholder of the SmartTown clothing chain, decides to accept a tender offer and sell the family business at a price almost double the market price of its shares. He describes this decision to his sister (SmartTown's treasurer), who conveys it to her daughter (who owns no stock in the family company at present), who tells her husband, Staple. Staple, however, tells his stockbroker, Alex Halsey, who immediately buys SmartTown stock for himself.

Comment: The information regarding the pending sale is both material and nonpublic. Staple has violated Standard II(A) by communicating the inside information to his broker. Halsey also has violated the standard by buying the shares on the basis of material nonpublic information.

Example 2 (Controlling Nonpublic Information)

Samuel Peter, an analyst with Scotland and Pierce Incorporated, is assisting his firm with a secondary offering for Bright Ideas Lamp Company. Peter participates, via telephone conference call, in a meeting with Scotland and Pierce investment banking employees and Bright Ideas' CEO. Peter is advised that the company's earnings projections for the next year have significantly dropped. Throughout the telephone conference call, several Scotland and Pierce salespeople and portfolio managers walk in and out of Peter's office, where the telephone call is taking place. As a result, they are aware of the drop in projected earnings for Bright Ideas. Before the conference call is concluded, the salespeople trade the stock of the company on behalf of the firm's clients and other firm personnel trade the stock in a firm proprietary account and in employees' personal accounts.

Comment: Peter has violated Standard II(A) because he failed to prevent the transfer and misuse of material nonpublic information to others in his firm. Peter's firm should have adopted information barriers to prevent the communication of nonpublic information among departments of the firm. The salespeople and portfolio managers who traded on the information have also violated Standard II(A) by trading on inside information.

Example 3 (Selective Disclosure of Material Information)

Elizabeth Levenson is based in Taipei and covers the Taiwanese market for her firm, which is based in Singapore. She is invited, together with the other 10 largest shareholders of a manufacturing company, to meet the finance director of that company. During the meeting, the finance director states that the company expects its workforce to strike next Friday, which will cripple productivity and distribution. Can Levenson use this information as a basis to change her rating on the company from "buy" to "sell"?

Comment: Levenson must first determine whether the material information is public. According to Standard II(A), if the company has not made this information public (a small group forum does not qualify as a method of public dissemination), she cannot use the information.

Example 4 (Determining Materiality)

Leah Fechtman is trying to decide whether to hold or sell shares of an oil-and-gas exploration company that she owns in several of the funds she manages. Although the company has underperformed the index for some time already, the trends in the industry sector signal that companies of this type might become takeover targets. While she is considering her decision, her doctor, who casually follows the markets, mentions that she thinks that the company in question will soon be bought out by a large multinational conglomerate and that it would be a good idea to buy the stock right now. After talking to various investment professionals and checking their opinions on the company as well as checking industry trends, Fechtman decides the next day to accumulate more stock in the oil-and-gas exploration company.

Comment: Although information on an expected takeover bid may be of the type that is generally material and nonpublic, in this case, the source of information is unreliable, so the information cannot be considered material. Therefore, Fechtman is not prohibited from trading the stock on the basis of this information.

Example 5 (Applying the Mosaic Theory)

Jagdish Teja is a buy-side analyst covering the furniture industry. Looking for an attractive company to recommend as a buy, he analyzes several furniture makers by studying their financial reports and visiting their operations. He also talks to some designers and retailers to find out which furniture styles are trendy and popular. Although none of the companies that he analyzes are a clear buy, he discovers that one of them, Swan Furniture Company (SFC), may be in financial trouble. SFC's extravagant new designs have been introduced at substantial cost. Even though these designs initially attracted attention, the public is now buying more conservative furniture from other makers. Based on this information and on a profit-and-loss analysis, Teja believes that SFC's next quarter earnings will drop substantially. He issues a sell recommendation for SFC. Immediately after receiving that recommendation, investment managers start reducing the SFC stock in their portfolios.

Comment: Information on quarterly earnings data is material and nonpublic. Teja arrived at his conclusion about the earnings drop on the basis of public information and on pieces of nonmaterial nonpublic information (such as opinions of designers and retailers). Therefore, trading based on Teja's correct conclusion is not prohibited by Standard II(A).

Example 6 (Mosaic Theory)

John Doll is a research analyst for a hedge fund that also sells its research to a select group of paying client investment firms. Doll's focus is medical technology companies and products, and he has been in the business long enough and has been successful enough to build up a very credible network of friends and experts in the business. Doll has been working on a major research report recommending Boyce Health, a medical device manufacturer. He recently ran into an old acquaintance at a wedding who is a senior executive at Boyce, and Doll asked about the business. Doll was drawn to a

© 2015 Wiley

statement that the executive, who has responsibilities in the new products area, made about a product: "I would not get too excited about the medium-term prospects; we have a lot of work to do first." Doll incorporated this and other information about the new Boyce product in his long-term recommendation of Boyce.

Comment: Doll's conversation with the senior executive is part of the mosaic of information used in recommending Boyce. When holding discussions with a firm executive, Doll would need to guard against soliciting or obtaining material nonpublic information. Before issuing the report, the executive's statement about the continuing development of the product would need to be weighed against the other known public facts to determine whether it would be considered material.

Example 7 (Materiality Determination)

Larry Nadler, a trader for a mutual fund, gets a text message from another firm's trader, whom he has known for years. The message indicates a software company is going to report strong earnings when the firm publicly announces in two days. Nadler has a buy order from a portfolio manager within his firm to purchase several hundred thousand shares of the stock. Nadler is aggressive in placing the portfolio manager's order and completes the purchases by the following morning, a day ahead of the firm's planned earnings announcement.

Comment: There are often rumors and whisper numbers before a release of any kind. The text message from the other trader would most likely be considered market noise. Unless Nadler knew that the trader had an ongoing business relationship with the public firm, he had no reason to suspect he was receiving material nonpublic information that would prevent him from completing the trading request of the portfolio manager.

Example 8 (Using an Expert Network)

Tom Watson is a research analyst working for a hedge fund. To stay informed, Watson relies on outside experts for information on such industries as technology and pharmaceuticals, where new advancements occur frequently. The meetings with the industry experts often are arranged through networks or placement agents that have specific policies and procedures in place to deter the exchange of material nonpublic information.

Watson arranges a call to discuss future prospects for one of the fund's existing technology company holdings, a company that was testing a new semiconductor product. The scientist leading the tests indicates his disappointment with the performance of the new semiconductor. Following the call, Watson relays the insights he received to others at the fund. The fund sells its current position in the company and writes many put options because the market is anticipating the success of the new semiconductor and the share price reflects the market's optimism.

Comment: Watson has violated Standard II(A) by passing along material nonpublic information concerning the ongoing product tests, which the fund used to trade in the securities and options of the related company. Watson cannot simply rely on the agreements signed by individuals who participate in expert networks that state that he has not received information that would prohibit his trading activity. He must make his own determination whether information he received through these arrangements reaches a materiality threshold that would affect his trading abilities.

© 2015 Wiley

Standard II(B) Market Manipulation

The Standard

Members and candidates must not engage in practices that distort prices or artificially inflate trading volume with the intent to mislead market participants.

Guidance

- Members and candidates must uphold market integrity by prohibiting market manipulation. Market manipulation includes practices that distort security prices or trading volume with the intent to deceive people or entities that rely on information in the market.
- Market manipulation includes (1) the dissemination of false or misleading information and (2) transactions that deceive or would be likely to mislead market participants by distorting the price-setting mechanism of financial instruments.

Information-Based Manipulation

- Information-based manipulation includes, but is not limited to, spreading false rumors to induce trading by others.
  - For example, members and candidates must refrain from "pumping up" the price of an investment by issuing misleading positive information or overly optimistic projections of a security's worth only to later "dump" the investment (i.e., sell it) once the price, fueled by the misleading information's effect on other market participants, reaches an artificially high level.

Transaction-Based Manipulation

- Transaction-based manipulation involves instances where a member or candidate knew or should have known that his or her actions could affect the pricing of a security. This type of manipulation includes, but is not limited to, the following:
  - Transactions that artificially affect prices or volume to give the impression of activity or price movement in a financial instrument, which represent a diversion from the expectations of a fair and efficient market.
  - Securing a controlling, dominant position in a financial instrument to exploit and manipulate the price of a related derivative and/or the underlying asset.

Note that Standard II(B) is not intended to preclude transactions undertaken on legitimate trading strategies based on perceived market inefficiencies. The intent of the action is critical to determining whether it is a violation of this standard.

Application of the Standard

Example 1 (Independent Analysis and Company Promotion)

The principal owner of Financial Information Services (FIS) entered into an agreement with two microcap companies to promote the companies' stock in exchange for stock and cash compensation. The principal owner caused FIS to disseminate e-mails, design and maintain several websites, and distribute an online investment newsletter—all of which recommended investment in the two companies. The systematic publication of purportedly independent analyses and recommendations containing inaccurate and

© 2015 Wiley

highly promotional and speculative statements increased public investment in the companies and led to dramatically higher stock prices.

Comment: The principal owner of FIS violated Standard II(B) by using inaccurate reporting and misleading information under the guise of independent analysis to artificially increase the stock price of the companies. Furthermore, the principal owner violated Standard V(A)—Diligence and Reasonable Basis by not having a reasonable and adequate basis for recommending the two companies and violated Standard VI(A)—Disclosure of Conflicts by not disclosing to investors the compensation agreements (which constituted a conflict of interest).

Example 2 (Personal Trading Practices and Price)

John Gray is a private investor in Belgium who bought a large position several years ago in Fame Pharmaceuticals, a German small-cap security with limited average trading volume. He has now decided to significantly reduce his holdings owing to the poor price performance. Gray is worried that the low trading volume for the stock may cause the price to decline further as he attempts to sell his large position.

Gray devises a plan to divide his holdings into multiple accounts in different brokerage firms and private banks in the names of family members, friends, and even a private religious institution. He then creates a rumor campaign on various blogs and social media outlets promoting the company.

Gray begins to buy and sell the stock using the accounts in hopes of raising the trading volume and the price. He conducts the trades through multiple brokers, selling slightly larger positions than he bought on a tactical schedule, and over time, he is able to reduce his holding as desired without negatively affecting the sale price.

Comment: Gray violated Standard II(B) by fraudulently creating the appearance that there was a greater investor interest in the stock through the online rumors. Additionally, through his trading strategy, he created the appearance that there was greater liquidity in the stock than actually existed. He was able to manipulate the price through both misinformation and trading practices.

Example 3 (Personal Trading and Volume)

Rajesh Sekar manages two funds—an equity fund and a balanced fund—whose equity components are supposed to be managed in accordance with the same model. According to that model, the funds' holdings in stock of Digital Design Inc. (DD) are excessive. Reduction of the DD holdings would not be easy, however, because the stock has low liquidity in the stock market. Sekar decides to start trading larger portions of DD stock back and forth between his two funds to slowly increase the price; he believes market participants will see growing volume and increasing price and become interested in the stock. If other investors are willing to buy the DD stock because of such interest, then Sekar will be able to get rid of at least some of his overweight position without inducing price decreases. In this way, the whole transaction will be for the benefit of fund participants, even if additional brokers' commissions are incurred.

Comment: Sekar's plan would be beneficial for his funds' participants but is based on artificial distortion of both trading volume and the price of the DD stock and thus constitutes a violation of Standard II(B).

© 2015 Wiley

Example 4 ("Pump-Priming" Strategy)

Sergei Gonchar is chairman of the ACME Futures Exchange, which is launching a new bond futures contract. To convince investors, traders, arbitrageurs, hedgers, and so on, to use its contract, the exchange attempts to demonstrate that it has the best liquidity. To do so, it enters into agreements with members in which they commit to a substantial minimum trading volume on the new contract over a specific period in exchange for substantial reductions of their regular commissions.

Comment: The formal liquidity of a market is determined by the obligations set on market makers, but the actual liquidity of a market is better estimated by the actual trading volume and bid–ask spreads. Attempts to mislead participants about the actual liquidity of the market constitute a violation of Standard II(B). In this example, investors have been intentionally misled to believe they chose the most liquid instrument for some specific purpose, but they could eventually see the actual liquidity of the contract significantly reduced after the term of the agreement expires. If the ACME Futures Exchange fully discloses its agreement with members to boost transactions over some initial launch period, it will not violate Standard II(B). ACME's intent is not to harm investors but, on the contrary, to give them a better service. For that purpose, it may engage in a liquidity-pumping strategy, but the strategy must be disclosed.

Example 5 (Pump and Dump Strategy)

In an effort to pump up the price of his holdings in Moosehead & Belfast Railroad Company, Steve Weinberg logs on to several investor chat rooms on the Internet to start rumors that the company is about to expand its rail network in anticipation of receiving a large contract for shipping lumber.

Comment: Weinberg has violated Standard II(B) by disseminating false information about Moosehead & Belfast with the intent to mislead market participants.

Example 6 (Information Manipulation)

Allen King is a performance analyst for Torrey Investment Funds. King believes that the portfolio manager for the firm's small- and microcap equity fund dislikes him because the manager never offers him tickets to the local baseball team's games but does offer tickets to other employees. To incite a potential regulatory review of the manager, King creates user profiles on several online forums under the portfolio manager's name and starts rumors about potential mergers for several of the smaller companies in the portfolio. As the prices of these companies' stocks increase, the portfolio manager sells the position, which leads to an investigation by the regulator as King desired.

Comment: King has violated Standard II(B) even though he did not personally profit from the market's reaction to the rumor. In posting the false information, King misleads others into believing the companies were likely to be acquired. Although his intent was to create trouble for the portfolio manager, his actions clearly manipulated the factual information that was available to the market.

© 2015 Wiley

LESSON 3: STANDARD III: DUTIES TO CLIENTS

A. Loyalty, Prudence, and Care
B. Fair Dealing
C. Suitability
D. Performance Presentation
E. Preservation of Confidentiality

Standard III(A) Loyalty, Prudence, and Care

The Standard

Members and candidates have a duty of loyalty to their clients and must act with reasonable care and exercise prudent judgment. Members and candidates must act for the benefit of their clients and place their clients' interests before their employer's or their own interests.

Guidance

- Standard III(A) clarifies that client interests are paramount. A member's or candidate's responsibility to a client includes a duty of loyalty and a duty to exercise reasonable care. Investment actions must be carried out for the sole benefit of the client and in a manner the member or candidate believes, given the known facts and circumstances, to be in the best interest of the client. Members and candidates must exercise the same level of prudence, judgment, and care that they would apply in the management and disposition of their own interests in similar circumstances.
- Prudence requires caution and discretion. The exercise of prudence by investment professionals requires that they act with the care, skill, and diligence that a reasonable person acting in a like capacity and familiar with such matters would use. In the context of managing a client's portfolio, prudence requires following the investment parameters set forth by the client and balancing risk and return. Acting with care requires members and candidates to act in a prudent and judicious manner in avoiding harm to clients.
- Standard III(A), however, is not a substitute for a member's or candidate's legal or regulatory obligations. As stated in Standard I(A), members and candidates must abide by the most strict requirements imposed on them by regulators or the Code and Standards, including any legally imposed fiduciary duty.
- Members and candidates must also be aware of whether they have "custody" or effective control of client assets. If so, a heightened level of responsibility arises. Members and candidates are considered to have custody if they have any direct or indirect access to client funds. Members and candidates must manage any pool of assets in their control in accordance with the terms of the governing documents (such as trust documents and investment management agreements), which are the primary determinant of the manager's powers and duties.

Understanding the Application of Loyalty, Prudence, and Care

- Standard III(A) establishes a minimum benchmark for the duties of loyalty, prudence, and care that are required of all members and candidates regardless of whether a legal fiduciary duty applies. Although fiduciary duty often encompasses the principles of loyalty, prudence, and care, Standard III(A) does not render all members and candidates fiduciaries. The responsibilities of members and

© 2015 Wiley

candidates for fulfilling their obligations under this standard depend greatly on the nature of their professional responsibilities and the relationships they have with clients.

- There is a large variety of professional relationships that members and candidates have with their clients. Standard III(A) requires them to fulfill the obligations outlined explicitly or implicitly in the client agreements to the best of their abilities and with loyalty, prudence, and care. Whether a member or candidate is structuring a new securitization transaction, completing a credit rating analysis, or leading a public company, he or she must work with prudence and care in delivering the agreed-on services.

Identifying the Actual Investment Client

- The first step for members and candidates in fulfilling their duty of loyalty to clients is to determine the identity of the "client" to whom the duty of loyalty is owed. In the context of an investment manager managing the personal assets of an individual, the client is easily identified. When the manager is responsible for the portfolios of pension plans or trusts, however, the client is not the person or entity who hires the manager but, rather, the beneficiaries of the plan or trust. The duty of loyalty is owed to the ultimate beneficiaries.
- Members and candidates managing a fund to an index or an expected mandate owe the duty of loyalty, prudence, and care to invest in a manner consistent with the stated mandate. The decisions of a fund's manager, although benefiting all fund investors, do not have to be based on an individual investor's requirements and risk profile. Client loyalty and care for those investing in the fund are the responsibility of members and candidates who have an advisory relationship with those individuals.

Developing the Client's Portfolio

- Professional investment managers should ensure that the client's objectives and expectations for the performance of the account are realistic and suitable to the client's circumstances and that the risks involved are appropriate. In most circumstances, recommended investment strategies should relate to the long-term objectives and circumstances of the client.
- When members and candidates cannot avoid potential conflicts between their firm and clients' interests, they must provide clear and factual disclosures of the circumstances to the clients.
- Members and candidates must follow any guidelines set by their clients for the management of their assets.
- Investment decisions must be judged in the context of the total portfolio rather than by individual investment within the portfolio. The member's or candidate's duty is satisfied with respect to a particular investment if the individual has thoroughly considered the investment's place in the overall portfolio, the risk of loss and opportunity for gains, tax implications, and the diversification, liquidity, cash flow, and overall return requirements of the assets or the portion of the assets for which the manager is responsible.

Soft Commission Policies

- An investment manager often has discretion over the selection of brokers executing transactions. Conflicts may arise when an investment manager uses client

© 2015 Wiley

brokerage to purchase research services, a practice commonly called "soft dollars" or "soft commissions." A member or candidate who pays a higher brokerage commission than he or she would normally pay to allow for the purchase of goods or services, without corresponding benefit to the client, violates the duty of loyalty to the client.

- From time to time, a client will direct a manager to use the client's brokerage to purchase goods or services for the client, a practice that is commonly called "directed brokerage." Because brokerage commission is an asset of the client and is used to benefit that client, not the manager, such a practice does not violate any duty of loyalty. However, a member or candidate is obligated to seek "best price" and "best execution" and be assured by the client that the goods or services purchased from the brokerage will benefit the account beneficiaries. In addition, the member or candidate should disclose to the client that the client may not be getting best execution from the directed brokerage.
    - "Best execution" refers to a trading process that seeks to maximize the value of the client's portfolio within the client's stated investment objectives and constraints.

Proxy Voting Policies

- Part of a member's or candidate's duty of loyalty includes voting proxies in an informed and responsible manner. Proxies have economic value to a client, and members and candidates must ensure that they properly safeguard and maximize this value.
- An investment manager who fails to vote, casts a vote without considering the impact of the question, or votes blindly with management on nonroutine governance issues (e.g., a change in company capitalization) may violate this standard. Voting of proxies is an integral part of the management of investments.
- A cost–benefit analysis may show that voting all proxies may not benefit the client, so voting proxies may not be necessary in all instances.
- Members and candidates should disclose to clients their proxy voting policies.

Recommended Procedures for Compliance

Regular Account Information

Members and candidates with control of client assets should:

- Submit to each client, at least quarterly, an itemized statement showing the funds and securities in the custody or possession of the member or candidate plus all debits, credits, and transactions that occurred during the period.
- Disclose to the client where the assets are to be maintained, as well as where or when they are moved.
- Separate the client's assets from any other party's assets, including the member's or candidate's own assets.

Client Approval

- If a member or candidate is uncertain about the appropriate course of action with respect to a client, the member or candidate should consider what he or she would expect or demand if the member or candidate were the client.
- If in doubt, a member or candidate should disclose the questionable matter in writing to the client and obtain client approval.

© 2015 Wiley

Firm Policies

Members and candidates should address and encourage their firms to address the following topics when drafting the statements or manuals containing their policies and procedures regarding responsibilities to clients:

- *Follow all applicable rules and laws:* Members and candidates must follow all legal requirements and applicable provisions of the Code and Standards.
- *Establish the investment objectives of the client:* Make a reasonable inquiry into a client's investment experience, risk and return objectives, and financial constraints prior to making investment recommendations or taking investment actions.
- *Consider all the information when taking actions:* When taking investment actions, members and candidates must consider the appropriateness and suitability of the investment relative to (1) the client's needs and circumstances, (2) the investment's basic characteristics, and (3) the basic characteristics of the total portfolio.
- *Diversify:* Members and candidates should diversify investments to reduce the risk of loss, unless diversification is not consistent with plan guidelines or is contrary to the account objectives.
- *Carry out regular reviews:* Members and candidates should establish regular review schedules to ensure that the investments held in the account adhere to the terms of the governing documents.
- *Deal fairly with all clients with respect to investment actions:* Members and candidates must not favor some clients over others and should establish policies for allocating trades and disseminating investment recommendations.
- *Disclose conflicts of interest:* Members and candidates must disclose all actual and potential conflicts of interest so that clients can evaluate those conflicts.
- *Disclose compensation arrangements:* Members and candidates should make their clients aware of all forms of manager compensation.
- *Vote proxies:* In most cases, members and candidates should determine who is authorized to vote shares and vote proxies in the best interests of the clients and ultimate beneficiaries.
- *Maintain confidentiality:* Members and candidates must preserve the confidentiality of client information.
- *Seek best execution:* Unless directed by the client as ultimate beneficiary, members and candidates must seek best execution for their clients. (Best execution is defined in the preceding text.)
- *Place client interests first:* Members and candidates must serve the best interests of clients.

Application of the Standard

Example 1 (Identifying the Client—Plan Participants)

First Country Bank serves as trustee for the Miller Company's pension plan. Miller is the target of a hostile takeover attempt by Newton, Inc. In attempting to ward off Newton, Miller's managers persuade Julian Wiley, an investment manager at First Country Bank, to purchase Miller common stock in the open market for the employee pension plan. Miller's officials indicate that such action would be favorably received and would probably result in other accounts being placed with the bank. Although Wiley believes the stock is overvalued and would not ordinarily buy it, he purchases the stock to support Miller's managers, to maintain Miller's good favor toward the bank, and to

© 2015 Wiley

realize additional new business. The heavy stock purchases cause Miller's market price to rise to such a level that Newton retracts its takeover bid.

Comment: Standard III(A) requires that a member or candidate, in evaluating a takeover bid, act prudently and solely in the interests of plan participants and beneficiaries. To meet this requirement, a member or candidate must carefully evaluate the long-term prospects of the company against the short-term prospects presented by the takeover offer and by the ability to invest elsewhere. In this instance, Wiley, acting on behalf of his employer, which was the trustee for a pension plan, clearly violated Standard III(A). He used the pension plan to perpetuate existing management, perhaps to the detriment of plan participants and the company's shareholders, and to benefit himself. Wiley's responsibilities to the plan participants and beneficiaries should have taken precedence over any ties of his bank to corporate managers and over his self-interest. Wiley had a duty to examine the takeover offer on its own merits and to make an independent decision. The guiding principle is the appropriateness of the investment decision to the pension plan, not whether the decision benefited Wiley or the company that hired him.

Example 2 (Client Commission Practices)

JNI, a successful investment counseling firm, serves as investment manager for the pension plans of several large regionally based companies. Its trading activities generate a significant amount of commission-related business. JNI uses the brokerage and research services of many firms, but most of its trading activity is handled through a large brokerage company, Thompson, Inc., because the executives of the two firms have a close friendship. Thompson's commission structure is high in comparison with charges for similar brokerage services from other firms. JNI considers Thompson's research services and execution capabilities average. In exchange for JNI directing its brokerage to Thompson, Thompson absorbs a number of JNI overhead expenses, including those for rent.

Comment: JNI executives are breaching their responsibilities by using client brokerage for services that do not benefit JNI clients and by not obtaining best price and best execution for their clients. Because JNI executives are not upholding their duty of loyalty, they are violating Standard III(A).

Example 3 (Brokerage Arrangements)

Charlotte Everett, a struggling independent investment adviser, serves as investment manager for the pension plans of several companies. One of her brokers, Scott Company, is close to consummating management agreements with prospective new clients whereby Everett would manage the new client accounts and trade the accounts exclusively through Scott. One of Everett's existing clients, Crayton Corporation, has directed Everett to place securities transactions for Crayton's account exclusively through Scott. But to induce Scott to exert efforts to send more new accounts to her, Everett also directs transactions to Scott from other clients without their knowledge.

Comment: Everett has an obligation at all times to seek best price and best execution on all trades. Everett may direct new client trades exclusively through Scott Company as long as Everett receives best price and execution on the trades or receives a written

© 2015 Wiley

statement from new clients that she is *not* to seek best price and execution and that they are aware of the consequence for their accounts. Everett may trade other accounts through Scott as a reward for directing clients to Everett only if the accounts receive best price and execution and the practice is disclosed to the accounts. Because Everett does not disclose the directed trading, Everett has violated Standard III(A).

Example 4 (Brokerage Arrangements)

Emilie Rome is a trust officer for Paget Trust Company. Rome's supervisor is responsible for reviewing Rome's trust account transactions and her monthly reports of personal stock transactions. Rome has been using Nathan Gray, a broker, almost exclusively for trust account brokerage transactions. When Gray makes a market in stocks, he has been giving Rome a lower price for personal purchases and a higher price for sales than he gives to Rome's trust accounts and other investors.

Comment: Rome is violating her duty of loyalty to the bank's trust accounts by using Gray for brokerage transactions simply because Gray trades Rome's personal account on favorable terms. Rome is placing her own interests before those of her clients.

Example 5 (Managing Family Accounts)

Adam Dill recently joined New Investments Asset Managers. To assist Dill in building a book of clients, both his father and brother opened new fee-paying accounts. Dill followed all the firm's procedures in noting his relationships with these clients and in developing their investment policy statements.

After several years, the number of Dill's clients has grown, but he still manages the original accounts of his family members. An IPO is coming to market that is a suitable investment for many of his clients, including his brother. Dill does not receive the amount of stock he requested, so to avoid any appearance of a conflict of interest, he does not allocate any shares to his brother's account.

Comment: Dill has violated Standard III(A) because he is not acting for the benefit of his brother's account as well as his other accounts. The brother's account is a regular fee-paying account comparable to the accounts of his other clients. By not allocating the shares proportionately across *all* accounts for which he thought the IPO was suitable, Dill is disadvantaging specific clients.

Dill would have been correct in not allocating shares to his brother's account if that account was being managed outside the normal fee structure of the firm.

Example 6 (Identifying the Client)

Donna Hensley has been hired by a law firm to testify as an expert witness. Although the testimony is intended to represent impartial advice, she is concerned that her work may have negative consequences for the law firm. If the law firm is Hensley's client, how does she ensure that her testimony will not violate the required duty of loyalty, prudence, and care to one's client?

© 2015 Wiley

Comment: In this situation, the law firm represents Hensley's employer and the aspect of "Who is the client?" is not well defined. When acting as an expert witness, Hensley is bound by the standard of independence and objectivity in the same manner as an independent research analyst would be bound. Hensley must not let the law firm influence the testimony she provides in the legal proceedings.

Example 7 (Client Loyalty)

After providing client account investment performance to the external-facing departments but prior to it being finalized for release to clients, Teresa Nguyen, an investment performance analyst, notices the reporting system missed a trade. Correcting the omission resulted in a large loss for a client that had previously placed the firm on "watch" for potential termination owing to underperformance in prior periods. Nguyen knows this news is unpleasant but informs the appropriate individuals that the report needs to be updated before releasing it to the client.

Comment: Nguyen's actions align with the requirements of Standard III(A). Even though the correction may to lead to the firm's termination by the client, withholding information on errors would not be in the best interest of the client.

Example 8 (Execution-Only Responsibilities)

Baftija Sulejman recently became a candidate in the CFA Program. He is a broker who executes client-directed trades for several high-net-worth individuals. Sulejman does not provide any investment advice and only executes the trading decisions made by clients. He is concerned that the Code and Standards impose a fiduciary duty on him in his dealing with clients and sends an e-mail to the CFA Ethics Helpdesk (ethics@cfainstitute.org) to seek guidance on this issue.

Comment: In this instance, Sulejman serves in an execution-only capacity and his duty of loyalty, prudence, and care is centered on the skill and diligence used when executing trades—namely, by seeking best execution and making trades within the parameters set by the clients (instructions on quantity, price, timing, etc.). Acting in the best interests of the client dictates that trades are executed on the most favorable terms that can be achieved for the client. Given this job function, the requirements of the Code and Standards for loyalty, prudence, and care clearly do not impose a fiduciary duty.

Standard III(B) Fair Dealing

The Standard

Members and candidates must deal fairly and objectively with all clients when providing investment analysis, making investment recommendations, taking investment action, or engaging in other professional activities.

Guidance

- Standard III(B) requires members and candidates to treat all clients fairly when disseminating investment recommendations or making material changes to prior

© 2015 Wiley

investment recommendations, or when taking investment action with regard to general purchases, new issues, or secondary offerings.

- The term "fairly" implies that the member or candidate must take care not to discriminate against any clients when disseminating investment recommendations or taking investment action. Standard III(B) does not state "equally" because members and candidates could not possibly reach all clients at exactly the same time. Further, each client has unique needs, investment criteria, and investment objectives, so not all investment opportunities are suitable for all clients.
- Members and candidates may provide more personal, specialized, or in-depth service to clients who are willing to pay for premium services through higher management fees or higher levels of brokerage. Members and candidates may differentiate their services to clients, but different levels of service must not disadvantage or negatively affect clients. In addition, the different service levels should be disclosed to clients and prospective clients and should be available to everyone (i.e., different service levels should not be offered selectively).

Investment Recommendations

- An investment recommendation is any opinion expressed by a member or candidate in regard to purchasing, selling, or holding a given security or other investment. The opinion may be disseminated to customers or clients through an initial detailed research report, through a brief update report, by addition to or deletion from a list of recommended securities, or simply by oral communication. A recommendation that is distributed to anyone outside the organization is considered a communication for general distribution under Standard III(B).
- Each member or candidate is obligated to ensure that information is disseminated in such a manner that all clients have a fair opportunity to act on every recommendation. Members and candidates should encourage their firms to design an equitable system to prevent selective or discriminatory disclosure and should inform clients about what kind of communications they will receive.
- The duty to clients imposed by Standard III(B) may be more critical when members or candidates change their recommendations than when they make initial recommendations. Material changes in a member's or candidate's prior investment recommendations because of subsequent research should be communicated to all current clients; particular care should be taken that the information reaches those clients who the member or candidate knows have acted on or been affected by the earlier advice.
- Clients who do not know that the member or candidate has changed a recommendation and who, therefore, place orders contrary to a current recommendation should be advised of the changed recommendation before the order is accepted.

Investment Action

- Members or candidates must treat all clients fairly in light of their investment objectives and circumstances. For example, when making investments in new offerings or in secondary financings, members and candidates should distribute the issues to all customers for whom the investments are appropriate in a

© 2015 Wiley

manner consistent with the policies of the firm for allocating blocks of stock. If the issue is oversubscribed, then the issue should be prorated to all subscribers. If the issue is oversubscribed, members and candidates should forgo any sales to themselves or their immediate families in order to free up additional shares for clients.
    - If the investment professional's family-member accounts are managed similarly to the accounts of other clients of the firm, however, the family-member accounts should not be excluded from buying such shares.
- Members and candidates must make every effort to treat all individual and institutional clients in a fair and impartial manner.
- Members and candidates should disclose to clients and prospective clients the documented allocation procedures they or their firms have in place and how the procedures would affect the client or prospect. The disclosure should be clear and complete so that the client can make an informed investment decision. Even when complete disclosure is made, however, members and candidates must put client interests ahead of their own. A member's or candidate's duty of fairness and loyalty to clients can never be overridden by client consent to patently unfair allocation procedures.
- Treating clients fairly also means that members and candidates should not take advantage of their position in the industry to the detriment of clients. For instance, in the context of IPOs, members and candidates must make bona fide public distributions of "hot issue" securities (defined as securities of a public offering that are trading at a premium in the secondary market whenever such trading commences because of the great demand for the securities). Members and candidates are prohibited from withholding such securities for their own benefit and must not use such securities as a reward or incentive to gain benefit.

Recommended Procedures for Compliance

Develop Firm Policies

- A member or candidate should recommend appropriate procedures to management if none are in place.
- A member or candidate should make management aware of possible violations of fair-dealing practices within the firm when they come to the attention of the member or candidate.
- Although a member or candidate need not communicate a recommendation to all customers, the selection process by which customers receive information should be based on suitability and known interest, not on any preferred or favored status.

A common practice to assure fair dealing is to communicate recommendations simultaneously within the firm and to customers. Members and candidates should consider the following points when establishing fair-dealing compliance procedures:

- Limit the number of people involved.
- Shorten the time frame between decision and dissemination.
- Publish guidelines for pre-dissemination behavior.
- Simultaneous dissemination.
- Maintain a list of clients and their holdings.

© 2015 Wiley

- Develop and document trade allocation procedures that ensure:
    - Fairness to advisory clients, both in priority of execution of orders and in the allocation of the price obtained in execution of block orders or trades.
    - Timeliness and efficiency in the execution of orders.
    - Accuracy of the member's or candidate's records as to trade orders and client account positions.

With these principles in mind, members and candidates should develop or encourage their firm to develop written allocation procedures, with particular attention to procedures for block trades and new issues. Procedures to consider are as follows:

- Requiring orders and modifications or cancellations of orders to be documented and time stamped.
- Processing and executing orders on a first-in, first-out basis with consideration of bundling orders for efficiency as appropriate for the asset class or the security.
- Developing a policy to address such issues as calculating execution prices and "partial fills" when trades are grouped, or in a block, for efficiency.
- Giving all client accounts participating in a block trade the same execution price and charging the same commission.
- When the full amount of the block order is not executed, allocating partially executed orders among the participating client accounts pro rata on the basis of order size while not going below an established minimum lot size for some securities (e.g., bonds).
- When allocating trades for new issues, obtaining advance indications of interest, allocating securities by client (rather than portfolio manager), and providing a method for calculating allocations.

Disclose Trade Allocation Procedures

- Members and candidates should disclose to clients and prospective clients how they select accounts to participate in an order and how they determine the amount of securities each account will buy or sell. Trade allocation procedures must be fair and equitable, and disclosure of inequitable allocation methods does not relieve the member or candidate of this obligation.

Establish Systematic Account Review

- Member and candidate supervisors should review each account on a regular basis to ensure that no client or customer is being given preferential treatment and that the investment actions taken for each account are suitable for each account's objectives.
- Because investments should be based on individual needs and circumstances, an investment manager may have good reasons for placing a given security or other investment in one account while selling it from another account and should fully document the reasons behind both sides of the transaction.
- Members and candidates should encourage firms to establish review procedures, however, to detect whether trading in one account is being used to benefit a favored client.

Disclose Levels of Service

- Members and candidates should disclose to all clients whether the organization offers different levels of service to clients for the same fee or different fees.
- Different levels of service should not be offered to clients selectively.

© 2015 Wiley

Application of the Standard

Example 1 (Selective Disclosure)

Bradley Ames, a well-known and respected analyst, follows the computer industry. In the course of his research, he finds that a small, relatively unknown company whose shares are traded over the counter has just signed significant contracts with some of the companies he follows. After a considerable amount of investigation, Ames decides to write a research report on the small company and recommend purchase of its shares. While the report is being reviewed by the company for factual accuracy, Ames schedules a luncheon with several of his best clients to discuss the company. At the luncheon, he mentions the purchase recommendation scheduled to be sent early the following week to all the firm's clients.

Comment: Ames has violated Standard III(B) by disseminating the purchase recommendation to the clients with whom he has lunch a week before the recommendation is sent to all clients.

Example 2 (Fair Dealing and IPO Distribution)

Dominic Morris works for a small regional securities firm. His work consists of corporate finance activities and investing for institutional clients. Arena, Ltd., is planning to go public. The partners have secured rights to buy an arena football league franchise and are planning to use the funds from the issue to complete the purchase. Because arena football is the current rage, Morris believes he has a hot issue on his hands. He has quietly negotiated some options for himself for helping convince Arena to do the financing through his securities firm. When he seeks expressions of interest, the institutional buyers oversubscribe the issue. Morris, assuming that the institutions have the financial clout to drive the stock up, then fills all orders (including his own) and decreases the institutional blocks.

Comment: Morris has violated Standard III(B) by not treating all customers fairly. He should not have taken any shares himself and should have prorated the shares offered among all clients. In addition, he should have disclosed to his firm and to his clients that he received options as part of the deal [see Standard VI(A)—Disclosure of Conflicts].

Example 3 (Fair Dealing and Transaction Allocation)

Eleanor Preston, the chief investment officer of Porter Williams Investments (PWI), a medium-size money management firm, has been trying to retain a client, Colby Company. Management at Colby, which accounts for almost half of PWI's revenues, recently told Preston that if the performance of its account did not improve, it would find a new money manager. Shortly after this threat, Preston purchases mortgage-backed securities (MBSs) for several accounts, including Colby's. Preston is busy with a number of transactions that day, so she fails to allocate the trades immediately or write up the trade tickets. A few days later, when Preston is allocating trades, she notes that some of the MBSs have significantly increased in price and some have dropped. Preston decides to allocate the profitable trades to Colby and spread the losing trades among several other PWI accounts.

© 2015 Wiley

Comment: Preston has violated Standard III(B) by failing to deal fairly with her clients in taking these investment actions. Preston should have allocated the trades prior to executing the orders, or she should have had a systematic approach to allocating the trades, such as pro rata, as soon as practical after they were executed. Among other things, Preston must disclose to the client that the adviser may act as broker for, receive commissions from, and have a potential conflict of interest regarding both parties in agency cross-transactions. After the disclosure, she should obtain from the client consent authorizing such transactions in advance.

Example 4 (Additional Services for Select Clients)

Jenpin Weng uses e-mail to issue a new recommendation to all his clients. He then calls his three largest institutional clients to discuss the recommendation in detail.

Comment: Weng has not violated Standard III(B) because he widely disseminated the recommendation and provided the information to all his clients prior to discussing it with a select few. Weng's largest clients received additional personal service because they presumably pay higher fees or because they have a large amount of assets under Weng's management. If Weng had discussed the report with a select group of clients prior to distributing it to all his clients, he would have violated Standard III(B).

Example 5 (Minimum Lot Allocations)

Lynn Hampton is a well-respected private wealth manager in her community with a diversified client base. She determines that a new 10-year bond being offered by Healthy Pharmaceuticals is appropriate for five of her clients. Three clients request to purchase US$10,000 each, and the other two request US$50,000 each. The minimum lot size is established at US$5,000, and the issue is oversubscribed at the time of placement. Her firm's policy is that odd-lot allocations, especially those below the minimum, should be avoided because they may affect the liquidity of the security at the time of sale.

Hampton is informed she will receive only US$55,000 of the offering for all accounts. Hampton distributes the bond investments as follows: The three accounts that requested US$10,000 are allocated US$5,000 each, and the two accounts that requested US$50,000 are allocated US$20,000 each.

Comment: Hampton has not violated Standard III(B), even though the distribution is not on a completely pro rata basis because of the required minimum lot size. With the total allocation being significantly below the amount requested, Hampton ensured that each client received at least the minimum lot size of the issue. This approach allowed the clients to efficiently sell the bond later if necessary.

Example 6 (Excessive Trading)

Ling Chan manages the accounts for many pension plans, including the plan of his father's employer. Chan developed similar but not identical investment policies for each client, so the investment portfolios are rarely the same. To minimize the cost to his father's pension plan, he intentionally trades more frequently in the accounts of other

© 2015 Wiley

clients to ensure the required brokerage is incurred to continue receiving free research for use by all the pensions.

Comment: Chan is violating Standard III(B) because his trading actions are disadvantaging his clients to enhance a relationship with a preferred client. All clients are benefiting from the research being provided and should incur their fair portion of the costs. This does not mean that additional trading should occur if a client has not paid an equal portion of the commission; trading should occur only as required by the strategy.

Example 7 (Fair Dealing among Clients)

Paul Rove, performance analyst for Alpha-Beta Investment Management, is describing to the firm's chief investment officer (CIO) two new reports he would like to develop to assist the firm in meeting its obligations to treat clients fairly. Because many of the firm's clients have similar investment objectives and portfolios, Rove suggests a report detailing securities owned across several clients and the percentage of the portfolio the security represents. The second report would compare the monthly performance of portfolios with similar strategies. The outliers within each report would be submitted to the CIO for review.

Comment: As a performance analyst, Rove likely has little direct contact with clients and thus has limited opportunity to treat clients differently. The recommended reports comply with Standard III(B) while helping the firm conduct after-the-fact reviews of how effectively the firm's advisers are dealing with their clients' portfolios. Reports that monitor the fair treatment of clients are an important oversight tool to ensure that clients are treated fairly.

Standard III(C) Suitability

The Standard

1. When Members and candidates are in an advisory relationship with a client, they must:
    a. Make a reasonable inquiry into a client's or prospective client's investment experience, risk and return objectives, and financial constraints prior to making any investment recommendation or taking investment action and must reassess and update this information regularly.
    b. Determine that an investment is suitable to the client's financial situation and consistent with the client's written objectives, mandates, and constraints before making an investment recommendation or taking investment action.
    c. Judge the suitability of investments in the context of the client's total portfolio.
2. When members and candidates are responsible for managing a portfolio to a specific mandate, strategy, or style, they must make only investment recommendations or take only investment actions that are consistent with the stated objectives and constraints of the portfolio.

Guidance

- Standard III(C) requires that members and candidates who are in an investment advisory relationship with clients consider carefully the needs, circumstances, and objectives of the clients when determining the appropriateness and suitability of a given investment or course of investment action.

© 2015 Wiley

- In judging the suitability of a potential investment, the member or candidate should review many aspects of the client's knowledge, experience related to investing, and financial situation. These aspects include, but are not limited to, the risk profile of the investment as compared with the constraints of the client, the impact of the investment on the diversity of the portfolio, and whether the client has the means or net worth to assume the associated risk. The investment professional's determination of suitability should reflect only the investment recommendations or actions that a prudent person would be willing to undertake. Not every investment opportunity will be suitable for every portfolio, regardless of the potential return being offered.
- The responsibilities of members and candidates to gather information and make a suitability analysis prior to making a recommendation or taking investment action fall on those members and candidates who provide investment advice in the course of an advisory relationship with a client. Other members and candidates who are simply executing specific instructions for retail clients when buying or selling securities, may not have the opportunity to judge the suitability of a particular investment for the ultimate client.

Developing an Investment Policy

- When an advisory relationship exists, members and candidates must gather client information at the inception of the relationship. Such information includes the client's financial circumstances, personal data (such as age and occupation) that are relevant to investment decisions, attitudes toward risk, and objectives in investing. This information should be incorporated into a written investment policy statement (IPS) that addresses the client's risk tolerance, return requirements, and all investment constraints (including time horizon, liquidity needs, tax concerns, legal and regulatory factors, and unique circumstances).
- The IPS also should identify and describe the roles and responsibilities of the parties to the advisory relationship and investment process, as well as schedules for review and evaluation of the IPS.
- After formulating long-term capital market expectations, members and candidates can assist in developing an appropriate strategic asset allocation and investment program for the client, whether these are presented in separate documents or incorporated in the IPS or in appendices to the IPS.

Understanding the Client's Risk Profile

- The investment professional must consider the possibilities of rapidly changing investment environments and their likely impact on a client's holdings, both individual securities and the collective portfolio.
- The risk of many investment strategies can and should be analyzed and quantified in advance.
- Members and candidates should pay careful attention to the leverage inherent in many synthetic investment vehicles or products when considering them for use in a client's investment program.

Updating an Investment Policy

- Updating the IPS should be repeated at least annually and also prior to material changes to any specific investment recommendations or decisions on behalf of the client.
    - For an individual client, important changes might include the number of dependents, personal tax status, health, liquidity needs, risk tolerance,

© 2015 Wiley

amount of wealth beyond that represented in the portfolio, and extent to which compensation and other income provide for current income needs.
    - For an institutional client, such changes might relate to the magnitude of unfunded liabilities in a pension fund, the withdrawal privileges in an employee savings plan, or the distribution requirements of a charitable foundation.
- If clients withhold information about their financial portfolios, the suitability analysis conducted by members and candidates cannot be expected to be complete; it must be based on the information provided.

The Need for Diversification

- The unique characteristics (or risks) of an individual investment may become partially or entirely neutralized when it is combined with other individual investments within a portfolio. Therefore, a reasonable amount of diversification is thus the norm for many portfolios.
- An investment with high relative risk on its own may be a suitable investment in the context of the entire portfolio or when the client's stated objectives contemplate speculative or risky investments.
- Members and candidates can be responsible for assessing the suitability of an investment only on the basis of the information and criteria actually provided by the client.

Addressing Unsolicited Trading Requests

- If an unsolicited request is expected to have only a minimum impact on the entire portfolio because the size of the requested trade is small or the trade would result in a limited change to the portfolio's risk profile, the member or candidate should focus on educating the investor on how the request deviates from the current policy statement, and then she may follow her firm's policies regarding the necessary client approval for executing unsuitable trades. At a minimum, the client should acknowledge the discussion and accept the conditions that make the recommendation unsuitable.
- If an unsolicited request is expected to have a material impact on the portfolio, the member or candidate should use this opportunity to update the investment policy statement. Doing so would allow the client to fully understand the potential effect of the requested trade on his or her current goals or risk levels.
- If the client declines to modify her policy statements while insisting an unsolicited trade be made, the member or candidate will need to evaluate the effectiveness of her services to the client. The options available to the members or candidates will depend on the services provided by their employer. Some firms may allow for the trade to be executed in a new unmanaged account. If alternative options are not available, members and candidates ultimately will need to determine whether they should continue the advisory arrangement with the client.

Managing to an Index or Mandate

Some members and candidates do not manage money for individuals but are responsible for managing a fund to an index or an expected mandate. The responsibility of these members and candidates is to invest in a manner consistent with the stated mandate.

© 2015 Wiley

Recommended Procedures for Compliance

Investment Policy Statement

In formulating an investment policy for the client, the member or candidate should take the following into consideration:

- *Client identification*—(1) type and nature of client, (2) the existence of separate beneficiaries, and (3) approximate portion of total client assets that the member or candidate is managing.
- *Investor objectives*—(1) return objectives (income, growth in principal, maintenance of purchasing power) and (2) risk tolerance (suitability, stability of values).
- *Investor constraints*—(1) liquidity needs; (2) expected cash flows (patterns of additions and/or withdrawals); (3) investable funds (assets and liabilities or other commitments); (4) time horizon; (5) tax considerations; (6) regulatory and legal circumstances; (7) investor preferences, prohibitions, circumstances, and unique needs; and (8) proxy voting responsibilities and guidance.
- *Performance measurement benchmarks.*

Regular Updates

- The investor's objectives and constraints should be maintained and reviewed periodically to reflect any changes in the client's circumstances.

Suitability Test Policies

- With the increase in regulatory required suitability tests, members and candidates should encourage their firms to develop related policies and procedures. The test procedures should require the investment professional to look beyond the potential return of the investment and include the following:
    - An analysis of the impact on the portfolio's diversification.
    - A comparison of the investment risks with the client's assessed risk tolerance.
    - The fit of the investment with the required investment strategy.

Application of the Standard

Example 1 (Investment Suitability—Risk Profile)

Caleb Smith, an investment adviser, has two clients: Larry Robertson, 60 years old, and Gabriel Lanai, 40 years old. Both clients earn roughly the same salary, but Robertson has a much higher risk tolerance because he has a large asset base. Robertson is willing to invest part of his assets very aggressively; Lanai wants only to achieve a steady rate of return with low volatility to pay for his children's education. Smith recommends investing 20% of both portfolios in zero-yield, small-cap, high-technology equity issues.

Comment: In Robertson's case, the investment may be appropriate because of his financial circumstances and aggressive investment position, but this investment is not suitable for Lanai. Smith is violating Standard III(C) by applying Robertson's investment strategy to Lanai because the two clients' financial circumstances and objectives differ.

© 2015 Wiley

Example 2 (Investment Suitability—Entire Portfolio)

Jessica McDowell, an investment adviser, suggests to Brian Crosby, a risk-averse client, that covered call options be used in his equity portfolio. The purpose would be to enhance Crosby's income and partially offset any untimely depreciation in the portfolio's value should the stock market or other circumstances affect his holdings unfavorably. McDowell educates Crosby about all possible outcomes, including the risk of incurring an added tax liability if a stock rises in price and is called away and, conversely, the risk of his holdings losing protection on the downside if prices drop sharply.

Comment: When determining suitability of an investment, the primary focus should be the characteristics of the client's entire portfolio, not the characteristics of single securities on an issue-by-issue basis. The basic characteristics of the entire portfolio will largely determine whether investment recommendations are taking client factors into account. Therefore, the most important aspects of a particular investment are those that will affect the characteristics of the total portfolio. In this case, McDowell properly considers the investment in the context of the entire portfolio and thoroughly explains the investment to the client.

Example 3 (Following an Investment Mandate)

Louis Perkowski manages a high-income mutual fund. He purchases zero-dividend stock in a financial services company because he believes the stock is undervalued and is in a potential growth industry, which makes it an attractive investment.

Comment: A zero-dividend stock does not seem to fit the mandate of the fund that Perkowski is managing. Unless Perkowski's investment fits within the mandate or is within the realm of allowable investments the fund has made clear in its disclosures, Perkowski has violated Standard III(C).

Example 4 (Submanager and IPS Reviews)

Paul Ostrowski's investment management business has grown significantly over the past couple of years, and some clients want to diversify internationally. Ostrowski decides to find a submanager to handle the expected international investments. Because this will be his first subadviser, Ostrowski uses the CFA Institute model "request for proposal" to design a questionnaire for his search. By his deadline, he receives seven completed questionnaires from a variety of domestic and international firms trying to gain his business. Ostrowski reviews all the applications in detail and decides to select the firm that charges the lowest fees because doing so will have the least impact on his firm's bottom line.

Comment: When selecting an external manager or subadviser, Ostrowski needs to ensure that the new manager's services are appropriate for his clients. This due diligence includes comparing the risk profile of the clients with the investment strategy of the manager. In basing the decision on the fee structure alone, Ostrowski may be violating Standard III(C).

When clients ask to diversify into international products, it is an appropriate time to review and update the clients' IPSs. Ostrowski's review may determine that the risk of international investments modifies the risk profiles of the clients or does not represent an appropriate investment.

See also Standard V(A)—Diligence and Reasonable Basis for further discussion of the review process needed in selecting appropriate submanagers.

Example 5 (Investment Suitability)

Andre Shrub owns and operates Conduit, an investment advisory firm. Prior to opening Conduit, Shrub was an account manager with Elite Investment, a hedge fund managed by his good friend Adam Reed. To attract clients to a new Conduit fund, Shrub offers lower-than-normal management fees. He can do so because the fund consists of two top-performing funds managed by Reed. Given his personal friendship with Reed and the prior performance record of these two funds, Shrub believes this new fund is a winning combination for all parties. Clients quickly invest with Conduit to gain access to the Elite funds. No one is turned away because Conduit is seeking to expand its assets under management.

Comment: Shrub has violated Standard III(C) because the risk profile of the new fund may not be suitable for every client. As an investment adviser, Shrub needs to establish an investment policy statement for each client and recommend only investments that match each client's risk and return profile in the IPS. Shrub is required to act as more than a simple sales agent for Elite.

Although Shrub cannot disobey the direct request of a client to purchase a specific security, he should fully discuss the risks of a planned purchase and provide reasons why it might not be suitable for a client. This requirement may lead members and candidates to decline new customers if those customers' requested investment decisions are significantly out of line with their stated requirements.

See also Standard V(A)—Diligence and Reasonable Basis.

Standard III(D) Performance Presentation

The Standard

When communicating investment performance information, members and candidates must make reasonable efforts to ensure that it is fair, accurate, and complete.

Guidance

- Members and candidates must provide credible performance information to clients and prospective clients and to avoid misstating performance or misleading clients and prospective clients about the investment performance of members or candidates or their firms.
- Standard III(D) covers any practice that would lead to misrepresentation of a member's or candidate's performance record, whether the practice involves performance presentation or performance measurement.

© 2015 Wiley

- Members and candidates should not state or imply that clients will obtain or benefit from a rate of return that was generated in the past.
- Research analysts promoting the success or accuracy of their recommendations must ensure that their claims are fair, accurate, and complete.
- If the presentation is brief, the member or candidate must make available to clients and prospects, on request, the detailed information supporting that communication. Best practice dictates that brief presentations include a reference to the limited nature of the information provided.

Recommended Procedures for Compliance

Apply the GIPS Standards

- Compliance with the GIPS standards is the best method to meet their obligations under Standard III(D).

Compliance without Applying GIPS Standards

Members and candidates can also meet their obligations under Standard III(D) by:

- Considering the knowledge and sophistication of the audience to whom a performance presentation is addressed.
- Presenting the performance of the weighted composite of similar portfolios rather than using a single representative account.
- Including terminated accounts as part of performance history with a clear indication of when the accounts were terminated.
- Including disclosures that fully explain the performance results being reported (for example, stating, when appropriate, that results are simulated when model results are used, clearly indicating when the performance record is that of a prior entity, or disclosing whether the performance is gross of fees, net of fees, or after tax).
- Maintaining the data and records used to calculate the performance being presented.

Application of the Standard

Example 1 (Performance Calculation and Length of Time)

Kyle Taylor of Taylor Trust Company, noting the performance of Taylor's common trust fund for the past two years, states in a brochure sent to his potential clients, "You can expect steady 25% annual compound growth of the value of your investments over the year." Taylor Trust's common trust fund did increase at the rate of 25% per year for the past year, which mirrored the increase of the entire market. The fund has never averaged that growth for more than one year, however, and the average rate of growth of all of its trust accounts for five years is 5% per year.

Comment: Taylor's brochure is in violation of Standard III(D). Taylor should have disclosed that the 25% growth occurred only in one year. Additionally, Taylor did not include client accounts other than those in the firm's common trust fund. A general claim of firm performance should take into account the performance of all categories of accounts. Finally, by stating that clients can expect a steady 25% annual compound growth rate, Taylor is also violating Standard I(C)—Misrepresentation, which prohibits assurances or guarantees regarding an investment.

© 2015 Wiley

Example 2 (Performance Calculation and Asset Weighting)

Anna Judd, a senior partner of Alexander Capital Management, circulates a performance report for the capital appreciation accounts for the years 1988 through 2004. The firm claims compliance with the GIPS standards. Returns are not calculated in accordance with the requirements of the GIPS standards, however, because the composites are not asset weighted.

Comment: Judd is in violation of Standard III(D). When claiming compliance with the GIPS standards, firms must meet *all* of the requirements, make mandatory disclosures, and meet any other requirements that apply to that firm's specific situation. Judd's violation is not from any misuse of the data but from a false claim of GIPS compliance.

Example 3 (Performance Calculation and Selected Accounts Only)

In a presentation prepared for prospective clients, William Kilmer shows the rates of return realized over a five-year period by a "composite" of his firm's discretionary accounts that have a "balanced" objective. This composite, however, consisted of only a few of the accounts that met the balanced criterion set by the firm, excluded accounts under a certain asset level without disclosing the fact of their exclusion, and included accounts that did not have the balanced mandate because those accounts would boost the investment results. In addition, to achieve better results, Kilmer manipulated the narrow range of accounts included in the composite by changing the accounts that made up the composite over time.

Comment: Kilmer violated Standard III(D) by misrepresenting the facts in the promotional material sent to prospective clients, distorting his firm's performance record, and failing to include disclosures that would have clarified the presentation.

Example 4 (Performance Attribution Changes)

Art Purell is reviewing the quarterly performance attribution reports for distribution to clients. Purell works for an investment management firm with a bottom-up, fundamentals-driven investment process that seeks to add value through stock selection. The attribution methodology currently compares each stock with its sector. The attribution report indicates that the value added this quarter came from asset allocation and that stock selection contributed negatively to the calculated return. Through running several different scenarios, Purell discovers that calculating attribution by comparing each stock with its industry and then rolling the effect to the sector level improves the appearance of the manager's stock selection activities. Because the firm defines the attribution terms and the results better reflect the stated strategy, Purell recommends that the client reports should use the revised methodology.

Comment: Modifying the attribution methodology without proper notifications to clients would fail to meet the requirements of Standard III(D). Purrell's recommendation is being done solely for the interest of the firm to improve its perceived ability to meet the stated investment strategy. Such changes are unfair to clients and obscure the facts regarding the firm's abilities. Had Purell believed the new methodology offered improvements to the original model, then he would have needed to report the results of both calculations to the client. The report should also include the reasons why the new methodology is preferred, which would allow the client to make a meaningful comparison to prior results and provide a basis for comparing future attributions.

© 2015 Wiley

Example 5 (Performance Calculation Methodology Disclosure)

While developing a new reporting package for existing clients, Alisha Singh, a performance analyst, discovers that her company's new system automatically calculates both time-weighted and money-weighted returns. She asks the head of client services and retention which value would be preferred given that the firm has various investment strategies that include bonds, equities, securities without leverage, and alternatives. Singh is told not to label the return value so that the firm may show whichever value is greatest for the period.

Comment: Following these instructions would lead to Singh violating Standard III(D). In reporting inconsistent return values, Singh would not be providing complete information to the firm's clients. Full information is provided when clients have sufficient information to judge the performance generated by the firm.

Example 6 (Performance Calculation Methodology Disclosure)

Richmond Equity Investors manages a long–short equity fund in which clients can trade once a week (on Fridays). For transparency reasons, a daily net asset value of the fund is calculated by Richmond. The monthly fact sheets of the fund report month-to-date and year-to-date performance. Richmond publishes the performance based on the higher of the last trading day of the month (typically, not the last business day) or the last business day of the month as determined by Richmond. The fact sheet mentions only that the data are as of the end of the month, without giving the exact date. Maggie Clark, the investment performance analyst in charge of the calculations, is concerned about the frequent changes and asks her supervisor whether they are appropriate.

Comment: Clark's actions in questioning the changing performance metric comply with Standard III(D). She has shown concern that these changes are not presenting an accurate and complete picture of the performance generated.

Standard III(E) Preservation of Confidentiality

The Standard

Members and candidates must keep information about current, former, and prospective clients confidential unless:

1. The information concerns illegal activities on the part of the client;
2. Disclosure is required by law; or
3. The client or prospective client permits disclosure of the information.

Guidance

- Members and candidates must preserve the confidentiality of information communicated to them by their clients, prospective clients, and former clients. This standard is applicable when (1) the member or candidate receives information because of his or her special ability to conduct a portion of the client's business or personal affairs and (2) the member or candidate receives information that arises

© 2015 Wiley

from or is relevant to that portion of the client's business that is the subject of the special or confidential relationship.
- If disclosure of the information is required by law or the information concerns illegal activities by the client, however, the member or candidate may have an obligation to report the activities to the appropriate authorities.

Status of Client
- This standard protects the confidentiality of client information even if the person or entity is no longer a client of the member or candidate. Therefore, members and candidates must continue to maintain the confidentiality of client records even after the client relationship has ended.
- If a client or former client expressly authorizes the member or candidate to disclose information, however, the member or candidate may follow the terms of the authorization and provide the information.

Compliance with Laws
- As a general matter, members and candidates must comply with applicable law. If applicable law requires disclosure of client information in certain circumstances, members and candidates must comply with the law. Similarly, if applicable law requires members and candidates to maintain confidentiality, even if the information concerns illegal activities on the part of the client, members and candidates should not disclose such information.
- When in doubt, members and candidates should consult with their employer's compliance personnel or legal counsel before disclosing confidential information about clients.

Electronic Information and Security
- Standard III(E) does not require members or candidates to become experts in information security technology, but they should have a thorough understanding of the policies of their employer.
- Members and candidates should encourage their firm to conduct regular periodic training on confidentiality procedures for all firm personnel, including portfolio associates, receptionists, and other non-investment staff who have routine direct contact with clients and their records.

Professional Conduct Investigations by CFA Institute
- The requirements of Standard III(E) are not intended to prevent members and candidates from cooperating with an investigation by the CFA Institute Professional Conduct Program (PCP). When permissible under applicable law, members and candidates shall consider the PCP an extension of themselves when requested to provide information about a client in support of a PCP investigation into their own conduct.

Recommended Procedures for Compliance

The simplest, most conservative, and most effective way to comply with Standard III(E) is to avoid disclosing any information received from a client except to authorized fellow employees who are also working for the client. In some instances, however, a member or candidate may want to disclose information received from clients that is outside the scope

© 2015 Wiley

of the confidential relationship and does not involve illegal activities. Before making such a disclosure, a member or candidate should ask the following:

- In what context was the information disclosed? If disclosed in a discussion of work being performed for the client, is the information relevant to the work?
- Is the information background material that, if disclosed, will enable the member or candidate to improve service to the client?

Communicating with Clients

- Members and candidates should make reasonable efforts to ensure that firm-supported communication methods and compliance procedures follow practices designed for preventing accidental distribution of confidential information.
- Members and candidates should be diligent in discussing with clients the appropriate methods for providing confidential information. It is important to convey to clients that not all firm-sponsored resources may be appropriate for such communications.

Application of the Standard

Example 1 (Possessing Confidential Information)

Sarah Connor, a financial analyst employed by Johnson Investment Counselors, Inc., provides investment advice to the trustees of City Medical Center. The trustees have given her a number of internal reports concerning City Medical's needs for physical plant renovation and expansion. They have asked Connor to recommend investments that would generate capital appreciation in endowment funds to meet projected capital expenditures. Connor is approached by a local businessman, Thomas Kasey, who is considering a substantial contribution either to City Medical Center or to another local hospital. Kasey wants to find out the building plans of both institutions before making a decision, but he does not want to speak to the trustees.

Comment: The trustees gave Connor the internal reports so she could advise them on how to manage their endowment funds. Because the information in the reports is clearly both confidential and within the scope of the confidential relationship, Standard III(E) requires that Connor refuse to divulge information to Kasey.

Example 2 (Disclosing Confidential Information)

Lynn Moody is an investment officer at the Lester Trust Company. She has an advisory customer who has talked to her about giving approximately US$50,000 to charity to reduce her income taxes. Moody is also treasurer of the Home for Indigent Widows (HIW), which is planning its annual giving campaign. HIW hopes to expand its list of prospects, particularly those capable of substantial gifts. Moody recommends that HIW's vice president for corporate gifts call on her customer and ask for a donation in the US$50,000 range.

Comment: Even though the attempt to help the Home for Indigent Widows was well intended, Moody violated Standard III(E) by revealing confidential information about her client.

© 2015 Wiley

Example 3 (Disclosing Possible Illegal Activity)

David Bradford manages money for a family-owned real estate development corporation. He also manages the individual portfolios of several of the family members and officers of the corporation, including the chief financial officer (CFO). Based on the financial records of the corporation and some questionable practices of the CFO that Bradford has observed, Bradford believes that the CFO is embezzling money from the corporation and putting it into his personal investment account.

Comment: Bradford should check with his firm's compliance department or appropriate legal counsel to determine whether applicable securities regulations require reporting the CFO's financial records.

Example 4 (Accidental Disclosure of Confidential Information)

Lynn Moody is an investment officer at the Lester Trust Company (LTC). She has stewardship of a significant number of individually managed taxable accounts. In addition to receiving quarterly written reports, about a dozen high-net-worth individuals have indicated to Moody a willingness to receive communications about overall economic and financial market outlooks directly from her by way of a social media platform. Under the direction of her firm's technology and compliance departments, she established a new group page on an existing social media platform specifically for her clients. In the instructions provided to clients, Moody asked them to "join" the group so they may be granted access to the posted content. The instructions also advised clients that all comments posted would be available to the public and thus the platform was not an appropriate method for communicating personal or confidential information.

Six months later, in early January, Moody posted LTC's year-end "Market Outlook." The report outlined a new asset allocation strategy that the firm is adding to its recommendations in the new year. Moody introduced the publication with a note informing her clients that she would be discussing the changes with them individually in their upcoming meetings.

One of Moody's clients responded directly on the group page that his family recently experienced a major change in their financial profile. The client described highly personal and confidential details of the event. Unfortunately, all clients that were part of the group were also able to read the detailed posting until Moody was able to have the comment removed.

Comment: Moody has taken reasonable steps for protecting the confidentiality of client information while using the social media platform. She provided instructions clarifying that all information posted to the site would be publicly viewable to all group members and warned against using this method for communicating confidential information. The accidental disclosure of confidential information by a client is not under Moody's control. Her actions to remove the information promptly once she became aware further align with Standard III(E).

In understanding the potential sensitivity clients express surrounding the confidentiality of personal information, this event highlights a need for further training. Moody might advocate for additional warnings or controls for clients when they consider using social media platforms for two-way communications.

© 2015 Wiley

LESSON 4: STANDARD IV: DUTIES TO EMPLOTERS

A. Loyalty
B. Additional Compensation Arrangements
C. Responsibilities of Supervisors

Standard IV(A) Loyalty

The Standard

In matters related to their employment, members and candidates must act for the benefit of their employer and not deprive their employer of the advantage of their skills and abilities, divulge confidential information, or otherwise cause harm to their employer.

Guidance

- Members and candidates should protect the interests of their firm by refraining from any conduct that would injure the firm, deprive it of profit, or deprive it of the member's or candidate's skills and ability.
- Members and candidates must always place the interests of clients above the interests of their employer but should also consider the effects of their conduct on the sustainability and integrity of the employer firm.
- In matters related to their employment, members and candidates must comply with the policies and procedures established by their employers that govern the employer–employee relationship—to the extent that such policies and procedures do not conflict with applicable laws, rules, or regulations or the Code and Standards.
- The standard does not require members and candidates to subordinate important personal and family obligations to their work.

Employer Responsibilities

- Employers must recognize the duties and responsibilities that they owe to their employees if they expect to have content and productive employees.
- Members and candidates are encouraged to provide their employer with a copy of the Code and Standards.
- Employers are not obligated to adhere to the Code and Standards. In expecting to retain competent employees who are members and candidates, however, they should not develop conflicting policies and procedures.

Independent Practice

- Members and candidates must abstain from independent competitive activity that could conflict with the interests of their employer.
- Members and candidates who plan to engage in independent practice for compensation must notify their employer and describe the types of services they will render to prospective independent clients, the expected duration of the services, and the compensation for the services.
- Members and candidates should not render services until they receive consent from their employer to all of the terms of the arrangement.
  - "Practice" means any service that the employer currently makes available for remuneration.
  - "Undertaking independent practice" means engaging in competitive business, as opposed to making preparations to begin such practice.

© 2015 Wiley

Leaving an Employer

- When members and candidates are planning to leave their current employer, they must continue to act in the employer's best interest. They must not engage in any activities that would conflict with this duty until their resignation becomes effective.
- Activities that might constitute a violation, especially in combination, include the following:
  - Misappropriation of trade secrets.
  - Misuse of confidential information.
  - Solicitation of the employer's clients prior to cessation of employment.
  - Self-dealing (appropriating for one's own property a business opportunity or information belonging to one's employer).
  - Misappropriation of clients or client lists.
- A departing employee is generally free to make arrangements or preparations to go into a competitive business before terminating the relationship with his or her employer as long as such preparations do not breach the employee's duty of loyalty.
- A member or candidate who is contemplating seeking other employment must not contact existing clients or potential clients prior to leaving his or her employer for purposes of soliciting their business for the new employer. Once notice is provided to the employer of the intent to resign, the member or candidate must follow the employer's policies and procedures related to notifying clients of his or her planned departure. In addition, the member or candidate must not take records or files to a new employer without the written permission of the previous employer.
- Once an employee has left the firm, the skills and experience that an employee obtained while employed are not "confidential" or "privileged" information. Similarly, simple knowledge of the names and existence of former clients is generally not confidential information unless deemed such by an agreement or by law.
- Standard IV(A) does not prohibit experience or knowledge gained at one employer from being used at another employer. Firm records or work performed on behalf of the firm that is stored in paper copy or electronically for the member's or candidate's convenience while employed, however, should be erased or returned to the employer unless the firm gives permission to keep those records after employment ends.
- The standard does not prohibit former employees from contacting clients of their previous firm as long as the contact information does not come from the records of the former employer or violate an applicable "noncompete agreement." Members and candidates are free to use public information after departing to contact former clients without violating Standard IV(A) as long as there is no specific agreement not to do so.

Use of Social Media

- Members and candidates should understand and abide by all applicable firm policies and regulations as to the acceptable use of social media platforms to interact with clients and prospective clients.
- Specific accounts and user profiles of members and candidates may be created for solely professional reasons, including firm-approved accounts for client engagements. Such firm-approved business-related accounts would be considered part of the firm's assets, thus requiring members and candidates to transfer or delete the accounts as directed by their firm's policies and procedures.

© 2015 Wiley

- Best practice for members and candidates is to maintain separate accounts for their personal and professional social media activities. Members and candidates should discuss with their employers how profiles should be treated when a single account includes personal connections and also is used to conduct aspects of their professional activities.

Whistleblowing

Sometimes, circumstances may arise (e.g., when an employer is engaged in illegal or unethical activity) in which members and candidates must act contrary to their employer's interests in order to comply with their duties to the market and clients. In such instances, activities that would normally violate a member's or candidate's duty to his or her employer (such as contradicting employer instructions, violating certain policies and procedures, or preserving a record by copying employer records) may be justified. However, such action would be permitted only if the intent is clearly aimed at protecting clients or the integrity of the market, not for personal gain.

Nature of Employment

- Members and candidates must determine whether they are employees or independent contractors in order to determine the applicability of Standard IV(A). This issue will be decided largely by the degree of control exercised by the employing entity over the member or candidate. Factors determining control include whether the member's or candidate's hours, work location, and other parameters of the job are set; whether facilities are provided to the member or candidate; whether the member's or candidate's expenses are reimbursed; whether the member or candidate seeks work from other employers; and the number of clients or employers the member or candidate works for.
- A member's or candidate's duties within an independent contractor relationship are governed by the oral or written agreement between the member and the client. Members and candidates should take care to define clearly the scope of their responsibilities and the expectations of each client within the context of each relationship. Once a member or candidate establishes a relationship with a client, the member or candidate has a duty to abide by the terms of the agreement.

Recommended Procedures for Compliance

Competition Policy

- A member or candidate must understand any restrictions placed by the employer on offering similar services outside the firm while employed by the firm.
- If a member's or candidate's employer elects to have its employees sign a non-compete agreement as part of the employment agreement, the member or candidate should ensure that the details are clear and fully explained prior to signing the agreement.

Termination Policy

- Members and candidates should clearly understand the termination policies of their employer. Termination policies should:
    - Establish clear procedures regarding the resignation process, including addressing how the termination will be disclosed to clients and staff and whether updates posted through social media platforms will be allowed.

- Outline the procedures for transferring ongoing research and account management responsibilities.
- Address agreements that allow departing employees to remove specific client-related information upon resignation.

Incident-Reporting Procedures

- Members and candidates should be aware of their firm's policies related to whistleblowing and encourage their firm to adopt industry best practices in this area.

Employee Classification

- Members and candidates should understand their status within their employer firm.

Application of the Standard

Example 1 (Soliciting Former Clients)

Samuel Magee manages pension accounts for Trust Assets, Inc., but has become frustrated with the working environment and has been offered a position with Fiduciary Management. Before resigning from Trust Assets, Magee asks four big accounts to leave that firm and open accounts with Fiduciary. Magee also persuades several prospective clients to sign agreements with Fiduciary Management. Magee had previously made presentations to these prospects on behalf of Trust Assets.

Comment: Magee violated the employee–employer principle requiring him to act solely for his employer's benefit. Magee's duty is to Trust Assets as long as he is employed there. The solicitation of Trust Assets' current clients and prospective clients is unethical and violates Standard IV(A).

Example 2 (Addressing Rumors)

Reuben Winston manages all-equity portfolios at Target Asset Management (TAM), a large, established investment counselor. Ten years previously, Philpott & Company, which manages a family of global bond mutual funds, acquired TAM in a diversification move. After the merger, the combined operations prospered in the fixed-income business but the equity management business at TAM languished. Lately, a few of the equity pension accounts that had been with TAM before the merger have terminated their relationships with TAM. One day, Winston finds on his voice mail the following message from a concerned client: "Hey! I just heard that Philpott is close to announcing the sale of your firm's equity management business to Rugged Life. What is going on?" Not being aware of any such deal, Winston and his associates are stunned. Their internal inquiries are met with denials from Philpott management, but the rumors persist. Feeling left in the dark, Winston contemplates leading an employee buyout of TAM's equity management business.

Comment: An employee-led buyout of TAM's equity asset management business would be consistent with Standard IV(A) because it would rest on the permission of the employer and, ultimately, the clients. In this case, however, in which employees suspect the senior managers or principals are not truthful or forthcoming, Winston should consult legal counsel to determine appropriate action.

© 2015 Wiley

Example 3 (Ownership of Completed Prior Work)

Emma Madeline, a recent college graduate and a candidate in the CFA Program, spends her summer as an unpaid intern at Murdoch and Lowell. The senior managers at Murdoch are attempting to bring the firm into compliance with the GIPS standards, and Madeline is assigned to assist in its efforts. Two months into her internship, Madeline applies for a job at McMillan & Company, which has plans to become GIPS compliant. Madeline accepts the job with McMillan. Before leaving Murdoch, she copies the firm's software that she helped develop because she believes this software will assist her in her new position.

Comment: Even though Madeline does not receive monetary compensation for her services at Murdoch, she has used firm resources in creating the software and is considered an employee because she receives compensation and benefits in the form of work experience and knowledge. By copying the software, Madeline violated Standard IV(A) because she misappropriated Murdoch's property without permission.

Example 4 (Starting a New Firm)

Geraldine Allen currently works at a registered investment company as an equity analyst. Without notice to her employer, she registers with government authorities to start an investment company that will compete with her employer, but she does not actively seek clients. Does registration of this competing company with the appropriate regulatory authorities constitute a violation of Standard IV(A)?

Comment: Allen's preparation for the new business by registering with the regulatory authorities does not conflict with the work for her employer if the preparations have been done on Allen's own time outside the office and if Allen will not be soliciting clients for the business or otherwise operating the new company until she has left her current employer.

Example 5 (Competing with Current Employer)

Several employees are planning to depart their current employer within a few weeks and have been careful to not engage in any activities that would conflict with their duty to their current employer. They have just learned that one of their employer's clients has undertaken a request for proposal (RFP) to review and possibly hire a new investment consultant. The RFP has been sent to the employer and all of its competitors. The group believes that the new entity to be formed would be qualified to respond to the RFP and be eligible for the business. The RFP submission period is likely to conclude before the employees' resignations are effective. Is it permissible for the group of departing employees to respond to the RFP for their anticipated new firm?

Comment: A group of employees responding to an RFP that their employer is also responding to would lead to direct competition between the employees and the employer. Such conduct violates Standard IV(A) unless the group of employees receives permission from their employer as well as the entity sending out the RFP.

© 2015 Wiley

Example 6 (Externally Compensated Assignments)

Alfonso Mota is a research analyst with Tyson Investments. He works part time as a mayor for his hometown, a position for which he receives compensation. Must Mota seek permission from Tyson to serve as mayor?

Comment: If Mota's mayoral duties are so extensive and time-consuming that they might detract from his ability to fulfill his responsibilities at Tyson, he should discuss his outside activities with his employer and come to a mutual agreement regarding how to manage his personal commitments with his responsibilities to his employer.

Example 7 (Soliciting Former Clients)

After leaving her employer, Shawna McQuillen establishes her own money management business. While with her former employer, she did not sign a noncompete agreement that would have prevented her from soliciting former clients. Upon her departure, she does not take any of her client lists or contact information and she clears her personal computer of any employer records, including client contact information. She obtains the phone numbers of her former clients through public records and contacts them to solicit their business.

Comment: McQuillen is not in violation of Standard IV(A) because she has not used information or records from her former employer and is not prevented by an agreement with her former employer from soliciting her former clients.

Example 8 (Leaving an Employer)

Laura Webb just left her position as portfolio analyst at Research Systems, Inc. (RSI). Her employment contract included a nonsolicitation agreement that requires her to wait two years before soliciting RSI clients for any investment-related services. Upon leaving, Webb was informed that RSI would contact clients immediately about her departure and introduce her replacement.

While working at RSI, Webb connected with clients, other industry associates, and friends through her LinkedIn network. Her business and personal relationships were intermingled because she considered many of her clients to be personal friends. Realizing that her LinkedIn network would be a valuable resource for new employment opportunities, she updated her profile several days following her departure from RSI. LinkedIn automatically sent a notification to Webb's entire network that her employment status had been changed in her profile.

Comment: Prior to her departure, Webb should have discussed any client information contained in her social media networks. By updating her LinkedIn profile after RSI notified clients and after her employment ended, she has appropriately placed her employer's interests ahead of her own personal interests. In addition, she has not violated the nonsolicitation agreement with RSI, unless it prohibited any contact with clients during the two-year period.

© 2015 Wiley

Example 9 (Confidential Firm Information)

Sam Gupta is a research analyst at Naram Investment Management (NIM). NIM uses a team-based research process to develop recommendations on investment opportunities covered by the team members. Gupta, like others, provides commentary for NIM's clients through the company blog, which is posted weekly on the NIM password-protected website. According to NIM's policy, every contribution to the website must be approved by the company's compliance department before posting. Any opinions expressed on the website are disclosed as representing the perspective of NIM.

Gupta also writes a personal blog to share his experiences with friends and family. As with most blogs, Gupta's personal blog is widely available to interested readers through various Internet search engines. Occasionally, when he disagrees with the team-based research opinions of NIM, Gupta uses his personal blog to express his own opinions as a counterpoint to the commentary posted on the NIM website. Gupta believes this provides his readers with a more complete perspective on these investment opportunities.

Comment: Gupta is in violation of Standard IV(A) for disclosing confidential firm information through his personal blog. The recommendations on the firm's blog to clients are not freely available across the internet, but his personal blog post indirectly provides the firm's recommendations.

Additionally, by posting research commentary on his personal blog, Gupta is using firm resources for his personal advantage. To comply with Standard IV(A), members and candidates must receive consent from their employer prior to using company resources.

Example 10 (Notification of Code and Standards)

Krista Smith is a relatively new assistant trader for the fixed-income desk of a major investment bank. She is on a team responsible for structuring collateralized debt obligations (CDOs) made up of securities in the inventory of the trading desk. At a meeting of the team, senior executives explain the opportunity to eventually separate the CDO into various risk-rated tranches to be sold to the clients of the firm. After the senior executives leave the meeting, the head trader announces various responsibilities of each member of the team and then says, "This is a good time to unload some of the junk we have been stuck with for a while and disguise it with ratings and a thick, unreadable prospectus, so don't be shy in putting this CDO together. Just kidding." Smith is worried by this remark and asks some of her colleagues what the head trader meant. They all respond that he was just kidding but that there is some truth in the remark because the CDO is seen by management as an opportunity to improve the quality of the securities in the firm's inventory.

Concerned about the ethical environment of the workplace, Smith decides to talk to her supervisor about her concerns and provides the head trader with a copy of the Code and Standards. Smith discusses the principle of placing the client above the interest of the firm and the possibility that the development of the new CDO will not adhere to this responsibility. The head trader assures Smith that the appropriate analysis will be conducted when determining the appropriate securities for collateral. Furthermore, the ratings are assigned by an independent firm and the prospectus will include full and factual disclosures. Smith is reassured by the meeting, but she also reviews the company's procedures and requirements for reporting potential violations of company policy and securities laws.

© 2015 Wiley

Comment: Smith's review of the company policies and procedures for reporting violations allows her to be prepared to report through the appropriate whistleblower process if she decides that the CDO development process involves unethical actions by others. Smith's actions comply with the Code and Standards principles of placing the client's interests first and being loyal to her employer. In providing her supervisor with a copy of the Code and Standards, Smith is highlighting the high level of ethical conduct she is required to adhere to in her professional activities.

Standard IV(B) Additional Compensation Arrangements

The Standard

Members and candidates must not accept gifts, benefits, compensation, or consideration that competes with or might reasonably be expected to create a conflict of interest with their employer's interest unless they obtain written consent from all parties involved.

Guidance

- Members and candidates must obtain permission from their employer before accepting compensation or other benefits from third parties for the services rendered to the employer or for any services that might create a conflict with their employer's interest.
  - Compensation and benefits include direct compensation by the client and any indirect compensation or other benefits received from third parties.
  - "Written consent" includes any form of communication that can be documented (for example, communication via e-mail that can be retrieved and documented).

Recommended Procedures for Compliance

- Members and candidates should make an immediate written report to their supervisor and compliance officer specifying any compensation they propose to receive for services in addition to the compensation or benefits received from their employer.
- The details of the report should be confirmed by the party offering the additional compensation, including performance incentives offered by clients.
- This written report should state the terms of any agreement under which a member or candidate will receive additional compensation; "terms" include the nature of the compensation, the approximate amount of compensation, and the duration of the agreement.

Application of the Standard

Example 1 (Notification of Client Bonus Compensation)

Geoff Whitman, a portfolio analyst for Adams Trust Company, manages the account of Carol Cochran, a client. Whitman is paid a salary by his employer, and Cochran pays the trust company a standard fee based on the market value of assets in her portfolio. Cochran proposes to Whitman that "any year that my portfolio achieves at least a 15% return before taxes, you and your wife can fly to Monaco at my expense and use my condominium during the third week of January." Whitman does not inform his employer of the arrangement and vacations in Monaco the following January as Cochran's guest.

© 2015 Wiley

Comment: Whitman violated Standard IV(B) by failing to inform his employer in writing of this supplemental, contingent compensation arrangement. The nature of the arrangement could have resulted in partiality to Cochran's account, which could have detracted from Whitman's performance with respect to other accounts he handles for Adams Trust. Whitman must obtain the consent of his employer to accept such a supplemental benefit.

Example 2 (Notification of Outside Compensation)

Terry Jones sits on the board of directors of Exercise Unlimited, Inc. In return for his services on the board, Jones receives unlimited membership privileges for his family at all Exercise Unlimited facilities. Jones purchases Exercise Unlimited stock for the client accounts for which it is appropriate. Jones does not disclose this arrangement to his employer because he does not receive monetary compensation for his services to the board.

Comment: Jones has violated Standard IV(B) by failing to disclose to his employer benefits received in exchange for his services on the board of directors. The nonmonetary compensation may create a conflict of interest in the same manner as being paid to serve as a director.

Example 3 (Prior Approval for Outside Compensation)

Jonathan Hollis is an analyst of oil-and-gas companies for Specialty Investment Management. He is currently recommending the purchase of ABC Oil Company shares and has published a long, well-thought-out research report to substantiate his recommendation. Several weeks after publishing the report, Hollis receives a call from the investor-relations office of ABC Oil saying that Thomas Andrews, CEO of the company, saw the report and really liked the analyst's grasp of the business and his company. The investor-relations officer invites Hollis to visit ABC Oil to discuss the industry further. ABC Oil offers to send a company plane to pick Hollis up and arrange for his accommodations while visiting. Hollis, after gaining the appropriate approvals, accepts the meeting with the CEO but declines the offered travel arrangements.

Several weeks later, Andrews and Hollis meet to discuss the oil business and Hollis's report. Following the meeting, Hollis joins Andrews and the investment relations officer for dinner at an upscale restaurant near ABC Oil's headquarters.

Upon returning to Specialty Investment Management, Hollis provides a full review of the meeting to the director of research, including a disclosure of the dinner attended.

Comment: Hollis's actions did not violate Standard IV(B). Through gaining approval before accepting the meeting and declining the offered travel arrangements, Hollis sought to avoid any potential conflicts of interest between his company and ABC Oil. Because the location of the dinner was not available prior to arrival and Hollis notified his company of the dinner upon his return, accepting the dinner should not impair his objectivity. By disclosing the dinner, Hollis has enabled Specialty Investment Management to assess whether it has any impact on future reports and recommendations by Hollis related to ABC Oil.

© 2015 Wiley

Standard IV(C) Responsibilities of Supervisors

The Standard

Members and candidates must make reasonable efforts to ensure that anyone subject to their supervision or authority complies with applicable laws, rules, regulations, and the Code and Standards.

Guidance

- Members and candidates must promote actions by all employees under their supervision and authority to comply with applicable laws, rules, regulations, and firm policies and the Code and Standards.
- A member's or candidate's responsibilities under Standard IV(C) include instructing those subordinates to whom supervision is delegated about methods to promote compliance, including preventing and detecting violations of laws, rules, regulations, firm policies, and the Code and Standards.
- At a minimum, Standard IV(C) requires that members and candidates with supervisory responsibility make reasonable efforts to prevent and detect violations by ensuring the establishment of effective compliance systems. However, an effective compliance system goes beyond enacting a code of ethics, establishing policies and procedures to achieve compliance with the code and applicable law, and reviewing employee actions to determine whether they are following the rules.
- To be effective supervisors, members and candidates should implement education and training programs on a recurring or regular basis for employees under their supervision. Further, establishing incentives—monetary or otherwise—for employees not only to meet business goals but also to reward ethical behavior offers supervisors another way to assist employees in complying with their legal and ethical obligations.
- A member or candidate with supervisory responsibility should bring an inadequate compliance system to the attention of the firm's senior managers and recommend corrective action. If the member or candidate clearly cannot discharge supervisory responsibilities because of the absence of a compliance system or because of an inadequate compliance system, the member or candidate should decline in writing to accept supervisory responsibility until the firm adopts reasonable procedures to allow adequate exercise of supervisory responsibility.

System for Supervision

- Members and candidates with supervisory responsibility must understand what constitutes an adequate compliance system for their firms and make reasonable efforts to see that appropriate compliance procedures are established, documented, communicated to covered personnel, and followed.
    - "Adequate" procedures are those designed to meet industry standards, regulatory requirements, the requirements of the Code and Standards, and the circumstances of the firm.
    - To be effective, compliance procedures must be in place prior to the occurrence of a violation of the law or the Code and Standards.
- Once a supervisor learns that an employee has violated or may have violated the law or the Code and Standards, the supervisor must promptly initiate an assessment to determine the extent of the wrongdoing. Relying on an employee's statements about the extent of the violation or assurances that the wrongdoing will not reoccur is not enough. Reporting the misconduct up the chain of command and warning the employee to cease the activity are also not enough. Pending the outcome of the investigation, a supervisor should take steps to ensure that the violation will not be repeated, such as placing limits on the employee's activities or increasing the monitoring of the employee's activities.

© 2015 Wiley

Supervision Includes Detection

- Members and candidates with supervisory responsibility must also make reasonable efforts to detect violations of laws, rules, regulations, firm policies, and the Code and Standards. If a member or candidate has adopted reasonable procedures and taken steps to institute an effective compliance program, then the member or candidate may not be in violation of Standard IV(C) if he or she does not detect violations that occur despite these efforts. The fact that violations do occur may indicate, however, that the compliance procedures are inadequate.
- In addition, in some cases, merely enacting such procedures may not be sufficient to fulfill the duty required by Standard IV(C). A member or candidate may be in violation of Standard IV(C) if he or she knows or should know that the procedures designed to promote compliance, including detecting and preventing violations, are not being followed.

Recommended Procedures for Compliance

Codes of Ethics or Compliance Procedures

- Members and candidates are encouraged to recommend that their employers adopt a code of ethics, and put in place specific policies and procedures needed to ensure compliance with the codes and with securities laws and regulations
- Members and candidates should encourage their employers to provide their codes of ethics to clients.

Adequate Compliance Procedures

Adequate compliance procedures should:

- Be contained in a clearly written and accessible manual that is tailored to the firm's operations.
- Be drafted so that the procedures are easy to understand.
- Designate a compliance officer whose authority and responsibility are clearly defined and who has the necessary resources and authority to implement the firm's compliance procedures.
- Describe the hierarchy of supervision and assign duties among supervisors.
- Implement a system of checks and balances.
- Outline the scope of the procedures.
- Outline procedures to document the monitoring and testing of compliance procedures.
- Outline permissible conduct.
- Delineate procedures for reporting violations and sanctions.

Once a compliance program is in place, a supervisor should:

- Disseminate the contents of the program to appropriate personnel.
- Periodically update procedures to ensure that the measures are adequate under the law.
- Continually educate personnel regarding the compliance procedures.
- Issue periodic reminders of the procedures to appropriate personnel.
- Incorporate a professional conduct evaluation as part of an employee's performance review.
- Review the actions of employees to ensure compliance and identify violators.
- Take the necessary steps to enforce the procedures once a violation has occurred.

© 2015 Wiley

Once a violation is discovered, a supervisor should:

- Respond promptly.
- Conduct a thorough investigation of the activities to determine the scope of the wrongdoing.
- Increase supervision or place appropriate limitations on the wrongdoer pending the outcome of the investigation.
- Review procedures for potential changes necessary to prevent future violations from occurring.

Implementation of Compliance Education and Training

- Regular ethics and compliance training, in conjunction with the adoption of a code of ethics, is critical to investment firms seeking to establish a strong culture of integrity and to provide an environment in which employees routinely engage in ethical conduct in compliance with the law.

Establish an Appropriate Incentive Structure

- Supervisors and firms must look closely at their incentive structure to determine whether the structure encourages profits and returns at the expense of ethically appropriate conduct. Only when compensation and incentives are firmly tied to client interests and *how* outcomes are achieved, rather than *how much* is generated for the firm, will employees work to achieve a culture of integrity.

Application of the Standard

Example 1 (Supervising Research Activities)

Jane Mattock, senior vice president and head of the research department of H&V, Inc., a regional brokerage firm, has decided to change her recommendation for Timber Products from buy to sell. In line with H&V's procedures, she orally advises certain other H&V executives of her proposed actions before the report is prepared for publication. As a result of Mattock's conversation with Dieter Frampton, one of the H&V executives accountable to Mattock, Frampton immediately sells Timber's stock from his own account and from certain discretionary client accounts. In addition, other personnel inform certain institutional customers of the changed recommendation before it is printed and disseminated to all H&V customers who have received previous Timber reports.

Comment: Mattock has violated Standard IV(C) by failing to reasonably and adequately supervise the actions of those accountable to her. She did not prevent or establish reasonable procedures designed to prevent dissemination of or trading on the information by those who knew of her changed recommendation. She must ensure that her firm has procedures for reviewing or recording any trading in the stock of a corporation that has been the subject of an unpublished change in recommendation. Adequate procedures would have informed the subordinates of their duties and detected sales by Frampton and selected customers.

Example 2 (Supervising Trading Activities)

David Edwards, a trainee trader at Wheeler & Company, a major national brokerage firm, assists a customer in paying for the securities of Highland, Inc., by using anticipated profits from the immediate sale of the same securities. Despite the fact that Highland is not on Wheeler's recommended list, a large volume of its stock

© 2015 Wiley

is traded through Wheeler in this manner. Roberta Ann Mason is a Wheeler vice president responsible for supervising compliance with the securities laws in the trading department. Part of her compensation from Wheeler is based on commission revenues from the trading department. Although she notices the increased trading activity, she does nothing to investigate or halt it.

Comment: Mason's failure to adequately review and investigate purchase orders in Highland stock executed by Edwards and her failure to supervise the trainee's activities violate Standard IV(C). Supervisors should be especially sensitive to actual or potential conflicts between their own self-interests and their supervisory responsibilities.

Example 3 (Supervising Trading Activities and Record Keeping)

Samantha Tabbing is senior vice president and portfolio manager for Crozet, Inc., a registered investment advisory and registered broker/dealer firm. She reports to Charles Henry, the president of Crozet. Crozet serves as the investment adviser and principal underwriter for ABC and XYZ public mutual funds. The two funds' prospectuses allow Crozet to trade financial futures for the funds for the limited purpose of hedging against market risks. Henry, extremely impressed by Tabbing's performance in the past two years, directs Tabbing to act as portfolio manager for the funds. For the benefit of its employees, Crozet has also organized the Crozet Employee Profit-Sharing Plan (CEPSP), a defined contribution retirement plan. Henry assigns Tabbing to manage 20% of the assets of CEPSP. Tabbing's investment objective for her portion of CEPSP's assets is aggressive growth. Unbeknownst to Henry, Tabbing frequently places S&P 500 Index purchase and sale orders for the funds and the CEPSP without providing the futures commission merchants (FCMs) who take the orders with any prior or simultaneous designation of the account for which the trade has been placed. Frequently, neither Tabbing nor anyone else at Crozet completes an internal trade ticket to record the time an order was placed or the specific account for which the order was intended. FCMs often designate a specific account only after the trade, when Tabbing provides such designation. Crozet has no written operating procedures or compliance manual concerning its futures trading, and its compliance department does not review such trading. After observing the market's movement, Tabbing assigns to CEPSP the S&P 500 positions with more favorable execution prices and assigns positions with less favorable execution prices to the funds.

Comment: Henry violated Standard IV(C) by failing to adequately supervise Tabbing with respect to her S&P 500 trading. Henry further violated Standard IV(C) by failing to establish record-keeping and reporting procedures to prevent or detect Tabbing's violations. Henry must make a reasonable effort to determine that adequate compliance procedures covering all employee trading activity are established, documented, communicated, and followed.

Example 4 (Supervising Research Activities)

Mary Burdette was recently hired by Fundamental Investment Management (FIM) as a junior auto industry analyst. Burdette is expected to expand the social media presence of the firm because she is active with various networks, including Facebook, LinkedIn, and Twitter. Although Burdette's supervisor, Joe Graf, has never used social media, he encourages Burdette to explore opportunities to increase FIM's online presence and ability to share content, communicate, and broadcast information to clients. In response to Graf's encouragement, Burdette is working on a proposal detailing the advantages of getting FIM onto Twitter in addition to launching a company Facebook page.

As part of her auto industry research for FIM, Burdette is completing a report on the financial impact of Sun Drive Auto Ltd.'s new solar technology for compact automobiles. This research report will be her first for FIM, and she believes Sun Drive's technology could revolutionize the auto industry. In her excitement, Burdette sends a quick tweet to FIM Twitter followers summarizing her "buy" recommendation for Sun Drive Auto stock.

Comment: Graf has violated Standard IV(C) by failing to reasonably supervise Burdette with respect to the contents of her tweet. He did not establish reasonable procedures to prevent the unauthorized dissemination of company research through social media networks. Graf must make sure all employees receive regular training about FIM's policies and procedures, including the appropriate business use of personal social media networks.

See Standard III(B) for additional guidance.

Example 5 (Supervising Research Activities)

Chen Wang leads the research department at YYRA Retirement Planning Specialists. Chen supervises a team of 10 analysts in a fast-paced and understaffed organization. He is responsible for coordinating the firm's approved process to review all reports before they are provided to the portfolio management team for use in rebalancing client portfolios.

One of Chen's direct reports, Huang Mei, covers the banking industry. Chen must submit the latest updates to the portfolio management team tomorrow morning. Huang has yet to submit her research report on ZYX Bank because she is uncomfortable providing a "buy" or "sell" opinion of ZYX on the basis of the completed analysis. Pressed for time and concerned that Chen will reject a "hold" recommendation, she researches various websites and blogs on the banking sector for whatever she can find on ZYX. One independent blogger provides a new interpretation of the recently reported data Huang has analyzed and concludes with a strong "sell" recommendation for ZYX. She is impressed by the originality and resourcefulness of this blogger's report.

Very late in the evening, Huang submits her report and "sell" recommendation to Chen without any reference to the independent blogger's report. Given the late time of the submission and the competence of Huang's prior work, Chen compiles this report with the recommendations from each of the other analysts and meets with the portfolio managers to discuss implementation.

Comment: Chen has violated Standard IV(C) by neglecting to reasonably and adequately follow the firm's approved review process for Huang's research report. The delayed submission and the quality of prior work do not remove Chen's requirement to uphold the designated review process. A member or candidate with supervisory responsibility must make reasonable efforts to see that appropriate procedures are established, documented, communicated to covered personnel, and followed.

© 2015 Wiley

LESSON 5: STANDARD V: INVESTMENT ANALYSIS, RECOMMENDATIONS AND ACTION

A. Diligence and Reasonable Basis
B. Communication with Clients and Prospective Clients
C. Record Retention

Standard V(A) Diligence and Reasonable Basis

The Standard

Members and candidates must:

1. Exercise diligence, independence, and thoroughness in analyzing investments, making investment recommendations, and taking investment actions.
2. Have a reasonable and adequate basis, supported by appropriate research and investigation, for any investment analysis, recommendation, or action.

Guidance

- The requirements for issuing conclusions based on research will vary in relation to the member's or candidate's role in the investment decision-making process, but the member or candidate must make reasonable efforts to cover all pertinent issues when arriving at a recommendation.
- Members and candidates enhance transparency by providing or offering to provide supporting information to clients when recommending a purchase or sale or when changing a recommendation.

Defining Diligence and Reasonable Basis

- As with determining the suitability of an investment for the client, the necessary level of research and analysis will differ with the product, security, or service being offered. The following list provides some, but definitely not all, examples of attributes to consider while forming the basis for a recommendation:
    - Global, regional, and country macroeconomic conditions.
    - A company's operating and financial history.
    - The industry's and sector's current conditions and the stage of the business cycle.
    - A mutual fund's fee structure and management history.
    - The output and potential limitations of quantitative models.
    - The quality of the assets included in a securitization.
    - The appropriateness of selected peer-group comparisons.
- The steps taken in developing a diligent and reasonable recommendation should minimize unexpected downside events.

Using Secondary or Third-Party Research

- If members and candidates rely on secondary or third-party research, they must make reasonable and diligent efforts to determine whether such research is sound.
    - Secondary research is defined as research conducted by someone else in the member's or candidate's firm.
    - Third-party research is research conducted by entities outside the member's or candidate's firm, such as a brokerage firm, bank, or research firm.

© 2015 Wiley

- Members and candidates should make reasonable inquiries into the source and accuracy of all data used in completing their investment analysis and recommendations.
- Criteria that a member or candidate can use in forming an opinion on whether research is sound include the following:
    - Assumptions used.
    - Rigor of the analysis performed.
    - Date/timeliness of the research.
    - Evaluation of the objectivity and independence of the recommendations.
- A member or candidate may rely on others in his or her firm to determine whether secondary or third-party research is sound and use the information in good faith unless the member or candidate has reason to question its validity or the processes and procedures used by those responsible for the research.
- A member or candidate should verify that the firm has a policy about the timely and consistent review of approved research providers to ensure that the quality of the research continues to meet the necessary standards. If such a policy is not in place at the firm, the member or candidate should encourage the development and adoption of a formal review practice.

Using Quantitatively Oriented Research

- Members and candidates must have an understanding of the parameters used in models and quantitative research that are incorporated into their investment recommendations. Although they are not required to become experts in every technical aspect of the models, they must understand the assumptions and limitations inherent in any model and how the results were used in the decision-making process.
- Members and candidates should make reasonable efforts to test the output of investment models and other pre-programmed analytical tools they use. Such validation should occur before incorporating the process into their methods, models, or analyses.
- Although not every model can test for every factor or outcome, members and candidates should ensure that their analyses incorporate a broad range of assumptions sufficient to capture the underlying characteristics of investments. The omission from the analysis of potentially negative outcomes or of levels of risk outside the norm may misrepresent the true economic value of an investment. The possible scenarios for analysis should include factors that are likely to have a substantial influence on the investment value and may include extremely positive and negative scenarios.

Developing Quantitatively Oriented Techniques

- Members and candidates involved in the development and oversight of quantitatively oriented models, methods, and algorithms must understand the technical aspects of the products they provide to clients. A thorough testing of the model and resulting analysis should be completed prior to product distribution.
- In reviewing the computer models or the resulting output, members and candidates need to pay particular attention to the assumptions used in the analysis and the rigor of the analysis to ensure that the model incorporates a wide range of possible input expectations, including negative market events.

© 2015 Wiley

Selecting External Advisers and Subadvisers

- Members and candidates must review managers as diligently as they review individual funds and securities.
- Members and candidates who are directly involved with the use of external advisers need to ensure that their firms have standardized criteria for reviewing these selected external advisers and managers. Such criteria would include, but would not be limited to, the following:
  - Reviewing the adviser's established code of ethics.
  - Understanding the adviser's compliance and internal control procedures.
  - Assessing the quality of the published return information.
  - Reviewing the adviser's investment process and adherence to its stated strategy.

Group Research and Decision Making

In some instances, a member or candidate will not agree with the view of the group. If, however, the member or candidate believes that the consensus opinion has a reasonable and adequate basis and is independent and objective, the member or candidate need not decline to be identified with the report. If the member or candidate is confident in the process, the member or candidate does not need to dissociate from the report even if it does not reflect his or her opinion.

Recommended Procedures for Compliance

Members and candidates should encourage their firms to consider the following policies and procedures to support the principles of Standard V(A):

- Establish a policy requiring that research reports, credit ratings, and investment recommendations have a basis that can be substantiated as reasonable and adequate.
- Develop detailed, written guidance for analysts (research, investment, or credit), supervisory analysts, and review committees that establishes the due diligence procedures for judging whether a particular recommendation has a reasonable and adequate basis.
- Develop measurable criteria for assessing the quality of research, the reasonableness and adequacy of the basis for any recommendation or rating, and the accuracy of recommendations over time.
- Develop detailed, written guidance that establishes minimum levels of scenario testing of all computer-based models used in developing, rating, and evaluating financial instruments.
- Develop measurable criteria for assessing outside providers, including the quality of information being provided, the reasonableness and adequacy of the provider's collection practices, and the accuracy of the information over time.
- Adopt a standardized set of criteria for evaluating the adequacy of external advisers.

Application of the Standard

Example 1 (Sufficient Due Diligence)

Helen Hawke manages the corporate finance department of Sarkozi Securities, Ltd. The firm is anticipating that the government will soon close a tax loophole that currently allows oil-and-gas exploration companies to pass on drilling expenses to holders of a certain class of shares. Because market demand for this tax-advantaged class of stock is currently high, Sarkozi convinces several companies to undertake new equity financings at once, before the loophole closes. Time is of the essence, but Sarkozi lacks sufficient resources to conduct adequate research on all the prospective issuing companies. Hawke decides to estimate the IPO prices on the basis of the relative size of each company and to justify the pricing later when her staff has time.

Comment: Sarkozi should have taken on only the work that it could adequately handle. By categorizing the issuers by general size, Hawke has bypassed researching all the other relevant aspects that should be considered when pricing new issues and thus has not performed sufficient due diligence. Such an omission can result in investors purchasing shares at prices that have no actual basis. Hawke has violated Standard V(A).

Example 2 (Sufficient Scenario Testing)

Babu Dhaliwal works for Heinrich Brokerage in the corporate finance group. He has just persuaded Feggans Resources, Ltd., to allow his firm to do a secondary equity financing at Feggans Resources' current stock price. Because the stock has been trading at higher multiples than similar companies with equivalent production, Dhaliwal presses the Feggans Resources managers to project what would be the maximum production they could achieve in an optimal scenario. Based on these numbers, he is able to justify the price his firm will be asking for the secondary issue. During a sales pitch to the brokers, Dhaliwal then uses these numbers as the base-case production levels that Feggans Resources will achieve.

Comment: When presenting information to the brokers, Dhaliwal should have given a range of production scenarios and the probability of Feggans Resources achieving each level. By giving the maximum production level as the likely level of production, he has misrepresented the chances of achieving that production level and seriously misled the brokers. Dhaliwal has violated Standard V(A).

Example 3 (Reliance on Third-Party Research)

Gary McDermott runs a two-person investment management firm. McDermott's firm subscribes to a service from a large investment research firm that provides research reports. McDermott's firm makes investment recommendations on the basis of these reports.

Comment: Members and candidates can rely on third-party research but must make reasonable and diligent efforts to determine that such research is sound. If McDermott undertakes due diligence efforts on a regular basis to ensure that the research produced by the large firm is objective and reasonably based, McDermott can rely on that research when making investment recommendations to clients.

Example 4 (Quantitative Model Diligence)

Barry Cannon is the lead quantitative analyst at CityCenter Hedge Fund. He is responsible for the development, maintenance, and enhancement of the proprietary models the fund uses to manage its investors' assets. Cannon reads several high-level mathematical publications and blogs to stay informed of current developments. One

© 2015 Wiley

blog, run by Expert CFA, presents some intriguing research that may benefit one of CityCenter's current models. Cannon is under pressure from firm executives to improve the model's predictive abilities, and he incorporates the factors discussed in the online research. The updated output recommends several new investments to the fund's portfolio managers.

Comment: Cannon has violated Standard V(A) by failing to have a reasonable basis for the new recommendations made to the portfolio managers. He needed to diligently research the effect of incorporating the new factors before offering the output recommendations. Cannon may use the blog for ideas, but it is his responsibility to determine the effect on the firm's proprietary models.

See Standard VII(B) regarding the violation by "Expert CFA" in the use of the CFA designation.

Example 5 (Selecting a Service Provider)

Ellen Smith is a performance analyst at Artic Global Advisors, a firm that manages global equity mandates for institutional clients. She was asked by her supervisor to review five new performance attribution systems and recommend one that would more appropriately explain the firm's investment strategy to clients. On the list was a system she recalled learning about when visiting an exhibitor booth at a recent conference. The system is highly quantitative and something of a "black box" in how it calculates the attribution values. Smith recommended this option without researching the others because the sheer complexity of the process was sure to impress the clients.

Comment: Smith's actions do not demonstrate a sufficient level of diligence in reviewing this product to make a recommendation for selecting the service. Besides not reviewing or considering the other four potential systems, she did not determine whether the "black box" attribution process aligns with the investment practices of the firm, including its investments in different countries and currencies. Smith must review and understand the process of any software or system before recommending its use as the firm's attribution system.

Example 6 (Subadviser Selection)

Craig Jackson is working for Adams Partners, Inc., and has been assigned to select a hedge fund subadviser to improve the diversification of the firm's large fund-of-funds product. The allocation must be in place before the start of the next quarter. Jackson uses a consultant database to find a list of suitable firms that claim compliance with the GIPS standards. He calls more than 20 firms on the list to confirm their potential interest and to determine their most recent quarterly and annual total return values. Because of the short turnaround, Jackson recommends the firm with the greatest total return values for selection.

Comment: By considering only performance and GIPS compliance, Jackson has not conducted sufficient review of potential firms to satisfy the requirements of Standard V(A). A thorough investigation of the firms and their operations should be conducted to ensure that their addition would increase the diversity of clients' portfolios and that they are suitable for the fund-of-funds product.

Example 7 (Manager Selection)

Timothy Green works for Peach Asset Management, where he creates proprietary models that analyze data from the firm request for proposal questionnaires to identify managers for possible inclusion in the firm's fund-of-funds investment platform. Various criteria must be met to be accepted to the platform. Because of the number of respondents to the questionnaires, Green uses only the data submitted to make a recommendation for adding a new manager.

Comment: By failing to conduct any additional outside review of the information to verify what was submitted through the request for proposal, Green has likely not satisfied the requirements of Standard V(A). The amount of information requested from outside managers varies among firms. Although the requested information may be comprehensive, Green should ensure sufficient effort is undertaken to verify the submitted information before recommending a firm for inclusion. This requires that he go beyond the information provided by the manager on the request for proposal questionnaire and may include interviews with interested managers, reviews of regulatory filings, and discussions with the managers' custodian or auditor.

Example 8 (Technical Model Requirements)

Jérôme Dupont works for the credit research group of XYZ Asset Management, where he is in charge of developing and updating credit risk models. In order to perform accurately, his models need to be regularly updated with the latest market data.

Dupont does not interact with or manage money for any of the firm's clients. He is in contact with the firm's U.S. corporate bond fund manager, John Smith, who has only very superficial knowledge of the model and who from time to time asks very basic questions regarding the output recommendations. Smith does not consult Dupont with respect to finalizing his clients' investment strategies.

Dupont's recently assigned objective is to develop a new emerging market corporate credit risk model. The firm is planning to expand into emerging credit, and the development of such a model is a critical step in this process. Because Smith seems to follow the model's recommendations without much concern for its quality as he develops his clients' investment strategies, Dupont decides to focus his time on the development of the new emerging market model and neglects to update the U.S. model.

After several months without regular updates, Dupont's diagnostic statistics start to show alarming signs with respect to the quality of the U.S. credit model. Instead of conducting the long and complicated data update, Dupont introduces new codes into his model with some limited new data as a quick "fix." He thinks this change will address the issue without needing to complete the full data update, so he continues working on the new emerging market model.

Several months following the quick "fix," another set of diagnostic statistics reveals nonsensical results and Dupont realizes that his earlier change contained an error. He quickly corrects the error and alerts Smith. Smith realizes that some of the prior trades he performed were due to erroneous model results. Smith rebalances the portfolio to remove the securities purchased on the basis of the questionable results without reporting the issue to anyone else.

© 2015 Wiley

Comment: Smith violated Standard V(A) because exercising "diligence, independence, and thoroughness in analyzing investments, making investment recommendations, and taking investment actions" means that members and candidates must understand the technical aspects of the products they provide to clients. Smith does not understand the model he is relying on to manage money. Members and candidates should also make reasonable inquiries into the source and accuracy of all data used in completing their investment analysis and recommendations.

Dupont violated Standard V(A) even if he does not trade securities or make investment decisions. Dupont's models give investment recommendations, and Dupont is accountable for the quality of those recommendations. Members and candidates should make reasonable efforts to test the output of pre-programmed analytical tools they use. Such validation should occur before incorporating the tools into their decision-making process.

See also Standard V(B)—Communication with Clients and Prospective Clients.

Standard V(B) Communication with Clients and Prospective Clients

The Standard

Members and candidates must:

1. Disclose to clients and prospective clients the basic format and general principles of the investment processes they use to analyze investments, select securities, and construct portfolios, and must promptly disclose any changes that might materially affect those processes.
2. Disclose to clients and prospective clients significant limitations and risks associated with the investment process.
3. Use reasonable judgment in identifying which factors are important to their investment analyses, recommendations, or actions, and include those factors in communications with clients and prospective clients.
4. Distinguish between fact and opinion in the presentation of investment analyses and recommendations.

Guidance

- Members and candidates should communicate in a recommendation the factors that were instrumental in making the investment recommendation. A critical part of this requirement is to distinguish clearly between opinions and facts.
- Follow-up communication of significant changes in the risk characteristics of a security or asset strategy is required.
- Providing regular updates to any changes in the risk characteristics is recommended.

Informing Clients of the Investment Process

- Members and candidates must adequately describe to clients and prospective clients the manner in which they conduct the investment decision-making process. Such disclosure should address factors that have positive and negative influences on the recommendations, including significant risks and limitations of the investment process used.

- The member or candidate must keep clients and other interested parties informed on an ongoing basis about changes to the investment process, especially newly identified significant risks and limitations.
- Members and candidates should inform the clients about the specialization or diversification expertise provided by the external adviser(s).

Different Forms of Communication

- Members and candidates using any social media service to communicate business information must be diligent in their efforts to avoid unintended problems because these services may not be available to all clients. When providing information to clients through new technologies, members and candidates should take reasonable steps to ensure that such delivery would treat all clients fairly and, if necessary, be considered publicly disseminated.
- If recommendations are contained in capsule form (such as a recommended stock list), members and candidates should notify clients that additional information and analyses are available from the producer of the report.

Identifying Risks and Limitations

- Members and candidates must outline to clients and prospective clients significant risks and limitations of the analysis contained in their investment products or recommendations.
- The appropriateness of risk disclosure should be assessed on the basis of what was known at the time the investment action was taken (often called an *ex ante* basis). Members and candidates must disclose significant risks known to them at the time of the disclosure. Members and candidates cannot be expected to disclose risks they are unaware of at the time recommendations or investment actions are made.
- Having no knowledge of a risk or limitation that subsequently triggers a loss may reveal a deficiency in the diligence and reasonable basis of the research of the member or candidate but may not reveal a breach of Standard V(B).

Report Presentation

- A report writer who has done adequate investigation may emphasize certain areas, touch briefly on others, and omit certain aspects deemed unimportant.
- Investment advice based on quantitative research and analysis must be supported by readily available reference material and should be applied in a manner consistent with previously applied methodology. If changes in methodology are made, they should be highlighted.

Distinction between Facts and Opinions in Reports

- Violations often occur when reports fail to separate the past from the future by not indicating that earnings estimates, changes in the outlook for dividends, or future market price information are *opinions* subject to future circumstances.
- In the case of complex quantitative analyses, members and candidates must clearly separate fact from statistical conjecture and should identify the known limitations of an analysis.
- Members and candidates should explicitly discuss with clients and prospective clients the assumptions used in the investment models and processes to generate the analysis. Caution should be used in promoting the perceived accuracy of any model or process to clients because the ultimate output is merely an estimate of future results and not a certainty.

© 2015 Wiley

Recommended Procedures for Compliance

- Members and candidates should encourage their firms to have a rigorous methodology for reviewing research that is created for publication and dissemination to clients.
- To assist in the after-the-fact review of a report, the member or candidate must maintain records indicating the nature of the research and should, if asked, be able to supply additional information to the client (or any user of the report) covering factors not included in the report.

Application of the Standard

Example 1 (Sufficient Disclosure of Investment System)

Sarah Williamson, director of marketing for Country Technicians, Inc., is convinced that she has found the perfect formula for increasing Country Technicians' income and diversifying its product base. Williamson plans to build on Country Technicians' reputation as a leading money manager by marketing an exclusive and expensive investment advice letter to high-net-worth individuals. One hitch in the plan is the complexity of Country Technicians' investment system—a combination of technical trading rules (based on historical price and volume fluctuations) and portfolio construction rules designed to minimize risk. To simplify the newsletter, she decides to include only each week's top five "buy" and "sell" recommendations and to leave out details of the valuation models and the portfolio structuring scheme.

Comment: Williamson's plans for the newsletter violate Standard V(B). Williamson need not describe the investment system in detail in order to implement the advice effectively, but she must inform clients of Country Technicians' basic process and logic. Without understanding the basis for a recommendation, clients cannot possibly understand its limitations or its inherent risks.

Example 2 (Proper Description of a Security)

Olivia Thomas, an analyst at Government Brokers, Inc., which is a brokerage firm specializing in government bond trading, has produced a report that describes an investment strategy designed to benefit from an expected decline in U.S. interest rates. The firm's derivative products group has designed a structured product that will allow the firm's clients to benefit from this strategy. Thomas's report describing the strategy indicates that high returns are possible if various scenarios for declining interest rates are assumed. Citing the proprietary nature of the structured product underlying the strategy, the report does not describe in detail how the firm is able to offer such returns or the related risks in the scenarios, nor does the report address the likely returns of the strategy if, contrary to expectations, interest rates rise.

Comment: Thomas has violated Standard V(B) because her report fails to describe properly the basic characteristics of the actual and implied risks of the investment strategy, including how the structure was created and the degree to which leverage was

© 2015 Wiley

embedded in the structure. The report should include a balanced discussion of how the strategy would perform in the case of rising as well as falling interest rates, preferably illustrating how the strategies might be expected to perform in the event of a reasonable variety of interest rate and credit risk–spread scenarios. If liquidity issues are relevant with regard to the valuation of either the derivatives or the underlying securities, provisions the firm has made to address those risks should also be disclosed.

Example 3 (Notification of Changes to the Investment Process)

RJZ Capital Management is an active value-style equity manager that selects stocks by using a combination of four multifactor models. The firm has found favorable results when back testing the most recent 10 years of available market data in a new dividend discount model (DDM) designed by the firm. This model is based on projected inflation rates, earnings growth rates, and interest rates. The president of RJZ decides to replace its simple model that uses price to trailing 12-month earnings with the new DDM.

Comment: Because the introduction of a new and different valuation model represents a material change in the investment process, RJZ's president must communicate the change to the firm's clients. RJZ is moving away from a model based on hard data toward a new model that is at least partly dependent on the firm's forecasting skills. Clients would likely view such a model as a significant change rather than a mere refinement of RJZ's process.

Example 4 (Notification of Changes to the Investment Process)

RJZ Capital Management loses the chief architect of its multifactor valuation system. Without informing its clients, the president of RJZ decides to redirect the firm's talents and resources toward developing a product for passive equity management—a product that will emulate the performance of a major market index.

Comment: By failing to disclose to clients a substantial change to its investment process, the president of RJZ has violated Standard V(B).

Example 5 (Sufficient Disclosure of Investment System)

Amanda Chinn is the investment director for Diversified Asset Management, which manages the endowment of a charitable organization. Because of recent staff departures, Diversified has decided to limit its direct investment focus to large-cap securities and supplement the needs for small-cap and mid-cap management by hiring outside fund managers. In describing the planned strategy change to the charity, Chinn's update letter states, "As investment director, I will directly oversee the investment team managing the endowment's large-capitalization allocation. I will coordinate the selection and ongoing review of external managers responsible for allocations to other classes." The letter also describes the reasons for the change and the characteristics external managers must have to be considered.

Comment: Standard V(B) requires the disclosure of the investment process used to construct the portfolio of the fund. Changing the investment process from managing all classes of investments within the firm to the use of external managers is one example of information that needs to be communicated to clients. Chinn and her firm have embraced

© 2015 Wiley

the principles of Standard V(B) by providing their client with relevant information. The charity can now make a reasonable decision about whether Diversified Asset Management remains the appropriate manager for its fund.

Example 6 (Notification of Risks and Limitations)

Quantitative analyst Yuri Yakovlev has developed an investment strategy that selects small-cap stocks on the basis of quantitative signals. Yakovlev's strategy typically identifies only a small number of stocks (10–20) that tend to be illiquid, but according to his backtests, the strategy generates significant risk-adjusted returns. The partners at Yakovlev's firm, QSC Capital, are impressed by these results. After a thorough examination of the strategy's risks, stress testing, historical back testing, and scenario analysis, QSC decides to seed the strategy with US$10 million of internal capital in order for Yakovlev to create a track record for the strategy.

After two years, the strategy has generated performance returns greater than the appropriate benchmark and the Sharpe ratio of the fund is close to 1.0. On the basis of these results, QSC decides to actively market the fund to large institutional investors. While creating the offering materials, Yakovlev informs the marketing team that the capacity of the strategy is limited. The extent of the limitation is difficult to ascertain with precision; it depends on market liquidity and other factors in his model that can evolve over time. Yakovlev indicates that given the current market conditions, investments in the fund beyond US$100 million of capital could become more difficult and negatively affect expected fund returns.

Alan Wellard, the manager of the marketing team, is a partner with 30 years of marketing experience and explains to Yakovlev that these are complex technical issues that will muddy the marketing message. According to Wellard, the offering material should focus solely on the great track record of the fund. Yakovlev does not object because the fund has only US$12 million of capital, very far from the US$100 million threshold.

Comment: Yakovlev and Wellard have not appropriately disclosed a significant limitation associated with the investment product. Yakovlev believes this limitation, once reached, will materially affect the returns of the fund. Although the fund is currently far from the US$100 million mark, current and prospective investors must be made aware of this capacity issue. If significant limitations are complicated to grasp and clients do not have the technical background required to understand them, Yakovlev and Wellard should either educate the clients or ascertain whether the fund is suitable for each client.

Example 7 (Notification of Risks and Limitations)

Brickell Advisers offers investment advisory services mainly to South American clients. Julietta Ramon, a risk analyst at Brickell, describes to clients how the firm uses value at risk (VaR) analysis to track the risk of its strategies. Ramon assures clients that calculating a VaR at a 99% confidence level, using a 20-day holding period, and applying a methodology based on an *ex ante* Monte Carlo simulation is extremely effective. The firm has never had losses greater than those predicted by this VaR analysis.

Comment: Ramon has not sufficiently communicated the risks associated with the investment process to satisfy the requirements of Standard V(B). The losses predicted by

© 2015 Wiley

a VaR analysis depend greatly on the inputs used in the model. The size and probability of losses can differ significantly from what an individual model predicts. Ramon must disclose how the inputs were selected and the potential limitations and risks associated with the investment strategy.

Example 8 (Notification of Risks and Limitations)

Lily Smith attended an industry conference and noticed that John Baker, an investment manager with Baker Associates, attracted a great deal of attention from the conference participants. On the basis of her knowledge of Baker's reputation and the interest he received at the conference, Smith recommends adding Baker Associates to the approved manager platform. Her recommendation to the approval committee includes the statement "John Baker is well respected in the industry, and his insights are consistently sought after by investors. Our clients are sure to benefit from investing with Baker Associates."

Comment: Smith is not appropriately separating facts from opinions in her recommendation to include the manager within the platform. Her actions conflict with the requirements of Standard V(B). Smith is relying on her opinions about Baker's reputation and the fact that many attendees were talking with him at the conference. Smith should also review the requirements of Standard V(A) regarding reasonable basis to determine the level of review necessary to recommend Baker Associates.

Standard V(C) Record Retention

The Standard
Members and candidates must develop and maintain appropriate records to support their investment analyses, recommendations, actions, and other investment-related communications with clients and prospective clients.

Guidance
- Members and candidates must retain records that substantiate the scope of their research and reasons for their actions or conclusions. The retention requirement applies to decisions to buy or sell a security as well as reviews undertaken that do not lead to a change in position.
- Records may be maintained either in hard copy or electronic form.

New Media Records
- Members and candidates should understand that although employers and local regulators are developing digital media retention policies, these policies may lag behind the advent of new communication channels. Such lag places greater responsibility on the individual for ensuring that all relevant information is retained. Examples of non-print media formats that should be retained include, but are not limited to e-mails, text messages, blog posts, and Twitter posts.

Records Are Property of the Firm
- As a general matter, records created as part of a member's or candidate's professional activity on behalf of his or her employer are the property of the firm.

© 2015 Wiley

- When a member or candidate leaves a firm to seek other employment, the member or candidate cannot take the property of the firm, including original forms or copies of supporting records of the member's or candidate's work, to the new employer without the express consent of the previous employer.
- The member or candidate cannot use historical recommendations or research reports created at the previous firm because the supporting documentation is unavailable.
- For future use, the member or candidate must re-create the supporting records at the new firm with information gathered through public sources or directly from the covered company and not from memory or sources obtained at the previous employer.

Local Requirements

- Local regulators and firms may also implement policies detailing the applicable time frame for retaining research and client communication records. Fulfilling such regulatory and firm requirements satisfies the requirements of Standard V(C).
- In the absence of regulatory guidance or firm policies, CFA Institute recommends maintaining records for at least seven years.

Recommended Procedures for Compliance

The responsibility to maintain records that support investment action generally falls with the firm rather than individuals. Members and candidates must, however, archive research notes and other documents, either electronically or in hard copy, that support their current investment-related communications.

Application of the Standard

Example 1 (Record Retention and Research Process)

Malcolm Young is a research analyst who writes numerous reports rating companies in the luxury retail industry. His reports are based on a variety of sources, including interviews with company managers, manufacturers, and economists; on-site company visits; customer surveys; and secondary research from analysts covering related industries.

Comment: Young must carefully document and keep copies of all the information that goes into his reports, including the secondary or third-party research of other analysts. Failure to maintain such files would violate Standard V(C).

Example 2 (Records as Firm, Not Employee, Property)

Martin Blank develops an analytical model while he is employed by Green Partners Investment Management, LLP (GPIM). While at the firm, he systematically documents the assumptions that make up the model as well as his reasoning behind the assumptions. As a result of the success of his model, Blank is hired to be the head of the research department of one of GPIM's competitors. Blank takes copies of the records supporting his model to his new firm.

Comment: The records created by Blank supporting the research model he developed at GPIM are the records of GPIM. Taking the documents with him to his new employer without GPIM's permission violates Standard V(C). To use the model in the future, Blank must re-create the records supporting his model at the new firm.

© 2015 Wiley

LESSON 6: STANDARD VI: CONFLICTS OF INTEREST

A. Disclosure of Conflicts
B. Priority of Transactions
C. Referral Fees

Standard VI(A) Disclosure of Conflicts

The Standard

Members and candidates must make full and fair disclosure of all matters that could reasonably be expected to impair their independence and objectivity or interfere with respective duties to their clients, prospective clients, and employer. Members and candidates must ensure that such disclosures are prominent, are delivered in plain language, and communicate the relevant information effectively.

Guidance

- Best practice is to avoid actual conflicts or the appearance of conflicts of interest when possible. Conflicts of interest often arise in the investment profession.
- When conflicts cannot be reasonably avoided, clear and complete disclosure of their existence is necessary.
- In making and updating disclosures of conflicts of interest, members and candidates should err on the side of caution to ensure that conflicts are effectively communicated.

Disclosure of Conflicts to Employers

- When reporting conflicts of interest to employers, members and candidates must give their employers enough information to assess the impact of the conflict.
- Members and candidates must take reasonable steps to avoid conflicts and, if they occur inadvertently, must report them promptly so that the employer and the member or candidate can resolve them as quickly and effectively as possible.
- Any potential conflict situation that could prevent clear judgment about or full commitment to the execution of a member's or candidate's duties to the employer should be reported to the member's or candidate's employer and promptly resolved.

Disclosure to Clients

- The most obvious conflicts of interest, which should always be disclosed, are relationships between an issuer and the member, the candidate, or his or her firm (such as a directorship or consultancy by a member; investment banking, underwriting, and financial relationships; broker/dealer market-making activities; and material beneficial ownership of stock).
- Disclosures should be made to clients regarding fee arrangements, subadvisory agreements, or other situations involving nonstandard fee structures. Equally important is the disclosure of arrangements in which the firm benefits directly from investment recommendations. An obvious conflict of interest is the rebate of a portion of the service fee some classes of mutual funds charge to investors.

© 2015 Wiley

Cross-Departmental Conflicts

- Other circumstances can give rise to actual or potential conflicts of interest. For instance:
  - A sell-side analyst working for a broker/dealer may be encouraged, not only by members of her or his own firm but by corporate issuers themselves, to write research reports about particular companies.
  - A buy-side analyst is likely to be faced with similar conflicts as banks exercise their underwriting and security-dealing powers.
  - The marketing division may ask an analyst to recommend the stock of a certain company in order to obtain business from that company.
- Members, candidates, and their firms should attempt to resolve situations presenting potential conflicts of interest or disclose them in accordance with the principles set forth in Standard VI(A).

Conflicts with Stock Ownership

- The most prevalent conflict requiring disclosure under Standard VI(A) is a member's or candidate's ownership of stock in companies that he or she recommends to clients or that clients hold. Clearly, the easiest method for preventing a conflict is to prohibit members and candidates from owning any such securities, but this approach is overly burdensome and discriminates against members and candidates. Therefore:
  - Sell-side members and candidates should disclose any materially beneficial ownership interest in a security or other investment that the member or candidate is recommending.
  - Buy-side members and candidates should disclose their procedures for reporting requirements for personal transactions.

Conflicts as a Director

- Service as a director poses three basic conflicts of interest.
  - A conflict may exist between the duties owed to clients and the duties owed to shareholders of the company.
  - Investment personnel who serve as directors may receive the securities or options to purchase securities of the company as compensation for serving on the board, which could raise questions about trading actions that might increase the value of those securities.
  - Board service creates the opportunity to receive material nonpublic information involving the company.
- When members or candidates providing investment services also serve as directors, they should be isolated from those making investment decisions by the use of firewalls or similar restrictions.

Recommended Procedures for Compliance

- Members or candidates should disclose special compensation arrangements with the employer that might conflict with client interests, such as bonuses based on short-term performance criteria, commissions, incentive fees, performance fees, and referral fees.
- Members' and candidates' firms are encouraged to include information on compensation packages in firms' promotional literature.

© 2015 Wiley

Application of the Standard

Example 1 (Conflict of Interest and Business Relationships)

Hunter Weiss is a research analyst with Farmington Company, a broker and investment banking firm. Farmington's merger and acquisition department has represented Vimco, a conglomerate, in all of Vimco's acquisitions for 20 years. From time to time, Farmington officers sit on the boards of directors of various Vimco subsidiaries. Weiss is writing a research report on Vimco.

Comment: Weiss must disclose in his research report Farmington's special relationship with Vimco. Broker/dealer management of and participation in public offerings must be disclosed in research reports. Because the position of underwriter to a company entails a special past and potential future relationship with a company that is the subject of investment advice, it threatens the independence and objectivity of the report writer and must be disclosed.

Example 2 (Conflict of Interest and Business Stock Ownership)

The investment management firm of Dover & Roe sells a 25% interest in its partnership to a multinational bank holding company, First of New York. Immediately after the sale, Margaret Hobbs, president of Dover & Roe, changes her recommendation for First of New York's common stock from "sell" to "buy" and adds First of New York's commercial paper to Dover & Roe's approved list for purchase.

Comment: Hobbs must disclose the new relationship with First of New York to all Dover & Roe clients. This relationship must also be disclosed to clients by the firm's portfolio managers when they make specific investment recommendations or take investment actions with respect to First of New York's securities.

Example 3 (Conflict of Interest and Personal Stock Ownership)

Carl Fargmon, a research analyst who follows firms producing office equipment, has been recommending purchase of Kincaid Printing because of its innovative new line of copiers. After his initial report on the company, Fargmon's wife inherits from a distant relative US$3 million of Kincaid stock. He has been asked to write a follow-up report on Kincaid.

Comment: Fargmon must disclose his wife's ownership of the Kincaid stock to his employer and in his follow-up report. Best practice would be to avoid the conflict by asking his employer to assign another analyst to draft the follow-up report.

Example 4 (Conflict of Interest and Personal Stock Ownership)

Betty Roberts is speculating in penny stocks for her own account and purchases 100,000 shares of Drew Mining, Inc., for US$0.30 a share. She intends to sell these shares at the sign of any substantial upward price movement of the stock. A week later, her employer asks her to write a report on penny stocks in the mining industry to be published in two weeks. Even without owning the Drew stock, Roberts would recommend it in her report

© 2015 Wiley

as a "buy." A surge in the price of the stock to the US$2 range is likely to result once the report is issued.

Comment: Although this holding may not be material, Roberts must disclose it in the report and to her employer before writing the report because the gain for her will be substantial if the market responds strongly to her recommendation. The fact that she has only recently purchased the stock adds to the appearance that she is not entirely objective.

Example 5 (Conflict of Interest and Compensation Arrangements)

Gary Carter is a representative with Bengal International, a registered broker/dealer. Carter is approached by a stock promoter for Badger Company, who offers to pay Carter additional compensation for sales of Badger Company's stock to Carter's clients. Carter accepts the stock promoter's offer but does not disclose the arrangements to his clients or to his employer. Carter sells shares of the stock to his clients.

Comment: Carter has violated Standard VI(A) by failing to disclose to clients that he is receiving additional compensation for recommending and selling Badger stock. Because he did not disclose the arrangement with Badger to his clients, the clients were unable to evaluate whether Carter's recommendations to buy Badger were affected by this arrangement. Carter's conduct also violated Standard VI(A) by failing to disclose to his employer monetary compensation received in addition to the compensation and benefits conferred by his employer. Carter was required by Standard VI(A) to disclose the arrangement with Badger to his employer so that his employer could evaluate whether the arrangement affected Carter's objectivity and loyalty.

Example 6 (Conflict of Interest and Directorship)

Carol Corky, a senior portfolio manager for Universal Management, recently became involved as a trustee with the Chelsea Foundation, a large not-for-profit foundation in her hometown. Universal is a small money manager (with assets under management of approximately US$100 million) that caters to individual investors. Chelsea has assets in excess of US$2 billion. Corky does not believe informing Universal of her involvement with Chelsea is necessary.

Comment: By failing to inform Universal of her involvement with Chelsea, Corky violated Standard VI(A). Given the large size of the endowment at Chelsea, Corky's new role as a trustee can reasonably be expected to be time consuming, to the possible detriment of Corky's portfolio responsibilities with Universal. Also, as a trustee, Corky may become involved in the investment decisions at Chelsea. Therefore, Standard VI(A) obligates Corky to discuss becoming a trustee at Chelsea with her compliance officer or supervisor at Universal before accepting the position, and she should have disclosed the degree to which she would be involved in investment decisions at Chelsea.

Example 7 (Conflict of Interest and Requested Favors)

Michael Papis is the chief investment officer of his state's retirement fund. The fund has always used outside advisers for the real estate allocation, and this information is clearly presented in all fund communications. Thomas Nagle, a recognized sell-side research analyst and Papis's business school classmate, recently left the investment bank he worked for to start his own asset management firm, Accessible Real Estate. Nagle is trying to build his assets under management and contacts Papis about gaining some of the retirement fund's allocation. In the previous few years, the performance of the retirement fund's real estate investments was in line with the fund's benchmark but was not extraordinary. Papis decides to help out his old friend and also to seek better returns by moving the real estate allocation to Accessible. The only notice of the change in adviser appears in the next annual report in the listing of associated advisers.

Comment: Papis has violated Standard VI(A) by not disclosing to his employer his personal relationship with Nagle. Disclosure of his past history with Nagle would allow his firm to determine whether the conflict may have impaired Papis's independence in deciding to change managers.

See also Standard IV(C)—Responsibilities of Supervisors, Standard V(A)—Diligence and Reasonable Basis, and Standard V(B)—Communication with Clients and Prospective Clients.

Example 8 (Conflict of Interest and Business Relationships)

Bob Wade, trust manager for Central Midas Bank, was approached by Western Funds about promoting its family of funds, with special interest in the service-fee class. To entice Central to promote this class, Western Funds offered to pay the bank a service fee of 0.25%. Without disclosing the fee being offered to the bank, Wade asked one of the investment managers to review the Western Funds family of funds to determine whether they were suitable for clients of Central. The manager completed the normal due diligence review and determined that the funds were fairly valued in the market with fee structures on a par with their competitors. Wade decided to accept Western's offer and instructed the team of portfolio managers to exclusively promote these funds and the service-fee class to clients seeking to invest new funds or transfer from their current investments. So as to not influence the investment managers, Wade did not disclose the fee offer and allowed that income to flow directly to the bank.

Comment: Wade is violating Standard VI(A) by not disclosing the portion of the service fee being paid to Central. Although the investment managers may not be influenced by the fee, neither they nor the client have the proper information about Wade's decision to exclusively market this fund family and class of investments. Central may come to rely on the new fee as a component of the firm's profitability and may be unwilling to offer other products in the future that could affect the fees received.

(See also Standard I(B)—Independence and Objectivity.)

Example 9 (Disclosure of Conflicts to Employers)

Yehudit Dagan is a portfolio manager for Risk Management Bank (RMB), whose clients include retirement plans and corporations. RMB provides a defined contribution retirement plan for its employees that offers 20 large diversified mutual fund investment options, including a mutual fund managed by Dagan's RMB colleagues. After being employed for six months, Dagan became eligible to participate in the retirement plan, and she intends to allocate her retirement plan assets in six of the investment options, including the fund managed by her RMB colleagues. Dagan is concerned

© 2015 Wiley

that joining the plan will lead to a potentially significant amount of paperwork for her (e.g., disclosure of her retirement account holdings and needing preclearance for her transactions), especially with her investing in the in-house fund.

Comment: Standard VI(A) would not require Dagan to disclosure her personal or retirement investments in large diversified mutual funds, unless specifically required by her employer. For practical reasons, the standard does not require Dagan to gain preclearance for ongoing payroll deduction contributions to retirement plan account investment options.

Dagan should ensure that her firm does not have a specific policy regarding investment—whether personal or in the retirement account—for funds managed by the company's employees. These mutual funds may be subject to the company's disclosure, preclearance, and trading restriction procedures to identify possible conflicts prior to the execution of trades.

Standard VI(B) Priority of Transactions

The Standard

Investment transactions for clients and employers must have priority over investment transactions in which a member or candidate is the beneficial owner.

Guidance

- This standard is designed to prevent any potential conflict of interest or the appearance of a conflict of interest with respect to personal transactions.
- Client interests have priority. Client transactions must take precedence over transactions made on behalf of the member's or candidate's firm or personal transactions.

Avoiding Potential Conflicts

- Although conflicts of interest exist, nothing is inherently unethical about individual managers, advisers, or mutual fund employees making money from personal investments as long as (1) the client is not disadvantaged by the trade, (2) the investment professional does not benefit personally from trades undertaken for clients, and (3) the investment professional complies with applicable regulatory requirements.
- Some situations occur in which a member or candidate may need to enter a personal transaction that runs counter to current recommendations or what the portfolio manager is doing for client portfolios. In these situations, the same three criteria given in the preceding paragraph should be applied in the transaction so as to not violate Standard VI(B).

Personal Trading Secondary to Trading for Clients

- The objective of the standard is to prevent personal transactions from adversely affecting the interests of clients or employers. A member or candidate having the same investment positions or being co-invested with clients does not always create a conflict.
- Personal investment positions or transactions of members or candidates or their firm should never, however, adversely affect client investments.

© 2015 Wiley

Standards for Nonpublic Information

- Standard VI(B) covers the activities of members and candidates who have knowledge of pending transactions that may be made on behalf of their clients or employers, who have access to nonpublic information during the normal preparation of research recommendations, or who take investment actions.
- Members and candidates are prohibited from conveying nonpublic information to any person whose relationship to the member or candidate makes the member or candidate a beneficial owner of the person's securities.
- Members and candidates must not convey this information to any other person if the nonpublic information can be deemed material.

Impact on All Accounts with Beneficial Ownership

- Members or candidates may undertake transactions in accounts for which they are a beneficial owner only after their clients and employers have had adequate opportunity to act on a recommendation.
- Personal transactions include those made for the member's or candidate's own account, for family (including spouse, children, and other immediate family members) accounts, and for accounts in which the member or candidate has a direct or indirect pecuniary interest, such as a trust or retirement account.
- Family accounts that are client accounts should be treated like any other firm account and should neither be given special treatment nor be disadvantaged because of the family relationship. If a member or candidate has a beneficial ownership in the account, however, the member or candidate may be subject to preclearance or reporting requirements of the employer or applicable law.

Recommended Procedures for Compliance

- Members and candidates should urge their firms to establish such policies and procedures.
- The specific provisions of each firm's standards will vary, but all firms should adopt certain basic procedures to address the conflict areas created by personal investing. These procedures include the following:
    - Limited participation in equity IPOs.
    - Restrictions on private placements.
    - Establish blackout/restricted periods.
    - Reporting requirements, including:
        - Disclosure of holdings in which the employee has a beneficial interest.
        - Providing duplicate confirmations of transactions.
        - Preclearance procedures.
    - Disclosure of policies to investors.

Application of the Standard

Example 1 (Personal Trading)

Research analyst Marlon Long does not recommend purchase of a common stock for his employer's account because he wants to purchase the stock personally and does not want to wait until the recommendation is approved and the stock is purchased by his employer.

Comment: Long has violated Standard VI(B) by taking advantage of his knowledge of the stock's value before allowing his employer to benefit from that information.

© 2015 Wiley

Example 2 (Trading for Family Member Account)

Carol Baker, the portfolio manager of an aggressive growth mutual fund, maintains an account in her husband's name at several brokerage firms with which the fund and a number of Baker's other individual clients do a substantial amount of business. Whenever a hot issue becomes available, she instructs the brokers to buy it for her husband's account. Because such issues normally are scarce, Baker often acquires shares in hot issues but her clients are not able to participate in them.

Comment: To avoid violating Standard VI(B), Baker must acquire shares for her mutual fund first and acquire them for her husband's account only after doing so, even though she might miss out on participating in new issues via her husband's account. She also must disclose the trading for her husband's account to her employer because this activity creates a conflict between her personal interests and her employer's interests.

Example 3 (Trading Prior to Report Dissemination)

A brokerage's insurance analyst, Denise Wilson, makes a closed-circuit TV report to her firm's branches around the country. During the broadcast, she includes negative comments about a major company in the insurance industry. The following day, Wilson's report is printed and distributed to the sales force and public customers. The report recommends that both short-term traders and intermediate investors take profits by selling that insurance company's stock. Seven minutes after the broadcast, however, Ellen Riley, head of the firm's trading department, had closed out a long "call" position in the stock. Shortly thereafter, Riley established a sizable "put" position in the stock. When asked about her activities, Riley claimed she took the actions to facilitate anticipated sales by institutional clients.

Comment: Riley did not give customers an opportunity to buy or sell in the options market before the firm itself did. By taking action before the report was disseminated, Riley's firm may have depressed the price of the calls and increased the price of the puts. The firm could have avoided a conflict of interest if it had waited to trade for its own account until its clients had an opportunity to receive and assimilate Wilson's recommendations. As it is, Riley's actions violated Standard VI(B).

Standard VI(C) Referral Fees

The Standard

Members and candidates must disclose to their employer, clients, and prospective clients, as appropriate, any compensation, consideration, or benefit received from or paid to others for the recommendation of products or services.

Guidance

- Members and candidates must inform their employer, clients, and prospective clients of any benefit received for referrals of customers and clients.
- Members and candidates must disclose when they pay a fee or provide compensation to others who have referred prospective clients to the member or candidate.

- Appropriate disclosure means that members and candidates must advise the client or prospective client, before entry into any formal agreement for services, of any benefit given or received for the recommendation of any services provided by the member or candidate. In addition, the member or candidate must disclose the nature of the consideration or benefit

Recommended Procedures for Compliance

- Members and candidates should encourage their employers to develop procedures related to referral fees. The firm may completely restrict such fees. If the firm does not adopt a strict prohibition of such fees, the procedures should indicate the appropriate steps for requesting approval.
- Employers should have investment professionals provide to the clients notification of approved referral fee programs and provide the employer regular (at least quarterly) updates on the amount and nature of compensation received.

Application of the Standard

Example 1 (Disclosure of Interdepartmental Referral Arrangements)

James Handley works for the trust department of Central Trust Bank. He receives compensation for each referral he makes to Central Trust's brokerage department and personal financial management department that results in a sale. He refers several of his clients to the personal financial management department but does not disclose the arrangement within Central Trust to his clients.

Comment: Handley has violated Standard VI(C) by not disclosing the referral arrangement at Central Trust Bank to his clients. Standard VI(C) does not distinguish between referral payments paid by a third party for referring clients to the third party and internal payments paid within the firm to attract new business to a subsidiary. Members and candidates must disclose all such referral fees. Therefore, Handley is required to disclose, at the time of referral, any referral fee agreement in place among Central Trust Bank's departments. The disclosure should include the nature and the value of the benefit and should be made in writing.

Example 2 (Disclosure of Referral Arrangements and Informing Firm)

Katherine Roberts is a portfolio manager at Katama Investments, an advisory firm specializing in managing assets for high-net-worth individuals. Katama's trading desk uses a variety of brokerage houses to execute trades on behalf of its clients. Roberts asks the trading desk to direct a large portion of its commissions to Naushon, Inc., a small broker/dealer run by one of Roberts's business school classmates. Katama's traders have found that Naushon is not very competitive on pricing, and although Naushon generates some research for its trading clients, Katama's other analysts have found most of Naushon's research to be not especially useful. Nevertheless, the traders do as Roberts asks, and in return for receiving a large portion of Katama's business, Naushon recommends the investment services of Roberts and Katama to its wealthiest clients. This arrangement is not disclosed to either Katama or the clients referred by Naushon.

Comment: Roberts is violating Standard VI(C) by failing to inform her employer of the referral arrangement.

© 2015 Wiley

Example 3 (Disclosure of Referral Arrangements and Outside Organizations)

Alex Burl is a portfolio manager at Helpful Investments, a local investment advisory firm. Burl is on the advisory board of his child's school, which is looking for ways to raise money to purchase new playground equipment for the school. Burl discusses a plan with his supervisor in which he will donate to the school a portion of his service fee from new clients referred by the parents of students at the school. Upon getting the approval from Helpful, Burl presents the idea to the school's advisory board and directors. The school agrees to announce the program at the next parent event and asks Burl to provide the appropriate written materials to be distributed. A week following the distribution of the fliers, Burl receives the first school-related referral. In establishing the client's investment policy statement, Burl clearly discusses the school's referral and outlines the plans for distributing the donation back to the school.

Comment: Burl has not violated Standard VI(C) because he secured the permission of his employer, Helpful Investments, and the school prior to beginning the program and because he discussed the arrangement with the client at the time the investment policy statement was designed.

Example 4 (Disclosure of Referral Arrangements and Outside Parties)

The sponsor of a state employee pension is seeking to hire a firm to manage the pension plan's emerging market allocation. To assist in the review process, the sponsor has hired Thomas Arrow as a consultant to solicit proposals from various advisers. Arrow is contracted by the sponsor to represent its best interest in selecting the most appropriate new manager. The process runs smoothly, and Overseas Investments is selected as the new manager.

The following year, news breaks that Arrow is under investigation by the local regulator for accepting kickbacks from investment managers after they are awarded new pension allocations. Overseas Investments is included in the list of firms allegedly making these payments. Although the sponsor is happy with the performance of Overseas since it has been managing the pension plan's emerging market funds, the sponsor still decides to have an independent review of the proposals and the selection process to ensure that Overseas was the appropriate firm for its needs. This review confirms that, even though Arrow was being paid by both parties, the recommendation of Overseas appeared to be objective and appropriate.

Comment: Arrow has violated Standard VI(C) because he did not disclose the fee being paid by Overseas. Withholding this information raises the question of a potential lack of objectivity in the recommendations Overseas is making; this aspect is in addition to questions about the legality of having firms pay to be considered for an allocation.

Regulators and governmental agencies may adopt requirements concerning allowable consultant activities. Local regulations sometimes include having a consultant register with the regulatory agency's ethics board. Regulator policies may include a prohibition on acceptance of payments from investment managers receiving allocations and require regular reporting of contributions made to political organizations and candidates. Arrow would have to adhere to these requirements as well as the Code and Standards.

© 2015 Wiley

LESSON 7: STANDARD VII: RESPONSIBILITIES AS A CFA INSTITUTE MEMBER OR CFA CANDIDATE

A. Conduct As Participants in the CFA Institute Program
B. Reference to CFA Institute, the CFA Designation, and the CFA Program

Standard VII(A) Conduct as Participants in CFA Institute Programs

The Standard

Members and candidates must not engage in any conduct that compromises the reputation or integrity of CFA Institute or the CFA designation or the integrity, validity, or security of CFA Institute programs.

Guidance

- Standard VII(A) prohibits any conduct that undermines the public's confidence that the CFA charter represents a level of achievement based on merit and ethical conduct.
- Conduct covered includes but is not limited to:
  - Giving or receiving assistance (cheating) on any CFA Institute examinations.
  - Violating the rules, regulations, and testing policies of CFA Institute programs.
  - Providing confidential program or exam information to candidates or the public.
  - Disregarding or attempting to circumvent security measures established for any CFA Institute examinations.
  - Improperly using an association with CFA Institute to further personal or professional goals.
  - Misrepresenting information on the Professional Conduct Statement or in the CFA Institute Continuing Education Program.

Confidential Program Information

- Examples of information that cannot be disclosed by candidates sitting for an exam include but are not limited to:
  - Specific details of questions appearing on the exam.
  - Broad topical areas and formulas tested or not tested on the exam.
- All aspects of the exam, including questions, broad topical areas, and formulas, tested or not tested, are considered confidential until such time as CFA Institute elects to release them publicly.

Additional CFA Program Restrictions

- Violating any of the testing policies, such as the calculator policy, personal belongings policy, or the Candidate Pledge, constitutes a violation of Standard VII(A).
- Examples of information that cannot be shared by members involved in developing, administering, or grading the exams include but are not limited to:
  - Questions appearing on the exam or under consideration.
  - Deliberation related to the exam process.
  - Information related to the scoring of questions.

© 2015 Wiley

Expressing an Opinion

- Standard VII(A) does *not* cover expressing opinions regarding CFA Institute, the CFA Program, or other CFA Institute programs.
- However, when expressing a personal opinion, a candidate is prohibited from disclosing content-specific information, including any actual exam question and the information as to subject matter covered or not covered in the exam.

Application of the Standard

Example 1 (Sharing Exam Questions)

Travis Nero serves as a proctor for the administration of the CFA examination in his city. In the course of his service, he reviews a copy of the Level II exam on the evening prior to the exam's administration and provides information concerning the exam questions to two candidates who use it to prepare for the exam.

Comment: Nero and the two candidates have violated Standard VII(A). By giving information about the exam questions to two candidates, Nero provided an unfair advantage to the two candidates and undermined the integrity and validity of the Level II exam as an accurate measure of the knowledge, skills, and abilities necessary to earn the right to use the CFA designation. By accepting the information, the candidates also compromised the integrity and validity of the Level II exam and undermined the ethical framework that is a key part of the designation.

Example 2 (Sharing Exam Content)

After completing Level II of the CFA exam, Annabelle Rossi posts on her blog about her experience. She posts the following: "Level II is complete! I think I did fairly well on the exam. It was really difficult, but fair. I think I did especially well on the derivatives questions. And there were tons of them! I think I counted 18! The ethics questions were really hard. I'm glad I spent so much time on the Code and Standards. I was surprised to see there were no questions at all about IPO allocations. I expected there to be a couple. Well, off to celebrate getting through it. See you tonight?"

Comment: Rossi did not violate Standard VII(A) when she wrote about how difficult she found the exam or how well she thinks she may have done. By revealing portions of the CBOK covered on the exam and areas not covered, however, she did violate Standard VII(A) and the Candidate Pledge. Depending on the time frame in which the comments were posted, Rossi not only may have assisted future candidates but also may have provided an unfair advantage to candidates yet to sit for the same exam, thereby undermining the integrity and validity of the Level II exam.

Example 3 (Sharing Exam Content)

Level I candidate Etienne Gagne has been a frequent visitor to an Internet forum designed specifically for CFA Program candidates. The week after completing the Level I examination, Gagne and several others begin a discussion thread on the forum about the most challenging questions and attempt to determine the correct answers.

© 2015 Wiley

Comment: Gagne has violated Standard VII(A) by providing and soliciting confidential exam information, which compromises the integrity of the exam process and violates the Candidate Pledge. In trying to determine correct answers to specific questions, the group's discussion included question-specific details considered to be confidential to the CFA Program.

Example 4 (Sharing Exam Content)

CFA4Sure is a company that produces test-preparation materials for CFA Program candidates. Many candidates register for and use the company's products. The day after the CFA examination, CFA4Sure sends an e-mail to all its customers asking them to share with the company the hardest questions from the exam so that CFA4Sure can better prepare its customers for the next exam administration. Marisol Pena e-mails a summary of the questions she found most difficult on the exam.

Comment: Pena has violated Standard VII(A) by disclosing a portion of the exam questions. The information provided is considered confidential until publicly released by CFA Institute. CFA4Sure is likely to use such feedback to refine its review materials for future candidates. Pena's sharing of the specific questions undermines the integrity of the exam while potentially making the exam easier for future candidates.

If the CFA4Sure employees who participated in the solicitation of confidential CFA Program information are CFA Institute members or candidates, they also have violated Standard VII(A).

Example 5 (Compromising CFA Institute Integrity as a Volunteer)

Jose Ramirez is an investor-relations consultant for several small companies that are seeking greater exposure to investors. He is also the program chair for the CFA Institute society in the city where he works. Ramirez schedules only companies that are his clients to make presentations to the society and excludes other companies.

Comment: Ramirez, by using his volunteer position at CFA Institute to benefit himself and his clients, compromises the reputation and integrity of CFA Institute and thus violates Standard VII(A).

Example 6 (Compromising CFA Institute Integrity as a Volunteer)

Marguerite Warrenski is a member of the CFA Institute GIPS Executive Committee, which oversees the creation, implementation, and revision of the GIPS standards. As a member of the Executive Committee, she has advance knowledge of confidential information regarding the GIPS standards, including any new or revised standards the committee is considering. She tells her clients that her Executive Committee membership will allow her to better assist her clients in keeping up with changes to the Standards and facilitating their compliance with the changes.

Comment: Warrenski is using her association with the GIPS Executive Committee to promote her firm's services to clients and potential clients. In defining her volunteer position at CFA Institute as a strategic business advantage over competing firms

© 2015 Wiley

and implying to clients that she would use confidential information to further their interests, Warrenski is compromising the reputation and integrity of CFA Institute and thus violating Standard VII(A). She may factually state her involvement with the Executive Committee but cannot infer any special advantage to her clients from such participation.

Standard VII(B) Reference to CFA Institute, the CFA Designation, and the CFA Program

The Standard

When referring to CFA Institute, CFA Institute membership, the CFA designation, or candidacy in the CFA Program, members and candidates must not misrepresent or exaggerate the meaning or implications of membership in CFA Institute, holding the CFA designation, or candidacy in the CFA Program.

Guidance

- Standard VII(B) is intended to prevent promotional efforts that make promises or guarantees that are tied to the CFA designation. Individuals may refer to their CFA designation, CFA Institute membership, or candidacy in the CFA Program but must not exaggerate the meaning or implications of membership in CFA Institute, holding the CFA designation, or candidacy in the CFA Program.
- Standard VII(B) is not intended to prohibit factual statements related to the positive benefit of earning the CFA designation. However, statements referring to CFA Institute, the CFA designation, or the CFA Program that overstate the competency of an individual or imply, either directly or indirectly, that superior performance can be expected from someone with the CFA designation are not allowed under the standard.
- Statements that highlight or emphasize the commitment of CFA Institute members, CFA charterholders, and CFA candidates to ethical and professional conduct or mention the thoroughness and rigor of the CFA Program are appropriate.
- Members and candidates may make claims about the relative merits of CFA Institute, the CFA Program, or the Code and Standards as long as those statements are implicitly or explicitly stated as the opinion of the speaker.
- Standard VII(B) applies to any form of communication, including but not limited to communications made in electronic or written form (such as on firm letterhead, business cards, professional biographies, directory listings, printed advertising, firm brochures, or personal resumes), and oral statements made to the public, clients, or prospects.

CFA Institute Membership

The term "CFA Institute member" refers to "regular" and "affiliate" members of CFA Institute who have met the membership requirements as defined in the CFA Institute Bylaws. Once accepted as a CFA Institute member, the member must satisfy the following requirements to maintain his or her status:

- Remit annually to CFA Institute a completed Professional Conduct Statement, which renews the commitment to abide by the requirements of the Code and Standards and the CFA Institute Professional Conduct Program.
- Pay applicable CFA Institute membership dues on an annual basis.

© 2015 Wiley

If a CFA Institute member fails to meet any of these requirements, the individual is no longer considered an active member. Until membership is reactivated, individuals must not present themselves to others as active members. They may state, however, that they were CFA Institute members in the past or refer to the years when their membership was active.

Using the CFA Designation

- Those who have earned the right to use the Chartered Financial Analyst designation may use the trademarks or registered marks "Chartered Financial Analyst" or "CFA" and are encouraged to do so but only in a manner that does not misrepresent or exaggerate the meaning or implications of the designation.
- The use of the designation may be accompanied by an accurate explanation of the requirements that have been met to earn the right to use the designation.
- "CFA charterholders" are those individuals who have earned the right to use the CFA designation granted by CFA Institute. These people have satisfied certain requirements, including completion of the CFA Program and required years of acceptable work experience. Once granted the right to use the designation, individuals must also satisfy the CFA Institute membership requirements (see above) to maintain their right to use the designation.
- If a CFA charterholder fails to meet any of the membership requirements, he or she forfeits the right to use the CFA designation. Until membership is reactivated, individuals must not present themselves to others as CFA charterholders. They may state, however, that they were charterholders in the past.
- Given the growing popularity of social media, where individuals may anonymously express their opinions, pseudonyms or online profile names created to hide a member's identity should not be tagged with the CFA designation.

Referring to Candidacy in the CFA Program

- Candidates in the CFA Program may refer to their participation in the CFA Program, but such references must clearly state that an individual is a *candidate* in the CFA Program and must not imply that the candidate has achieved any type of partial designation. A person is a candidate in the CFA Program if:
    - The person's application for registration in the CFA Program has been accepted by CFA Institute, as evidenced by issuance of a notice of acceptance, and the person is enrolled to sit for a specified examination; or
    - The registered person has sat for a specified examination but exam results have not yet been received.
- If an individual is registered for the CFA Program but declines to sit for an exam or otherwise does not meet the definition of a candidate as described in the CFA Institute Bylaws, then that individual is no longer considered an active candidate. Once the person is enrolled to sit for a future examination, his or her CFA candidacy resumes.
- CFA candidates must never state or imply that they have a partial designation as a result of passing one or more levels, or cite an expected completion date of any level of the CFA Program. Final award of the charter is subject to meeting the CFA Program requirements and approval by the CFA Institute Board of Governors.
- If a candidate passes each level of the exam in consecutive years and wants to state that he or she did so, that is not a violation of Standard VII(B) because it is a statement of fact. If the candidate then goes on to claim or imply superior ability by obtaining the designation in only three years, however, he or she is in violation of Standard VII(B).

© 2015 Wiley

Proper and Improper References to the CFA Designation

Proper References	Improper References
"Completion of the CFA Program has enhanced my portfolio management skills."	"CFA charterholders achieve better performance results."
"John Smith passed all three CFA examinations in three consecutive years."	"John Smith is among the elite, having passed all three CFA examinations in three consecutive attempts."
"The CFA designation is globally recognized and attests to a charterholder's success in a rigorous and comprehensive study program in the field of investment management and research analysis."	"As a CFA charterholder, I am the most qualified to manage client investments."
"The credibility that the CFA designation affords and the skills the CFA Program cultivates are key assets for my future career development."	"As a CFA charterholder, Jane White provides the best value in trade execution."
"I enrolled in the CFA Program to obtain the highest set of credentials in the global investment management industry."	"Enrolling as a candidate in the CFA Program ensures one of becoming better at valuing debt securities."
"I passed Level I of the CFA exam."	"CFA, Level II"
"I am a 2010 Level III candidate in the CFA Program."	"CFA, Expected 2011" "Level III CFA Candidate"
"I passed all three levels of the CFA Program and will be eligible for the CFA charter upon completion of the required work experience."	"CFA, Expected 2011" "John Smith, Charter Pending"
"As a CFA charterholder, I am committed to the highest ethical standards."	

Proper Usage of the CFA Marks

- Upon obtaining the CFA charter from CFA Institute, charterholders are given the right to use the CFA marks, including Chartered Financial Analyst®, CFA®, and the CFA logo (a certification mark).
- The Chartered Financial Analyst and CFA marks must always be used either after a charterholder's name or as adjectives (never as nouns) in written documents or oral conversations. For example, to refer to oneself as "a CFA" or "a Chartered Financial Analyst" is improper.
- Members and candidates must not use a pseudonym or fictitious phrase meant to hide their identity in conjunction with the CFA designation. CFA Institute can verify only that a specific individual has earned the designation according to the name that is maintained in the membership database.
- The CFA logo certification mark is used by charterholders as a distinctive visual symbol of the CFA designation that can be easily recognized by employers, colleagues, and clients. As a certification mark, it must be used only to directly refer to an individual charterholder or group of charterholders.

© 2015 Wiley

Correct and Incorrect Use of the Chartered Financial Analyst and CFA Marks

Correct	Incorrect	Principle
He is one of two CFA charterholders in the company.	He is one of two CFAs in the company.	The CFA and Chartered Financial Analyst designations must always be used as adjectives, never as nouns or common names.
He earned the right to use the Chartered Financial Analyst designation.	He is a Chartered Financial Analyst.	
Jane Smith, CFA	Jane Smith, C.F.A. John Doe, cfa	No periods. Always capitalize the letters "CFA."
	John, a CFA-type portfolio manager.	
John Jones, CFA	The focus is on Chartered Financial Analysis.	Do not alter the designation to create new words or phrases.
	CFA-equivalent program. Swiss-CFA.	
John Jones, Chartered Financial Analyst	Jones Chartered Financial Analysts, Inc.	The designation must not be used as part of the name of a firm.
Jane Smith, CFA John Doe, Chartered Financial Analyst	Jane Smith, **CFA** John Doe, **Chartered Financial Analyst**	The CFA designation should not be given more prominence (e.g., larger or bold font) than the charterholder's name.
Level I candidate in the CFA Program.	Chartered Financial Analyst (CFA), September 2011.	Candidates in the CFA Program must not cite the expected date of exam completion and award of charter.
Passed Level I of the CFA examination in 2010.	CFA Level I. CFA degree expected in 2011.	No designation exists for someone who has passed Level I, Level II, or Level III of the exam. The CFA designation should not be referred to as a degree.
I have passed all three levels of the CFA Program and may be eligible for the CFA charter upon completion of the required work experience.	CFA (Passed Finalist) CFA Charter Pending Pending CFA Charterholder	A candidate who has passed Level III but has not yet received his or her charter cannot use the CFA or Chartered Financial Analyst designation.

© 2015 Wiley

Correct	Incorrect	Principle
CFA Charter, 2009, CFA Institute (optional: Charlottesville, Virginia, USA)	CFA Charter, 2009, CFA Society of the UK	In citing the designation in a resume, a charterholder should use the date that he or she received the designation and should cite CFA Institute as the conferring body.
John Smith, CFA	Crazy Bear CFA (Online social media user name)	Charterholders should not attach the CFA designation to anonymous or fictitious names meant to conceal their identity.

Application of the Standard

Example 1 (Passing Exams in Consecutive Years)

An advertisement for AZ Investment Advisors states that all the firm's principals are CFA charterholders and all passed the three examinations on their first attempt. The advertisement prominently links this fact to the notion that AZ's mutual funds have achieved superior performance.

Comment: AZ may state that all principals passed the three examinations on the first try as long as this statement is true, but it must not be linked to performance or imply superior ability. Implying that (1) CFA charterholders achieve better investment results and (2) those who pass the exams on the first try may be more successful than those who do not violates Standard VII(B).

Example 2 (Right to Use CFA Designation)

Five years after receiving his CFA charter, Louis Vasseur resigns his position as an investment analyst and spends the next two years traveling abroad. Because he is not actively engaged in the investment profession, he does not file a completed Professional Conduct Statement with CFA Institute and does not pay his CFA Institute membership dues. At the conclusion of his travels, Vasseur becomes a self-employed analyst accepting assignments as an independent contractor. Without reinstating his CFA Institute membership by filing his Professional Conduct Statement and paying his dues, he prints business cards that display "CFA" after his name.

Comment: Vasseur has violated Standard VII(B) because his right to use the CFA designation was suspended when he failed to file his Professional Conduct Statement and stopped paying dues. Therefore, he no longer is able to state or imply that he is an active CFA charterholder. When Vasseur files his Professional Conduct Statement, resumes paying CFA Institute dues to activate his membership, and completes the CFA Institute reinstatement procedures, he will be eligible to use the CFA designation.

© 2015 Wiley

Example 3 (Order of Professional and Academic Designations)

Tatiana Prittima has earned both her CFA designation and a PhD in finance. She would like to cite both her accomplishments on her business card but is unsure of the proper method for doing so.

Comment: The order of designations cited on such items as resumes and business cards is a matter of personal preference. Prittima is free to cite the CFA designation either before or after citing her PhD.

Example 4 (Use of Fictitious Name)

Barry Glass is the lead quantitative analyst at CityCenter Hedge Fund. Glass is responsible for the development, maintenance, and enhancement of the proprietary models the fund uses to manage its investors' assets. Glass reads several high-level mathematical publications and blogs to stay informed on current developments. One blog, run by Expert CFA, presents some intriguing research that may benefit one of CityCenter's current models. Glass is under pressure from firm executives to improve the model's predictive abilities, and he incorporates the factors discussed in the online research. The updated output recommends several new investments to the fund's portfolio managers.

Comment: "Expert CFA" has violated Standard VII(B) by using the CFA designation inappropriately. As with any research report, authorship of online comments must include the charterholder's full name along with any reference to the CFA designation.

See also Standard V(A)—Diligence and Reasonable Basis, which Glass has violated for guidance on diligence and reasonable basis.

© 2015 Wiley

READING 3: INTRODUCTION TO THE GLOBAL INVESTMENT PERFORMANCE STANDARDS (GIPS®)

LESSON 1: INTRODUCTION TO THE GLOBAL INVESTMENT PERFORMANCE STANDARDS (GIPS)

LOS 3a: Explain why the GIPS standards were created, what parties the GIPS standards apply to, and who is served by the standards.

Vol 1, pp 195–197

Individual and institutional investors typically use past investment performance to gauge a fund manager's ability, and to make investment decisions. Questions relating to the accuracy and credibility of the data used in investment performance presentation make comparisons difficult. Other misleading practices that have been common in performance presentation include:

Representative accounts: Use of only the best performing portfolios to represent the firm's overall performance.

Survivorship bias: Historical data relating to investment performance excludes the performance of those accounts that faired poorly and were consequently terminated. This results in an overstatement of investment performance.

Varying time periods: Presenting performance relating only to those time periods during which the fund outperformed its benchmark or had exceptional performance.

The GIPS standards aim to provide clients and prospective clients with comparable and representative investment performance data. They establish an industry-wide, standard approach for calculation and presentation of investment performance. This forces complying firms to avoid misrepresentation and to communicate all relevant information that prospective clients should know to make informed investment decisions.

Who Can Claim Compliance?

Compliance with GIPS standards for any firm is *voluntary* and not required by any legal or regulatory authorities. However, only investment management firms that actually manage assets can claim compliance. Plan sponsors and consultants cannot claim to comply with GIPS if they do not manage any assets. They can only endorse the standards or require their investment managers to comply with them. Further, compliance is a firm-wide process that cannot be achieved on a single product or composite. In order to claim compliance, the firm needs to comply with all requirements of GIPS standards; there is no such thing as partial compliance to GIPS.

Who Benefits from Compliance?

The GIPS standards benefit two main groups—investment management firms and prospective clients.

1. Compliance with GIPS assures clients that the historical records presented by a firm are both complete and fairly presented so it helps investment management firms in their marketing activities. Further, compliance with GIPS may also strengthen the firm's internal controls.

2. Investors are provided with credible data for different investment firms and can therefore, easily compare firms' performance to make an informed decision regarding the selection of investment managers.

© 2015 Wiley

LOS 3b: Explain the construction and purpose of composites in performance reporting. Vol 1, p 197

The GIPS standards require the use of composites. A composite is formed by combining discretionary portfolios into one group that represents a particular investment objective or strategy. A composite representing a particular strategy must include all discretionary portfolios managed according to that strategy.

To ensure that the firm does not include only its best performing funds when presenting its investment performance, GIPS standards require that the criteria for classifying portfolios into composites are decided before performance is known (i.e., on an ex-ante basis), not after the fact.

LOS 3c: Explain the requirements for verification. Vol 1, pp 197–198

Firms that claim compliance with GIPS standards are responsible for ensuring that they really are compliant and maintaining their compliant status going forward. After claiming compliance, firms may hire an independent third party to verify that they are compliant to add credibility to their claim. Verification may also increase the knowledge of the firm's performance measurement team and improve the consistency and quality of the firm's compliant presentations.

Verification assures that the investment manager is compliant with GIPS standards on a firm-wide basis. Verification needs to be performed on the entire firm rather than specific composites. Verification tests:

- Whether the investment firm has complied with all the composite construction requirements on a firm-wide basis; and
- Whether the firm's processes and procedures calculate and present performance information according to GIPS standards.

Verification is optional, and it cannot be performed by the firm itself.

The Structure of the GIPS Standards

The provisions within the 2010 edition of the GIPS standards are divided into the following nine sections:

0 Fundamentals of Compliance
1 Input Data
2 Calculation Methodology
3 Composite Construction
4 Disclosure
5 Presentation and Reporting
6 Real Estate
7 Private Equity
8 Wrap Fee/Separately Managed Account (SMA) Portfolios

These provisions are further divided into requirements and recommendations.

© 2015 Wiley

Reading 4: Global Investment Performance Standards (GIPS®)

Lesson 1: Global Investment Performance Standards (GIPS)

LOS 4a: Describe the key features of the GIPS standards and the fundamentals of compliance. Vol 1, pp 201–202, 207–208

Financial markets around the world have become more integrated in recent years. With the dynamic growth in assets under management for investment companies, prospective clients and investors require a consistent standard for performance measurement and presentation, so that they can make well-informed decisions when choosing an investment manager to manage their assets.

Investment managers who adhere to investment performance standards help assure investors that the firm's investment performance is complete and fairly presented. Further, by adhering to a global standard, firms in countries with minimal or no investment performance standards will be able to compete for business on an equal footing with firms from countries with more developed standards.

Objectives of GIPS

- To establish investment industry best practices for calculating and presenting investment performance that promote investor interests and instill investor confidence.
- To obtain worldwide acceptance of a single standard for the calculation and presentation of investment performance based on the principles of fair representation and full disclosure.
- To promote the use of accurate and consistent investment performance data.
- To encourage fair, global competition among investment firms without creating barriers to entry.
- To foster the notion of industry "self-regulation" on a global basis.

Overview

GIPS standards have the following key features:

- GIPS standards are ethical standards to ensure full disclosure and fair representation of investment performance. In order to claim compliance, firms must adhere to all the requirements of the GIPS standards.
- Apart from adhering to the minimum requirements of the GIPS standards, firms should try to adhere to the recommendations of the GIPS standards to achieve best practice in the calculation and presentation of performance.
- Firms should include all actual, discretionary, fee-paying portfolios in at least one composite defined by investment mandate, objective, or strategy in order to prevent firms from cherry-picking their best performance.
- The accuracy of performance presentation is dependent on the accuracy of input data. The underlying valuations of portfolio holdings drive the portfolio's performance. Therefore, it is essential for these and other inputs to be accurate. The GIPS standards require firms to adhere to certain calculation methodologies and to make specific disclosures along with the firm's performance.
- Firms must comply with all requirements of the GIPS standards, including any updates, Guidance Statements, interpretations, Questions & Answers, and clarifications published by CFA Institute and the GIPS Executive Committee, which are available on the GIPS website as well as in the GIPS Handbook.

© 2015 Wiley

The GIPS standards do not address every aspect of performance measurement or cover unique characteristics of each asset class. However, they will continue to evolve over time to address additional areas of investment performance.

Fundamentals of Compliance

The fundamentals of compliance include both recommendations and requirements.

Requirements

- Firms must comply with all the requirements of the GIPS standards, including any updates, Guidance Statements, interpretations, Questions & Answers, and clarifications published by CFA Institute and the GIPS Executive Committee, which are available on the GIPS website as well as in the GIPS Handbook.
- Firms must comply with all applicable laws and regulations regarding the calculation and presentation of performance.
- Firms must not present performance or performance-related information that is false or misleading.
- The GIPS standards must be applied on a firm-wide basis.
- Firms must document their policies and procedures used in establishing and maintaining compliance with the GIPS standards, including ensuring the existence and ownership of client assets, and must apply them consistently.
- If the firm does not meet all the requirements of the GIPS standards, it must not represent or state that it is "in compliance with the Global Investment Performance Standards except for…" or make any other statements that may indicate partial compliance with the GIPS standards.
- Statements referring to the calculation methodology as being "in accordance," "in compliance," or "consistent with" the GIPS standards, or similar statements, are prohibited.
- Statements referring to the performance of a single, existing client portfolio as being "calculated in accordance with the GIPS standards" are prohibited, except when a GIPS-compliant firm reports the performance of an individual client's portfolio to that particular client.
- Firms must make every reasonable effort to provide a compliant presentation to all prospective clients. Firms must not choose whom they present a compliant presentation to. As long as a prospective client has received a compliant presentation within the previous 12 months, the firm has met this requirement.
- Firms must provide a complete list of composite descriptions to any prospective client that makes such a request. They must include terminated composites on their list of composite descriptions for at least five years after the composite termination date.
- Firms must provide a compliant presentation for any composite listed on their list of composite descriptions to any prospective client that makes such a request.

© 2015 Wiley

- Firms must be defined as an investment firm, subsidiary, or division held out to clients or prospective clients as a distinct business entity.

- For periods beginning on or after January 1, 2011, total firm assets must be aggregate fair value of all discretionary and non-discretionary assets managed by the firm. This includes both fee-paying and non-fee-paying portfolios.

- Total firm assets must include assets assigned to a sub-advisor, provided that the firm has discretion over the selection of the sub-advisor.

- Changes in a firm's organization must not lead to alteration of historical composite performance.

- When the firm jointly markets with other firms, the firm claiming compliance with the GIPS standards must ensure that it is clearly defined and separate from the other firms being marketed, and that it is clear which firm is claiming compliance.

Recommendations

- Firms should comply with the recommendations of the GIPS standards, including recommendations in any updates, Guidance Statements, interpretations, Questions & Answers, and clarifications published by CFA Institute and the GIPS Executive Committee, which will be made available on the GIPS website as well as in the GIPS Handbook.

- Firms should be verified.

- Firms should adopt the broadest, most meaningful definition of the firm, encompassing all geographical offices operating under the same brand name regardless of the actual name of the individual investment management company.

- Firms should provide to each existing client, on an annual basis, a compliant presentation of the composite in which the client's portfolio is included.

LOS 4b: Describe the scope of the GIPS standards with respect to an investment firm's definition and historical performance record. Vol 1, pp 202–203

Compliance with GIPS standards facilitates an investment firm participation in the global investment management industry. To claim compliance, investment management firms must define an entity that claims compliance (the firm). This firm must be defined as an investment firm, subsidiary or a division held out to clients and prospects as a "distinct business entity."

Firms are required to present a minimum of five years of GIPS-compliant historical investment performance. If the firm or composite has been in existence for less than five years, the presentation should include performance since inception. After initiating compliance with GIPS standards, the firm must add one year of compliant performance each year, so that the firm eventually presents a (minimum) performance record for 10 years.

© 2015 Wiley

Firms may link non-GIPS-compliant performance records to their compliant history as long as the non-compliant record is not for data after January 1, 2000. In such a case the firm must disclose the period of non-compliant data and disclose how the performance presentation differs from GIPS standards.

Firms that manage private equity, real estate, and/or wrap fee/separately managed account (SMA) portfolios must also comply with Sections 6, 7, and 8, respectively, of the Provisions of the GIPS standards that became effective as of January 1, 2006.

The effective date for the 2010 edition of the GIPS standards is 1 January 2011. Compliant presentations that include performance for periods that begin on or after January 1, 2011 must be prepared in accordance with the 2010 edition of the GIPS standards. Prior editions of the GIPS standards may be found on the GIPS website.

LOS 4c: Explain how the GIPS standards are implemented in countries with existing standards for performance reporting and describe the appropriate response when the GIPS standards and local regulations conflict.

Vol 1, pp 203–204

The GIPS Executive Committee strongly encourages countries without an investment performance standard to promote the GIPS standards as the local standard and translate them into the local language when necessary.

Local sponsoring organizations provide an important link between the GIPS Executive Committee, the governing body for the GIPS standards, and the local markets in which investment managers operate.

In countries where laws and regulations regarding performance presentation do exist, firms are encouraged to adhere to GIPS in addition to their local laws. In case of a conflict, local laws are applicable and firms are required to disclose the conflict.

LOS 4d: Describe the nine major sections of the GIPS standards.

Vol 1, pp 205–208

The nine major sections of the GIPS standards are:

0. Fundamentals of compliance which discusses issues pertaining to definition of a firm, documentation of policies and procedures, maintaining compliance with any updates and ensuring proper reference to claim of compliance with GIPS and references to verification of GIPS.
1. Input data which specifies standards for input data to be used to calculate investment performance. For periods beginning on or after January 1, 2011, all portfolios must be valued in accordance with the definition of fair value and the GIPS Valuation Principles.
2. Calculation methodology includes definitions of specific methods for return calculations of portfolios and composites.
3. Composite construction: Composites should be constructed to achieve consistency and fair presentation. Details were discussed in LOS 3b.
4. Disclosures Requirements for disclosure of information pertaining to a firm's policies and performance presentation.

© 2015 Wiley

5. Presentation and reporting: Performance presentation must be according to GIPS requirements.
6. Real estate standards must be applied to present performance relating to real estate investments.
7. Private equity: GIPS Private Equity Valuation Principles must be used to value private equity investments, except for open-end and evergreen funds.
8. Wrap Fee/Separately Managed Account (SMA) Portfolios: Firms must include the performance record of all wrap fee/SMA portfolios in appropriate composites in accordance with the firm's established portfolio inclusion policies.

© 2015 Wiley

Study Session 2: Quantitative Methods—Basic Concepts

© 20˙5 Wiley

Reading 5: The Time Value of Money

LESSON 1: INTRODUCTION, INTEREST RATES, FUTURE VALUE AND PRESNT VALUE

The Financial Calculator

It is very important for you to be able to use a financial calculator when working with TVM problems. CFA Institute allows only two types of calculators for the exam—the TI BA II Plus™ (including the TI BA II Plus™ Professional) and the HP 12C (including the HP 12C Platinum). We highly recommend that you choose the TI BA II Plus™ or the TI BA II Plus™ Professional, and the keystrokes defined in our readings cater exclusively to TI BA II Plus™ users. However, if you already own an HP 12C and would like to use it, by all means continue to do so.

The TI BA II Plus™ comes preloaded from the factory with the periods per year (P/Y) function set to 12. This feature is not appropriate for most TVM problems, so before moving ahead please set the "P/Y" setting of your calculator to "1" by using the following keystrokes:

[2nd] [I/Y] "1" [ENTER] [2nd] [CPT]

Your calculator's P/Y setting will remain at 1 even when you switch it off. However, if you replace its batteries you will have to reset the P/Y setting to "1". If you wish to check this setting at any time, simply press [2nd] [I/Y] and the display should read "P/Y = 1."

With these setting in place, you can think of "I/Y" as the interest rate per compounding period, and of "N" as the number of compounding periods. Please take the time to familiarize yourself with the following keys on your TI Calculator:

N = Number of compounding periods
I/Y = Periodic interest rate
PV = Present Value
FV = Future Value
PMT = Constant periodic payment
CPT = Compute

Timelines

To illustrate some examples, we will use timelines to present the information more clearly. It is very important for you to recognize that the cash flows occur at the end of the period depicted on the timeline. Further, the end of one period is the same as the beginning of the next period. For example, a cash flow that occurs at the beginning of Year 4 is equivalent to cash flow that occurs at the end of Year 3, and will appear at $t = 3$ on the timeline.

Sign Convention

Finally, pay attention to the signs when working through TVM questions. Think of inflows as positive numbers and outflows as negative numbers. We will continue to emphasize this point through the first few examples in this reading so that you get the hang of it.

Suppose you were offered a choice between receiving \$100 today or \$110 a year from today. If you are indifferent between the two options, you are attaching the same value to receiving \$110 a year from today as you are to receiving \$100 today. It is obvious that the cash flow that will be received in the future must be discounted to account for the passage of time. An interest rate, *r*, is the rate of return that shows the relationship between two differently dated cash flows. The interest rate implied in the tradeoff above is 10%.

Present value (PV) is the current worth of sum of money or stream of cash flows that will be received in the future, given the interest rate. For example, given an interest rate of 10%, the PV of \$110 that will be received in one year is \$100.

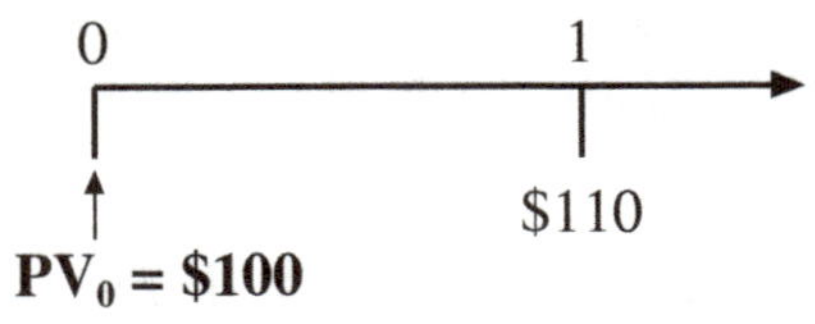

Future value (FV) is the value of a sum of money or a stream of cash flows at a specified date in the future. For example, assuming a 10% interest rate, the FV of \$100 received today is \$110.

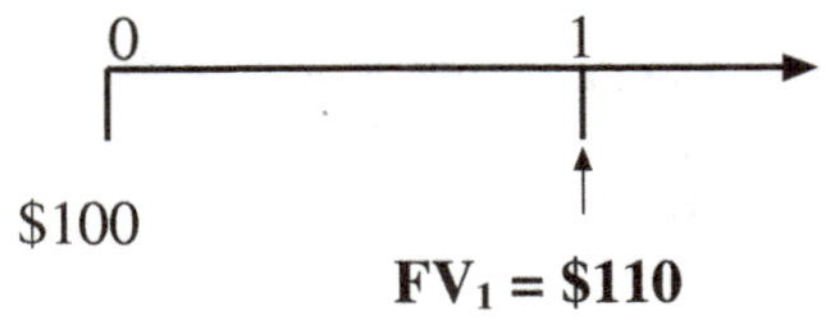

LOS 5a: Interpret interest rates as required rates of return, discount rates, or opportunity costs. Vol 1, p 278

Interest rates can be thought of in three ways:

- The minimum rate of return that you require to accept a payment at a later date.
- The discount rate that must be applied to a future cash flow in order to determine its present value.
- The opportunity cost of spending the money today as opposed to saving it for a certain period and earning a return on it.

© 2015 Wiley

LOS 5b: Explain an interest rate as the sum of a real risk-free rate, and premiums that compensate investors for bearing distinct types of risk.
Vol 1, p 279

Interest rates are determined by the demand and supply of funds. They are composed of the real risk-free rate plus compensation for bearing different types of risks:

- The real risk-free rate is the single-period return on a risk-free security assuming zero inflation. With no inflation, every dollar holds on to its purchasing power, so this rate purely reflects individuals' preferences for current versus future consumption.
- An inflation premium is added to the real risk-free rate to reflect the expected loss in purchasing power over the term of a loan. The real risk-free rate plus the inflation premium equals the *nominal risk-free rate.*
- The default risk premium compensates investors for the risk that the borrower might fail to make promised payments in full in a timely manner.
- The liquidity premium compensates investors for any difficulty that they might face in converting their holdings readily into cash at their fair value. Securities that trade infrequently or with low volumes require a higher liquidity premium than those that trade frequently with high volumes.
- The maturity premium compensates investors for the higher sensitivity of the market values of longer term debt instruments to changes in interest rates.

LOS 5e: Calculate and interpret the future value (FV) and present value (PV) of a single sum of money, an ordinary annuity, an annuity due, a perpetuity (PV only), and a series of unequal cash flows. **Vol 1, pp 280–284, 288–302**

We shall go through LOS 5c after LOS 5e.

The Future Value of a Single Cash Flow

Let's start off with a relatively simple concept. If you had \$100 in your pocket right now, and interest rates were 6%, what would be the future value of your money in one year, and in two years?

$$FV_N = PV(1+r)^N$$

In one year the value of \$100 will be:
$\$100 \times (1+0.06)^1 = \$106$

Or using your calculator:
PV = −100; I/Y = 6; N = 1; CPT FV → FV = \$106.

TI calculator keystrokes:
[2nd] [FV] "−100" [PV] "6" [I/Y] "1" [N] [CPT] [FV]

We have shown the PV as a negative number so that the resulting FV is positive. Basically, an investment (outflow) of \$100 today at 6% would result in the receipt (inflow) of \$106 in one year.

© 2015 Wiley

> In solving time value of money problems remember that the stated interest rate, I/Y, and the number of compounding periods, N, should be compatible. For example if N is stated in **days**, I/Y must be the unannualized **daily** interest rate.

In two years the value of $100 will be:
$100 \times (1+0.06)^2 = \$112.36$.

Or using your calculator:
PV = – 100; I/Y = 6; N = 2; CPT FV → FV = $112.36

TI calculator keystrokes:
[2nd][FV] "–100" [PV] "6" [I/Y] "2" [N] [CPT] [FV]

On your investment of $100 you earn 0.06 × 100 = $6 in simple interest each year. In the second year, the $6 simple interest earned in Year 1 also earns interest in addition to the principal. This $6 × 0.06 = $0.36 of additional interest earned is compound interest. Over the two years, total interest earned equals $6 + $6 + $0.36 = $12.36

Drawing up timelines will help you avoid careless mistakes when handling TVM questions. A general timeline for the future value concept looks like this:

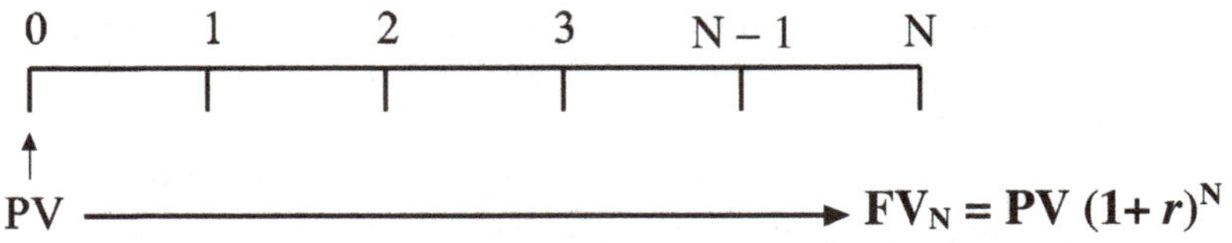

If we wanted to determine the future value after 15 periods, the PV and FV would be separated by a future value factor of $(1 + r)^{15}$, where r would be the interest rate corresponding to the length of each period.

Since PV and FV are separated in time, remember the following:

- We can add sums of money only if they are being valued at exactly the same point in time.
- For a given interest rate, the future value *increases* as the number of periods *increases.*
- For a given number of periods, the future value *increases* as the interest rate *increases.*

> An investment (outflow) of $750 today at 7% would result in the receipt (inflow) of $1,689.14 in 12 years.

Example 1-1: Calculate the FV of $750 at the end of 12 years if the annual interest rate is 7%.

Solution
PV = –$750; N = 12; I/Y = 7; CPT FV → FV = $1,689.14

> Important: After each problem, get into the habit of clearing your TI calculator's memory by pressing [2nd] [FV] and [2nd] [CE|E].

Example 1-2: Calculate the value after 20 years of an investment of $500, which will be made after 7 years. The expected annual rate of return is 8%.

Solution
PV = –$500; N = 13; I/Y = 8; CPT FV → FV = $1,359.81
Note: The investment will earn interest for 13 periods.

© 2015 Wiley

The Present Value of a Single Cash Flow

Calculating the present value involves determining the value in today's terms of a cash flow or cash flow stream that will be received in the future. If you were offered a payment of $106 a year from today, and interest rates were 6%, calculating the PV of this cash flow would involve determining the amount, which invested today at 6%, would yield $106 in a year.

$$PV = \frac{FV_N}{(1+r)^N}$$

In the example above, FV = 106; I/Y = 6; N = 1 and PV = –$100

Example 1-3: Given a discount rate of 10%, what is the PV of a $1,500 cash flow that will be received in 6 years?

Solution
FV = $1,500; I/Y = 10; N = 6; CPT PV → PV = –$846.71 (ignore the negative sign)

In order to receive $1,500 (inflow) in 6 years, an investment (outflow) of $846.71 at 10% is required.

Example 1-4: What is the present value of a cash flow of $1,200 that will be received in 15 years if the discount rate is 8%?

Solution
N = 15; I/Y = 8; FV = $1,200; CPT → PV = –$378.29 (ignore the negative sign)

- For a given discount rate, the *longer* the time period till the future amount is received, the *lower* the present value.
- For a given time period, the *higher* the discount rate, the *lower* the present value of the amount.

FV and PV of a Series of Cash Flows

Ordinary Annuities

An *annuity* is a finite set of level sequential cash flows.

An *ordinary annuity* is an annuity where the cash flows occur at the *end* of each compounding period.

Calculating future values and present values for annuities is different from calculating future values and present values for single sums because we have to find the value of a stream of periodic payments, each of which is denoted by the variable, PMT, on your calculator. Make sure you pay attention to the signs of PV, PMT, and FV when performing these calculations.

PMT is the single periodic payment, not the sum of all the payments that will be received from the annuity.

© 2015 Wiley

> We are calculating the amount that we will get back (inflow) if we were to invest $500 in each of the next 5 years (outflows). Therefore, we put a minus sign in front of the payments and obtain a positive future value.

Future Value of an Ordinary Annuity

Suppose we have an ordinary annuity that pays $500 every year for 5 years. Interest rates equal 6%. What is the future value of this annuity at the end of Year 5?

We are given the annual payment (PMT = –$500), the number of payments (N = 5), the periodic interest rate (I/Y = 6), and we need to calculate how much the cash flow stream is worth in the future:

PMT = –$500; N = 5; I/Y = 6; CPT FV → FV = $2,818.55

Example 1-5: What is the future value after 10 years of seven $1,000 payments to be received at the end of each of the first 7 years assuming that the interest rate is 4%?

Solution

It is advisable to draw up timelines to handle such problems:

Timeline:

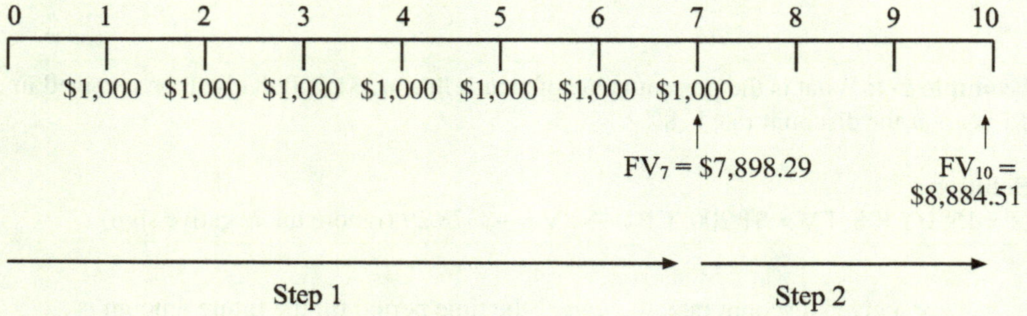

> The future value at the end of Year 7 calculated in Step 1 is used as the present value in Step 2.

Step 1: Find the value of this 7-year annuity at the end of Year 7:
N = 7; I/Y = 4; PMT = –$1,000; CPT FV → FV_7 = $7,898.29

Step 2: Find the future value at t = 10 of FV_7:
N = 3; I/Y = 4; PMT = 0; PV_7 = –$7,898.29; CPT → FV = FV_{10} = $8,884.51

> In Step 2, we have changed the sign for FV_7 ($7,897.29) to a minus sign just so that our FV is positive. You could choose to have the PV as an inflow of $7,898.29 in Step 2, and simply ignore the minus sign from the resulting FV.

Present Value of an Ordinary Annuity

Let's calculate the PV of the ordinary annuity in Example 1-5.

The sign for PMT and PV must be different. We will put a minus sign in the PMT so that we obtain a positive number for PV. However, you can easily choose not to put the minus sign in the PMT and ignore the resulting minus sign in PV.

N = 7; I/Y = 4; PMT = –$1,000; FV = 0; CPT → PV = PV_0 = $6,002.05

© 2015 Wiley

Example 1-6: What is the present value of seven annual payments of $1,000 if the first payment will be received after 4 years and the interest rate is 4%?

Solution

Timeline:

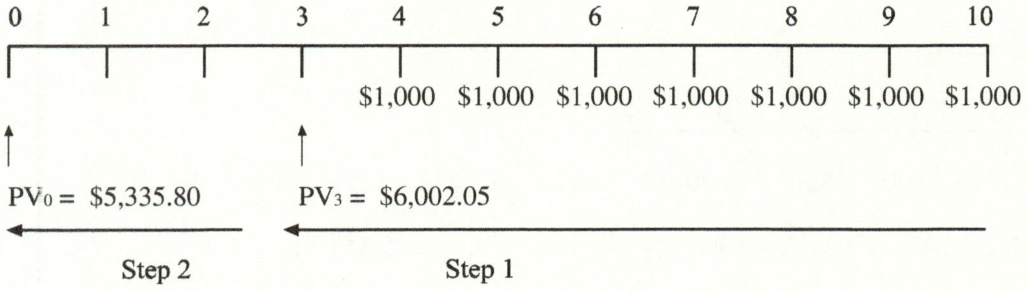

Step 1: Find the value of this 7-year annuity at the end of Year 3:
N = 7; I/Y = 4; PMT = –$1,000; CPT PV → PV_3 = $6,002.05

Step 2: Find the value of PV_3 as of today:
N = 3; I/Y = 4; PMT = 0; FV_3 = –$6,002.05; CPT → PV = PV_0 = $5,335.80

> Since payments start at the end of Year 4, the PV calculated in Step 1 is as of the end of Year 3.

> The present value calculated in Step 1 (at the end of Year 3) is used as the future value in Step 2.

> We have changed the sign for the FV ($6,002.50) in Step 2 to a minus sign just so that our PV figure comes out positive. You could choose to have the FV as an inflow of $6002.05 in Step 2, and simply ignore the minus sign in front of the resulting PV.

Annuities Due

An *annuity due* is an annuity where the periodic cash flows occur at the *beginning* of every period. There are two ways to calculate the present and future values of annuities due.

1. You can set your calculator in (BGN) mode and then insert all the variables as you normally would. Your calculators are usually in (END) mode, but nothing shows up on your calculator screens to indicate this. However, when you switch to (BGN) mode, you will see "BGN" on your calculator screens. Be very diligent about this—make sure that your calculators are always in (END) mode, and only switch to (BGN) mode when you encounter annuity due problems. Of course, remember to switch back to (END) mode once you are done with the annuity due problem.

2. You can treat the cash flow stream as an ordinary annuity over N compounding periods, and simply multiply the resulting PV or FV by (1+ periodic interest rate). Given an ordinary annuity and an annuity due with the same annual payment (PMT), number of payments (N), and periodic interest rate (I/Y), the value of the annuity due must be *greater* because each cash flow is received one period earlier.

Therefore,

$$PV_{\text{Annuity Due}} = PV_{\text{Ordinary Annuity}} \times (1+r)$$
$$FV_{\text{Annuity Due}} = FV_{\text{Ordinary Annuity}} \times (1+r)$$

© 2015 Wiley

The FV for an annuity due is the value of the cash flow stream at the end of the year in which the last payment occurs. Therefore, the FV is the value one period after the last cash flow.

Future Value of an Annuity Due

Example 1-7: What is the value at the end of Year 4 of an annuity that pays $500 at the beginning of each of the next 4 years, starting today. Assume that the cash flows can be invested at an annual rate of 8%?

Solution

Timeline:

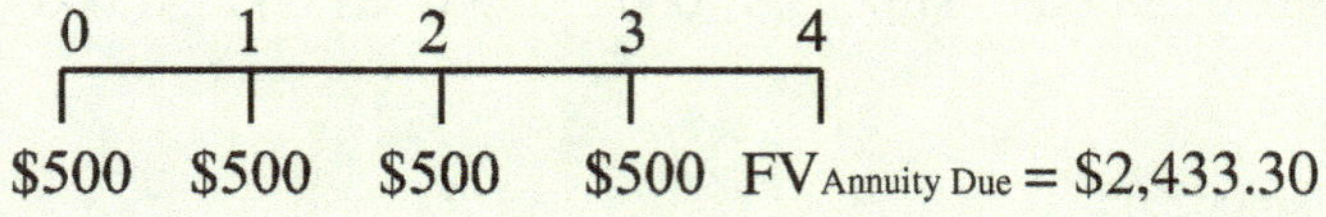

N = 4; I/Y = 8; PMT = –$500; CPT → $FV_{Annuity\ Due}$ = $2,433.30

We have performed this calculation in "BGN" mode. Make sure you change the mode on your calculator as well:

TI calculator keystrokes to shift to BGN Mode: [2nd] [PMT] [2nd] [ENTER] [2nd] [CPT]

TI calculator keystrokes to shift back to END Mode: [2nd] [PMT] [2nd] [ENTER] [2nd] [QUIT]

Example 1-8: If you make an investment of $1,500 at the beginning of each of the next 4 years, how much will you have 10 years from today assuming a 5% interest rate?

Solution

Note: The calculations for this example have been performed in (END) mode. Change the mode in you calculators back to (END) mode to follow these calculations.

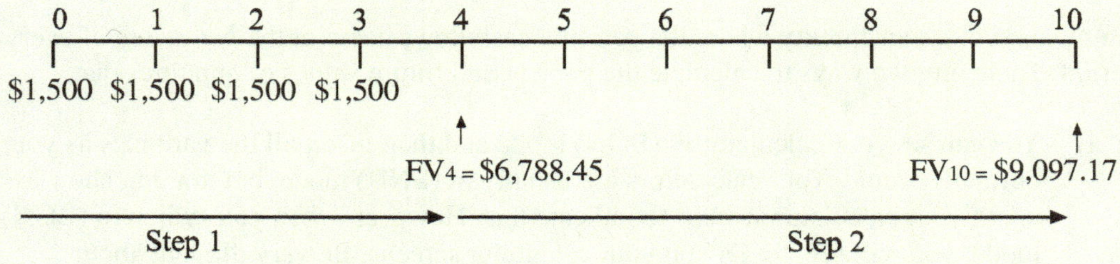

Step 1: Find the value of the 4-year annuity due as of the end of Year 4 (FV_4):
N = 4; I/Y = 5; PMT = –$1,500; CPT FV → $FV_{4\text{-Ordinary annuity}}$ = $6,465.19

The value of this ordinary annuity must be multiplied by (1 + r) to determine the FV of an annuity due: $6,465.19 × (1.05) = $FV_{4\text{-Annuity due}}$ = $6,788.45

Step 2: Find the future value of $FV_{4\text{-Annuity due}}$ 6 years from Year 4 (FV_{10}):
N = 6; I/Y = 5; PV = –$6,788.45; CPT → FV = FV_{10} = $9,097.17

© 2015 Wiley

Present Value of an Annuity Due

> The PV of an annuity due is the value of the payment stream today or on the day the first payment is received.

Example 1-9: What is the present value of a 5-year annuity that makes a series of payments of \$300 at the beginning of each of the next 5 years starting today? The discount rate is 8%.

Solution

Note: The calculations for this example have been performed in (END) mode.

Timeline:

0	1	2	3	4	5
\$300	\$300	\$300	\$300	\$300	

↑

$PV_{\text{Annuity Due}}$ = \$1,293.64

We solve this question by first calculating the value of the cash flow stream as an ordinary annuity and then converting it into the value of an annuity due.

N = 5; I/Y = 8; PMT = –\$300; CPT → $PV_{\text{Ordinary Annuity}}$ = \$1,197.81

Therefore,

$PV_{\text{Annuity Due}} = PV_{\text{Ordinary Annuity}} \times (1 + r) = \$1{,}197.81 \times (1.08) = \$1{,}293.64$

Example 1-10: An investor expects to receive an annuity of \$1,000 at the beginning of each year for 7 years. The first payment will be received 3 years from today. At a 6% discount rate, what is this annuity worth today?

Solution

Note: The calculations for this example have been performed in (END) mode.

Timeline:

0	1	2	3	4	5	6	7	8	9	10
			\$1,000	\$1,000	\$1,000	\$1,000	\$1,000	\$1,000	\$1,000	
↑			↑							
PV_0 = \$4,968.30			PV_3 = \$5,917.32							
← Step 2			← Step 1							

Step 1: Find the value of this 7-year annuity due at the end of Year 3:

N = 7; I/Y = 6; PMT = –\$1,000; CPT PV → $PV_{3\text{-Ordinary Annuity}}$ = \$5,582.38.

$PV_{3\text{-Annuity Due}} = PV_{3\text{-Ordinary Annuity}} \times (1 + r) = \$5{,}582.38 \times (1.06) = \$5{,}917.32$

Step 2: Find the value PV_3 as of today PV_0:

N = 3; I/Y = 6; FV = –\$5,917.32; CPT → PV = PV_0 = \$4,968.30

© 2015 Wiley

Present Value of a Perpetuity

A perpetuity is a never ending series of level payments, where the first cash flow occurs in the next period (at $t = 1$).

$$PV = \frac{PMT}{I/Y}$$

Example 1-11: ABC Corporation pays a $10 per share annual dividend on its preferred stock. Given a 5% rate of return and assuming that this dividend policy will continue forever, what is the value of ABC stock?

Solution

Value of ABC's preferred stock = $PV_{perpetuity}$ = \$10/0.05 = \$200

Example 1-12: Using ABC Stock from Example 1-11, determine the rate of return an investor would realize if the price of the stock were $250.

Solution

Rearranging the formula for $PV_{perpetuity}$, we get:

$$r = PMT / PV_{perpetuity}$$

$$= \$10 / \$250 = 0.04 = 4\%$$

Present and Future Value of Unequal Cash Flows

In an annuity, all cash flows are identical. Faced with a series of unequal cash flows, you will have to calculate the future value of each individual cash flow separately (by using the single sum future value formula) and add up the future values. The calculator shortcuts are illustrated in Example 1-13.

© 2015 Wiley

Example 1-13: Compute the future value, as of the end of Year 6, of the uneven cash flow stream illustrated in the timeline below. Assume that the periodic discount rate is 5%.

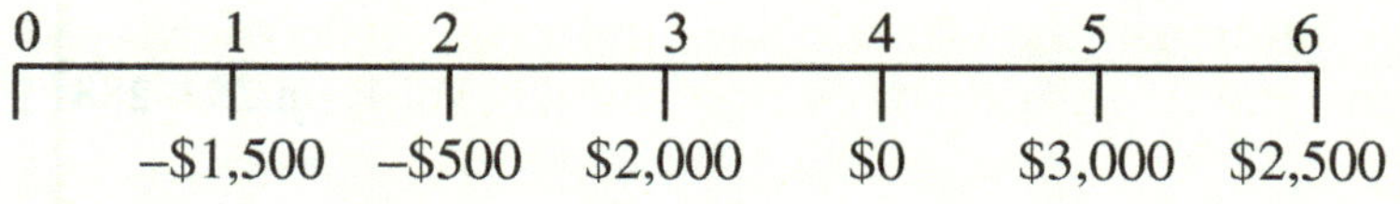

Solution

The FV of the cash flow stream is calculated by first calculating the FV of each of the individual cash flows, and then adding them up.

$FV_{1:}$ PV = –$1,500; I/Y = 5; N = 5; CPT FV → FV_1 = –$1,914.42
$FV_{2:}$ PV = –$500; I/Y = 5; N = 4; CPT FV → FV_2 = –$607.75
$FV_{3:}$ PV = $2,000; I/Y = 5; N = 3; CPT FV → FV_3 = $2,315.25
$FV_{4:}$ PV = $0; I/Y = 5; N = 2; CPT FV → FV_4 = $0
$FV_{5:}$ PV = $3,000; I/Y = 5; N = 1; CPT FV → FV_5 = $3,150
$FV_{6:}$ PV = $2,500; I/Y = 5; N = 0; CPT FV → FV_6 = $2,500

Make sure you insert the correct sign for each of the individual cash flows. Attach the same sign to the FV as the sign of the cash flow in the question.

FV of cash flow stream = Sum of individual future values = **$5,443.08**

The PV of the cash flow stream is calculated by first calculating the PV of each individual cash flow, and then adding up the resulting present values.

$PV_{1:}$ FV = –$1,500; I/Y = 5; N = 1; CPT PV → PV_1 = –$1,428.57
$PV_{2:}$ FV = –$500; I/Y = 5; N = 2; CPT PV → PV_2 = –$453.51
$FV_{3:}$ FV = $2,000; I/Y = 5; N = 3; CPT PV → PV_3 = $1,727.68
$PV_{4:}$ FV = $0; I/Y = 5; N = 4; CPT PV → PV_4 = 0
$PV_{5:}$ FV = $3,000; I/Y = 5; N = 5; CPT PV →PV_5 = $2,350.58
$PV_{6:}$ FV = $2,500; I/Y = 5; N = 6; CPT PV → PV_6 = $1,865.54

Make sure you insert the correct sign for each of the individual cash flows. Attach the same sign to the PV as the sign of the cash flow in the question.

PV of cash flow stream = Sum of individual present values = **$4,061.71**

Do it the shorter way: TI BA II Plus™ Calculator Keystrokes

The TI BAII Plus **Professional** will give a Net Future Value [NFV] of $5,443.07 if you press the ↓ key, and then press [CPT]

Key Strokes	Explanation	Display
[CF][2nd][CE|C]	Clear CF Memory Registers	CF0 = 0.0000
0 [+/–][ENTER]	Initial Cash Outlay	CF0 = 0.0000
[↓] –1500 [ENTER]	Period 1 Cash Flow	C01 = –1,500.0000
[↓] [↓] –500 [ENTER]	Period 2 Cash Flow	C02 = –500.0000
[↓] [↓] 2000 [ENTER]	Period 3 Cash Flow	C03 = 2,000.0000
[↓] [↓] 0 [ENTER]	Period 4 Cash Flow	C04 = 0.0000
[↓] [↓] 3000 [ENTER]	Period 5 Cash Flow	C05 = 3,000.0000
[↓] [↓] 2500 [ENTER]	Period 6 Cash Flow	C06 = 2,500.0000
[NPV] 5 [ENTER]	5% Discount Rate	I = 5
[↓] [CPT]	Calculate NPV	NPV = 4,061.71

Pressing the [↓] key twice takes you past F01, F02, etc. These refer to the frequency of the cash flow, and are set to equal 1 by default. If the Period 3 cash flow ocurred twice (at $t = 3$ and $t = 4$), we would insert F03 as 2 to account for both these cash flows. The next input, C04, would correspond to the cash flow at $t = 5$.

© 2015 Wiley

LESSON 2: STATED ANNUAL INTEREST RATES, COMPOUNDING FREQUENCY, EFFECTIVE ANNUAL RATES AND ILLUSTRATIONS OF TVM PROBLEMS

LOS 5c: Calculate and interpret the effective annual rate, given the stated annual interest rate and the frequency of compounding. Vol 1, pp 284–288

LOS 5d: Solve time value of money problems for different frequencies of compounding. Vol 1, pp 284–288

The Frequency of Compounding

Compounding and Future Values

(1 + stated annual interest rate) is not the future value factor when compounding is more frequent than annual.

Remember: When stated annual interest rates are compounded at a rate other than annually, you have to unannualize the quoted rate to bring compatibility between interest rates (I/Y) and the number of periods (N).

Now we shall turn our attention toward investments where payments are made more than once a year. If interest payments are made monthly, the interest rate is not quoted on a monthly basis, but is the *stated annual interest rate*. This rate must be *unannualized* to bring compatibility between the periodic interest rate, I/Y and the number of compounding periods, N.

For example, if an investment is quoted as paying 8% compounded monthly, 8% is simply the stated annual interest rate. Since the number of compounding periods per year is 12, the relevant periodic (monthly) interest rate will be calculated as 8%/12 = 0.667%.

Note that the 8% (expressing interest rates on an annual basis) is only the quoting convention. The annual rate actually applicable in this case equals $(1+0.00667)^{12} - 1 = 8.3\%$; not 8%.

"N" equals the number of compounding periods. Quarterly compounding implies 4 compounding periods per year.

"I/Y" equals the quoted annual rate divided by the number of compounding periods per year.

Pay attention to the compatibility between I/Y and N; I/Y is the periodic interest rate, while N equals the number of periods in the investment horizon.

Example 2-1: Compute the FV after 5 years of \$5,000 invested at 13% assuming quarterly compounding.

Solution

PV = \$5,000; N = 5 × 4 = 20; I/Y = 13/4 = 3.25; CPT FV; FV → –\$9,479.19

The future value can also be calculated as:

$FV = \$5{,}000(1+0.0325)^{20} = \$9{,}479.19$

Continuous Compounding and Future Values

So far, all our examples have involved discrete compounding, where the number of compounding periods is finite and defined. In continuous compounding, the number of compounding periods is infinite, and the expression for the FV of an amount after N years is given as:

$$FV_N = PVe^{r_s \times N}$$

Example 2-2: Calculate the FV after 3 years of an investment of \$5,000 at an interest rate of 7% assuming continuous compounding.

Solution

$FV = 5{,}000 \times e^{(0.07\times3)} = \$6{,}168.39$

© 2015 Wiley

Effective Annual Rates

In Table 2-1, we calculate the returns realized on an investment of $100 for one year at a stated annual interest rate of 8% assuming different compounding frequencies.

r_s is the stated annual interest rate.

Table 2-1: Calculation of Effective Annual Rates

Frequency	Periodic Interest Rate (I/Y)	Number of Compounding Periods (N)	Future Value of $100
Annual	0.08/1 = 0.08	1 × 1 = 1	$100 \times (1 + 0.08) = 108$
Semiannual	0.08/2 = 0.04	1 × 2 = 2	$100 \times (1 + 0.04)^2 = 108.16$
Quarterly	0.08/4 = 0.02	1 × 4 = 4	$100 \times (1 + 0.02)^4 = 108.2432$
Monthly	0.08/12 = 0.00667	1 × 12 = 12	$100 \times (1 + 0.00667)^{12} = 108.30$
Daily	0.08/365 = 0.000219	1 × 365 = 365	$100 \times (1 + 0.000219)^{365} = 108.3278$
Continuous			$100 \times e^{(0.08 \times 1)} = 108.3287$

The effective annual rate with monthly compounding is 8.3%.

FV (annual compounding): N = 1; I/Y = 8; PV = −100; CPT FV; FV → $108

FV (semiannual compounding): N = 2; I/Y = 4; PV = −100; CPT FV; FV → $108.16
(N equals number of years multiplied by 2 and I/Y equals the stated annual interest rate (8%) divided by 2)

FV (quarterly compounding): N = 4; I/Y = 2; PV = −100; CPT FV; FV → $108.24
(N equals number of years multiplied by 4 and I/Y equals the stated annual interest rate (8%) divided by 4)

FV (monthly compounding): N = 12; I/Y = 0.667; PV = −100; CPT FV; FV → $108.30
(N equals number of years multiplied by 12 and I/Y equals the stated annual interest rate (8%) divided by 12)

FV (daily compounding): N = 365; I/Y = 0.0219; PV = −100, CPT FV; FV → $108.3278
(N equals number of years multiplied by 365 and I/Y equals the stated annual interest rate (8%) divided by 365)

FV (continuous compounding): $100(e^{0.08}) = \$108.3287$

Notice that as the number of compounding periods *increases,* the future value of the investment increases. 8% is the stated annual rate, but the effective annual rate (EAR) *rises* as compounding frequency *increases.* The expression for EAR is given as:

$$\text{EAR} = (1 + \text{Periodic interest rate})^N - 1$$

© 2015 Wiley

Compounding Frequency	Periodic Interest Rate (I/Y)	EAR
Annual	8%	$(1 + 0.08) - 1 = 8\%$
Semiannual	4%	$(1 + 0.04)^2 - 1 = 8.16\%$
Quarterly	2%	$(1 + 0.02)^4 - 1 = 8.24\%$
Monthly	0.667%	$(1 + 0.00667)^{12} - 1 = 8.3\%$
Daily	0.0219%	$(1 + 0.000219)^{365} - 1 = 8.3278\%$
Continuous		$e^{0.08} - 1 = 8.3287\%$

Compounding and Present Value

Example 2-3: Calculate the PV of a payment of $7,000 that will be received after 9 years if the interest rate is 6% compounded monthly.

Solution

N = (9×12) = 108; I/Y = (6/12) = 0.5; FV = –$7,000; CPT PV; PV → $4,084.73

Continuous Compounding and Present Value

Example 2-4: Calculate the PV of a payment of $7,000 that will be received after 9 years if the interest rate is 5% compounded continuously.

Solution

$$PV = \frac{FV}{e^{0.05\times 9}} = \$4,463.40$$

Now let's calculate the PV of $100 to be received in one year using different compounding frequencies.

PV (annual compounding): N = 1; I/Y = 8; FV = –$100; CPT PV; PV→ $92.59

PV (semiannual compounding): N = 2; I/Y = 4; FV = –$100; CPT PV; PV→ $92.456

PV (quarterly compounding): N = 4; I/Y = 2; FV = –$100; CPT PV; PV→ $92.385

PV (monthly compounding): N = 12; I/Y = 0.67; FV = –$100; CPT PV; PV→ $92.336

PV (daily compounding): N = 365; I/Y = 0.0219; FV = –$100; CPT PV; PV→ $92.312

$$PV \text{ (continuous compounding)} = \frac{100}{e^{0.08\times 1}} = \$92.312$$

Notice that as the number of compounding periods *increases*, the present value of the investment *decreases*. 8% is the stated annual rate, but the effective annual rate *rises* as compounding frequency *increases* and calculated present values *fall*.

© 2015 Wiley

LOS 5f: Demonstrate the use of a timeline in modeling and solving time value of money problems. Vol 1, pp 302–311

Loan Payments and Amortization

Loan amortization is the process of retiring loan obligations through predetermined equal monthly payments. Each of these payments includes an interest component, which is based on the principal balance outstanding at the beginning of the period, and a principal repayment component. The relative proportion of the payment that is attributable to the interest and principal components changes with each payment. Specifically, the principal repayment component increases with the passage of time, and the interest payment component declines over time in line with the decreasing amount of principal outstanding.

Example 2-5: Loan Payment Calculations with Annual Payments

A company borrows $75,000 at a rate of 10%. The loan will be paid off in three equal end-of-year installments. Calculate the amount of the annual payment.

Solution

We are given the number of discounting periods (N = 3), the periodic interest rate (I/Y = 10), and the amount that the company borrows today (PV = $75,000). Infer that when the loan is paid back in full, the remaining amount (FV) will be zero.

N = 3; I/Y = 10; PV = –$75,000; FV = 0; CPT PMT; PMT → $30,158.61

The loan will be fully paid off or amortized after 3 payments of $30,158.61 have been made.

Example 2-6: Loan Payment Calculations with Monthly Payments

A company borrows $75,000 at a rate of 10%. The loan will be paid off through equal monthly installments over 3 years. Calculate the monthly payment required to pay off the loan.

Solution

The number of compounding periods (N) is now 36 (12 × 3), the periodic interest rate (I/Y) equals 0.833% (10/12), the amount borrowed today (PV) equals $75,000 and the amount outstanding at the end of the loan (FV) equals zero.

N = 36; I/Y = 0.833; PV = –75,000; FV = 0; CPT → PMT = $2,420.04

The monthly payment that must be made in order to retire the loan in 36 months equals $2,420.04.

© 2015 Wiley

Example 2-7: Constructing an Amortization Schedule

Ben Company borrows $25,000 at an interest rate of 7%. The amount will be paid back in semiannual installments over 14 years. Calculate the outstanding balance of the loan after the second payment is made.

Solution

First we must determine the payment that must be made every six months. We are given the amount borrowed today (PV) as $25,000, the periodic interest rate (I/Y) as 3.5% (7/2), the number of discounting periods (N) as 28 (14×2), and the loan balance remaining at the end of the term (FV = 0).

PV = -$25,000; I/Y = 3.5; N = 28; FV = 0; CPT → PMT = $1,415.07

Now we must construct an amortization schedule for the first two years.

Payment: Calculated above

Interest Component: Beginning of period loan balance multiplied by the periodic interest rate

Principal Component: Amount of monthly payment minus the interest component of each monthly payment

Ending Balance: The excess of the monthly payment over the interest component serves to reduce the balance of the liability

Period	Beginning Balance	Payment	Interest Component	Prinicipal Component	Ending Balance
1	25,000	1,415.07	875	540.07	24,459.93
2	24,459.93	1,415.07	856.10	558.97	23,901

The outstanding loan balance after the second payment is made (at the end of Year 1) equals $23,901.

***Shortcut*:** The principal outstanding at any payment date equals the present value of the remaining payments discounted at the periodic interest rate. Once we have determined the monthly payment, this calculation is fairly straightforward. The balance outstanding at the end of Year 1 (after the second semiannual payment has been made) equals:

N = 26; I/Y = 3.5; PMT = -$1,415.07; FV = 0; CPT PV; PV → $23,901

Example 2-8: Computing the Annuity Payment Needed to Achieve a Given FV

A couple wants to accumulate $5,000 over the next 10 years. How much should they deposit in the bank every year given that the expected rate of return in 8%?

Solution

We have been given the desired FV ($5,000), the number of compounding periods (10), and the periodic interest rate (8%), so we can calculate the annual payment required as:

FV = -$5,000; N = 10; I/Y = 8; PV = 0; CPT PMT; PMT → $345.15

© 2015 Wiley

Example 2-9: Computing the Fixed Monthly Payment on a Loan

Robert has taken a loan of $10,000 that he will repay through 15 equal yearly installments. Given an annual interest rate of 7%, how much must he pay every year?

Solution

We have been given the amount borrowed (PV) as $10,000 the number of compounding periods (N) as 15 and the periodic interest rate (I/Y) as 7%, so the annual payment assuming that the loan will be paid off (FV = 0) in 15 years is calculated as:

N = 15; I/Y = 7; PV = -$10,000; FV = 0; CPT PMT; PMT → $1,097.95

Example 2-10: Computing the Number of Periods in an Annuity

Jack needs to accumulate at least $1,000 with annual deposits of $80 into his bank account. If the annual interest rate is 10%, how many end-of-year payments are required?

Solution

We have been given the amount needed eventually (FV) as $1,000, the periodic payment (PMT) as $80 and the periodic discount rate (I/Y) as 10%, so we can calculate the number of periodic payments required (N) as:

FV = –$1,000; PMT = $80; I/Y = 10; PV = 0; CPT N; N → 8.51 years.
Therefore, 9 deposits are needed to accumulate more than $1,000 in the bank account with annual deposits of $80.

(PMT and FV should have opposite signs; otherwise the calculator will give an error)

Example 2-11: Computing the Number of Years in an Ordinary Annuity

Suri has $500 in the bank on which she earns an annual 10% return. How many annual end-of-year withdrawals of $120 can she make?

Solution

We have been given the amount invested today (PV) as $500, the periodic discount rate (I/Y) as 10, the annual withdrawal (PMT) as $120, and need to calculate the number of withdrawals (N) that can be made.

I/Y = 10; PMT = $120; PV = –$500; CPT N; N → 5.66, which means that 5 end-of-year withdrawals of $120 can be made.

Example 2-12: Computing the Rate of Return for an Annuity

Suppose that we have the opportunity to invest $150 at the end of each of the next 5 years in exchange for $850 after 5 years. What is the annual rate of return on this investment?

Solution

We have been given the annual payment (PMT) that must be made as $150, the number of annual payments (N) as 5, the amount that we will receive after 5 years (FV) as $850, and need to calculate the periodic interest rate (I/Y).

PMT = –$150; N = 5; FV = $850; CPT I/Y; I/Y→ 6.26%

© 2015 Wiley

Example 2-13: Computing the Discount Rate for an Annuity

What rate of return will we earn on an ordinary annuity that requires a $900 deposit today and promises to pay $150 at the end of every year for the next 10 years?

Solution

We are given the amount we need to pay today (PV) as –$900, the annual payment we will receive (PMT) as $150, the number of payments we will receive (N) as 10, and need to calculate the periodic interest rate. We will not receive anything beyond the 10 annual payments so FV equals zero.

PV = -$900; PMT = $150; N = 10; FV = 0; CPT I/Y; I/Y → 10.56%

Funding a Future Obligation

There are many TVM applications where we might need to calculate the periodic payment that must be made for a number of years to fund a cash flow stream that will be required to provide retirement income or fund future college tuition payments.

Example 2-14: Computing the Required Payment to Fund an Annuity Due

Suppose we have to make 5 annual payments of $1,500 starting at the beginning of Year 5. To accumulate the money to meet these obligations, we want to make 4 equal annual deposits beginning at the end of Year 1. Assuming a 12% rate of return, what amount must be deposited for 4 years to satisfy the eventual payment obligations?

Solution

Timeline:

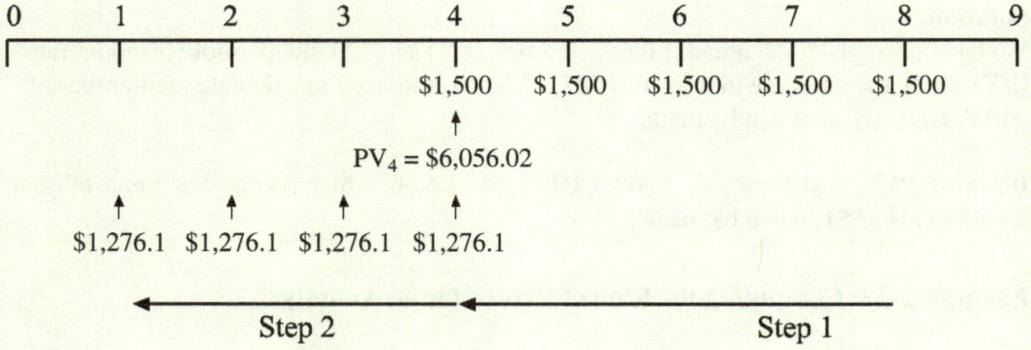

From the timeline we can infer that the FV, at the end of Year 4, of a 4-payment ordinary annuity (the money we are going to deposit) must equal the present value, at the end of Year 4, of a 5-payment annuity due whose first payment occurs at the beginning of Year 5 (end of Year 4).

Step 1: Determine the amount of money that must be available at the beginning of Year 5 (end of Year 4) in order to satisfy the payment requirements. There are two ways of solving for this amount.

© 2015 Wiley

Option 1: We recommend this approach as it does not require a change in calculator settings. Leave the calculator in END mode. First compute the PV, at the end of Year 4, of a 5-year *ordinary annuity* as:

N = 5; I/Y = 12; PMT = –$1,500; CPT PV; PV → $5,407.16

And then calculate the PV of an annuity due as:
$PV_{\text{Annuity Due}} = PV_{\text{Ordinary Annuity}} \times (1 + r) = \$5{,}407.16 \times (1.12) = \$6{,}056.02$

Option 2: Set the calculator to BGN mode and calculate PV:
N = 5; I/Y = 12; PMT = –$1,500; CPT PV; PV → $6,056.02

Step 2: Now that we have calculated the value (as of the end of Year 4) of the payments we will need to make, we can calculate the FV of the required contributions. If you have used BGN mode in Step 1, make sure that your calculator is in END mode now. Then calculate the annual deposit required under an ordinary annuity to accumulate $6,056.02 by the end Year 4 as:

N = 4; I/Y = 12; FV = –$6,056.02; CPT PMT; PMT → $1,267.13

Example 2-15: Funding a Retirement Plan

Assume that 20-year old Janet wants to retire in 40 years at the age of 60. She expects to earn 10% on deposits prior to retirement and 8% thereafter. How much must she deposit at the end of each of the next 40 years in order to be able to withdraw $15,000 every year at the beginning of each year for 30 years from the age of 60 to 90?

Solution

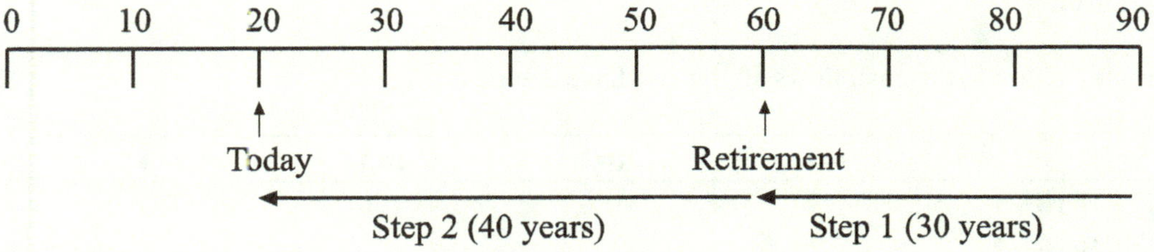

Step 1: We should first calculate the amount that must be held in the retirement account at the end of Year 40 (there are 40 years from the age of 20 to 60) in order to fund the 30 year, $15,000 annuity due (30 withdrawals will be made at the beginning of each year).

Option 1: Make sure your calculator is in END mode. The required amount equals the PV (at retirement) of the 30 year annuity with payments of $15,000 starting at the beginning of Year 41 (end of Year 40).

N = 30; I/Y = 8; PMT = –$15,000; CPT PV; $PV_{\text{Ordinary Annuity}}$ → $168,866.75

Then compute the value of the annuity due:
$\$168{,}866.75\ (1.08) = PV_{\text{Annuity Due}} = \$182{,}376.09$
Janet will need $182,376.09 in her account when she is 60 years old.

Option 2: We can also perform the calculation in BGN mode.
Set the calculator in BGN mode with the following strokes:
[2nd] [PMT] [2nd] [ENTER] [2nd] [CPT]

N = 30; PMT = –$15,000; I/Y = 8; CPT PV; PV → $182,376.09

Step 2: Now calculate the annual payment that Janet must start depositing to accumulate $182,379.06 over 40 years till she is 60 years old.

N = 40; I/Y = 10; FV = -$182,376.09; CPT PMT; PMT → $412.06

The Cash Flow Additivity Principle

The additivity principle has various applications in time value of money problems. It states that the present value of any stream of cash flows equals the sum of the present values of the individual cash flows. If we have two streams of cash flows, the sum of the present values of the two streams at any point in time is the same as the present value of the two series combined by adding cash flows that occur at the same point in time. The cash flow stream can also be divided in any desired manner, and the present value of the pieces will equal the present value of the series.

Example 2-16: Additivity Principle

Robin will make the following payments in the next 4 years: $150, $500, $150 and $150. Calculate the PV of the cash flows using the concept of present value of an annuity assuming that the discount rate equals 8%.

Solution

First we divide the cash flows so that we have 2 series:

	t=1	*t*=2	*t*=3	*t*=4
Series 1	150	150	150	150
Series 2	0	350	0	0
	150	500	150	150

Next we calculate the PV of both the series:
Series 1: N = 4; PMT = –$150; FV = 0; I/Y = 8; CPT → PV = $496.82
Series 2: N = 2; PMT = 0; FV = –$350; I/Y = 8; CPT → PV = $300.07

The sum of the PVs of the two series ($496.82 + $300.07 = **$796.89**) gives us the PV of our cash flow stream.

The PV is the same when we discount the individual cash flows of the original series.

$$\frac{150}{(1.08)} + \frac{500}{(1.08)^2} + \frac{150}{(1.08)^3} + \frac{150}{(1.08)^4} = \mathbf{\$796.89}$$

© 2015 Wiley

Reading 6: Discounted Cash Flow Applications

LESSON 1: NET PRESENT VALUE AND INTERNAL RATE OF RETURN

LOS 6a: Calculate and interpret the net present value (NPV) and the internal rate of return (IRR) of an investment. Vol 1, pp 332–337

LOS 6b: Contrast the NPV rule to the IRR rule, and identify problems associated with the IRR rule. Vol 1, pp 337–339

The net present value (NPV) of an investment equals the present value of all expected inflows from the investment minus the present value of all expected outflows. The rate used to discount the cash flows is the appropriate cost of capital, which reflects the opportunity cost of undertaking the particular investment and compensates investors for various risks inherent in the investment.

To calculate a project's NPV: $\sum_{t=0}^{N} \frac{CF_t}{(1+r)^t}$

where
CF_t = the expected net cash flow at time t
N = the investment's projected life
r = the discount rate or cost of capital

Calculating a project's NPV requires the following steps:

1. Identify all cash inflows and outflows associated with the investment.
2. Determine the appropriate discount rate.
3. Compute the PV of all cash flows.
4. Aggregate all the present values, with inflows as positive values, and outflows as negative values.

After the NPV has been calculated, the NPV rule is applied to determine whether the project under consideration should be undertaken.

1. Positive NPV projects increase shareholder wealth and should be accepted.
2. Negative NPV projects decrease shareholder wealth and should be rejected.
3. For mutually exclusive projects (where only one project may be chosen from several options) the project with the highest, positive NPV should be chosen as it would add the most value to the firm.

Example 1-1: Computing NPV

Calculate the NPV of an investment project with an initial cost of $10 million. This project generates positive cash flows of $3 million at the end of Year 1, $4.8 million at the end of Year 2 and $5.5 million at the end of Year 3. Use a 10% discount rate.

Solution
To calculate the NPV we must calculate the PVs of the individual cash flows and then add them up.

$$NPV = -\$10 + \frac{\$3}{(1.10)^1} + \frac{\$4.8}{(1.10)^2} + \frac{\$5.5}{(1.10)^3}$$

$$NPV = -\$10 + \$2.727 + \$3.966 + \$4.132$$

NPV = $0.826446 million or **$826,446**

Calculating NPV with the TI BA II Plus:

KeyStrokes	Explanation	Display
[CF][2nd][CE|C]	Clear CF Memory Registers	CF0 = 0.0000
10 [+/–][ENTER]	Initial Cash Outlay	CF0 = –10.0000
[↓] 3 [ENTER]	Period 1 Cash Flow	C01 = 3.0000
[↓] [↓] 4.8 [ENTER]	Period 2 Cash Flow	C02 = 4.8000
[↓] [↓] 5.5 [ENTER]	Period 3 Cash Flow	C03 = 5.5000
[NPV] 10 [ENTER]	10% Discount Rate	I/Y = 10
[↓] [CPT]	Calculate NPV	NPV = 0.826

Example 1-2: Applying the NPV Rule

ABC Corporation is preparing a feasibility study for a project that has an initial cost of $8 million. It will generate no cash flows in the first year. However, the project will generate positive cash flows of $2 million at the end of the second year, $3.2 million at the end of third year and $3.3 million at the end of fourth year. Assume that the discount rate is 12%. Calculate the NPV of the project and determine whether the company should invest in it.

Solution

$$NPV = -\$8 + \$0 + \frac{\$2.0}{(1.12)^2} + \frac{\$3.2}{(1.12)^3} + \frac{\$3.3}{(1.12)^4}$$

$$NPV = -\$8 + \$0 + \$1.594 + \$2.277 + \$2.097$$

$$NPV = -\$2.030706 \text{ million}$$

The company should NOT pursue the project because it has a negative NPV.

TI BA II Plus™ Calculator Keystrokes:

KeyStrokes	Explanation	Display
[CF][2nd][CE|C]	Clear CF Memory Registers	CF0 = 0.0000
8[+/–][ENTER]	Initial Cash Outlay	CF0 = –8.0000
[↓] 0 [ENTER]	Period 1 Cash Flow	C01 = 0.0000
[↓] [↓] 2 [ENTER]	Period 2 Cash Flow	C02 = 2.0000
[↓] [↓] 3.2 [ENTER]	Period 3 Cash Flow	C03 = 3.2000
[↓] [↓] 3.3 [ENTER]	Period 3 Cash Flow	C03 = 3.3000
[NPV] 12 [ENTER]	12% Discount Rate	I/Y = 12
[↓] [CPT]	Calculate NPV	NPV = –2.03071

© 2015 Wiley

Internal Rate of Return (IRR)

The internal rate of return (IRR) of a project is the discount rate that equates the project's NPV to zero. Effectively, it is the discount rate that equates the present value of all inflows from a project to the present value of all project-related outflows. Calculating IRR only requires forecasts of cash flows in the future; there is no need for externally generated market data to determine appropriate discount rates. An important thing to remember regarding IRR is that it assumes that all cash flows from the project will be reinvested at the IRR.

The IRR rule dictates that:

- Projects for which the IRR *exceeds* the required rate of return should be accepted.
- Projects for which the IRR is *lower* than the required rate of return should be rejected.

Example 1-3: Computing IRR

Calculate the IRR of an investment project with an initial cost of $10 million. This project generates positive cash flows of $3 million at the end of Year 1, $4.8 million at the end of Year 2 and $5.5 million at the end of Year 3.

Solution

$$0 = -\$10 + \frac{\$3}{(1+\text{IRR})^1} + \frac{\$4.8}{(1+\text{IRR})^2} + \frac{\$5.5}{(1+\text{IRR})^3}$$

Solving this equation through trial and error provides an IRR of **14.2%**.

TI BA II Plus™ Calculator Keystrokes:

KeyStrokes	Explanation	Display
[CF][2nd][CE|C]	Clear CF Memory Registers	CF0 = 0.0000
10 [+/–][ENTER]	Initial Cash Outlay	CF0 = –10.0000
[↓] 3 [ENTER]	Period 1 Cash Flow	C01 = 3.0000
[↓] [↓] 4.8 [ENTER]	Period 2 Cash Flow	C02 = 4.8000
[↓] [↓] 5.5 [ENTER]	Period 3 Cash Flow	C03 = 5.5000
[IRR] [CPT]	Calculate IRR	IRR = 14.2

© 2015 Wiley

Example 1-4: Calculating IRR

A project generates a positive cash flow of $5.2 million at the end of Year 1, no cash flows in the second year and $3.1 million at the end of Year 3. It requires an initial cash outflow of $6 million. Calculate the IRR of this project.

Solution

$$0 = -\$6 + \frac{\$5.2}{(1+\text{IRR})^1} + \frac{\$0}{(1+\text{IRR})^2} + \frac{\$3.1}{(1+\text{IRR})^3}$$

Through trial and error we determine that the IRR of the project is **21.6%**.

TI BA II Plus™ Calculator Keystrokes:

KeyStrokes	Explanation	Display
[CF][2nd][CE|C]	Clear CF Memory Registers	CF0 = 0.0000
6 [+/–][ENTER]	Initial Cash Outlay	CF0 = –6.0000
[↓] 5.2 [ENTER]	Period 1 Cash Flow	C01 = 5.2000
[↓] [↓] 0 [ENTER]	Period 2 Cash Flow	C02 = 0.0000
[↓] [↓] 3.1 [ENTER]	Period 3 Cash Flow	C03 = 3.1000
[IRR] [CPT]	Calculate IRR	IRR = 21.6

In deciding whether a single project should be undertaken, IRR and NPV will offer the same recommendation.

- If IRR is *greater* than the required rate of return, NPV is *positive.*
- If IRR is *less* than the required rate of return, NPV is *negative.*

Problems Associated with the IRR

When only one of two or more projects can be accepted, the projects are said to be *mutually exclusive.* For mutually exclusive projects, NPV and IRR may offer conflicting conclusions. This can happen in two scenarios:

1. When the projects' initial cash outlays are different.
2. When there is a difference in the timing of cash flows across the projects.

NPV assumes that interim cash flows from the project will be reinvested at the required rate of return, whereas IRR assumes that they will be reinvested at the IRR. When choosing between mutually exclusive projects, use the NPV rule if the recommendations of the NPV and IRR rules conflict. Examples 1-5 and 1-6 illustrate scenarios in which the methods of capital budgeting can offer different investment recommendations.

© 2015 Wiley

Example 1-5: When Initial Cash Outflows for the Projects are Different

Project	Initial Cash Outflow	Cash flow at t = 1	IRR	NPV at 12%
A	−50,000	75,000	50%	16,964
B	−20,000	32,000	60%	8,571

A company can only invest in one of the two projects listed above. Which one should the company invest in?

Solution

Project A has an initial cash outflow of $50,000, and generates a cash flow of $75,000 in Year 1. It has an IRR of 50% and adds $16,964 to the value of the firm assuming that the firm's cost of capital is 12%.

Project B has a much lower initial cash outflow of $20,000, and generates $32,000 in Year 1. It has an IRR of 60% (higher than Project A's), but an NPV of only $8,571 (lower than Project A's).

The NPV and IRR rules are in conflict. In such cases the NPV rule is given preference. The company should choose Project A as it adds more to shareholder wealth.

Example 1-6: When the Timing of Cash Flows is Different

Project	Initial Cash Outflow	CF at t = 1	CF at t = 2	IRR	NPV at 12%
B	−20,000	32,000	0	60%	8,571
C	−20,000	0	38,000	38%	10,293

Given that the two projects are mutually exclusive, which one should the company invest in?

Solution

The NPV rule recommends that the company should choose Project C, while the IRR rule suggests that Project B should be undertaken. When the two are in conflict, the NPV rule is given preference. Therefore, the company should invest in Project C as it adds more to company value.

There are two additional problems with IRR.

Multiple IRR problem: Projects with a nonconventional cash flow pattern may have more than one IRR. There maybe two discount rates that will produce an NPV of zero.

No IRR problem: It is also possible to have a positive NPV project with no IRR meaning that there is no discount rate that results in a zero NPV.

Note: These additional problems of IRR are discussed in the Corporate Finance section.

Conclusion: When choosing between mutually exclusive projects, use the NPV rule if the recommendations of the NPV and IRR rules conflict.

© 2015 Wiley

LESSON 2: PORTFOLIO RETURN MEASUREMENT

LOS 6c: Calculate and interpret a holding period return (total return). Vol 1, pp 339–340

We are required to calculate and interpret two methods of measuring portfolio performance. In order to understand them, we will first describe the holding period yield (HPY), which is also known as the holding period return. HPY is quite simply the return earned on an investment over the entire investment horizon.

For example, if an investor purchases a share of stock for $100, receives a dividend of $5, and sells the stock for $110 in 9 months, her HPY on the investment is calculated as:

$$\text{HPY} = \frac{\$110 + \$5 - \$100}{\$100} \times 100 = 15\%$$

LOS 6d: Calculate and compare the money-weighted and time-weighted rates of return of a portfolio and evaluate the performance of portfolios based on these measures. Vol 1, pp 340–346

The money-weighted rate of return is simply the internal rate of return of an investment. It accounts for the timing and amount of all dollar flows into and out of the portfolio.

Example 2-1: Money-Weighted Rate of Return

An investor purchases a share for $50 today. At the end of the year, she purchases another share for $60. At the end of Year 2, she sells both shares for $65 each. At the end of each year during the holding period, she also receives a dividend of $1 per share. What is her money-weighted rate of return on the investment?

Solution

Step 1: Determine the timing and nature of the cash flow. Inflows are positive cash flows while outflows are negative cash flows.

t = 0	Purchase of first share	–	**50**
t = 1	Dividend from first share	+	1
	Purchase of second share	–	60
	Net cash flow at t=1	–	**59**
t = 2	Dividend from two shares	+	2
	Proceeds from selling shares	+	130
	Net cash flow at t=2	+	**132**

Step 2: Equate the PV of cash outflows to the PV of cash inflows:

PV of outflows = PV of inflows

$$50 + \frac{59}{(1+r)^1} = \frac{132}{(1+r)^2}$$

© 2015 Wiley

Step 3: Calculate the value of *r* to find the money-weighted return. There are 2 ways to calculate *r*.

1. Trial and error.
2. Using the IRR function on a financial calculator.

TI BA II Plus™ Calculator Keystrokes:

KeyStrokes	Explanation	Display
[CF][2nd][CE|C]	Clear CF Memory registers	CF0 = 0.0000
50 [ENTER]	Initial Cash Outlay	CF0 = –50.0000
[↓] 59 [+/–][ENTER]	Period 1 cash flow	C01 = –59.0000
[↓] [↓] 132 [ENTER]	Period 2 cash flow	C02 = 132.0000
[IRR] [CPT]	Calculate IRR	**IRR = 13.86**

The money-weighted rate of return is 13.86%.

The time-weighted rate of return measures the compounded rate of growth of an investment over a stated measurement period. In contrast to money-weighted return, the time-weighted return:

1. Is not affected by cash withdrawals or contributions to the portfolio.
2. Averages the holding period returns over time.

The standard in the investment management industry is to express returns on a time-weighted basis.

Example 2-2: Time-Weighted Return

An investor purchases a share for $50 today. At the end of the year, she purchases another share for $60. At the end of Year 2, she sells the shares for $65 each. At the end of each year in the holding period, she also receives $1 per share as dividend. What is her time-weighted rate of return?

Solution

Step 1: Break down the cash flows into 2 holding periods based on the their timing:

Holding period 1	Beginning price	50	
	Dividends received	1	
	Ending price	**60**	
Holding period 2	Beginning price	120	(2 shares)
	Dividends received	2	(1 per share)
	Ending price	**130**	(2 shares)

Step 2: Calculate the HPY for each period.

$$HPY_1 = [(60 + 1)/50] - 1 = 22\%$$
$$HPY_2 = [130 + 2)/120] - 1 = 10\%$$

Step 3: Finally, calculate the compounded annual rate that would produce the same return as the investment over the two-year period.

$$(1 + \text{time-weighted rate of return})^2 = (1 + HPY_1)(1 + HPY_2) = (1.22)(1.10)$$
$$\text{Time-weighted rate of return} = [(1.22)\ (1.10)]^{0.5} - 1 = 15.84\%.$$

Important Takeaways

- The time-weighted rate of return is preferred because it is not affected by the timing and amount of cash inflows and outflows. In the Examples 2-1 and 2-2, the time-weighted return is higher than the money-weighted return. This is because the money-weighted return gave more weight to the return in the second year as the value of the portfolio was greater in the second year. Since the portfolio return was lower in the second year, the money-weighted return was lower.

- Decisions regarding contributions and withdrawals from a portfolio are usually made by clients. Since these decisions are not typically in investment managers' hands, it would be inappropriate to evaluate their performance based on money-weighted returns. If a manager does have discretion over withdrawals and contributions of funds in a portfolio, money-weighted return might be a more appropriate measure of portfolio performance.

- If funds are deposited into the investment portfolio prior to a period of superior performance, money-weighted return will be *higher* than time-weighted return.

- If funds are deposited into the investment portfolio just before a period of relatively poor performance, money-weighted return will be *lower* than time-weighted return.

LESSON 3: MONEY MARKET YIELDS

LOS 6e: Calculate and interpret the bank discount yield, holding period yield, effective annual yield, and money market yield for U.S. Treasury bills and other money market instruments. Vol 1, pp 346–351

LOS 6f: Convert among holding period yields, money market yields, effective annual yields, and bond equivalent yields. Vol 1, pp 346–351

Market Yields

Bank Discount Yield: This quoting convention is used primarily for quoting Treasury bills. The bank discount yield (BDY) annualizes the discount on the instrument as a percentage of *par or face value* over a *360-day* period. It is computed as:

© 2015 Wiley

$$r_{BD} = \frac{D}{F} \times \frac{360}{t}$$

where:
r_{BD} = the annualized yield on a bank discount basis.
D = the dollar discount (face value – purchase price)
F = the face value of the bill
t = number of days remaining until maturity

Yields presented on a bank discount basis do not hold much meaning to investors for the following reasons:

1. Investors want to evaluate returns based on the amount invested when purchasing the instrument; BDY calculates returns based on par.
2. Returns are based on a 360-day year rather than a 365-day year.
3. BDY assumes simple interest. In doing so it ignores the interest earned on interest (compound interest).

Example 3-1: Bank Discount Yield

Calculate the bank discount yield for a T-bill with a face value of $1,000 that is currently priced at $960 and has 240 days remaining till maturity.

Solution

Bank discount yield = (D/F) × (360/t)
D = $1,000 – $960 = $40; F = $1,000; t = 240

Bank discount yield = (40/1,000) × (360/240) = **6%**

Example 3-2: Bank Discount Yield

What is the bank discount yield of a T-bill that is selling for $98,000, has 95 days remaining till maturity and a face value of $100,000?

Solution

D = $100,000 – $98,000 = $2,000; F = $100,000; t = 95

Bank discount yield = (2,000/100,000) × (360/95) = **7.58%**

Holding Period Yield: The holding period yield equals the return realized on an investment over the entire horizon that it is held (which can either be till maturity or sale). It is an unannualized return measure that is calculated as follows:

© 2015 Wiley

$$HPY = \frac{P_1 - P_0 + D_1}{P_0} = \frac{P_1 + D_1}{P_0} - 1$$

where:
P_0 = initial price of the investment.
P_1 = price received from the instrument at maturity/sale.
D_1 = interest or dividend received from the investment.

Example 3-3: Holding Period Yield

Calculate the holding period yield on a T-bill with a face value of $1,000 that is currently trading for $960 and has 240 days remaining till maturity.

Solution

In this example, D_1 is zero as T-bills make no interest payments.

$$HPY = \frac{P_1 - P_0 + D_1}{P_0} = \frac{(1{,}000 - 960) + 0}{960} = 40/960 = \mathbf{4.17\%}$$

Effective Annual Yield (EAY): The effective annual yield is an annualized return measure that accounts for compounding over *365-day* period. It is calculated as follows:

$$EAY = (1 + HPY)^{365/t} - 1$$

where:
HPY = holding period yield
t = numbers of days remaining till maturity

We can also convert an EAY to HPY using the following formula:

$$HPY = (1 + EAY)^{t/365} - 1$$

Example 3-4: Calculating the Effective Annual Yield

Compute the EAY when the HPY of a T-bill is 2.3% and there are 240 days remaining till maturity.

Solution

$$EAY = (1 + HPY)^{365/t} - 1$$
$$EAY = (1 + 0.023)^{365/240} - 1 = \mathbf{3.52\%}$$

© 2015 Wiley

Example 3-5: Calculating HPY from EAY

Compute the HPY of a T-bill when its EAY is 1.8% and there are 240 days left to maturity.

Solution

$$HPY = (1 + 0.018)^{240/365} - 1 = \mathbf{1.18\%}$$

Money Market Yield or CD Equivalent Yield: The money market yield (R_{MM}) is the holding period yield annualized on a *360-day* basis. Further, it does not consider the effects of compounding. It is different from the bank discount yield as it is based on the *purchase price*, not par value. For Treasuries, the money-market yield can be obtained from the bank discount yield using the following formula.

$$R_{MM} = \frac{360 \times r_{BD}}{360 - (t \times r_{BD})}$$

And more conveniently:

$$R_{MM} = HPY \times (360/t)$$

Example 3-6: Money Market Yield

What is the money market yield for a T-bill that has 90 days to maturity if it is selling for $99,500 and has a face value of $100,000?

Solution

The simpler way is to use the second formula and calculate the HPY to compute the money market yield.

$$HPY = \frac{P_1 - P_0 + D_1}{P_0} = \frac{(100{,}000 - 99{,}500)}{99{,}500} = 500/99{,}500 = \mathbf{0.5025\%}$$

$$R_{MM} = HPY \times (360/t)$$

$$R_{MM} = 0.5025\% \times (360/90) = \mathbf{2.01\%}$$

© 2015 Wiley

Example 3-7: Money-Market Yields

What is the money market yield for a 240 day T-bill that has a bank discount yield of 5%?

Solution

$$R_{MM} = \frac{360 \times r_{BD}}{360 - (t \times r_{BD})}$$

$$R_{MM} = \frac{360 \times 0.05}{360 - (240 \times 0.05)} = \mathbf{5.17\%}$$

An easier way to get through these problems is to first calculate the HPY and then convert the HPY into the required return measure.

- The HPY is the actual unannualized return an investor realizes over a holding period.
- The EAY is the HPY annualized on a *365-day* year *with* compounding.
- The R_{MM} is the HPY annualized on a *360-day* year *without* compounding.

Example 3-8: Converting HPY into Other Yield Measures

An investor purchases a T-bill for $950 when the money market yield on the T-bill is 5.2% and there are 180 days left to maturity. Compute HPY and EAY for the T-bill.

Solution

Calculation of HPY:

$$R_{MM} = HPY \times (360/t)$$

$$HPY = R_{MM} \times (t/360)$$

$$HPY = 5.2 \times (180/360)$$

$$HPY = \mathbf{2.6\%}$$

Calculation of EAY:

$$EAY = (1 + HPY)^{365/t} - 1$$

$$EAY = (1 + 0.026)^{365/180} - 1 = \mathbf{5.34\%}$$

© 2015 Wiley

Bond Equivalent Yield

The bond equivalent yield (BEY) is simply the semiannual discount rate multiplied by two. This convention comes from the U.S. where bonds are quoted at twice the semiannual rate because coupon payments are made semiannually.

Example 3-9: Bond Equivalent Yield

A 3-month loan has a holding period yield of 3%. What is the yield on a bond equivalent basis?

Solution

The first step in any BEY calculation is to determine the yield on a semiannual basis. Next, we double the semiannual yield to obtain the bond equivalent yield.

Step 1: Semiannual yield = $(1 + \text{3-month yield})^2 - 1 = (1.03)^2 - 1 = 6.09\%$

Step 2: BEY = $2 \times 6.09\% =$ **12.18%**

Example 3-10: Bond Equivalent Yield

The EAY (effective annual yield) on an investment is 7%. What is the yield on a bond-equivalent basis?

Solution

Step 1: Convert the effective annual yield to an effective semiannual yield:

Semiannual yield = $(1 + \text{EAY})^{0.5} - 1 = 1.07^{0.5} - 1 = 3.44\%$

Step 2: Double the effective semiannual yield:

BEY = Semiannual yield $\times$ 2 = 3.44% $\times$ 2 = **6.88%**

© 2015 Wiley

READING 7: STATISTICAL CONCEPTS AND MARKET RETURNS

LESSON 1: FUNDAMENTAL CONCEPTS, FREQUENCY DISTRIBUTIONS AND THE GRAPHICAL PRESENTATION OF DATA

LOS 7a: Distinguish between descriptive statistics and inferential statistics, between a population and a sample, and among the types of measurement scales. Vol 1, pp 362–364

Statistics refers to data and also to methods of analyzing data. A company's average earnings growth rate of 8% over the last 5 years is an example of a statistic (data). If we use this information to forecast the company's dividend payments going forward, the methods of collecting and analyzing data are also called statistics.

- Descriptive statistics refer to how large volumes of data are converted into useful, readily understood information by summarizing their important characteristics. Our focus in this reading will be on descriptive statistics.
- Inferential statistics (or statistical inference) refer to methods used to make forecasts, estimates, or draw conclusions about a larger set of data based on a smaller representative set. In subsequent readings we will focus on inferential statistics.

A population includes *all* the members of a particular group. The return on the entire set of companies trading on the NASDAQ is an example of a population. A descriptive measure of a population characteristic is known as a parameter. Investment analysts are usually interested in only a few parameters, including the mean and variance of asset returns.

It is usually very costly and time consuming to obtain data for each member of the population. Therefore, information about a small subset of the population, called a sample, is collected and conclusions about the population are drawn from the information obtained from the sample. For a population that includes the return on every stock listed on the NASDAQ, an example of a sample would be the return on any 25 stocks listed on the NASDAQ. The average return (mean) on the stocks in the sample is an example of a sample statistic.

In order to determine which statistical method to use, we need to distinguish between the different measurement scales or levels of measurement. The four major categories of measurement scales are nominal scales, ordinal scales, interval scales, and ratio scales.

Use the mnemonic "NOIR" to remember the types of measurement scales in order of precision.

- Nominal scales represent the weakest level of measurement. They categorize or count data but do not rank them. An example of a nominal scale would be assigning integers to the various kinds of stocks available in the market. Value stocks might be assigned the number, 1, while the number, 2, might refer to growth stocks, and so on.

- Ordinal scales represent a stronger level of measurement than nominal scales. They sort data in categories that are ranked according to a certain characteristic. For example, if we assign the number, 1, to stocks with the lowest returns, and numbers 2, 3, and 4 to stocks with increasingly higher returns, we would be using an ordinal scale. We can conclude that a stock assigned the number, 4, offers a higher return than one that is assigned the number, 3. However, the scale tells us nothing about the magnitude of the difference in returns between stocks in different categories, nor does it tell us whether the difference in returns between stocks ranked 4 and 5 is the same as the difference between stocks ranked 1 and 2.

© 2015 Wiley

- Interval scales rank observations in such a manner that the differences between scale values are equal so that values can be added and subtracted meaningfully. Temperature scales are an example of interval scales. Not only do we know that 6°C is hotter than 5°C, but we also know that the difference between 51°C and 53°C is the same as the difference between 63°C and 65°C. However, a measurement of 0 with an interval scale does not indicate the absence of the value being measured. Therefore, ratios calculated using this scale are meaningless. 0°C does not indicate an absence of temperature; it is just the specific temperature at which water freezes. Further, although 60°C is a number 6 times as large as 10°C, it does not represent 6 times as much temperature.

- Ratio scales represent the strongest level of measurement. They have all the characteristics of interval scales and have a true zero point as the origin. Therefore, meaningful ratios can also be computed with ratio scales. Purchasing power measured in terms of money is an example of a ratio scale. If one has $0, she has no purchasing power. Further, one who has $20 has twice as much purchasing power as one with only $10.

LOS 7b: Define a parameter, a sample statistic, and a frequency distribution. Vol 1, pp 365–368

We have already defined a parameter and a sample statistic in the previous section. A frequency distribution is a tabular illustration of data categorized into a relatively small number of intervals or classes. The intervals must be such that each observation must fall into only one interval (mutually exclusive), and the set of intervals must cover the entire range of values represented in the data (all inclusive). The data presented in a frequency distribution may be measured using any type of measurement scale.

Example 1-1: Construction of a Frequency Distribution

The scores of 20 students on a 100-point exam are 80, 15, 26, 51, 90, 95, 45, 70, 65, 58, 76, 54, 10, 27, 33, 76, 81, 54, 56, and 61. Construct a frequency distribution for this data.

Solution

Step 1: Define the size of the intervals.

In order to define the size of each interval we first determine the range of values in which all the data lie. In this case, the lowest possible score is 1 and highest possible score is 100. Next, we must decide on the number of intervals. The number of categories must be such that the information can be summarized effectively without losing any of its importance. If we assume that four categories are sufficient, each interval would have a width of 25 points (100/4).

Step 2: Tally and count the observations.

We start by constructing a table with three columns. In the first column we list the intervals in ascending order. In the second we tally the information by assigning each observation to an interval. Finally, we count the number of observations that fall in each interval and list the totals in the third column. These totals are called frequencies.

© 2015 Wiley

Interval	Tallies	Frequency
$0 < x \leq 25$	II	2
$25 < x \leq 50$	IIII	4
$50 < x \leq 75$	~~IIII~~ III	8
$75 < x \leq 100$	~~IIII~~ I	6
Total		20

The interval with the highest frequency is known as the **modal interval** or **modal class**. In this example, the modal interval is $50 < x \leq 75$. Notice, that the intervals are defined in such a manner that each observation only falls in one interval. For example, the score of 25 falls in the interval, $0 < x \leq 25$; not in the interval, $25 < x \leq 50$.

LOS 7c: Calculate and interpret relative frequencies and cumulative relative frequencies, given a frequency distribution. **Vol 1, pp 368–373**

LOS 7d: Describe the properties of a data set presented as a histogram or a frequency polygon. **Vol 1, pp 373–377**

Other useful ways of summarizing data include relative frequency, cumulative frequency, and cumulative relative frequency.

- The relative frequency for an interval is the proportion or fraction of total observations that lies in that particular interval. Each interval's relative frequency is calculated by dividing its absolute frequency by the total number of observations.

- The cumulative absolute frequency or cumulative frequency for an interval is the number of observations that are less than the upper bound of the interval. Alternatively, it is the sum of the frequencies of all intervals less than and including the said interval. In Example 1-1, the cumulative frequency for the $50 < x \leq 75$ interval is the sum of the frequencies of the $0 < x \leq 25$, $25 < x \leq 50$ and $50 < x \leq 75$ intervals, which equals 14.

- The cumulative relative frequency for an interval is the proportion of total observations that is less than the upper bound of the interval. It is calculated by adding the relative frequencies of all intervals lower than, and including the said interval. The cumulative relative frequency can also be calculated by dividing the cumulative absolute frequency of the interval by the total number of observations.

Table 1-1 lists the relative frequency, cumulative frequency and cumulative relative frequency for each interval in Example 1-1.

Table 1-1: Frequency Distributions for the Data in Example 1-1

Interval	Tallies	Absolute Frequency	Relative Frequency	Cumulative Frequency	Cumulative Relative Frequency
0 < x ≤ 25	II	2	10%	2	10%
25 < x ≤ 50	IIII	4	20%	6	30%
50 < x ≤ 75	~~IIII~~ III	8	40%	14	70%
75 < x ≤ 100	~~IIII~~ I	6	30%	20	100%
Total		20			

Histograms and Frequency Polygons

A histogram is used to graphically represent the data contained in frequency distribution. To construct a histogram, the intervals are listed on the horizontal axis, while the frequencies are scaled on the vertical axis. The histogram for the frequency distribution in Example 1-1 is illustrated in Figure 1-1.

Figure 1-1: Histogram of Students' Scores on the Exam

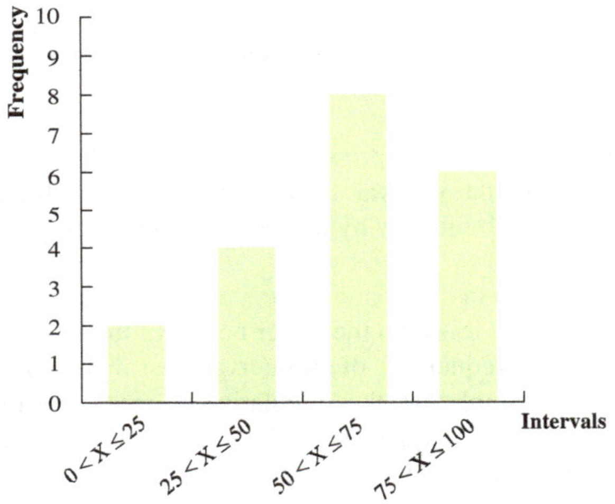

The advantage of illustrating data in a histogram is that users can quickly recognize where most of the data are concentrated.

A frequency polygon also graphically illustrates the data in a frequency distribution. Each coordinate or point on the frequency polygon is the frequency of each interval plotted against the midpoint of the interval. Figure 1-2 illustrates the frequency polygon for the data in Example 1-1.

© 2015 Wiley

Figure 1-2: Frequency Polygon Representing Students' Scores on the Exam

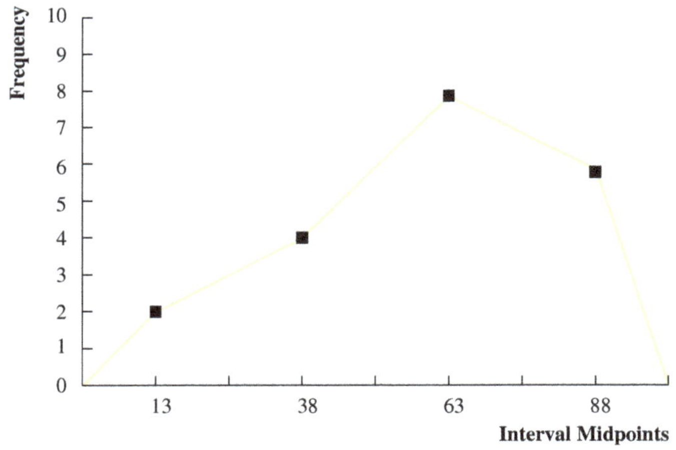

Both frequency polygons and histograms show how absolute frequency varies with each interval. Another way of looking at the distribution of data is to plot the cumulative frequency of each interval against the upper bound of the interval. Drawing a smooth curve through each of the coordinates gives us the cumulative frequency distribution (Figure 1-3).

Figure 1-3: Cumulative Frequency Distribution of Students' Scores on the Exam

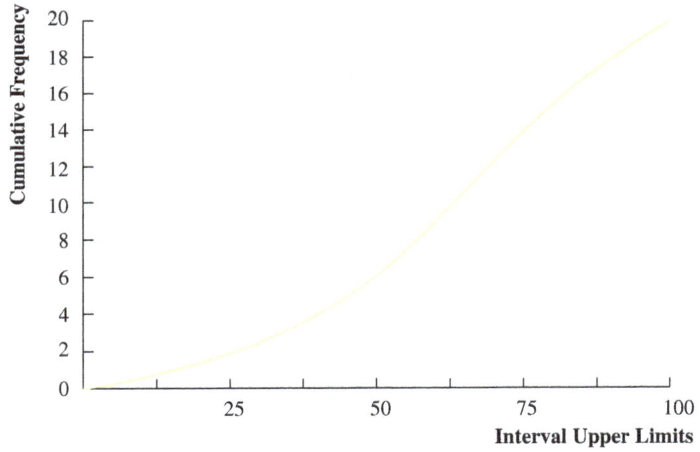

Cumulative frequency distributions tend to flatten out when returns are extremely negative or extremely positive.

LESSON 2: MEASURES OF CENTRAL TENDENCY, OTHER MEASURES OF LOCATION (QUANTILES) AND MEASURES OF DISPERSION

LOS 7e: Calculate and interpret measures of central tendency, including the population mean, sample mean, arithmetic mean, weighted average or mean, geometric mean, harmonic mean, median, and mode. Vol 1, pp 378–395

A measure of central tendency looks to identify the "middle" or "expected value" of a data set. The arithmetic mean is the most frequently used measure of central tendency. It is simply the sum of all the observations in a data set divided by the total number of observations. The arithmetic mean can be calculated for the entire population (μ) and for a sample ($\overline{X}$).

© 2015 Wiley

For population consisting of N observations the population mean is calculated as:

$$\mu = \frac{\sum_{i=1}^{N} X_i}{N}$$

where,
X_i = is the *i*th observation.

The sample mean for a sample of size, n, is calculated as:

$$\overline{X} = \frac{\sum_{i=1}^{n} X_i}{n}$$

The arithmetic mean of a sample is the best estimate of the value of the next observation.

Example 2-1: Computing the Population Mean and Sample Mean

The scores of 20 students on a 100-point exam are given as 77, 90, 57, 85, 68, 31, 45, 86, 46, 98, 25, 10, 57, 67, 88, 77, 34, 89, 47, and 77. Calculate the population mean and the mean for a sample including only the first 5 observations. Show that the sum of the deviations from the sample mean equals zero.

Solution

$$\mu = \frac{\sum_{i=1}^{N} X_i}{N}$$

$$= 1{,}254/20 = 62.7$$

$$\overline{X} = \frac{\sum_{i=1}^{n} X_i}{n}$$

$$= (77+90+57+85+68)/5 = 377/5 = 75.4$$

$$\sum_{i=1}^{n}(X_i - \overline{X})$$

$$= (77-75.4)+(90-75.4)+(57-75.4)+(85-75.4)+(68-75.4) = 0$$

© 2015 Wiley

Properties of the Arithmetic Mean

- All observations are used in the computation of the arithmetic mean.
- All interval and ratio data sets have an arithmetic mean.
- The sum of the deviations from the arithmetic mean is always 0: $\sum_{i=1}^{n}(X_i - \overline{X}) = 0$
- An arithmetic mean is unique i.e., a data set only has one arithmetic mean.

A potential problem with the arithmetic mean is its sensitivity to extreme values. Because each and every observation is used in its computation, a disproportionately small or large value can drag the arithmetic mean towards itself. For example, a data set consisting of observations of 5, 8, 7, 10, 12, and 143 has an arithmetic mean of 30.83, which is significantly larger in magnitude than the bulk of the data (the first 5 observations). In this case, there are doubts regarding how well the arithmetic mean represents the data.

The **median** is the value of the middle item of a data set once it has been arranged in ascending or descending order. For a data set where the total number of observations, n, is an odd number, the median is the value of the item in [(n+1)/2] position. In an even-numbered data set, the median is the average of items occupying positions (n/2) and [(n+2)/2].

The advantage of using the median is that unlike the mean, it is not sensitive to extreme values and is most useful when dealing with skewed distributions. However, the median does not use all information about the size and magnitude of observations and only focuses on their relative positions.

Example 2-2: Calculation of the Median

Calculate the median score of the 20 scores listed in Example 2-1.

Solution

First we must arrange the scores in ascending or descending order. We'll go with ascending order.

10, 25, 31, 34, 45, 46, 47, 57, 57, **67**, **68**, 77, 77, 77, 85, 86, 88, 89, 95, 98.

Because this is an even-numbered data set (20 observations), the median equals the average of the 10th (n/2) and 11th [(n+2)/2] observations. The median for this data set is therefore, 67.5 [(67+68)/2].

The **mode** of a data set is its most frequently occurring value. In the data set in Example 2-2, the mode is 77 as it occurs most frequently (3 times). A data set that has one mode is said to be *unimodal*, while one that has two modes is said to be *bimodal*. It is also possible for a data set to have no mode, where all values are different and no value occurs more frequently than others. For grouped data, the **modal interval** is the interval with the highest frequency. The mode is the only measure of central tendency that can be used with nominal data.

© 2015 Wiley

Other Concepts of the Mean

The weighted mean ($\bar{X}_w$) is calculated by assigning *different* weights to observations in the data set to account for the disproportionate effect of certain observations on the arithmetic mean. The arithmetic mean assigns an *equal* weight to every observation in the data set, which makes it very sensitive to extreme values.

Example 2-3: Calculating the Weighted Mean

An individual invests 30% of her portfolio in Stock A, 40% in Stock B, and 30% in Stock C. The expected returns on Stock A, B, and C are 10%, 14%, and 6%, respectively. What is the portfolio's expected return?

Solution

$$\bar{X}_w = \sum_{i=1}^{n} w_i X_i = (w_A X_A + w_B X_B + w_C X_C)$$
$$= (0.3 \times 0.1) + (0.4 \times 0.14) + (0.3 \times 0.06)$$
$$= 10.4\%$$

The geometric mean is frequently used to average rates of change over time or to calculate the growth rate of a variable over a period. In the investment arena it is used to average rates of return over multiple periods or to compute the growth rate of a variable. The geometric mean, G, of a set of *n* observations is calculated as:

$$G = \sqrt[n]{X_1 \times X_2 \times X_3 \times \ldots \times X_n}$$
$$\text{with } X_i \geq 0 \text{ for } i = 1, 2, \ldots, n.$$

In order to calculate the geometric mean for investment returns data, we must add 1 to each return observation (expressed as a decimal) and then subtract 1 from the result. This is because returns can be negative (up to –100%) and the nth root of a negative number cannot be computed. The geometric mean, R_G, is computed as:

$$1 + R_G = \sqrt[T]{(1+R_1) \times (1+R_2) \times \ldots \times (1+R_T)} \quad \text{OR}$$

$$R_G = \left[\prod_{t=1}^{T}(1+R_t)\right]^{\frac{1}{T}} - 1$$

© 2015 Wiley

Example 2-4: Computing the Geometric Mean

The returns on XYZ common stock in the years 2000, 2001, 2002 and 2003 were 15.3%, 6.7%, –10% and –2.3% respectively. Compute the geometric mean of these returns.

Solution

$$1+R_G=\sqrt[4]{(1+0.153)\times(1+0.067)\times(1-0.1)\times(1-0.023)}$$
$$1+R_G=\sqrt[4]{1.153\times1.067\times0.9\times0.977}$$
$$1+R_G=\sqrt[4]{1.0817}=(1.0817)^{1/4}=1.0198$$
$$R_G=1.0198-1=0.0198\text{ or }1.98\%$$

Remember the following important relationships between the arithmetic mean and geometric mean of a particular data set:

- The geometric mean is always less than, or equal to the arithmetic mean.
- The geometric mean equals the arithmetic mean only when all the observations are identical.
- The difference between the geometric and arithmetic mean *increases* as the dispersion in observed values increases.

The harmonic mean is a relatively specialized concept that is used in the investment management arena to determine the average cost of shares purchased over time. It may be viewed as a special type of weighted mean, where the weight of an observation is inversely proportional to its magnitude. The harmonic mean is calculated as:

$$\text{Harmonic mean: } \overline{X}_H=\frac{N}{\sum_{i=1}^{N}\frac{1}{X_i}} \quad \text{with } X_i>0 \text{ for } i=1,2,\ldots,N.$$

Example 2-5: Harmonic Mean

An investor purchased $5,000 worth of RPS Stock each month over the last 4 months at prices of $4, $5, $6, and $7. Determine the average cost of the shares acquired.

Solution

$$\overline{X}_H=\frac{4}{1/4+1/5+1/6+1/7}=\$5.27$$

To check this result, calculate the total number of shares purchased and compute the average price.

$$\frac{5{,}000}{4}+\frac{5{,}000}{5}+\frac{5{,}000}{6}+\frac{5{,}000}{7}=3{,}797.619\text{ shares}$$

The average price equals $\frac{\$20{,}000}{3797.619}=\$5.27$

We can also use the weighted mean to compute the average cost of shares in Example 2-5. The weights on the purchase prices would be the number of shares purchased in each period.

Note that if the individual had invested different amounts in RPS Stock each month, we would not be able to use the harmonic mean formula to compute the average cost of shares.

Mathematically, unless all the observations in the data set are identical (equal in value), the harmonic mean will always be less than the geometric mean, which itself will be less than the arithmetic mean.

LOS 7f: Calculate and interpret quartiles, quintiles, deciles, and percentiles. Vol 1, pp 395–400

Quantiles

A quantile is a value at, or below which a stated proportion of the observations in a data set lie. Examples of quantiles include:

- quartiles, which divide the distribution in quarters or four equal parts.
- quintiles, which divide the distribution into fifths.
- deciles, which divide the data into tenths.
- percentiles, which divide the distribution into hundredths.

The most commonly used quantiles are percentiles. Other types of quantiles can also be expressed in terms of percentiles. For example, the second quintile (at or below which two-fifths of the observations lie) is also the 40th percentile.

The formula for the position of a percentile in a data set with *n* observations sorted in ascending order is:

$$L_y = \frac{(n+1)y}{100}$$

where:
y = percentage point at which we are dividing the distribution
L_y = location (L) of the percentile (P_y) in the data set sorted in ascending order

Example 2-6: Quartiles

1. Calculate the first quartile of a distribution that consists of the following asset returns: 10%, 23%, 13%, 17%, 19%, 5%, 4%.

2. If we include one more return observation of 10% in our data set, what is the new value of the first quartile?

Solution

1. First, arrange the data in ascending order:
   4%, 5%, 10%, 13%, 17%, 19%, 23%

   The first quartile = (7+1)(25/100) = 2nd item in the data set.

   One-fourth or 25% of the observed returns lie below the second observation from the left, which is 5%.

© 2015 Wiley

2. Once again we begin by arranging the data in ascending order:
   4%, 5%, 10%, 10%, 13%, 17%, 19%, 23%

   The first quartile = (8 + 1)(25/100) = 2.25

   This means that once the data set has been rearranged in ascending order, the first quartile is the second observation from the left plus 0.25 times the difference between the 2nd and 3rd observations. Therefore, one-fourth of the observed returns are below 6.25%. [5% + 0.25(10% – 5%)]

Part 2 illustrates how linear interpolation is used to determine P_y when L_y is not an integer.

Quantiles are used in portfolio performance evaluation (to rank the performance of portfolio managers relative to their peers) as well as investment strategy development and research (to classify companies according to certain quantifiable characteristics).

LOS 7g: Calculate and interpret 1) a range and a mean absolute deviation and 2) the variance and standard deviation of a population and of a sample. Vol 1, pp 401–402

Dispersion refers to the variability or spread of a random variable around its central tendency. In finance, the mean represents the expected reward (return) from an investment and the dispersion measures the risk in the investment.

The **range** is one of the most basic measures of variability of data. It is simply the difference between the highest and lowest values in a data set.

Range = Maximum value - Minimum value

Example 2-7: Calculating the Range

Calculate the range of the following data set that contains average returns earned by a portfolio manager over the last 6 years:
4%, 1%, 8%, 10%, 3%, 15%

Solution

Range = 15% – 1% = 14%

The **mean absolute deviation (MAD)** is the average of the *absolute* values of deviations of observations in a data set from its mean. Recall that the sum of the deviations from the arithmetic mean equals zero. Therefore, absolute values of deviations are used in this calculation.

© 2015 Wiley

$$MAD = \frac{\sum_{i=1}^{n} |X_i - \overline{X}|}{n}$$

where:
n = number of items in the data set
$\overline{X}$ = the arithmetic mean of the sample

Example 2-8: Calculating the Mean Absolute Deviation

Calculate the mean absolute deviation of the data set used in Example 2-7.

Solution

$$\text{Mean} = \overline{X} = (4+1+8+10+3+15)/6 = 6.83\%$$

$$MAD = (|4-6.83|+|1-6.83|+|8-6.83|+|10-6.83|+|3-6.83|+|15-6.83|)/6 = 4.167\%$$

On average, the observations in the data set deviate 4.167% from the mean return of 6.83%.

Population Variance and Standard Deviation

A more commonly used measure of dispersion is the variance, which equals the sum of the squares of deviations from the mean. The standard deviation is the positive square root of the variance. While the variance has no units, the standard deviation is expressed in the same units as the random variable itself. The variance and standard deviation can be calculated for both populations and samples.

The variance calculated using all the observations in a population is called the population variance (σ^2) and is calculated as:

The variance takes care of the problem of negative deviations from the mean canceling out positive deviations. Squaring the differences between observations and the mean results in a positive value regardless of whether the difference is positive or negative.

$$\sigma^2 = \frac{\sum_{i=1}^{N} (X_i - \mu)^2}{N}$$

where:
X_i = observation i
μ = population mean
N = size of the population

The population standard deviation (σ) is the positive square root of the population variance.

$$\sigma = \sqrt{\frac{\sum_{i=1}^{N} (X_i - \mu)^2}{N}}$$

© 2015 Wiley

Example 2-9: Calculating Population Variance and Standard Deviation

Calculate the variance and standard deviation of the scores of five golfers assuming that they represent the entire population of golfers participating in a particular tournament. Their scores are 67, 71, 72, 75, and 68.

Solution

$$\text{Population mean} = \mu = \frac{[67+71+72+75+68]}{5} = 70.6$$

$$\sigma^2 = \frac{\left[(67-70.6)^2+(71-70.6)^2+(72-70.6)^2+(75-70.6)^2+(68-70.6)^2\right]}{5} = 8.24$$

The average score of the 5 golfers is 70.6 strokes. The variance however, is 8.24 strokes squared. There is no such thing as strokes squared, which makes interpreting the variance very difficult. Therefore, the variance (which is always in squared units) is converted to a standard deviation, which equals the square root of the variance and is always presented in the same unit as the observations in the data set.

$$\text{Standard deviation} = \sigma = \sqrt{8.24} = 2.871 \text{ strokes.}$$

Conclusion: The average score of the 5 golfers is 70.6 strokes, and the standard deviation of their scores is 2.87 strokes.

The mean absolute deviation (MAD) will always be less than or equal to the standard deviation. This is because, by squaring all deviations from the mean, the standard deviation attaches a greater weight to larger deviations from the mean.

Sample Variance and Standard Deviation

When only sample data is available, we calculate the sample mean ($\overline{X}$), and sample variance (s^2) as follows:

$$\text{Sample mean} = \overline{X} = \frac{\sum_{i=1}^{n} X_i}{n}$$

$$\text{Sample variance} = s^2 = \frac{\sum_{i=1}^{n}(X_i-\overline{X})^2}{n-1}$$

where:
n = sample size.

Using n instead of n − 1 in the sample variance formula would result in the sample variance underestimating the true population variance.

Notice that the measure of central tendency used in the numerator to calculate the sample variance is ($\overline{X}$); not (μ) as is the case in the formula for population variance. Further, the divisor in the formula for sample variance is (n−1), whereas the divisor in the formula for population variance is N. The divisor is lower in the formula for sample variance in order to make it an unbiased (more accurate) estimate for the population variance. For our purposes, we just need to remember the difference in the divisors in the variance formulas. A more detailed knowledge of the reason for this difference is not required.

The **sample standard deviation (s)** is the positive square root of the sample variance and is calculated as:

$$s = \sqrt{\frac{\sum_{i=1}^{n}(X_i - \overline{X})^2}{n-1}}$$

Example 2-10: Calculating Sample Variance and Standard Deviation

Calculate the variance and standard deviation for the golfers' scores in Example 2-9. However, assume that the 5 scores that are presented are the scores of a representative sample of golfers from the entire population of golfers who participated in the tournament.

Solution

$$\overline{X} = \frac{[67+71+72+75+68]}{5} = 70.6$$

$$s^2 = \frac{\left[(67-70.6)^2+(71-70.6)^2+(72-70.6)^2+(75-70.6)^2+(68-70.6)^2\right]}{5-1} = 10.3$$

$$s = \sqrt{10.3} = 3.21$$

Sometimes, investors are only concerned with *downside risk* (e.g., the risk of obtaining returns below the mean). In these situations, it is quite helpful to compute the semivariance, which is the average of squared deviations below the mean, and the semideviation, which equals the positive square root of the semivariance. The target semivariance refers to the sum of the squared deviations from a specific target return, and its square root is known as the target semideviation.

© 2015 Wiley

LOS 7h: Calculate and interpret the proportion of observations falling within a specified number of standard deviations of the mean using Chebyshev's inequality. Vol 1, pp 402–414

Chebyshev's inequality is a method of calculating an approximate value for the proportion of observations in a data set that lie within *k* standard deviations from the mean.

Proportion of observations within *k* standard deviations from mean = $1 - 1/k^2$ for all $k > 1$

Example 2-11: Chebyshev's Inequality

Determine the minimum percentage of observations in a data set that lie within 1.5 standard deviations from the mean.

Solution

Chebyshev's inequality = $1 - 1/k^2$

$1 - 1/k^2 = 1 - 1/1.5^2 = 1 - 1/2.25 = 0.5556$ or 55.56%

The advantage of Chebyshev's inequality is that it holds for samples and populations and for discrete and continuous data regardless of the shape of the distribution.

LOS 7i: Calculate and interpret the coefficient of variation and the Sharpe ratio. Vol 1, pp 414–419

The standard deviation is more easily interpreted than the variance because it is expressed in the same units as the data. However, it may sometimes be difficult to determine what standard deviation means in terms of relative dispersion of the data when:

- The data sets being compared have significantly different means.
- The data sets have different units of measurement.

For example, suppose that we need to decide between two investments. One offers an expected return of 10% and has a standard deviation (risk) of 15%, while the other has an expected return of 18% and a standard deviation of 33%. We can compare the **relative dispersion** of returns on the two investments using the coefficient of variation, which is the ratio of the standard deviation of the data set to its mean.

$$CV = \frac{s}{\overline{X}}$$

where:

s = sample standard deviation

$\overline{X}$ = the sample mean.

In the investment arena, CV is used to measure the *risk per unit of return* in various investments.

Remember: The CV measures **risk per unit of return.** Further it is a scale-free measure (it has no units of measurement).

Example 2-12: Coefficient of Variation

Calculate the coefficient of variation for the following stocks and interpret the results:

	Mean Return	Standard Deviation
Stock A	12%	13%
Stock B	5%	4%
Stock C	10%	8%

Solution

$CV_A = 13/12 = 1.083$
$CV_B = 4/5 = 0.8$
$CV_C = 8/10 = 0.8$

Stock A has the *highest* risk per unit of return so it is the *least* attractive investment. Stock B and C are equally attractive as their CVs are identical.

The **Sharpe ratio** is the ratio of excess return over the risk-free rate from an investment to its standard deviation of returns. It basically measures excess return per unit of risk.

The Sharpe ratio measures **excess return per unit of risk.**

$$\text{Sharpe ratio} = \frac{\bar{r}_p - r_f}{s_p}$$

where:
$\bar{r}_p$ = mean portfolio return
r_f = risk-free return
s_p = standard deviation of portfolio returns

Example 2-13: Sharpe Ratio

Calculate the Sharpe ratio for a portfolio with a mean return of 12.5% and standard deviation of 10% given that the risk-free rate is 6%.

Solution

$$\text{Sharpe ratio} = \frac{12.5 - 6}{10} = 0.65$$

© 2015 Wiley

Issues with the Sharpe Ratio

- All other factors remaining the same, for portfolios with positive Sharpe ratios, the Sharpe ratio decreases if we increase risk. A portfolio with a higher positive Sharpe ratio offers a better risk-adjusted return. However, for portfolios with negative Sharpe ratios, the ratio increases (to a negative number closer to zero) if we increase risk. With negative Sharpe ratios we cannot always assume that the portfolio with the higher Sharpe ratio (closer to zero) offers a better risk-adjusted performance. If the standard deviation of two portfolios with negative Sharpe ratios is the same, the one with the higher ratio offers the better risk-adjusted performance.

- The standard deviation (which is used in the Sharpe ratio as a measure of risk) is an appropriate measure of risk only for investments and strategies that have approximately symmetric distributions. Use of the Sharpe ratio to evaluate the performance of hedge funds and options strategies (that have an asymmetric returns distribution) would give inaccurate results.

LESSON 3: SYMMETRY, SKEWNESS AND KURTOSIS IN RETURN DISTRIBUTIONS AND ARITHMETIC VERSUS GEOMETRIC MEANS

LOS 7j: Explain skewness and the meaning of a positively or negatively skewed return distribution. **Vol 1, pp 402–425**

LOS 7k: Describe the relative locations of the mean, median, and mode for a unimodal, nonsymmetrical distribution. **Vol 1, pp 420–422**

A distribution is said to be symmetrical about its mean when the distribution on either side of the mean is the mirror image of the other. Loss and gain intervals exhibit the same frequencies for a symmetrical distribution. For example, the frequency of a loss between 2% and 5% is identical to the frequency of a gain between 2% and 5%. Figure 3-1 illustrates a distribution that is symmetrical about its mean. It is known as the normal distribution and is one you will encounter frequently in the readings that follow.

Figure 3-1: Symmetrical Distribution (Normal Distribution)

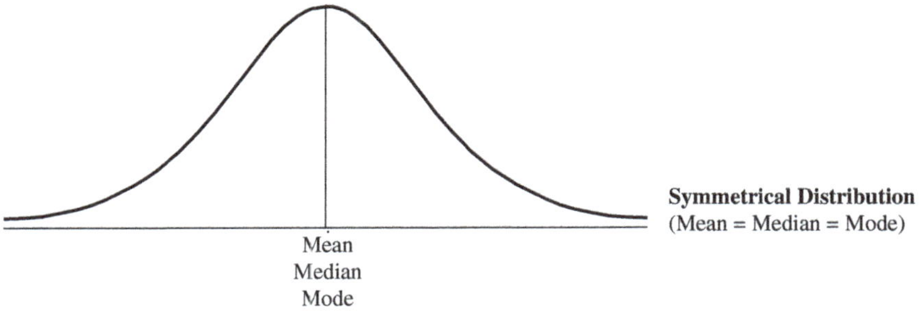

For a symmetrical distribution, the mean, median, and mode are equal.

When a distribution is nonsymmetrical it is said to be *skewed*. Skewness can be negative or positive. A distribution that is *positively skewed* (or skewed to the right) has a long tail on the right side, which suggests that there are certain observations that are much larger in value than most of the observations in the data set. Figure 3-2 illustrates a positively skewed distribution.

© 2015 Wiley

Figure 3-2: Positively Skewed Distribution

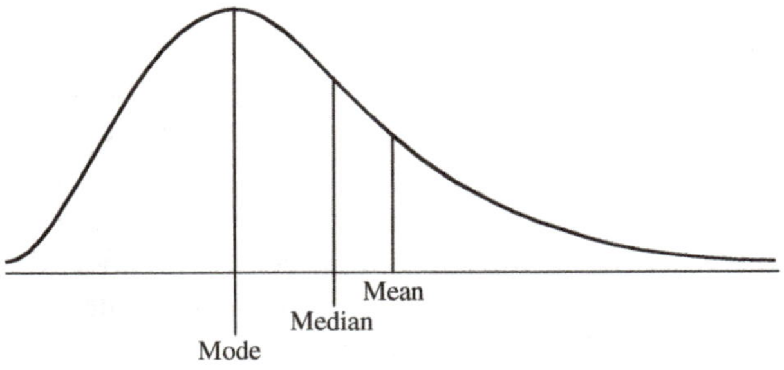

Positively (right) Skewed Distribution
(Mean > Median > Mode)

For positively skewed distributions, the mode is *less* than the median, which is *less* than the mean. The mean is affected the most by the extreme values (outliers) in the tail on the right side, and is "pulled" towards them.

A return distribution with positive skewness has frequent small losses and few large gains.

A return distribution with negative skewness has frequent small gains and few large losses.

Distributions of population incomes are generally skewed to the right. A large proportion of people have modest incomes, while a very small percentage have much higher incomes than the rest. This causes the average household income (mean) to be higher than the income earned by the majority (mode).

A *negatively skewed* distribution, on the other hand, has a long tail on the left side, which suggests that there are outliers that are much smaller in value than the majority of the observations in the distribution. Figure 3-3 illustrates a negatively skewed distribution.

Figure 3-3: Negatively Skewed Distribution

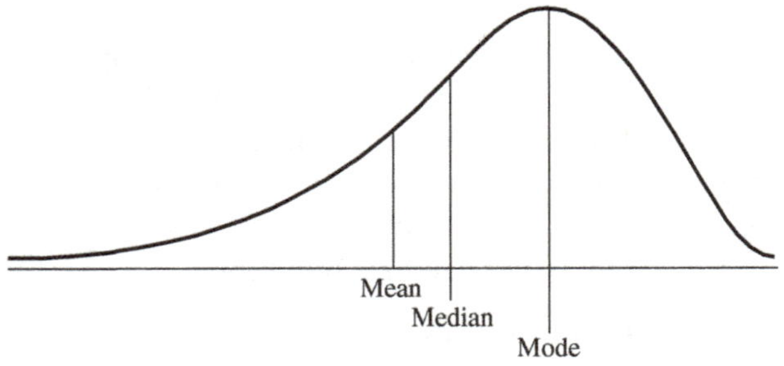

Negatively (left) Skewed Distribution
(Mean < Median < Mode)

For a negatively skewed distribution, the mode is *greater* than the median, which is *greater* than the mean. The mean is "pulled" lower by the outliers in the tail in the left side of the distribution.

© 2015 Wiley

LOS 71: Explain measures of sample skewness and kurtosis. Vol 1, pp 425–429

Sample skewness, also known as sample relative skewness, is calculated as:

$$S_K = \left[\frac{n}{(n-1)(n-2)}\right]\frac{\sum_{i=1}^{n}(X_i - \overline{X})^3}{s^3}$$

As n becomes large, the expression reduces to the mean cubed deviation.

$$S_K \approx \frac{1}{n}\frac{\sum_{i=1}^{n}(X_i - \overline{X})^3}{s^3}$$

where:
s = sample standard deviation

Some researchers believe that all other factors remaining the same, investors should prefer positive skewness i.e., portfolios that have a higher probability of earning relatively large profits.

- When the distribution is positively (right) skewed, sample skewness is positive because the numerator of the formula will be a positive number (the average of deviations above the mean is larger than the average of deviations below the mean).
- When the distribution is negatively (left) skewed, sample skewness is negative because the numerator of the formula will be a negative number (the average of deviations below the mean is larger than the average of deviations above the mean).
- Sample skewness of zero indicates that the data set follows a symmetrical distribution.
- Absolute values of skewness greater than 0.5 suggest that the data set is significantly skewed.

Kurtosis measures the extent to which a distribution is more or less peaked than a normal distribution. A normal distribution has a kurtosis of 3. Statistical packages usually report excess kurtosis (K_E) of any given distribution, which is the kurtosis of the distribution minus the kurtosis of the normal distribution (3).

- A leptokurtic distribution is *more* peaked and has *fatter* tails than a normal distribution and has an excess kurtosis greater than zero. (Figure 3-4)
- A platykurtic distribution is *less* peaked and has *thinner* tails than a normal distribution and has an excess kurtosis less than zero.
- A mesokurtic distribution is identical to a normal distribution and has an excess kurtosis of zero.

Skewness and kurtosis are extremely important concepts in the risk management arena. Generally speaking, greater positive kurtosis and/or more negative skewness in distribution of returns indicates higher risk.

A leptokurtic distribution has a greater proportion of small deviations from the mean and a greater proportion of large deviations from the mean compared to a normal distribution.

© 2015 Wiley

Figure 3-4: Leptokurtic Distribution

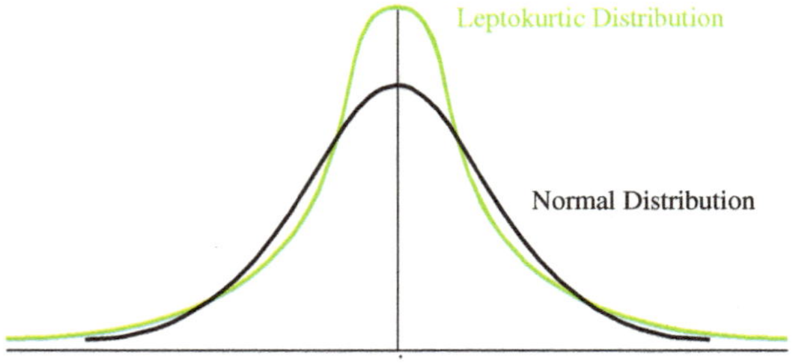

Sample Kurtosis uses standard deviations to the fourth power. Sample excess kurtosis is calculated as:

$$K_E = \left(\frac{n(n+1)}{(n-1)(n-2)(n-3)} \frac{\sum_{i=1}^{n}(X_i - \overline{X})^4}{s^4} \right) - \frac{3(n-1)^2}{(n-2)(n-3)}$$

As n becomes large the equation simplifies to:

$$K_E \approx \frac{1}{n} \frac{\sum_{i=1}^{n}(X_i - \overline{X})^4}{s^4} - 3$$

where:

s = sample standard deviation

For a sample size greater than 100, a sample excess kurtosis of greater than 1.0 would be considered unusually high. Most equity return series have been found to be leptokurtic.

LOS 7m: Compare the use of arithmetic and geometric means when analyzing investment returns. Vol 1, pp 429–430

For reporting historical returns, the geometric mean is more appropriate because it equals the rate of growth an investor would have to earn each year to match the actual cumulative investment performance. The geometric mean is an excellent measure of past performance. On the other hand, the arithmetic mean can distort evaluation of past performance.

- If we want to gauge performance over a single period, the arithmetic mean should be used because the arithmetic mean is the average of one-period returns.
- If we want to estimate returns over more than one period, we should use the geometric mean as it measures how investment returns are linked over time.

© 2015 Wiley

To calculate expected equity risk premiums (in a forward-looking context) use of the arithmetic mean is more appropriate. Let's go over a brief example to illustrate the use of the arithmetic and geometric means in a forward-looking context. Suppose you have \$100 that you plan to invest for 2 years and there is an equal chance of a 100% return or a –50% return in each year. With a 100% return in one year and a 50% return in the other year, the geometric mean return would equal $(2 \times 0.5)^{0.5} - 1 = 0$, while the arithmetic mean return would equal (100% – 50%)/2 = 25%.

The arithmetic mean wealth at the end of two periods may also be calculated as [(400 + 100 + 100 + 25) / 4] = \$156.25.

From Figure 3-5, notice that the geometric mean accurately predicts the median and modal wealth in this example (\$100). However, the arithmetic mean return better predicts the arithmetic mean ending wealth. In our example, actual returns over the two-period horizon might be 300%, 0%, 0%, or –75%, with a two-period arithmetic mean return of (300 + 0 + 0 – 75) / 4 = 56.25%. The arithmetic mean return predicts the arithmetic mean ending wealth at the end of two periods to be \$156.25. Based on the two-period arithmetic mean return of 56.25%, we can calculate the arithmetic mean rate per period to be $(1 + 0.5625)^{0.5} - 1 = 25\%$.

Figure 3-5: Arithmetic vs. Geometric Mean

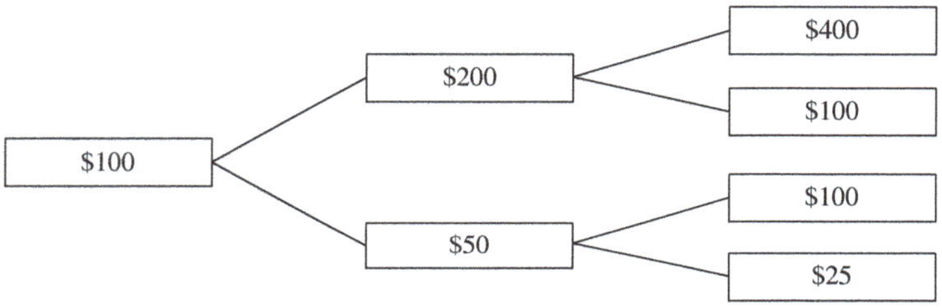

- Uncertainty in cash flows or returns causes the arithmetic mean to be larger than the geometric mean. The more the uncertainty, the greater the divergence between the two.
- Zero variance or zero uncertainty would result in the geometric and arithmetic mean returns being approximately equal.
- Studies have shown that the geometric mean return approximately equals the arithmetic mean minus half the variance of returns.

© 2015 Wiley

Reading 8: Probability Concepts

LESSON 1: PROBABILITY, EXPECTED VALUE AND VARIANCE

LOS 8a: Define a random variable, an outcome, an event, mutually exclusive events, and exhaustive events. Vol 1, pp 458–459

Let's first work with a simple example so that we can familiarize ourselves with the terminology that we will use extensively in the readings ahead. Suppose you are going to roll a six-sided fair die.

When you roll the die, you have no control over the result. It could be any one of six numbers and the one that comes up is a random variable. If you roll a 3, it is an outcome. Rolling an odd number and rolling a 5 are examples of events. Rolling a 3 and rolling a 4 are mutually exclusive events because you cannot roll a 3 and a 4 on the same throw. Finally, rolling a 1, 2, 3, 4, 5, and 6 are mutually exclusive and exhaustive events because they cover the entire spectrum of possible outcomes from the throw.

Now let's formally define some of the terms introduced above:

- A random variable is one whose possible values or results are *uncertain.*
- An outcome is the observed value of a random variable.
- An event could be a single outcome or a set of outcomes.
- Mutually exclusive events are events that cannot happen simultaneously. The occurrence of one precludes the occurrence of the other.
- Exhaustive events cover the range of *all possible outcomes* of an event.

LOS 8b: State the two defining properties of probability and distinguish among empirical, subjective, and a priori probabilities. Vol 1, pp 459–461

A probability is a number between 0 and 1 that reflects the chance of a certain event occurring. A probability of zero means that it is impossible for the event to occur, while a probability of 1 means that the event will definitely occur, and that the outcome is not random.

There are two basic defining principles of probability:

1. The probability of any event, E, is a number from 0 to 1. Therefore, $0 \leq P(E_i) \leq 1$, where $P(E_i)$ is the probability of event, i, occurring.
2. The sum of the probabilities of mutually exclusive exhaustive events equals 1. Thus $\sum P(E_i) = 1$.

The chances of rolling a particular number when rolling a die are 1 in 6 or 1/6 = 0.167. Rolling a 1, 2, 3, 4, 5, or 6 covers the entire range of possible outcomes, so the probability of rolling a 1, 2, 3, 4, 5, or 6 equals 1. One of the outcomes in this set of events will definitely occur.

Methods of Estimating Probabilities

- An empirical probability estimates the probability of an event based on the frequency of its occurrence in the past. For example, if it has rained for 20 days on average in June for the past 5 years, the probability of rain on any particular day this June is 67%.

© 2015 Wiley

- A subjective probability draws on subjective reasoning and personal judgment to estimate probabilities. If you think the probability of rain on a particular day is 80%, you are stating a subjective probability.

- An a priori probability is based on formal analysis and reasoning rather than personal judgment. An example of this would be if we were to look at the meteorological conditions leading up to, and on a particular day to determine the probability of rain to be 70%.

LOS 8c: State the probability of an event in terms of odds for and against the event. Vol 1, pp 460–461

Probabilities are sometimes stated in the form of odds for or odds against an event. John might assert that the odds *for* the market going up tomorrow are 1 to 4, to which Mary may respond by saying that the odds *for* the market rising are 1 to 7. What do these statements really mean?

The odds *for* an event are stated as the probability of the event occurring to the probability of the event not occurring.

- Odds *for* event, E, are stated as P(E) to [1 - P(E)]

  If the odds for are given as "a to b," then:

$$P(E) = \frac{a}{(a+b)}$$

The odds *against* an event are stated as the probability of the event not occurring to the probability of the event occurring.

- Odds *against* event, E, are stated in the form of [1 - P(E)] to P(E).

  If the odds *against* are given as "a to b," then:

$$P(E) = \frac{b}{(a+b)}$$

Given the odds for an outcome, the odds against the outcome are simply the *reciprocal* of the odds for. For example, if the odds for an event are given as "a to b," the odds against the event are simply "b to a."

So now let's determine what John and Mary are really saying about the probability of the market rising tomorrow:

John:
- He thinks the probability of the market going up tomorrow is 1/(1+4) = 0.2.
- This implies that in his view the probability of the market *not* going up tomorrow is 1 – 0.2 = 0.8.
- John would offer odds *against* the market going up of 4 to 1.

© 2015 Wiley

Mary:

- She thinks that the probability of the market going up tomorrow is 1/(1+7) = 0.125.
- This implies that, in her view, the probability of the market not going up tomorrow is 1 – 0.125 = 0.875.
- She would offer odds *against* the market going up of 7 to 1.

If Susan thinks that the probability of the market rising tomorrow is 0.40, what odds would she offer *for* the market rising, and *against* the market rising?

Susan's odds for the market rising = 0.4/(1 – 0.4) = 2 to 3
Susan's odds against market rising: (1 – 0.4)/0.4 = 3 to 2

If you were to bet *against* John that the stock market will go up, John would offer you odds of 4 to 1 *against* him. If you bet $1 and the market rises, you will have a profit of $4 and get your $1 back. If the market does not rise, you will lose your $1 stake. Remember that the expected return on the bet is always zero. Your expected return if you were to bet against John equals ($-1)(0.8) + ($4)(0.2) = 0.

Profiting from Inconsistent Probabilities

Suppose you, as an analyst, are evaluating two companies, ABC and XYZ that operate in the same industry. Both will benefit equally from a governmental decision to allow them to export their products. ABC's stock price reflects a 50% probability of the export ban being lifted, while XYZ's stock price reflects a 75% probability of the ban being lifted.

A trade in two closely-related stocks that involves short selling one and purchasing the other is known as a **pairs arbitrage trade**.

If the 50% probability (reflected in ABC's stock price) is accurate, ABC stock is fairly valued, while XYZ stock is overvalued. On the other hand, if the 75% chance (reflected in XYZ's stock price) is accurate, then XYZ is accurately valued and ABC is undervalued.

If you were to be conservative in your investment strategy, you would purchase ABC and perhaps reduce your holdings in XYZ. A more aggressive stance would be to purchase ABC and short sell XYZ. The Dutch Book Theorem states that if the probabilities reflected in the stock prices are not consistent, they give rise to profit opportunities. As investors take positions to take advantage of such opportunities, the inconsistency is eventually eliminated.

LOS 8d: Distinguish between unconditional and conditional probabilities. **Vol 1, pp 462**

LOS 8e part 1: Explain the multiplication , addition, and total probability rules. **Vol 1, pp 462–465**

LOS 8f: Calculate and interpret 1) the joint probability of two events, 2) the probability that at least one of two events will occur, given the probability of each and the joint probability of the two events, and 3) a joint probability of any number of independent events. **Vol 1, pp 466–470**

Unconditional and conditional probabilities answer different questions, and are calculated, estimated, and interpreted differently.

Unconditional or marginal probabilities estimate the probability of an event irrespective of the occurrence of other events. They can be thought of as stand-alone probabilities and answer questions like "What is probability of a return on a stock above 10%?" or "What are the chances of getting a 3 on a roll of the die?"

Conditional probabilities express the probability of an event occurring *given* that another event has occurred. They answer questions like "What is the probability of the return on the stock being above 10% *given* that the return is above the risk free rate?" or "What is the probability of rolling a 3 *given* that an odd number is rolled?"

Before stating an exact definition of a conditional probability, we need to define the **joint probability, P(AB)**, which answers the question, "What is the probability of *both* A **and** B occurring?"

- If A and B are *mutually exclusive* events, the joint probability P(AB) equals zero. This is because mutually exclusive events cannot occur simultaneously.

  Example:
  Event A = Getting a 3 upon rolling the die.
  Event B = Getting a 4 on the same throw.
  Since a 3 and a 4 cannot be obtained on the same throw, P(AB) = 0.

- If A is contained within the set of possible outcomes for B, P(AB) = P(A)

  Example:
  Event A = Getting a 3 upon rolling the die.
  Event B = Getting an odd number upon rolling the die.
  Rolling a 3 can only occur if an odd number is rolled. Therefore, the probability of rolling a 3 *and* rolling an odd number, P(AB), is simply the probability of rolling a 3, P(A).

Now that we have a better understanding of joint probabilities, we can define a conditional probability, P(A|B) (the probability of event A occurring given that event B has occurred) as the joint probability, P(AB), divided by the unconditional probability of event B occurring, P(B).

Mathematically the conditional probability, P(A|B), is expressed as:

$$P(A|B) = \frac{P(AB)}{P(B)} \text{ given that } P(B) \neq 0$$

© 2015 Wiley

Let's differentiate between a conditional and an unconditional probability using an example. Let's calculate the unconditional probability of rolling a 3, and the conditional probability of rolling a 3 *given* that an odd number is rolled.

Unconditional probability of rolling a 3:

$$P(3) = 1/6 = 0.167$$

Conditional probability of rolling a 3 *given* that an odd number is rolled:

$$P(3|\text{odd number is rolled}) = \frac{P(AB)}{P(B)} = \frac{P(\text{rolling a 3 and rolling an odd number})}{P(\text{rolling an odd number})}$$

$$= \frac{0.167}{0.5} = 0.334$$

The multiplication rule for probability to calculate joint probabilities can be derived from the conditional probability formula by simply rearranging it:

$$P(AB) = P(A|B) \times P(B)$$

Example 1-1: Calculating a Joint Probability Using the Multiplication Rule

We are given the following information:

- Probability that the state of economy is good, $P(E_G) = 0.3$
- Probability that stock performance is good *given* a good economic environment, $P(S_G|E_G) = 0.8$

What is the probability of having a good economic environment *and* good stock performance?

Solution

$$P(S_GE_G) = P(S_G|E_G) \times P(E_G)$$

$$P(S_GE_G) = 0.3 \times 0.8 = 0.24$$

Calculating the Probability that at Least One of Two Events Will Occur

Sometimes we want to determine the probability of event A **or** event B occurring, P(A or B). Here, we need to invoke the addition rule for probabilities, which calculates the probability of *at least one* of A and B occurring.

$$P(A \text{ or } B) = P(A) + P(B) - P(AB)$$

© 2015 Wiley

Given that A and B share some outcomes, if we simply add P(B) to P(A) we would be double counting the shared outcomes. In order to remove the shared outcomes from the sum of the probabilities of A and B, we subtract P(AB).

If A and B are mutually exclusive events, the joint probability of A and B, P(AB), equals zero. In this case, P(A or B) simply equals P(A) + P(B).

Figure 1-1: Venn Diagrams Illustrating the Addition Rule

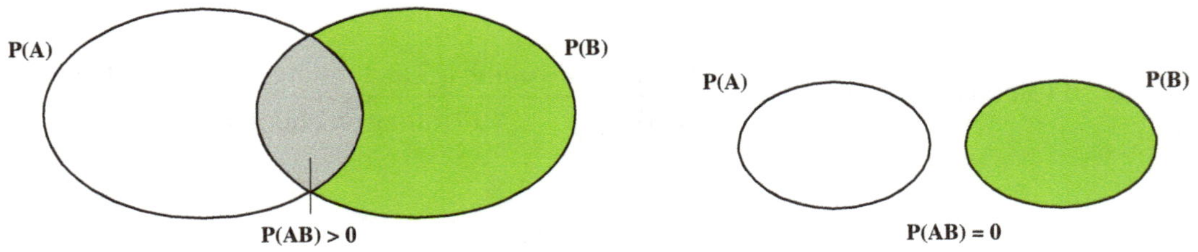

1a. Not Mutually Exclusive Events **1b. Mutually Exclusive Events**

Example 1-2: Addition Rule for Calculating Probabilities

We are given the following information:

- Probability that the state of economy is bad, $P(E_B) = 0.28$
- Probability that stock performance is good, $P(S_G) = 0.3$
- Probability that stock performance is good and the state of economy is bad, $P(S_G E_B) = P(E_B S_G) = 0.12$

Determine the probability that either the stock performance is good or the state of economy is bad.

Solution

P(A or B) = P(A) + P(B) – P(AB)

$P(S_G \text{ or } E_G) = 0.28 + 0.3 - 0.12 = 0.46$

LOS 8g: Distinguish between dependent and independent events.

Vol 1, pp 467–470

Dependent and Independent Events

With two dependent events, the occurrence of one is related to the occurrence of the other. For example, the probability of doing well on an exam is related to the probability of preparing well for it.

© 2015 Wiley

Two events are independent if the occurrence of one does *not* have any bearing on the occurrence of the other. For example, the probability of doing well on an exam is unrelated to the probability of there being exactly 5 trees in the park nearby.

When two events are independent:

$$P(A|B) = P(A), \text{ or equivalently}, P(B|A) = P(B)$$

If we are trying to forecast an event, information about a dependent event may be useful, but information about an independent event will not be useful. The results of three throws of the die are independent of each other. The probability of getting a 3 on the second throw is not related to the outcome of the first throw. The probability of rolling a 4 on each of the throws is equal.

P(getting a 4 on the first *and* a 4 on the second *and* a 4 on the third throw)

$$= P(4) \times P(4) \times P(4) = (1/6) \times (1/6) \times (1/6) = 0.00463$$

With independent events, the word *and* implies multiplication, and the word *or* implies addition. Therefore:

$$P(A \text{ or } B) = P(A) + P(B) - P(AB)$$
$$P(A \text{ and } B) = P(A) \times P(B)$$

Example 1-3: Joint Probability for More Than Two Independent Events

It is observed that the probability of a high school student failing her senior year is 0.15. Further, it has been determined that the probability of failing in a given year is independent of the probability of failing the previous year. Compute the probability of a student failing for 4 years?

Solution

P(Student failing for 4 years) = $0.15 \times 0.15 \times 0.15 \times 0.15 = 0.00051$

LOS 8e part 2: Explain the total probability rule. Vol 1, pp 470–471

LOS 8h: Calculate and interpret an unconditional probability using the total probability rule. Vol 1, pp 470–474

The total probability rule expresses the unconditional probability of an event in terms of conditional probabilities for mutually exclusive and exhaustive events. In the simple case, we will assume that only two outcomes are possible, S and not S, which we define as S^c (the complement of S).

$P(S) + P(S^c) = 1$ (this means that the events are exhaustive)

$P(S \text{ and } S^c) = 0$ (this means that the events are mutually exclusive)

© 2015 Wiley

In this case:

$$P(A) = P(AS) + P(AS^c)$$

Replacing the joint probabilities on the right hand side of the equation above with conditional probabilities using the multiplication rule, the probability of A can be reformulated as:

$$P(A) = P(A \mid S) \times P(S) + P(A \mid S^c) \times P(S^c)$$

The probability of event A, P(A) is expressed as a weighted average in the total probability rule. The weights applied to the conditional probabilities are the probabilities of the scenarios. For example, the weight attached to the conditional probability, P(A|S), is the probability of scenario S, P(S). Remember, for this rule to apply, the scenarios must be mutually exclusive and exhaustive.

Total probability rule for *n* possible scenarios:

$$P(A) = P(A \mid S_1) \times P(S_1) + P(A \mid S_2) \times P(S_2) + \ldots + P(A \mid S_n) \times P(S_n)$$

where the set of events $\{S_1, S_2, \ldots, S_n\}$ is mutually exclusive and exhaustive.

Example 1-4: Total Probability Rule

We have been given the following information:

- Probability of monetary authorities increasing money supply, $P(MS_{INC}) = 0.36$
- Probability of the monetary authorities *not* increasing money supply, $P(MS^C_{INC}) = 0.64$
- Probability of depreciation of currency given that money supply is increased, $P(D|MS_{INC}) = 0.52$
- Probability of depreciation of currency given that money supply is *not* increased, $P(D|MS^C_{INC}) = 0.74$

Assume that the currency can depreciate (D) in either scenario. The events, increase in money supply (MS_{INC}) and no increase in money supply (MS^C_{INC}) are mutually exclusive and exhaustive. Therefore, the sum of the two joint probabilities (i.e., $P(DMS_{INC})$ and $P(DMS^C_{INC})$) must equal the unconditional probability of a depreciation in the currency (using the total probability rule). The probability of currency depreciation equals the sum of the probability of currency depreciation with money supply increasing, and the probability of currency depreciation with money supply not increasing.

$$P(D) = P(DMS_{INC}) + P(DMS^C_{INC})$$

Replacing the joint probabilities with the conditional probabilities using the multiplication rule, we can reformulate the above equation as:

$$P(D) = P(D \mid MS_{INC}) \times P(MS_{INC}) + P(D \mid MS^C_{INC}) \times P(MS^C_{INC})$$
$$P(D) = 0.52 \times 0.36 + 0.74 \times 0.64$$
$$P(D) = 0.1872 + 0.4736 = 0.6608$$

© 2015 Wiley

Figure 1-2: Unconditional, Conditional, and Joint Probabilities

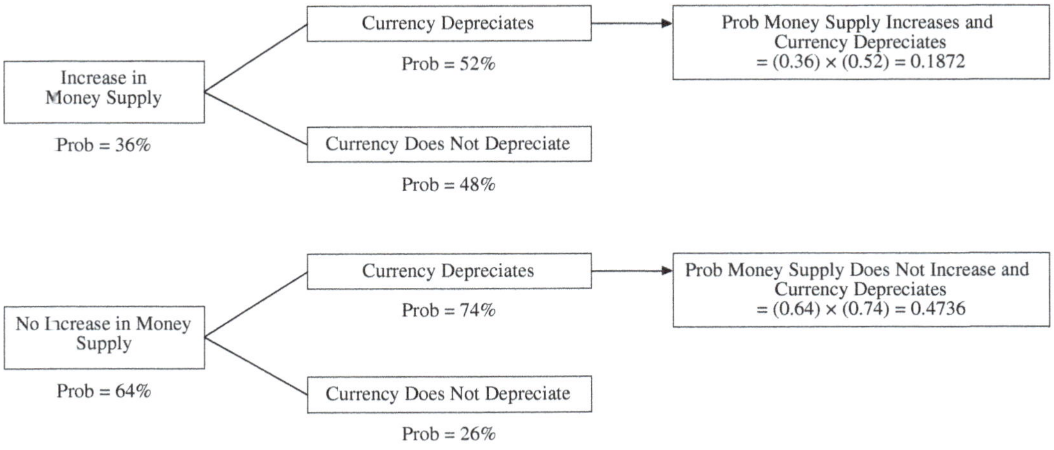

The unconditional probability ofthe currency depreciating equals 0.1872 + 0.4736 = 0.66

Expected Value

The expected value of a random variable is the probability-weighted average of all possible outcomes for the random variable. Remember that the sum of all the weights (probabilities) should equal 1.

$$E(X) = P(X_1)X_1 + P(X_2)X_2 + \ \ldots\ldots\ P(X_n)X_n$$

$$E(X) = \sum_{i=1}^{n} P(X_i)X_i$$

Where:
X_i = one of *n* possible outcomes.

Expected values are forecasts of what we think might happen based on probabilities. Sample and population means are based on historical observations. For rolling a die, the expected value for the outcome equals:

$$(1/6 \times 1) + (1/6 \times 2) + (1/6 \times 3) + (1/6 \times 4) + (1/6 \times 5) + (1/6 \times 6) = 3.5$$

It is impossible to roll a 3.5 on the die. However, the expected value represents our best guess of the average of all outcomes over the long run. By calculating expected values in this manner, the difference between actual outcomes and forecasts is minimized.

© 2015 Wiley

Example 1-5: Expected Value

At the upcoming Federal Reserve Board meeting, the probability that the Fed will increase money supply is 0.3, while the probability of no increase in money supply is 0.7. Historically, stocks have risen 4% on the day of the Fed announcement when money supply has been increased and have fallen by 5% on the day when money supply has not been increased. What is the expected value of stock returns on the day of the Fed announcement. Assuming that no other variables have any impact on stock returns on the day of announcement.

Solution

The probability of stocks rising on the day of the meeting equals the probability of money supply increasing (0.3). Similarly, the probability of stocks falling on the day of the announcement equals the probability of money supply not being increased (0.7).

Event	P(X)	X	P(X)×X
Money supply increased (stocks rise)	0.3	0.04	0.012
Money supply not increased (stocks fall)	0.7	–0.05	–0.035
Expected value			0.012 + (–0.035) = –0.023

The expected value of stock returns on the day of a Fed announcement equals –2.3%.

Variance and Standard Deviation

The variance of a random variable around its expected value is the probability weighted sum of the squared differences between each outcome and the expected value. If variance equals zero, there is no dispersion in the distribution. In this case, the outcome is certain, and the variable, X, is not a random variable.

$$\sigma^2(X) = E\{[X - E(X)]^2\}$$

$$\sigma^2(X) = \sum_{i=1}^{n} P(X_i)[X_i - E(X)]^2$$

Standard deviation is the positive square root of the variance. The variance has no units while the standard deviation is expressed in the same unit as the expected value and the random variable itself.

© 2015 Wiley

Example 1-6: Variance and Standard Deviation

Calculate the variance and standard deviation of coal prices given the following possible outcomes and their associated probabilities:

Coal Price (X)	Probability P(X)
$40	8%
$50	15%
$60	40%
$70	25%
$80	12%

To calculate the variance, we first need to calculate the expected price of coal:

E(Coal price) = $(0.08\times40) + (0.15\times50) + (0.40\times60) + (0.25\times70) + (0.12\times80) = \$61.80$

The variance of coal prices around the expected value is calculated as:

$$\sigma^2 = 0.08(40-61.8)^2 + 0.15(50-61.8)^2 + 0.40(60-61.8)^2 + 0.25(70-61.8)^2 + 0.12(80-61.8)^2 = 116.76$$

The standard deviation of coal prices is calculated as:

$$\sigma = \sqrt{116.76} = \$10.81$$

Notice that standard deviation is expressed in dollars (the same unit as the random variable and its expected value) while the variance has no unit.

LOS 8i: Explain the use of conditional expectation in investment applications. Vol 1, pp 474–475

In evaluating investments, analysts make use of all available relevant information to make forecasts. Forecasts are often refined in light of new information or events. In such cases, analysts use conditional expected values that are calculated using conditional probabilities. The goal is to calculate the expected value of a random variable given all the possible scenarios that can occur.

Similar to the total probability rule, which states unconditional probabilities in terms of conditional probabilities, there is a way to state (unconditional) expected values in terms of conditional expected values. This principle is known as the total probability rule for expected value and is given as:

1. $E(X) = E(X|S)P(S) + E(X|S^c)P(S^c)$
2. $E(X) = E(X|S_1) \times P(S_1) + E(X|S_2) \times P(S_2) + \ldots + E(X|S_n) \times P(S_n)$

Where:
$E(X)$ = the unconditional expected value of X
$E(X|S_1)$ = the expected value of X given Scenario 1
$P(S_1)$ = the probability of Scenario 1 occurring
The set of events $\{S_1, S_2,\ldots, S_n\}$ is mutually exclusive and exhaustive.

© 2015 Wiley

Like expected value, variance also has a conditional counterpart to the unconditional concept. Conditional variance can be used to assess the risk of a particular scenario.

Given that there are only two possible scenarios, the expected value of X equals the expected value of X given Scenario A, $E(X|S_A)$, multiplied by the probability of Scenario A, $P(S_A)$, plus the expected value of X given Scenario B, $E(X|S_B)$, times the probability of Scenario B, $P(S_B)$. The set of possible scenarios (A and B) must be *mutually exclusive and exhaustive* for the total probability rule for expected value to hold.

Example 1-7: Conditional Expected Value

The probability of monetary authorities increasing or not increasing the money supply in an economy depends on whether the state of economy is good or bad.

Given a "good economy" the conditional probabilities are as follows:

- P(Money supply increase|good economy) = 0.25
- P(Money supply not increase|good economy) = 0.75

Given a "bad" economy, the conditional probabilities are as follows:

- P(Money supply increase|bad economy) = 0.64
- P(Money supply not increase|bad economy) = 0.36

Compute the conditional expected value for stock returns for each possible state of the economy. The stock market goes up 4% if money supply is increased, but falls by 5% when money supply is not increased.

Solution

The expected value of stock returns given the state of the economy is good:

$$E(X|\text{good economy}) = (0.25)(0.04) + (0.75)(-0.05) = -0.0275 \text{ or } -2.75\%$$

The expected value of stock returns given the state of the economy is bad:

$$E(X|\text{bad economy}) = (0.64)(0.04) + (0.36)(-0.05) = 0.0076 \text{ or } 0.76\%$$

© 2015 Wiley

LOS 8j: Explain the use of a tree diagram to represent an investment problem. Vol 1, p 475

Example 1-8: Expected Value and Tree Diagrams

Supercar Inc's EPS was $5.76 in 2009. Its 2010 earnings depend on the state of the economy. There is a 0.7 probability of a "good" economy in 2010 and 0.3 probability of the economy being "not good."

- If there is a good economy in 2010, the probability that EPS will be $7.20 is estimated at 0.6, and the probability that EPS will be $6.4 is estimated at 0.4
- If there is a "not good" economy in 2010, the probability of a $5.80 EPS is estimated at 0.25, and the probability of EPS being $4.90 is estimated at 0.75

Use a tree diagram to model this problem and calculate the expected value of Supercar Inc's EPS for 2010.

Solution

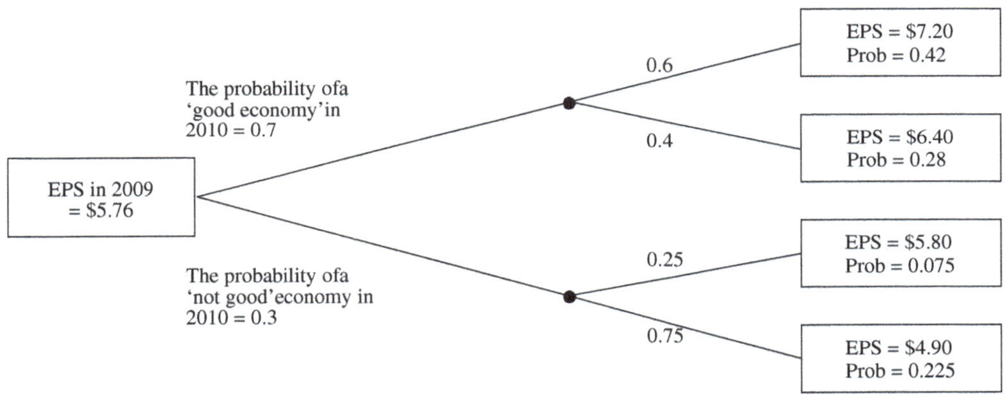

The unconditional probability in the top right box P(EPS = $7.20) = 0.42 is the same as the joint probability of a good economy and an EPS of $7.20, P(EPS = $7.20 and Good economy). It is calculated as the probability of a $7.20 EPS given a good economy, P(EPS = $7.20)|Good economy) times the unconditional probability of a good economy, P(Good economy).

P(EPS = $7.20) = P(EPS = $7.20 and Good economy)
= (EPS = $7.20)|Good economy) × P(Good economy)
= (0.7)(0.6) = 0.42

The expected value of EPS in 2010 is calculated as:

E(2010 EPS) = ($7.20)(0.42) + ($6.40)(0.28) + ($5.80)(0.075) + ($4.90)(0.225) = $6.35

Note that the sum of the probabilities of the four possible outcomes for EPS equals one.

What we are "really" calculating is the probability of a good economy AND an EPS of $7.20 (using the multiplication rule). The point to notice is that an EPS of $7.20 is a subset of a good economy (try drawing a Venn diagram). You can only have an EPS of $7.20 if the economy is good. Therefore, the probability of a good economy AND an EPS of $7.20 is essentially the same as the probability of an EPS of $7.20. You cannot have an EPS of $7.20 outside of a good economy.

© 2015 Wiley

LESSON 2: COVARIANCE AND CORRELATION AND CALCULATING PORTFOLIO EXPECTED RETURN AND VARIANCE

LOS 8k: Calculate and interpret covariance and correlation. Vol 1, pp 479–488

Covariance is a measure of the extent to which two random variables move together. For two random variables, X and Y, that have expected values of E(X) and E(Y) respectively, the covariance is calculated as:

$$\text{Cov}(XY) = E\{[X - E(X)][Y - E(Y)]\}$$

We can also write the covariance formula in terms of the returns on Asset A and Asset B:

$$\text{Cov}(R_A, R_B) = E\{[R_A - E(R_A)][R_B - E(R_B)]\}$$

Properties of Covariance

- Covariance is a similar concept to variance. The difference lies in the fact that variance measures how a random variable varies with itself, while covariance measures how a random variable varies with another random variable.
- Covariance is symmetric, i.e. Cov(X,Y) = Cov (Y, X).
- Covariance can range from positive infinity to negative infinity. Variance, on the other hand, is always positive.
- The covariance of X with itself, Cov(X,X), is equal to variance of X, Var(X).
- When the covariance of returns of two assets is *negative*, it means that when the return on one asset is above its expected value, the return on the other tends to be below its expected value. There is an *inverse* relationship between the two variables.
- When the covariance of returns of two assets is *positive*, it means that when the return on one asset is above its expected value, the return on the other also tends to be above its expected value.
- Covariance of returns is zero if the returns are unrelated.

Limitations of Covariance

- Because the unit that covariance is expressed in depends on the unit that the data is presented in, it is difficult to compare covariance across data sets that have different scales.
- In practice, it is difficult to interpret covariance as it can take on extreme large values.
- Covariance does not tell us anything about the strength of the relationship between the two variables.

Covariance can also be calculated using probabilistic data. Example 2-1 illustrates this.

The formula for calculating the covariance between random variables R_A and R_B is:

$$\text{Cov}(R_A, R_B) = \sum_i \sum_j P(R_{A,i}, R_{B,j})(R_{A,i} - ER_A)(R_{B,j} - ER_B)$$

© 2015 Wiley

Example 2-1: Calculating Covariance

Calculate and interpret the covariance of the returns for Stock A and Stock B given three possible states of the economy-expansion, normal and recession. The returns of Stock A and Stock B under each state and the probability of each state are listed below.

State	P(S)	R_A	R_B
Expansion	0.25	0.04	0.02
Normal	0.36	0.08	0.01
Recession	0.39	0.01	0.04
	$\Sigma(P) = 1.0$		

Solution

First we calculate the expected return on the two stocks:

$$E(R_A) = (0.25)(0.04) + (0.36)(0.08) + (0.39)(0.01) = 0.0427$$
$$E(R_B) = (0.25)(0.02) + (0.36)(0.01) + (0.39)(0.04) = 0.0242$$

State	P(S)	R_A	R_B	$P(S)\,[R_A - E(R_A)]\,[R_B - E(R_B)]$
Expansion	0.25	0.04	0.02	$(0.25)(0.04-0.0427)(0.02-0.0242) = 0.00000284$
Normal	0.36	0.08	0.01	$(0.36)(0.08-0.0427)(0.01-0.0242) = -0.000191$
Recession	0.39	0.01	0.04	$(0.39)(0.01-0.0427)(0.04-0.0242) = -0.000201$

The covariance of the returns of the two assets is calculated as:

$$0.00000284 + (-0.000191) + (-0.000201) = -0.000389$$

The only thing that the covariance tells us is that the returns on the two assets are inversely related (indicated by the negative sign). Covariance does not tell us anything about the strength of the relationship between the two variables.

Correlation Coefficient

The correlation coefficient measures the strength and direction of the linear relationship between two random variables. It is obtained by dividing (standardizing) the covariance of the two random variables by the product of their standard deviations.

$$\text{Corr}(R_A, R_B) = \rho(R_A, R_B) = \frac{\text{Cov}(R_A, R_B)}{(\sigma_A)(\sigma_B)}$$

Properties of the Correlation Coefficient

- It measures the strength of the relationship between two random variables.
- It has no unit.
- It lies between –1 and +1
- A correlation coefficient of +1 indicates a perfect positive correlation between two random variables.
- A correlation coefficient of –1 indicates a perfect negative correlation between two random variables.
- A correlation coefficient of zero indicates no linear relationship between two random variables.

A shortcoming of the correlation coefficient is the fact that it does not specify which factor or variable causes the linear relationship between the two variables.

Example 2-2: Correlation Coefficient

Using the data in Example 2-1, compute the correlation coefficient given that the variance of Stock A is 0.123 and the variance of Stock B is 0.325.

$$\sigma_A = \sqrt{0.123} = 0.351$$
$$\sigma_B = \sqrt{0.325} = 0.57$$
$$\text{Corr}(R_A, R_B) = -0.000389 / (0.351)(0.57) = -0.00195$$

The correlation between the returns on the two assets is very close to zero. We can conclude that their returns are uncorrelated.

LOS 8l: Calculate and interpret the expected value, variance, and standard deviation of a random variable and of returns on a portfolio. **Vol 1, pp 485–486**

The expected return and the variance of returns for a portfolio of assets are based on the properties of the individual assets in the portfolio. The first step in calculating portfolio expected return and variance is to compute the weights of the individual assets comprising the portfolio.

$$\text{Weight of asset i} = \frac{\text{Market value of investment i}}{\text{Market value of portfolio}}$$

The expected value of returns on a portfolio is a function of the returns on the individual assets and of their respective weights.

$$E(R_p) = \sum_{i=1}^{N} w_i E(R_i) = w_1 E(R_1) + w_2 E(R_2) + \ldots + w_N E(R_N)$$

© 2015 Wiley

Calculating the variance of a portfolio is more complicated. The variance is not only a function of individual asset weights and variances, but also of the covariance of the assets with each other.

$$\text{Var}(R_p) = \sum_{i=1}^{N}\sum_{j=1}^{N} w_i w_j \text{Cov}(R_i, R_j)$$

The variance of a 2-asset portfolio that contains only Asset A and Asset B is given as:

$$\text{Var}(R_p) = w_A^2\sigma^2(R_A) + w_B^2\sigma^2(R_B) + 2w_A w_B \text{Cov}(R_A, R_B)$$

We can also replace Cov (R_A,R_B) with $\rho(R_A,R_B)\sigma(R_A)\sigma(R_B)$ and reformulate the equation above as:

$$\text{Var}(R_p) = w_A^2\sigma^2(R_A) + w_B^2\sigma^2(R_B) + 2w_A w_B \rho(R_A, R_B)\sigma(R_A)\sigma(R_B)$$

The variance of a 3-asset portfolio is given as:

$$\text{Var}(R_p) = w_A^2\sigma^2(R_A) + w_B^2\sigma^2(R_B) + w_C^2\sigma^2(R_C) + 2w_A w_B \text{Cov}(R_A, R_B) + 2w_B w_C \text{Cov}(R_B, R_C) + 2w_C w_A \text{Cov}(R_C, R_A)$$

We do not think you will have to calculate the variance of a portfolio with more than three assets. For a portfolio with more than three assets, you might be asked to determine the number of unique covariances that must be computed to calculate portfolio variance. Calculating the variance for a portfolio containing *n* different assets requires the computation of *n(n-1)/2* unique covariances.

LOS 8m: Calculate and interpret covariance given a joint probability function.
Vol 1, pp 486–487

Example 2-3: Calculating Covariance Using a Joint Probability Function

What is the expected value, variance and covariance for a portfolio that consists of an investment of $250 in Stock A and $750 in Stock B? The joint probabilities of returns for the two assets are given in the table below.

Joint Probabilities	$R_B = 0.3$	$R_B = 0.5$	$R_B = 0.1$
$R_A = 0.45$	0.2	0	0
$R_A = 0.21$	0	0.35	0
$R_A = 0.04$	0	0	0.45

© 2015 Wiley

Solution

Asset weights:

$$w_A = 250 / (250 + 750) = 0.25$$
$$w_B = 750 / (250 + 750) = 0.75$$

Expected return on the individual assets:

$$E(R_A) = P(\text{Scenario}_1) \times R_{A1} + P(\text{Scenario}_2) \times R_{A2} + P(\text{Scenario}_3) \times R_{A3}$$
$$E(R_A) = (0.2)(0.45) + (0.35)(0.21) + (0.45)(0.04) = 0.1815$$

$$E(R_B) = P(\text{Scenario}_1) \times R_{B1} + P(\text{Scenario}_2) \times R_{B2} + P(\text{Scenario}_3) \times R_{B3}$$
$$E(R_B) = (0.2)(0.3) + (0.35)(0.5) + (0.45)(0.1) = 0.28$$

Variance of the individual assets:

$$Var(R_A) = P(\text{Scenario}_1)\{(R_{A1} - E(R_A)\}^2 + P(\text{Scenario}_2)\{(R_{A2} - E(R_A)\}^2 + P(\text{Scenario}_3)\{(R_{A3} - E(R_A)\}^2$$
$$Var(R_A) = (0.2)(0.45\text{-}0.1815)^2 + (0.35)(0.21\text{-}0.1815)^2 + (0.45)(0.04\text{-}0.1815)^2$$
$$Var(R_A) = 0.0237$$

$$Var(R_B) = P(\text{Scenario}_1)\{(R_{B1} - E(R_B)\}^2 + P(\text{Scenario}_2)\{(R_{B2} - E(R_B)\}^2 + P(\text{Scenario}_3)\{(R_{B3} - E(R_B)\}^2$$
$$Var(R_B) = (0.2)(0.3\text{-}0.28)^2 + (0.35)(0.5\text{-}0.28)^2 + (0.45)(0.1\text{-}0.28)^2$$
$$Var(R_B) = 0.0316$$

Covariance of the asset returns:

$$Cov(R_A, R_B) = P(\text{Scenario}_1)[R_{A1}\text{-}E(R_A)][R_{B1}\text{-}E(R_{AB})] + P(\text{Scenario}_2)[R_{A2}\text{-}E(R_A)][R_{B2}\text{-}E(R_{AB})] + P(\text{Scenario}_3)[R_{A3}\text{-}E(R_A)][R_{B3}\text{-}E(R_{AB})]$$

$$Cov(R_A, R_B) = (0.2)(0.45\text{-}0.1815)(0.3\text{-}0.28) + (0.35)(0.21\text{-}0.1815)(0.5\text{-}0.28) + (0.45)(0.04\text{-}0.1815)(0.1\text{-}0.28)$$
$$Cov(R_A, R_B) = 0.01473$$

The positive value for covariance suggests that's returns on Assets A and B move in the same direction.

© 2015 Wiley

Expected return of the portfolio

$$E(R_p) = w_A \times E(R_A) + w_B \times E(R_B)$$
$$= (0.25)(0.1815) + (0.75)(0.28) = 0.2554$$

Variance of the portfolio

$$Var(R_p) = w_A^2 \sigma^2(R_A) + w_B^2 \sigma^2(R_B) + 2w_A w_B Cov(R_A, R_B)$$
$$= (0.25)^2(0.0237) + (0.75)^2(0.0316) + 2(0.25)(0.75)(0.01473)$$
$$= 0.02478$$

Correlation coefficient between returns on Asset A and Asset B

$$Corr(R_i, R_j) = \frac{Cov(R_i, R_j)}{\sigma(R_i)\sigma(R_j)}$$

$$\rho = \frac{0.01473}{(0.1539)(0.1777)} = 0.5383$$

The correlation coefficient tells us that there is a moderate, positive relationship between the returns on the two assets.

Finally, the expected value of the products of uncorrelated random variables equals the product of their expected values.

$E(XY) = E(X)E(Y)$ if X and Y are uncorrelated.

Example 2-4: Covariance Matrix

Assume you have a portfolio which is 60% invested in U.S. Treasury Bills and 40% invested in equities. Using the covariance matrix provided below, compute the standard deviation of returns on the portfolio.

	T-Bills	**Equities**
T-Bills	169	121
Equities	121	324

Solution

$$Var(R_P) = w_A^2 \sigma^2(R_A) + w_B^2 \sigma^2(R_B) + 2w_A w_B Cov(R_A, R_B)$$
$$= (0.6)^2(169) + (0.4)^2(324) + 2(0.6)(0.4)(121)$$
$$= 112.68 + 58.08 = 170.76$$

$$\sigma(R_P) = (170.76)^{0.5} = 13.07\%.$$

© 2015 Wiley

LESSON 3: TOPICS IN PROBABILITY: BAYES' FORMULA AND COUNTING RULES

LOS 8n: Calculate and interpret an updated probability using Bayes' formula. **Vol 1, pp 488–492**

Bayes' formula relates the conditional and marginal probabilities of two random events. Let's derive it first:

- **Step 1:**
  P(A|B) = P(AB) / P(B) from the conditional probability formula of **A given B**
  Make P(AB) the subject to get:
  P(AB) = P(A|B) × P(B) …(i)

- **Step 2:**
  P(B|A) = P(BA) / P(A) from the conditional probability formula of **B given A**
  Make P(BA) the subject to get:
  P(BA) = P(B|A) × P(A) …(ii)

- **Step 3:**
  Since the joint probabilities P(AB) and P(BA) are equal, we can equate expressions (i) and (ii).
  P(A|B) × P(B) = P(B|A) × P(A)

  Make P(B|A) the subject to get:
  P(B|A) = P(A|B) × P(B) / P(A)

The updated probability is also known as the posterior probability.

Essentially, by using Bayes' formula, we can reverse the "given that probability" P(A|B) and convert it into P(B|A) using P(A) and P(B). Bear in mind that you will probably have to use the total probability rule to calculate P(A).

Replacing B with Event, and A with Information, Bayes' formula can be translated to:

$$P(\text{Event} \mid \text{Information}) = \frac{P(\text{Information} \mid \text{Event}) \times P(\text{Event})}{P(\text{Information})}$$

© 2015 Wiley

Example 3-1: Bayes' Formula

In a particular school, there are 54% boys and 46% girls. The girl students wear blue sweaters or red sweaters in equal numbers, while the boys all wear blue sweaters. An observer sees a (random) student from a distance, and all she can see is that the student is wearing a blue sweater. What is the probability that the student is a girl?

Solution

It is clear that the probability is less than 46% (the probability of the student being a girl), but by how much? Is it half that, because only half the girls wear blue sweaters? The correct answer can be computed using Bayes' theorem.

The event that we are interested in determining the probability of is that the student observed is a girl, and the information given is that the student observed is wearing a blue sweater. To compute P(B|A), we must determine:

- P(B): The unconditional probability that the student is a girl. This equals 0.46.
- $P(B^c)$: The probability that the student is a boy (B^c is the complementary event to B). This equals 0.54.
- P(A|B): The probability of the student wearing a blue sweater given that the student is a girl. Girls are as likely to wear red sweaters as they are to wear blue sweaters. Therefore, P(A|B) is 0.5. We can also calculate this as P(AB)/P(B). The joint probability of a student being a girl and wearing a blue sweater, P(AB), equals 0.23 (0.46 × 0.5), while the probability of a student being a girl, P(B), equals 0.46.
- $P(A|B^c)$: The probability of the student wearing a blue sweater given that the student is a boy. This is given as 1.
- P(A): The unconditional probability of a randomly selected student wearing a blue sweater. This can be calculated using the total probability rule:

$$P(A) = P(A|B) \times P(B) + P(A|B^c) \times P(B^c) = 0.5 \times 0.46 + 1 \times 0.54 = 0.77$$

Given all this information, the probability of the observer having spotted a girl given that the observed student is wearing a blue sweater can be computed as:

$$\begin{aligned} P(B|A) &= [P(A|B) \times P(B)] / P(A) \\ &= (0.5 \times 0.46) / 0.77 \\ &= 0.2987 \end{aligned}$$

As expected, the probability of a random student being a girl, given that he/she is wearing blue sweaters is less than 46%, but more than just half of 46%.

Another way to solve this problem is as follows: Assume that there are 100 students—54 boys and 46 girls. 54 boys and 23 girls wear blue sweaters. All together there are 77 blue sweater-wearers, of which 23 are girls. Therefore the chance that a random blue sweater-wearer is a girl equals 23/77 = 0.2987.

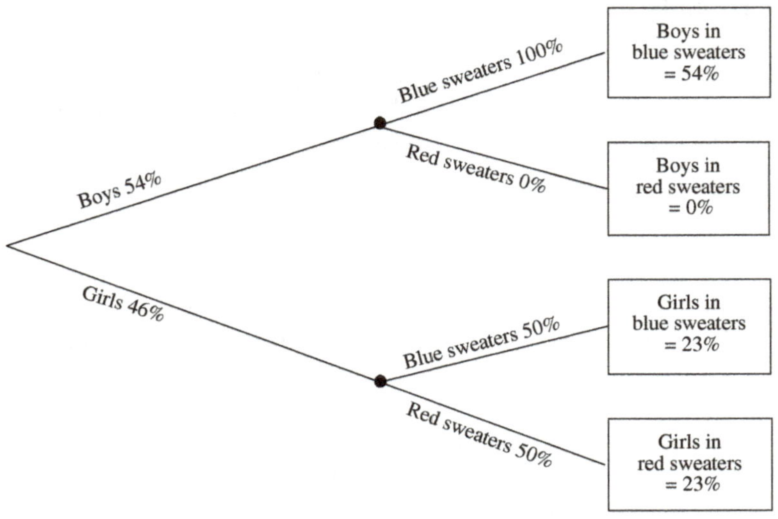

LOS 8o: Identify the most appropriate method to solve a particular counting problem, and solve counting problems using factorial, combination, and permutation concepts. Vol 1, pp 492–495

Multiplication Rule of Counting

Suppose there are k tasks that must be done. The first one can be done in n_1 ways; the second, given how the first was done, can be done in n_2 ways, and the third, given how the first two tasks were done, can be done in n_3 ways. The number of different ways that the k tasks can be done equals $n_1 \times n_2 \times n_3 \times \ldots n_k$.

Example 3-2: Multiplication Rule of Counting

There are 5 different musicians who can play any of 5 different instruments in a band. In how many ways can these 5 musicians be allocated different instruments?

Solution

Once the first musician has been given particular instrument, the second one can only get one of the 4 remaining instruments. When the first two have been given instruments, the third can only get one of the 3 remaining instruments. The total number of different ways that the 5 instruments can be assigned to band members equals $5 \times 4 \times 3 \times 2 \times 1 = 120$, or 5 factorial (5!). If we have n musicians, the number of ways we can assign different instruments equals:

$$n! = n(n-1)(n-2)(n-3)\ldots\ldots 1$$

The factorial of a number can be calculated using your BA II plus financial calculator. It is programmed as the 2nd function of the [×] button (e.g., 5! can be calculated as [5] [2ND] [×])

© 2015 Wiley

Labeling Problems

These refer to situations where there are n items, each of which can receive one of k different labels. We give each object in the group a label to place it in a category. n_1 items can be given the first label, n_2 receive the second label, and so on.

Example 3-3: Labeling

The conductor must determine which instruments to hand to the 12 members of his band. 4 of them will play the drums, 6 of them will play the saxophone, and 2 will play the bagpipes. How many ways can these 12 musicians be organized in the band?

Solution

There are 12! ways that the 12 musicians can be allotted the different instruments. Crucially however, the order that they fill these sections is not important. For example, it does not matter which of the 6 who will play the saxophone is the first to be "labeled." To eliminate the counting of these redundancies, we divide the total number of possibilities (12!) by the number of redundancies (6! × 4! × 2!). Therefore, the number of different ways to position (label) the 12 musicians is:

$$\frac{12!}{6! \times 4! \times 2!} = 13{,}860$$

If the number of labels equals the number of objects (n equals k), there are no redundancies and we simply have (n!/1) = n!. The number of ways to assign n different labels to n items is simply n! (as we saw in Example 3-1).

Combinations

The combination formula is used in a special case of the labeling problem. Specifically, the combination formula is used when the number of labels that can be assigned, k, equals 2. In such a situation, any item can only be labeled as one or the other, so $n_1 + n_2 = \boldsymbol{n}$. Suppose the number of objects that receive the first label, n_1, equals r. The number of objects that receive the second label will then equal n-r. Using the same formula as the one we used for labeling problems and inserting r and n-r in the denominator, the formula for combinations can be stated as:

$$_{n}C_{r} = \binom{n}{r} = \frac{n!}{(n-r)!(r!)}$$

Here, $_{n}C_{r}$ and $\binom{n}{r}$ are shorthand notations for n!/(n-r)!(r!). They are read as n choose r or n combination r.

Remember: The combination formula is used when the order in which the items are assigned the labels is NOT important.

© 2015 Wiley

Example 3-4: Combinations

There are 20 people on a trial for a soccer team out of which only 11 will be chosen. It does not matter who gets chosen first and who is the eleventh one to be chosen—all 11 will be in the team. The remaining 9, unfortunately will not be in the team. How many different ways can the 11-member team be chosen from the 20 aspirants?

Solution

We are looking for the number of different ways that 20 players (n) can be chosen for the 11-man team (r).

$$_{20}C_{11} = \frac{20!}{(9)!(11!)} = 167{,}960$$

Calculator keystrokes on the TI:
"20" [2ND] [+] "11" [=]

Permutations

When the order in which labels are assigned to two groups is an important consideration, the permutation formula is used. The number of permutations of *r* objects from *n* items equals:

$$_{n}P_{r} = \frac{n!}{(n-r)!}$$

Example 3-5: Permutations

Let's continue with the same example that we used for combinations. 20 players are trying out for a soccer team when only 11 will be chosen. Further, the eventual list of 11 should rank players from 1 to 11 with a higher rank indicating a more skillful player. How many ways can the eleven players be selected given that the order is important?

$$_{n}P_{r} = \frac{n!}{(n\text{-}r)!} = \frac{20!}{9!} = 6{,}704{,}425.728 \text{ million.}$$

Calculator keystrokes on the TI Calculator:

"20" [2nd] [-] "11" [=] 6,704,425.728

Notice how large the number for possible permutations is relative to the number of possible combinations.

© 2015 Wiley

Tips:

- Factorials are used when there is only one group i.e., we are simply arranging a given set or group of *n* items. Given *n* items, there are n! ways of arranging them.
- The labeling formula is used for three or more groups of predetermined size. Each item must be labeled as a member of one of the groups.
- The combination formula is used when there are only two groups of predetermined size and crucially, the order or rank of labeling is NOT important.
- The permutation formula is used when there are only two groups of predetermined size, and the order or rank IS important.

© 2015 Wiley

Study Session 3: Quantitative Methods—Application

© 2015 Wiley

READING 9: COMMON PROBABILITY DISTRIBUTIONS

LESSON 1: DISCRETE RANDOM VARIABLES, THE DISCRETE UNIFORM DISTRIBUTION AND THE BINOMIAL DISTRIBUTION

LOS 9a: Define a probability distribution and distinguish between discrete and continuous random variables and their probability functions. **Vol 1, p 514**

LOS 9b: Describe the set of possible outcomes of a specified discrete random variable. **Vol 1, p 515**

LOS 9c: Interpret a cumulative distribution function. **Vol 1, p 516**

LOS 9d: Calculate and interpret probabilities for a random variable, given its cumulative distribution function. **Vol 1, pp 516–517**

Let's first revisit our definition of a random variable. A random variable is a variable whose outcome cannot be predicted (e.g., the number of cars that will cross a traffic light during a given 10-minute period).

A discrete random variable is one that can take on a countable number of values. Each outcome has a specific probability of occurring, which can be measured. Common examples of discrete random variables include the toss of a coin, which has only two possible outcomes, and the throw of a fair die, which has 6 possible outcomes. Other examples of discrete random variables are listed below:

- The number of cars sold by a salesman in a week; x = 0, 1, 2 ....
- The number of customers waiting in line for a bank clerk at a point in time; x = 0, 1, 2 ....
- The number of bids put in for an item on Swoopo; x = 0, 1, 2....
- The number of people in a sample of 1,000 who prefer Coke™ over Pepsi™: x = 0, 1, 2, ...1,000

The probability distribution of a random variable identifies the probability of each of the possible outcomes of a random variable.

All probability distributions have the following two properties:

1. $0 \leq p(x) \leq 1$: The probability of a given outcome cannot be less than zero. If the outcome is not possible, its probability will equal zero; p(x) = 0. The probability of an outcome cannot exceed 1. If the particular outcome is the only outcome possible, the probability of the outcome equals 1; p(x) = 1.
2. $\sum p(x) = 1$: The sum of the probabilities of all possible outcomes equals 1.

For a discrete random variable the probability of each possible outcome can be listed in the form of a probability function, p(x), which expresses the probability that "X," the random variable, takes on a specific value of "x." A probability function can also be stated as P(X=x).

"X" is the random variable while "x" represents the different values it can take.

- p(x) or P(X=x) = 0 means that the random variable cannot take the particular value of x.

© 2015 Wiley

- p(x) or P(X=x) > 0 means that the specified value of x is present in the set of possible outcomes that the random variable can take.
- p(x) or P(X=x) = 1 means that x is the only possible outcome.

For example, if the random variable, X, is the number of days it snows this December, the probability of there being 5 days of snow, p(5), or P(X=5) is greater than zero but less than one. However, p(40) or P(x=40) equals zero because it is impossible for it to snow for 40 days in a 31-day period.

A continuous random variable is one for which the number of possible outcomes cannot be counted (there are infinite possible outcomes) and therefore, probabilities cannot be attached to specific outcomes. For example, consider the length of time it takes to get served at a particular restaurant (a random variable), which can be anywhere between 25 and 40 minutes (possible outcomes). While the probability of the waiting period being between 25 and 30 minutes can be measured, the probability of waiting for exactly 25 minutes and 15 seconds is zero because time can be measured in seconds, half seconds, even thousandths of seconds. The actual period of time taken to get served can take an infinite number of values as the unit of measurement gets smaller. Other examples of continuous random variables are:

- The amount of liquid poured into a glass that can hold 10 ounces. The random variable X can lie anywhere between, and including, zero and 10 ounces. The amount of liquid can be measured in ounces, half ounces, thousandths of ounces and in even smaller units. The number of possible outcomes is therefore, infinite.
- The return on a stock for a particular year. This random variable can take any value between –100% and infinity.

For continuous random variables, the probability of a specific outcome within a range of infinite outcomes is essentially zero: p(x) or P(X=x) = 0. Therefore, we use a probability density function (pdf), which is denoted by f(x) to interpret their probability structure. A pdf can be used to determine the probability that the outcome lies within a specified range of possible values. On a graphical illustration of the pdf (Figure 1-1), the probability that the outcome lies between *a* and *b* equals the area under the density function between the two points.

Figure 1-1: Probability Density Function

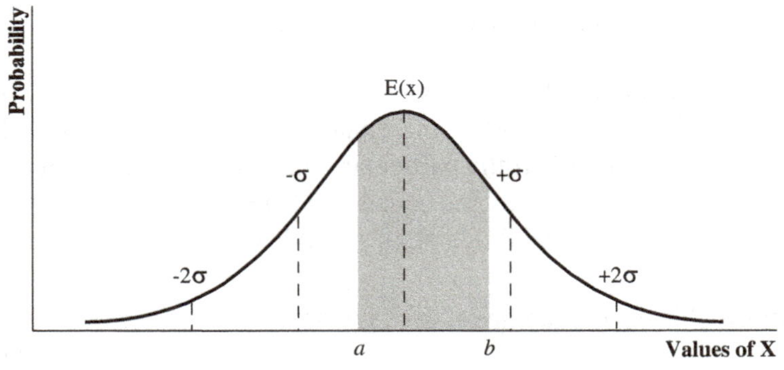

© 2015 Wiley

For a discrete distribution:

- $p(x) = 0$ when x cannot occur; and
- $p(x) > 0$ if x is a possible outcome.

$p(x)$ is read as "the probability that the random variable, X, equals x."

For a continuous distribution:

- $p(x) = 0$ even though x can occur.
- We can only consider $P(x_1 \leq X \leq x_2)$ where x_1 and x_2 are actual numbers.

A cumulative distribution function (cdf), also known as a distribution function, expresses the probability that a random variable, X, takes on a value *less than or equal to* a specific value, x. It represents the sum of the probabilities of all outcomes that are less than or equal to the specified value of x. A cdf is denoted by $F(x) = P(X \leq x)$.

Example 1-1: Probability Functions and Cumulative Distribution Functions

The set of possible values that a random variable, X, can take is given by: X = (5,10,15,20)
For all other values of X, $p(x) = 0$.
The probability function for the random variable is given as: $p(x) = x/50$

Calculate the following probabilities:

a. p(5)
b. p(15)
c. p(17)
d. F(10)
e. F(20)

Solution

a. $p(5) = 5/50 = 0.1$
b. $p(15) = 15/50 = 0.3$
c. $p(17) = 0$
d. $F(10) = p(5) + p(10) = 0.1 + 0.2 = 0.3$
e. $F(20) = p(5) + p(10) + p(15) + p(20) = 0.1 + 0.2 + 0.3 + 0.4 = 1.0$

The probability of numerous values of x (e.g., p(1), p(2), p(3), p(4), p(6), etc.) equals zero because these are not present in the set of possible outcomes for the distribution. Therefore, we have not explicitly mentioned them in calculating F(10) and F(20).

© 2015 Wiley

LOS 9e: Define a discrete uniform random variable, a Bernoulli random variable, and a binomial random variable. **Vol 1, pp 516–520**

LOS 9f: Calculate and interpret probabilities given the discrete uniform and the binomial distribution functions. **Vol 1, pp 520–524**

LOS 9g: Construct a binomial tree to describe stock price movement. **Vol 1, pp 525–527**

A discrete uniform distribution is one in which the probability of each of the possible outcomes is the same. The best example of a uniform distribution is the probability distribution of the outcomes from the roll of a fair die. The probability of each outcome equals 1/6. The cumulative distribution function of the distribution for a roll of a fair die increases in steps as shown in Figure 1-2. Another thing to notice about this particular distribution is that:

$F(x) = n \times p(x)$ for the *n*th observation.

Figure 1-2: Cumulative Distribution Function

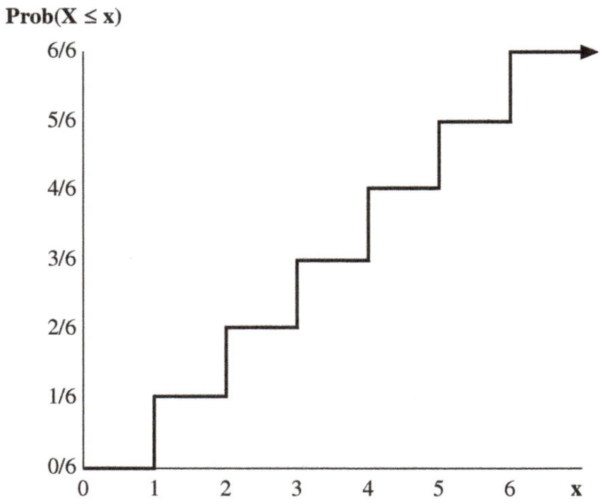

Example 1-2: Discrete Uniform Distribution

For a roll of a fair die:

a) Calculate the probability that the outcome is less than or equal to 2.
b) Calculate the probability that the outcome is greater than 2 but less than or equal to 5.
c) State the probability function, p(x), of this random variable.

© 2015 Wiley

Solution

Shortcut: The cumulative distribution function for the number observed when a die is thrown, F(x), equals x/6.

a) For the outcome, x = 2, we calculate the probability that the observed outcome is less than or equal to x by inserting 2 in the equation F(x) = x/6. Thus, F(2) = 2/6 = 1/3. Alternatively, we could simply add p(1) and p(2). Each of them equals 1/6 so F(2) = 1/3.

b) The probability that the observed value is less than or equal to 5 is F(5), which equals 5/6. We use the answer in part (a) above to calculate the required probability by subtracting F(2) from F(5).

$$F(5) - F(2) = P(2 < x \leq 5)$$
$$5/6 - 1/3 = 1/2.$$

Alternatively, we could simple add p(3), p(4), and p(5) to get a value of 0.5.

c) The probability of each outcome is 1/6 i.e., p(1) = p(2) = p(3) = p(4) = p(5) = p(6) = 1/6. Therefore, the probability function is denoted as p(x) = 1/6.

The Binomial Distribution

Suppose an experiment has only 2 possible outcomes which are labeled "success" and "failure." Further, these two outcomes are:

- mutually exclusive, which means that the occurrence of one outcome precludes the occurrence of the other.
- collectively exhaustive, which means that no other outcomes are possible.

Such an experiment is called a Bernoulli trial. If this experiment is carried out *n* times, the number of successes, X, is called a Bernoulli random variable and the distribution that X follows is known as the binomial distribution. The probability of success, *p*, is equal for all trials and the trials are independent i.e., the result of one trial has no effect on the outcome of another.

Under these assumptions a random variable that follows the Binomial distribution is defined by *n* and *p* as:

$X \sim B(n, p)$, which is read as:
The random variable "X" follows a binomial distribution with the number of trials, *n*, and a probability of success, *p*.

© 2015 Wiley

The probability of x successes in *n* trials is given by:

$$P(X=x) = {}_nC_x (p)^x (1-p)^{n-x}$$

where:
p = probability of success
1 − p = probability of failure
${}_nC_x$ = number of possible combinations of having *x* successes in *n* trials. Stated differently, it is the number of ways to choose *x* from *n* when the order does not matter.

Note: $${}_nC_x = \frac{n!}{(n-x)!x!}$$

We use the combination formula in binomial experiments because the number of labels equals 2 (success and failure) and we are not concerned about the order in which these successes occur. For example, if a trial is carried out 4 times and we want to determine the probability of 2 successes, the successes can occur in any of the following 6 ways: SSFF, SFSF, FFSS, FSFS, FSSF, SFFS. This is why we multiply the probability of achieving 2 successes in 4 trials by the number of possible combinations of having 2 successes in 4 trials (${}_4C_2$).

Example 1-3: Binomial Distribution

A door-to-door salesman visits 7 houses everyday. The probability of making a sale to any customer is 0.4. Compute the probability of making exactly 3 sales on a given day.

Solution

The possible outcomes from a visit to a potential customer are:

- Making a sale (success), which has a probability 0.4.
- Not making a sale (failure), which has a probability 0.6.

The number of sales made in a day follows a binomial distribution with p = 0.4 and n = 7.

$$X \sim B(7, 0.4)$$

$$P(X=x) = {}_nC_x (p)^x (1-p)^{n-x}$$

$$P(X=3) = p(3) = \frac{7!}{4!*3!}(0.4)^3(0.6)^4 = 0.29$$

There are 35 (${}_7C_3$) different ways to have 3 successes (sales) from 7 trials (visits). The probability of making sales to only 3 people and not making sales to the other 4 is 0.00829, which is calculated as $[(0.4)^3(0.6)^4]$ or [(0.4)(0.4)(0.4)(0.6)(0.6)(0.6)(0.6)].

© 2015 Wiley

The expected value of a binomial random variable, X, is the product of p and n. In Example 1-3, the salesman's daily expected sales would equal $0.4 \times 7 = 2.8$. The binomial distribution is a discrete distribution, and sales of 2.8 on any given day are not possible. However, the expected value tells us that if we were to track sales for several days, the average number of daily sales would equal 2.8.

Note: the expected value E(X) is also the mean (μ_x) of the variable.

The variance of a binomial random variable is given by:

$$\sigma_x^2 = n \times p \times (1 - p)$$

The variance of the salesman's daily sales is calculated as 7(0.4)(0.6), which equals 1.68. The standard deviation of daily sales is $\sqrt{1.68}$ or 1.296.

Binomial Trees

Binomial trees may be drawn to illustrate possible stock price movements. Figure 1-3 illustrates a three-period tree, where the stock can either rise by a factor of 1.1 (u = 1.1), or go down by a factor of 1/1.1 (d = 1/u = 0.9091) over a given period. The probability of a rise in price is constant through the periods and is given as 0.4, while the probability of a fall in price equals 0.6.

Figure 1-3: A Binomial Tree

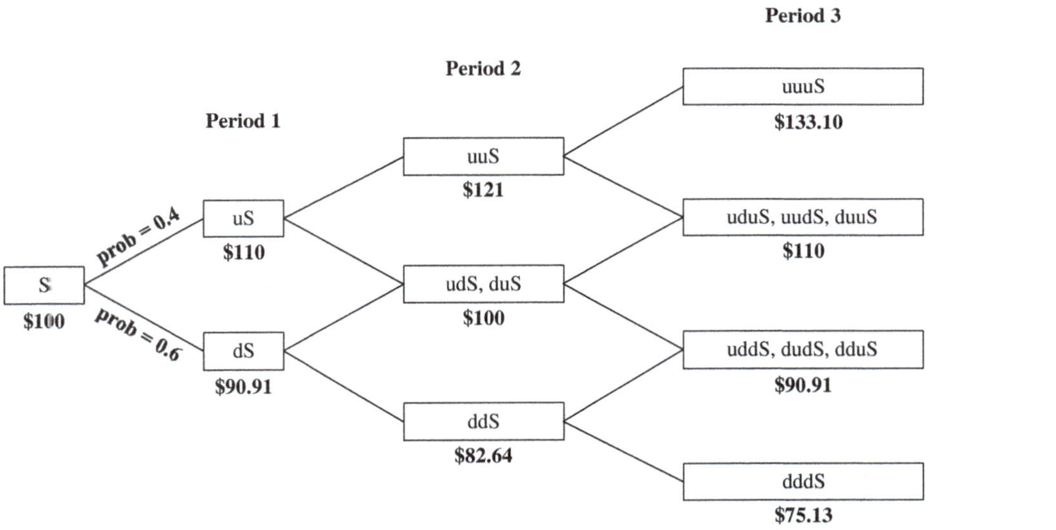

The tree tells us that after 3 periods, the stock price can take four different values: \$133.10, \$110, \$90.91 and \$75.13. The probability that the stock price equals any of these given values is given by a binomial distribution. For example, at the end of Period 3, the stock price can end up at \$110 in 3 possible ways; up-down-up, up-up-down and down-up-up. Each of these possibilities has 2 up-moves and 1 down-move. Therefore, the number of different ways of having 2 successes (up moves) from 3 trials (periods) is calculated using the combination formula ${}_3C_2$, which equals 3. The probability of a sequence containing two up moves and one down move is calculated as $p^2(1 - p)$, which equals 0.096. Therefore, the probability of a stock price of \$110 at the end of Period 3 equals $3 \times 0.096 = 0.288$.

Binomial stock price models are extensively used in option pricing.

Skewness and the Binomial Distribution

- If the probability of success is 0.50, the binomial distribution is symmetric.
- If the probability of success is less than 0.50, the binomial distribution is skewed to the right.
- If the probability of success is more than 0.50, the binomial distribution is skewed to the left.

LOS 9h: Calculate and interpret tracking error. Vol 1, pp 524–525

Tracking Error

Tracking error is a measure of how closely a portfolio's returns match the returns of the index to which it is benchmarked. It is the difference between the total return on the portfolio (before deducting fees) and the total return on the benchmark index.

Tracking error = Gross return on portfolio – Total return on benchmark index

We'll work with an example to describe how the binomial distribution is applied to evaluate the performance of investment managers with respect to the tracking errors of their portfolios.

Example 1-4: Tracking Error

Alex Karev, CFA is directed to keep the tracking error of the portfolios under his management within a band of 50 basis points. His supervisor expects Alex to be able to keep the tracking error of his portfolio within this band 90% of the time. Alex has met his objective in 3 of the previous 4 quarters.

It is fairly obvious from the numbers above that Alex has a 75% success rate. However, for our purposes here, we are more concerned with how Alex's actual performance related to the expectation of a 90% success rate, given the sample size of only 4 observations. Interpreting the tracking error requires us to answer the following question:

Given that the investment manager has the ability to achieve a success ratio of 90%, what is the probability that he will achieve his actual results (75% success rate) or worse?

© 2015 Wiley

Solution

In order to answer this question we make use of the binomial distribution. More specifically, we look to find the probability that given the underlying success rate of 90%, whether Alex's performance could have been as bad or worse than his actual performance (3 "successful" quarters out of 4).

Calculation of the probability of 3 or less successful quarters out of 4 given a probability of success of 0.9:

$$P(X \leq 3) = P(X = 0) + P(X = 1) + P(X = 2) + P(X = 3)$$

Always remember to calculate P(X=0) too.

$$P(X = 0) = {}_4C_0(0.90)^0(0.10)^4 = 0.0001$$
$$P(X = 1) = {}_4C_1(0.90)^1(0.10)^3 = 0.0036$$
$$P(X = 2) = {}_4C_2(0.90)^2(0.10)^2 = 0.0486$$
$$P(X = 3) = {}_4C_3(0.90)^3(0.10)^1 = 0.2916$$

$$P(X \leq 3) = 0.3439$$

Interpretation: There is a 34% probability that Alex would report the performance that he actually reported or worse (3 or less quarters out of 4 with a tracking error within the desired band) if he had the skill to meet his supervisor's expectations 90% of the time.

LESSON 2: CONTINUOUS RANDOM VARIABLES, THE CONTINUOUS UNIFORM DISTRIBUTION, THE NORMAL DISTRIBUTION AND THE LOGNORMAL DISTRIBUTION

LOS 9i: Define the continuous uniform distribution and calculate and interpret probabilities, given a continuous uniform distribution.

Vol 1, pp 527–531

A continuous uniform distribution is described by a lower limit, *a,* and an upper limit, *b*. These limits serve as the parameters of the distribution. The probability of any outcome or range of outcomes outside these limits is 0. Being a continuous distribution, individual outcomes also have a probability of 0. The distribution is often denoted as U(*a*,*b*).

- The probability of the random variable taking on any set of values outside the parameters, a and b, equals zero.
  - $P(X < a),\ P(X > b) = 0$
- The probability that the random variable will take a value that falls between x_1 and x_2 that both lie within the range, *a* to *b*, is the proportion of the total area taken up by the range, x_1 to x_2.
  - $P(x_1 \leq X \leq x_2) = \dfrac{x_2 - x_1}{b - a}$

Example 2-1: Continuous Uniform Distribution

X is a uniformly distributed continuous random variable that cannot take values lower than 2 or greater than 10. Calculate the probability that X will fall between 5 and 7.

Solution

$$P(5 \le X \le 7) = \frac{7-5}{10-2} = \frac{2}{8} = 0.25$$

Figure 2-1: Continuous Uniform Distribution

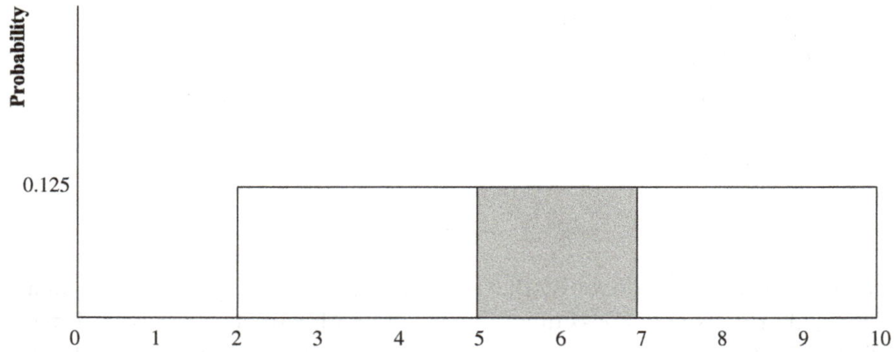

Figure 2-2: CDF for a Continuous Uniform Variable

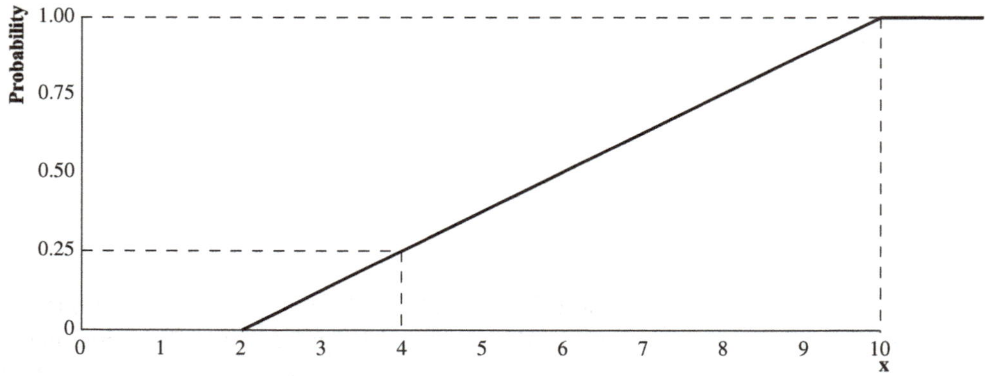

Remember that $P(X \ge x)$ is the same as $P(X > x)$ or this distribution because it is a continuous distribution where $P(X = x)$ equals zero.

LOS 9j: Explain the key properties of the normal distribution.

Vol 1, pp 531–532

LOS 9k: Distinguish between a univariate and a multivariate distribution, and explain the role of correlation in the multivariate normal distribution.

Vol 1, pp 531–533

© 2015 Wiley

The normal distribution is a continuous distribution that plays a central role in quantitative analysis. A continuous random variable that follows the normal distribution has a bell-shaped probability distribution. See Figure 2-3. A normal distribution has the following properties:

- It is completely described by its mean (μ) and variance (σ^2). The distribution is stated as $X \sim N(\mu,\sigma^2)$, which is read as the random variable X follows the normal distribution with mean, μ and variance, σ^2.
- The distribution has a skewness of 0, which means that it is symmetric about its mean. $P(X \leq \text{mean}) = P(X \geq \text{mean}) = 0.5$, and the mean, median and mode are the same.
- Kurtosis equals 3 and excess kurtosis equals 0.
- A linear combination of normally distributed random variables is also normally distributed. For example, if the returns on each stock in a portfolio are normally distributed, the returns on the portfolio will also be normally distributed.
- The probability of the random variable lying in ranges further away from the mean gets smaller and smaller, but never goes to zero. The tail on either side extends to infinity.

Figure 2-3: The Probability Density Function of the Normal Distribution

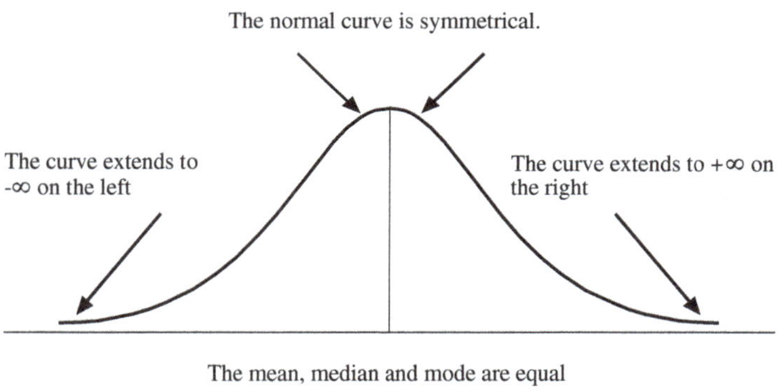

Univariate distributions describe the distribution of a single random variable. Up to this point, our discussion has been based on univariate random variables only.

Multivariate distributions specify probabilities associated with a group of random variables taking into account the interrelationships that may exist between them. As mentioned in the properties of normally distributed random variables, a linear combination of normally distributed random variables is also normally distributed. Therefore, the return on a portfolio of assets whose individual returns are normally distributed will also be normally distributed. The portfolio is said to have a multivariate normal distribution.

A multivariate normal distribution for the return on a portfolio with *n* stocks is completely defined by the following three parameters:

- The mean returns on all the *n* individual stocks $(\mu_1, \mu_2, \ldots, \mu_n)$
- The variances of returns of all *n* individual stocks $(\sigma_1^2, \sigma_2^2, \ldots, \sigma_n^2)$
- The return correlations between each possible pair of stocks. There will be $n(n-1)/2$ pairwise correlations in total. (Correlation is a measure of the strength of the linear relationship between 2 variables).

© 2015 Wiley

The need to determine correlations is what differentiates multivariate normal distributions from univariate normal distributions. If we are studying returns on a portfolio consisting of 4 assets, we will use 4 means, 4 variances, and the 6 correlations to describe the multivariate distribution.

LOS 91: Determine the probability that a normally distributed random variable lies inside a given interval. Vol 1, pp 534–535

A confidence interval represents the range of values within which a certain population parameter is expected to lie in a specified percentage of the time. A 95% confidence interval between 4 and 8 implies that we can be 95% confident that the relevant parameter lies between 4 and 8 (the probability that the parameter lies between 4 and 8 equals 0.95). Alternatively, we can conclude that there is a 5% chance that the parameter does not lie between 4 and 8. (See Figure 2-4.)

In practice, we do not usually know the values for population parameters, so we estimate them. We estimate the population mean, μ using the sample mean, $\overline{x}$, and estimate the population standard deviation, σ, using the sample standard deviation, s. The three confidence intervals that we will encounter most frequently are given below:

For a random variable X that follows the normal distribution:
The 90% confidence interval is $\overline{x} - 1.65s$ to $\overline{x} + 1.65s$
The 95% confidence interval is $\overline{x} - 1.96s$ to $\overline{x} + 1.96s$
The 99% confidence interval is $\overline{x} - 2.58s$ to $\overline{x} + 2.58s$

Example 2-2: Confidence Intervals

The average annual return on a stock is 15% and the standard deviation of returns equals 5%. Given that the stock's returns are distributed normally, calculate the 90% confidence interval for the return in any given year.

Solution

The 90% confidence interval is calculated as:

$$15 \pm 1.65(5) = 6.75\% \text{ to } 23.25\%$$

Interpretation: The probability that the return on the stock for a given year lies between 6.75% and 23.25% equals 0.90, or $P(6.75\% < x < 23.25\%) = 0.90$.

The following probability statements can be made about normal distributions:

- Approximately 50% of all observations lie in the interval $\mu \pm (2/3)\sigma$
- Approximately 68% of all observations lie in the interval $\mu \pm 1\sigma$
- Approximately 95% of all observations lie in the interval $\mu \pm 2\sigma$
- Approximately 99% of all observations lie in the interval $\mu \pm 3\sigma$

© 2015 Wiley

Figure 2-4: Confidence Intervals for a Normal Distribution

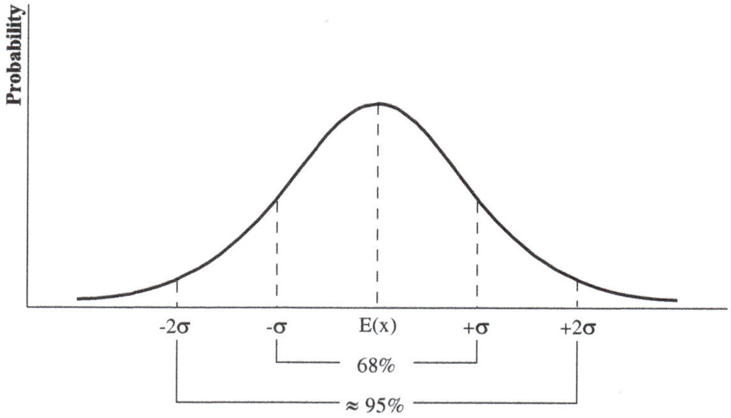

LOS 9m: Define the standard normal distribution, explain how to standardize a random variable, and calculate and interpret probabilities using the standard normal distribution. Vol 1, pp 532–535

We would need an infinite number of normal curves if we were to draw one for every possible combination of means and standard deviations. Through the process of standardizing, probability statements for any kind of normally distributed random variable can be made by referring to a single normal curve. This standard normal distribution curve is a normal distribution that has been standardized so that it has a mean of zero and a standard deviation of 1. To standardize a given observation of a normally distributed random variable, its z-score must be calculated. This is done by subtracting the mean of the population from the observed value of the random variable, and dividing the result by the standard deviation.

$$z = (\text{observed value} - \text{population mean})/\text{standard deviation} = (x - \mu)/\sigma$$

Essentially, the z-value represents the number of standard deviations away from the population mean, a given observation lies. Keeping this in mind will make the remaining readings of quantitative methods much easier to understand.

Example 2-3: Calculating Z-Values

Assume that the monthly salaries of the employees of Nippon Enterprises are normally distributed with a mean of $1,500 and standard deviation of $500. What are the z-scores for salaries of $1,200 and $3,000?

Solution

For x = $1,200, the z-score equals ($1,200 – $1,500) / $500 = –0.6
For x = $3,000, the z-score equals ($3,000 – $1,500) / $500 = 3

Interpretation: A z-score of -0.6 indicates that a salary of $1,200 lies 0.6 standard deviations *below* the mean. Similarly, a salary of $3,000 lies 3 standard deviations *above* the mean.

© 2015 Wiley

Calculating Probabilities Using Z-Scores

When we standardize an observed value of a normally distributed random variable, we essentially express the value in terms of standard deviations from the mean. Suppose we are looking at a security whose returns are normally distributed with an expected return of 15% and standard deviation of 30%. To find the probability of returns lower than 18%, we are looking for the probability of a return *less* than 0.1 (calculated as (18-15)/30) standard deviations *above* the mean. To find the probability of the observed return on the stock being less than 0.1 standard deviations above the mean, we refer to the cumulative density function for a standard normal distribution, F(Z), or simply the z-table.

Table 1-1 shows the probability of a random variable having a standardized value lower than or equal to the given standardized value, or $P(Z \leq z)$. The probability that returns will be less than or equal to 0.1 standard deviations above the mean equals 0.5398. If we were interested in calculating the probability of a return *greater* than 0.1 standard deviations above the mean (a return greater than 18%) we would compute it as 1 – 0.5398, which equals 0.4602.

Table 2-1: Z-Table Extract

	0	**0.01**	**0.02**	**0.03**	**0.04**	**0.05**	**0.06**	**0.07**	**0.08**	**0.09**
0	0.5000	0.5040	0.5080	0.5120	0.5160	0.5199	0.5239	0.5279	0.5319	0.5359
0.1	0.5398	0.5438	0.5478	0.5517	0.5557	0.5596	0.5636	0.5675	0.5714	0.5753
0.2	0.5793	0.5832	0.5871	0.5910	0.5948	0.5987	0.6026	0.6064	0.6103	0.6141
0.3	0.6179	0.6217	0.6255	0.6293	0.6331	0.6368	0.6406	0.6443	0.6480	0.6517
0.4	0.6554	0.6591	0.6628	0.6664	0.6700	0.6736	0.6772	0.6808	0.6844	0.6879
0.5	0.6915	0.6950	0.6985	0.7019	0.7054	0.7088	0.7123	0.7157	0.7190	0.7224
0.6	0.7257	0.7291	0.7324	0.7357	0.7389	0.7422	0.7454	0.7486	0.7517	0.7549
0.7	0.7580	0.7611	0.7642	0.7673	0.7704	0.7734	0.7764	0.7794	0.7823	0.7852
0.8	0.7881	0.7910	0.7939	0.7967	0.7995	0.8023	0.8051	0.8078	0.8106	0.8133
0.9	0.8159	0.8186	0.8212	0.8238	0.8264	0.8289	0.8315	0.8340	0.8365	0.8389
1	0.8413	0.8438	0.8461	0.8485	0.8508	0.8531	0.8554	0.8577	0.8599	0.8621
1.1	0.8643	0.8665	0.8686	0.8708	0.8729	0.8749	0.8770	0.8790	0.8810	0.8830
1.2	0.8849	0.8869	0.8888	0.8907	0.8925	0.8944	0.8962	0.8980	0.8997	0.9015
1.3	0.9032	0.9049	0.9066	0.9082	0.9099	0.9115	0.9131	0.9147	0.9162	0.9177
1.4	0.9192	0.9207	0.9222	0.9236	0.9251	0.9265	0.9279	0.9292	0.9306	0.9319

In most z-tables, probability values are only given for positive values. However, because of the symmetry of the normal distribution, we can deduce that $F(-Z) = 1 - F(Z)$. The calculations in Example 2-4 will facilitate your understanding of z-tables.

© 2015 Wiley

Example 2-4: Calculating Probabilities of Normally Distributed Variables

The points, X, scored by students in a class on their final exam are normally distributed with a mean of 60 and standard deviation of 15. What is the probability that the points scored by a given student will be:

a. less than 80
b. more than 70
c. less than 40
d. between 40 and 70.

Solution

a. We first calculate the z-score (standardized value) for the observed value of 80 points:

$$z = \frac{x - \mu}{\sigma} = \frac{80 - 60}{15} = 1.33$$

We are interested in P(X < 80), which is the area under the curve to the *left* of 80 in the figure below. This area equals the area to the left of 1.33 on the standard normal curve. The probability corresponding to 1.33 in the z-table is 0.9082, which is written as:

$$F(1.33) = P(Z < 1.33) = P(X < 80) = 0.9082$$

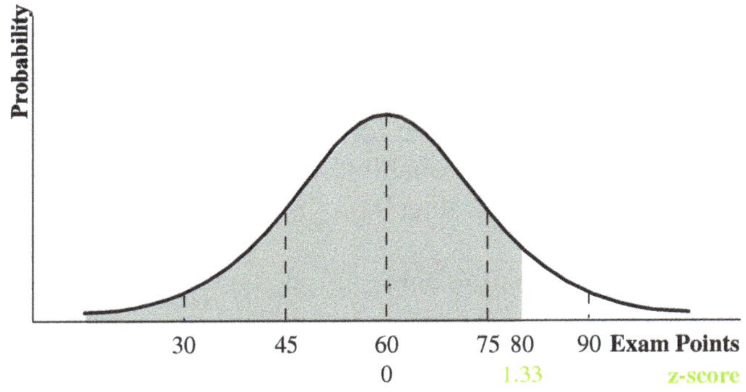

The probability of a student's score on the exam being lower than 80 (or less than 1.33 standard deviations above the mean) is 90.82%.

b. We first calculate the z-score (standardized value) for X = 70:

$$z = \frac{x - \mu}{\sigma} = \frac{70 - 60}{15} = 0.67$$

Here we are interested in P(X > 70), which is the area under the curve to the *right* of 70 on the population's distribution. On the standardized normal curve, the area we are interested in is to the right of 0.67 standard deviations *above* the mean. The value corresponding to

© 2015 Wiley

a z-score of 0.67 in the z-table is 0.7486. This, however, is the probability of a given student scoring *below* 0.67 standard deviations above the mean [P(Z < 0.67)]. In order to obtain the probability of a student scoring *more than* 0.67 standard deviations above the mean, we must subtract 0.7486 from 1:

$$P(Z > 0.67) = 1 - F(0.67) = 1 - 0.7486 = 0.2514$$

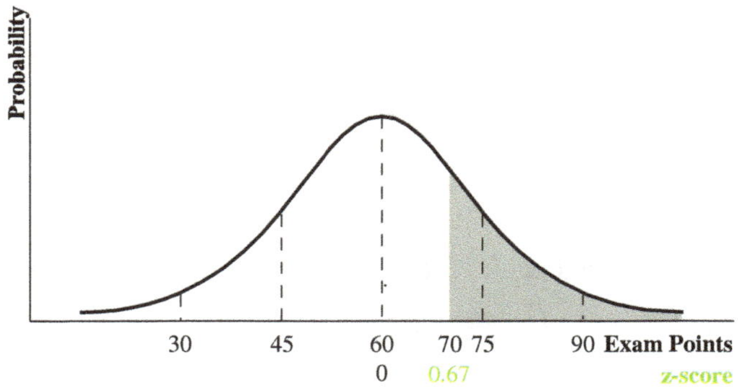

The probability of a student's score on the exam being higher than 70 (or more than 0.67 standard deviations above the mean) is 25.14%.

c. We first calculate the z-value (standardized value) for X = 40:

$$z = \frac{x - \mu}{\sigma} = \frac{40 - 60}{15} = -1.33$$

Now we want to calculate the probability that a given student's score will be *less* than 1.33 standard deviations *below* the mean. We know that for a normal distribution, half of the observed values lie below the mean, so the probability of a score lower than 1.33 standard deviations *below* the mean should be less than 0.5.

Because of the symmetry of the normal distribution curve, $F(-1.33) = 1 - F(1.33)$.

Therefore, $P(X < 40) = 1 - 0.9082 = 0.0918$.

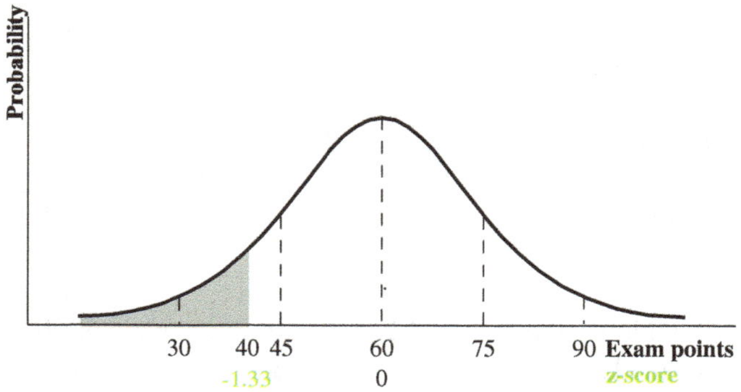

The probability of a student's score being lower than 40 (or lower than 1.33 standard deviations below the mean) is 9.18%.

© 2015 Wiley

d. Finally, we want to compute the proportion of students who scored less than 70, but not less than 40 on the exam. From part b above we know that 25.14% of students scored more than 70 on the exam. This means that 74.86% of students scored less than 70 (100% – 25.14%). From part c above we know that 9.18% of students scored below 40. Therefore, the percentage of students that scored between 40 and 70 on the exam is simply 65.68%. (74.86% – 9.18%)

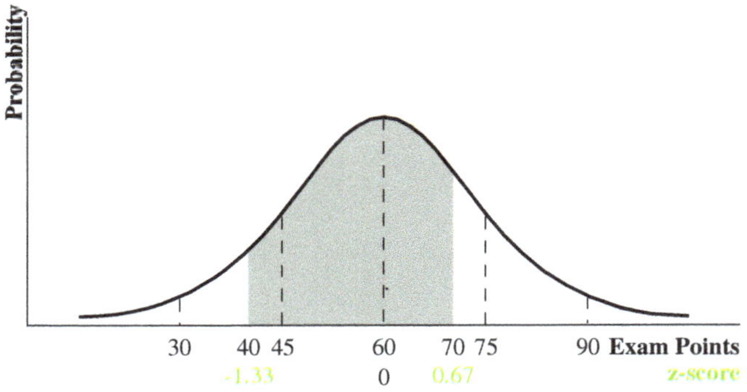

Remember for continuous random variables X > x is equal to X ≥ x.

LOS 9n: Define shortfall risk, calculate the safety-first ratio, and select an optimal portfolio using Roy's safety-first criterion. Vol 1, pp 537–539

Shortfall risk refers to the probability that a portfolio's value or return, $E(R_P)$, will fall below a particular target value or return (R_T) over a given period.

Roy's safety-first criterion states that an optimal portfolio minimizes the probability that the actual portfolio return, R_p, will fall below the target return, R_T.

Minimize $P(R_P < R_T)$
where:
R_P = portfolio return
R_T = target return

This minimum target level is also called the "threshold" level. If the portfolio's returns are normally distributed with a mean of $E(R_P)$ and standard deviation of σ_p, we can calculate the probability that returns will be lower than the threshold level by standardizing the portfolio return and looking up the probability of achieving a standardized return below the calculated z-score.

The SF Ratio provides a new perspective on the Sharpe ratio. Assuming that returns are distributed normally, the portfolio with the highest Sharpe ratio is the one that minimizes the probability of a return less than the risk-free rate.

$$\text{Shortfall ratio (SF Ratio) or z-score} = \frac{E(R_P) - R_T}{\sigma_P}$$

When making comparisons across portfolios, we can just look at their SF Ratios (z-scores) and conclude that the *higher* the value of the SF Ratio, the better the risk-return tradeoff the portfolio offers, given the investor's threshold level. A portfolio with a *higher* SF Ratio also has a *lower* probability of attaining returns lower than the threshold level.

© 2015 Wiley

Example 2-5: Using Roy's Safety-First Criterion to Select the Optimal Portfolio

An investor has $1,000 dollars to invest. His minimum acceptable portfolio value at the end of the year is $1,050. He is considering two portfolios, A and B. Portfolio A has an expected return of 8% and a standard deviation of 10%, while Portfolio B has an expected return of 12% and a standard deviation of 15%. Using Roy's safety-first criterion select the optimal portfolio, and calculate the probability that the portfolio's return will fall short of its target.

Solution

The investor is looking for a target or threshold return of:

$\$1,050 / \$1,000 - 1 = 0.05$ or 5%.

Portfolio A

$\text{SF Ratio} = (8-5)/10 = 0.3$

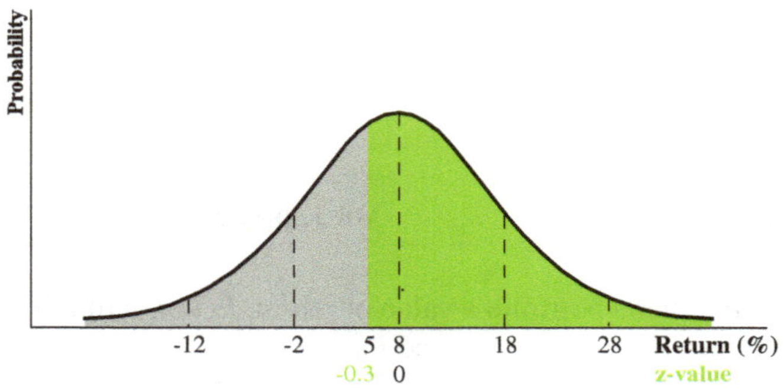

Portfolio A

Portfolio B

$\text{SF Ratio} = (12-5)/15 = 0.467$

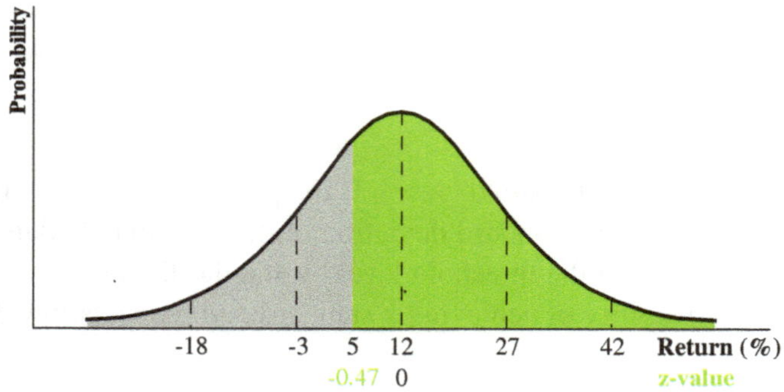

Portfolio B

Portfolio B has the higher SF Ratio so it is preferred to Portfolio A. We can also arrive at this conclusion by calculating the probability of earning a return 0.3 standard deviations *below* the mean for portfolio A, and 0.467 standard deviations *below* the mean for portfolio B. This is because the probability of not meeting the target return requirement for a given shortfall ratio is the probability to the left of -SF Ratio or F(-SF Ratio).

© 2015 Wiley

Portfolio A

$F(-0.3) = 0.3821 = 38.21\%$

Portfolio B

$F(-0.467) = 0.3228 = 32.28\%$

Portfolio B has a *lower* probability of falling short of the target return. Therefore, it offers the more appropriate investment opportunity for this particular investor.

Conclusion: Portfolios with *higher* SF Ratios are preferred to those that have a *lower* SF ratio. *Higher* SF Ratio portfolios have a *lower* probability of not meeting their target returns.

LOS 9o: Explain the relationship between normal and lognormal distributions and why the lognormal distribution is used to model asset prices. Vol 1, pp 539–541

A random variable, *Y*, follows the lognormal distribution if its natural logarithm, ln Y, is normally distributed. The reverse is also true: If the natural logarithm of random variable *Y*, ln *Y*, is normally distributed, then *Y* follows the lognormal distribution.

Three important features differentiate the lognormal distribution from the normal distribution:

1. It is bounded by zero on the lower end.
2. The upper end of its range is unbounded.
3. It is skewed to the right (positively skewed).

The lognormal distribution is frequently used to model the probability distribution of asset prices because it is bounded by zero on the lower side.

The holding period return on any asset can range between –100% and + ∞. In Figure 2-5, notice that distribution of holding period returns of an asset is skewed to the right.

Figure 2-5: Distribution of HPR of an Asset

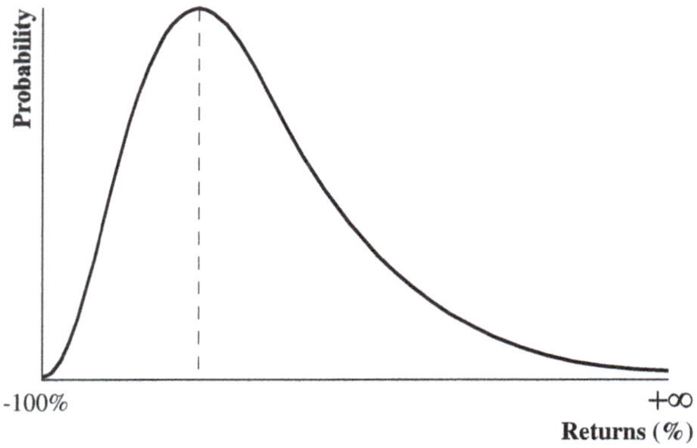

Instead of using the return on the investment as the random variable, if we were to use the ratio of the ending value of the investment to its beginning value, the distribution will still be skewed, but with a lower bound of zero, and no upper bound (Figure 2-6).

$$0 \leq \frac{V_t}{V_0} \leq +\infty$$

Notice that $\frac{V_t}{V_0}$ equals (1 + holding period return)

© 2015 Wiley

Figure 2-6: Lognormal Distribution of a Profitability Index (V_t / V_0)

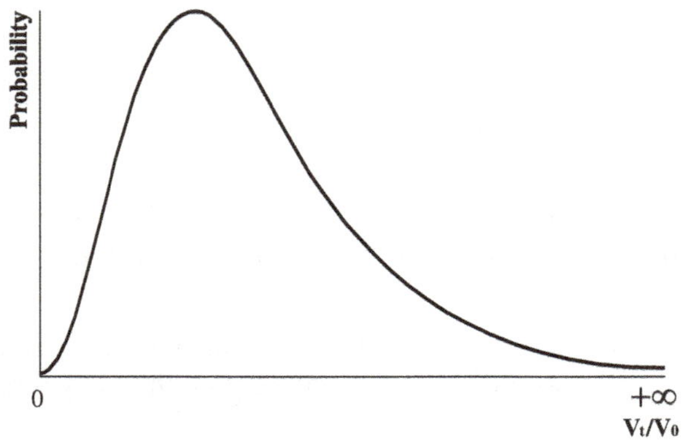

Finally, if we were to take the distribution of the natural logarithm of (V_t/V_0) we would find that the distribution is unbounded at both ends. Bear in mind that ln (V_t/V_0) is the same as ln (1 + HPR). As you will learn in the next LOS, these quantities represent the continuously compounded rate of return.

$$\text{If } V_t = 0,\ \ln\frac{V_t}{V_0} = \ln 0 \geq -\infty$$

$$\text{If } V_t = \infty,\ \ln\frac{V_t}{V_0} = \ln\infty \geq +\infty$$

Takeaway: While the distribution of the variable (V_t/V_0) follows the lognormal distribution, (Figure 2-6) (lower bound = 0; no upper bound), the distribution of the natural logarithm of (V_t/V_0) is normally distributed (Figure 2-7) with a lower bound of $-\infty$ and upper bound of $+\infty$.

Figure 2-7: Distribution of $\ln(V_t / V_0)$

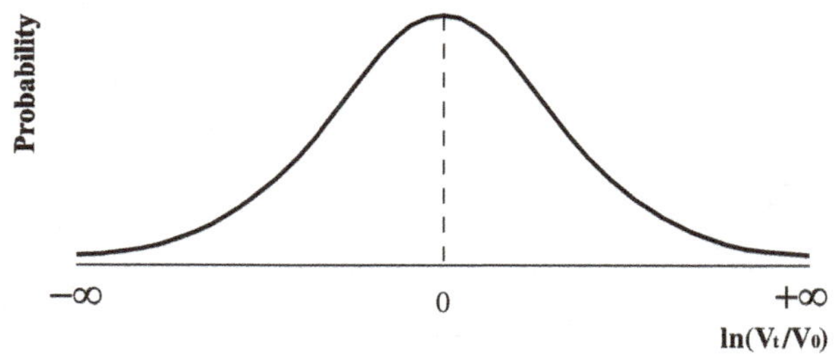

Conclusion: The lognormal distribution can be (and is frequently) used to model the distribution of asset prices because it is bounded from below by zero. The normal distribution, on the other hand, can be (and is frequently) used as an approximation for returns. If a stock's continuously compounded return is normally distributed, then future stock price must be lognormally distributed.

© 2015 Wiley

LOS 9p: Distinguish between discretely and continuously compounded rates of return, and calculate and interpret a continuously compounded rate of return, given a specific holding period return. **Vol 1, pp 541–545**

Discretely compounded returns are based on discrete or defined compounding periods, such as 12 months or 6 months. As the compounding periods get shorter and shorter, the effective annual rate (EAR) rises. With continuous compounding, the effective annual rate is given as:

$$EAR = e^{r_{cc}} - 1 \qquad r_{cc} = \text{continuously compounded annual rate}$$

If the stated rate equals 5%, the EAR based on continuous compounding is simply ($e^{0.05}$–1), which equals 5.127%.

The TI BA II keystrokes for solving ($e^{0.05}$ – 1) are:
"0.05" [2nd] [ln] [-] "1"

By reorganizing the EAR equation above, we can define an expression for calculating the continuously compounded stated annual rate:

$$EAR = e^{r_{cc}} - 1$$
$$\ln(EAR + 1) = \ln e^{r_{cc}}$$
$$\ln(EAR + 1) = r_{cc} \times \ln e$$

(ln e) equals 1. Therefore:

$$r_{cc} = \ln(EAR + 1)$$

For example, if the effective annual rate is given as 5.127%, the continuously compounded stated annual rate would be calculated as:

$$r_{cc} = \ln\ (1.05127) = 5\%$$

The TI BA II keystrokes for solving ln(1.05127) are:
"1.05127" [ln] = 0.05 or 5%.

Notice that the continuously compounded stated annual rate is *lower* than the effective annual rate (or the associated holding period return).

If continuously compounded returns are normally distributed, asset prices are lognormally distributed. This relationship is used to move back and forth between the distributions for return and price. Because of the central limit theorem, continuously compounded returns need not be normally distributed for asset prices to be reasonably well described by a lognormal distribution.

© 2015 Wiley

We can use the method described above to calculate the continuously compounded stated annual rate of return given a holding period return.

$$r_{cc} = \ln\ (1 + HPR)$$

(1 + HPR) simply equals (V_t/V_0). Therefore, the continuously compounded rate of return can also be calculated as:

$$r_{cc} = \ln\left(\frac{V_t}{V_0}\right)$$

Example 2-6: Continuously Compounded Returns

A stock that was purchased for $65 one year ago was sold for $86 today. What was the continuously compounded return on this investment?

Solution

$$r_{cc} = \ln\frac{V_t}{V_0} = \ln\frac{86}{65} = 0.28 \text{ or } 28\%$$

Alternatively, if we were given the HPY of 32.31%:

$$r_{cc} = \ln(1 + 0.3231) = 0.28 \text{ or } 28\%$$

The relationship between holding period return (HPR) and the continuously compounded rate is given as:

$$HPR_t = e^{r_{cc} \times t} - 1$$

Example 2-7: Continuously Compounded Returns

An investment of $1,000 appreciates to a value of $1,250 in 2 years. Calculate the continuously compounded return on this investment.

Solution

The HPR equals 25%

$$0.25 = e^{r_{cc} \times 2} - 1$$
$$r_{cc} = \frac{\ln(0.25 + 1)}{2}$$
$$= 11.16\%$$

© 2015 Wiley

Example 2-8: Volatility as Used in Option Pricing Models

The table below lists closing prices for XYZ Stock over the course of 5 days.

XYZ Stock Closing Prices

Date	Closing Price ($)
24-Sep-12	49.40
25-Sep-12	49.95
26-Sep-12	50.64
27-Sep-12	51.14
28-Sep-12	50.60

1. Estimate the volatility of XYZ shares. (Annualize volatility based on 250 days in a year)
2. Identify the probability distribution for XYZ share prices if continuously compounded daily returns follow the normal distribution.

Solution:

1. First, we calculate continuously compounded daily returns, $\mathbf{X_t = ln(y_t/y_{t-1})}$, using the closing prices provided. This is done in Column 3 below:

(1) Date	(2) Closing Price ($)	(3) $X_t = \ln(y_t/y_{t-1})$	(4) $(X_t - \bar{X})^2$
24-Sep-12	49.40		
25-Sep-12	49.95	0.011072	0.000026
26-Sep-12	50.64	0.013719	0.000060
27-Sep-12	51.14	0.009825	0.000015
28-Sep-12	50.60	-0.010620	0.000276
	Sum	**0.024001**	**0.000376**

Then, we divide the sum of the continuously compounded returns (in Column 3) by the number of daily **returns** (4) in the sample to determine the sample mean ($\bar{X}$).

Sample mean = 0.024001 / (5 − 1) = **0.006**

Next, the sample mean is used to compute the squared deviation ojfeach daily continuously compounded return observation (X_t) from its mean ($\bar{X}$). The sum of the squared deviations $(X_t - \bar{X})^2$ is then used to calculate the variance and standard deviation of continuously compounded daily returns.

Variance = 0.000376 / (4 − 1) = **0.000125**;
Standard deviation = $(0.000125)^{0.5}$ = **0.011195**

There are 4 daily **return** observations in the data set, so n−1 = 3 is used as the divisor to calculate the variance and standard deviation.

© 2015 Wiley

Annualize XYZ Stock price volatility based on a 250-day year is calculated as:

$$\text{Annualized volatility} = \text{Daily standard deviation} \times (250)^{0.5}$$
$$= 0.011195 \times (250)^{0.5} = \mathbf{0.177016142}$$

2. Since continuously compounded daily returns of XYZ Stock follow the normal distribution, XYZ Stock prices should follow the lognormal distribution.

LESSON 3: MONTE CARLO SIMULATION

LOS 9q: Explain Monte Carlo simulation and describe its major applications and limitations. Vol 1, pp 545–551

LOS 9r: Compare Monte Carlo simulation and historical simulation. Vol 1, pp 545–551

Monte Carlo simulation generates random numbers and operator inputs to synthetically create probability distributions for variables. It is used to calculate expected values and dispersion measures of random variables, which are then used for statistical inference. Let us consider the valuation of a call option on a stock to illustrate the specific steps involved in Monte Carlo simulation:

Specifying the Simulation

- Step 1: Specify the the quantity of interest (option price) along with the underlying variables (e.g., stock price).
- Step 2: Specify a time period and break it down into a number of subperiods.
- Step 3: Specify the distributional assumptions for the risk factors affecting the underlying variables.

Running the Simulation

- Step 4: Use a computer program or a spreadsheet function to draw random values for each risk factor.
- Step 5: Based on the random values generated in Step 4, calculate the values for the underlying variables, and then calculate the average of those values.
- Step 6: Based on the average values of the underlying variables calculated in Step 5 calculate the value of the stock option.
- Step 7: Iteratively go back to Step 4 until a sufficient number of trials has been performed.

Investment Applications

- To experiment with a proposed policy before actually implementing it.
- To provide a probability distribution that is used to estimate investment risk (e.g., VAR).
- To provide expected values of investments that can be difficult to price.
- To test models and investment tools and strategies.

© 2015 Wiley

Limitations

- Answers are only as good as the assumptions and model used.
- Does not provide cause-and-effect relationships.

Historical simulation assumes that the distribution of the random variable going forward depends on its distribution in the past. This method of forecasting has an advantage in that the distribution of risk factors does not have to be estimated. However, it faces the following limitations:

- A risk factor that was not represented in historical data will not be considered in the simulation.
- It does not facilitate "what if" analysis when the "if" factor has not occurred in the past. Monte Carlo simulation *can* be used for "what if" analysis.
- It assumes that the future will be similar to the past.
- It does not provide any cause-and-effect relationship information.

© 2015 Wiley

Reading 10: Sampling And Estimation

LESSON 1: SAMPLING, SAMPLING ERROR, AND THE DISTRIBUTION OF THE SAMPLE MEAN

In this reading, the idea is to draw information about a population (all members of a specified group) from a sample (a representative portion of the entire group). The information that we try to obtain about the population usually concerns the value of a parameter (e.g., the mean and variance). When we use sample data to estimate the value of a population parameter, we make use of sample statistics. For example, in order to estimate the average SAT score of all students in the U.S. we could use the average score of a sample of 1,000 students.

LOS 10a: Define simple random sampling and a sampling distribution. **Vol 1, pg 567–568**

LOS 10b: Explain sampling error. **Vol 1, pg 567**

In a simple random sample, each member of the population has the same probability or likelihood of being included in the sample. For example, assume that our population consists of 10 balls labeled with numbers 1 to 10. Drawing a *random* sample of 3 balls from this population of 10 balls would require that each ball has an equal chance of being chosen in the sample, and each combination of balls has an identical chance of being the chosen sample as any other combination.

In practice, random samples are generated using random number tables or computer random-number generators. Systematic sampling is often used to generate approximately random samples. In systematic sampling, every *k*th member in the population list is selected until the desired sample size is reached.

Sampling Error

Sampling error is the error caused by observing a sample instead of the entire population to draw conclusions relating to population parameters. It equals the difference between a sample statistic and the corresponding population parameter. The sampling error of the mean is given as:

$$\text{Sampling error of the mean} = \text{Sample mean} - \text{Population mean} = \bar{x} - \mu$$

Sampling Distribution

A sampling distribution is the probability distribution of a given sample statistic under repeated sampling of the population. Suppose that a random sample of 50 stocks is selected from a population of 10,000 stocks, and the average return on the 50-stock sample is calculated. If this process were repeated several times with samples of the same size (50), the sample mean (estimate of the population mean) calculated will be different each time due to the different individual stocks making up each sample. The distribution of these sample means is called the sampling distribution of the mean.

Remember that all the samples drawn from the population must be random, and of the same size. Also note that the sampling distribution is different from the distribution of returns of each of the components of the population (each of the 10,000 stocks) and has different parameters.

© 2015 Wiley

LOS 10c: Distinguish between simple random and stratified random sampling. Vol 1, pg 567–569

Stratification is the process of grouping members of the population into relatively homogeneous subgroups, or strata, before drawing samples. The strata should be *mutually exclusive* i.e., each member of the population must be assigned to only one stratum. The strata should also be *collectively exhaustive* i.e., no population element should be excluded from the sampling process. Once this is accomplished, random sampling is applied within each stratum and the number of observations drawn from each stratum is based on the size of the stratum relative to the population. This often improves the *representativeness* of the sample by *reducing* sampling error.

Example 1-1: Stratified Random Sampling

In a college, there are:

- 150 males studying full-time
- 50 males studying part-time
- 125 females studying full-time
- 25 females studying part-time
- A total of 350 students

Construct a stratified random sample of 40 students.

Solution

The first step is to calculate the percentage of students in each group (stratum).

- male, full-time = (150/350) × 100 = 42.86%
- male, part-time = (50/350) × 100 = 14.29%
- female, full-time = (125/350) × 100 = 35.71%
- female, part-time = (25/350) × 100 = 7.14%

Therefore, in our sample of 40, we will choose:

- 43% of 40 = 17.2 ≈ 17 male full-time students.
- 14% of 40 = 5.6 ≈ 6 male part-time student.
- 36% of 40 = 14.4 ≈ 14 female-full time student.
- 7% of 40 = 2.8 ≈ 3 female part-time students.

Remember that within each stratum, observations are selected randomly.

© 2015 Wiley

LOS 10d: Distinguish between time-series and cross-sectional data. Vol 1, pg 569–571

- Time-series data consists of observations measured over a period of time, spaced at uniform intervals. The monthly returns on a particular stock over the last 5 years are an example of time-series data.
- Cross-sectional data refers to data collected by observing many subjects (such as individuals, firms, or countries/regions) at the same point in time. Analysis of cross-sectional data usually consists of comparing the differences among the subjects. The returns of individual stocks over the last year are an example of cross-sectional data.

Data sets can have both time-series and cross-sectional data in them. Examples of such data sets are:

- Longitudinal data, which is data collected over time about multiple characteristics of the same observational unit. The various economic indicators—unemployment levels, inflation, GDP growth rates (multiple characteristics) of a particular country (observational unit) over a decade (period of time) are examples of longitudinal data.
- Panel data, which refers to data collected over time about a single characteristic of multiple observational units. The unemployment rate (single characteristic) of a number of countries (multiple observational units) over time are examples of panel data.

LOS 10e: Explain the central limit theorem and its importance. Vol 1, pg 572

Earlier in this reading, we referred to an analyst who was trying to estimate the average return on a population of 10,000 stocks using the average return on a sample of 50 stocks. How would the analyst determine the accuracy of the sample mean in estimating the population mean? The sample is taken at random from a population, so the sample mean itself is a random variable with a distribution. To gauge how closely the sample mean reflects the population mean, the analyst must understand the sampling distribution of the mean (distribution of sample means).

The central limit theorem allows us to make accurate statements about the population mean and variance using the sample mean and variance *regardless of the distribution of the population*, as long as the sample size is adequate. An adequate sample size is defined as one that has more than 30 observations ($n \geq 30$).

The important properties of the central limit theorem are:

- Given a population with *any* probability distribution, with mean, μ, and variance, σ^2, the sampling distribution of the sample mean $\bar{x}$, computed from sample size, *n*, will approximately be *normal* with mean, μ (the population mean), and variance, σ^2/n (population variance divided by sample size), when the sample size is greater than or equal to 30.

© 2015 Wiley

- No matter what the distribution of the population, for a sample whose size is greater than or equal to 30, the sample mean will be normally distributed.

$$\bar{x} \sim N\left(\mu, \frac{\sigma^2}{n}\right)$$

- The mean of the population (μ) and the mean of the distribution of sample means $\bar{x}$ are equal.
- The variance of the distribution of sample means equals σ^2/n, or population variance divided by sample size.

Let's go back to estimating the average return on a population of 10,000 stocks using samples of 50 stocks. If we know that the population mean return is 5% and population standard deviation is 10%, through the central limit theorem we can conclude that a distribution of the means of all the possible samples of 50 stocks will be normally distributed with a mean of 5% and standard deviation of 1.41%($10/\sqrt{50}$).

LOS 10f: Calculate and interpret the standard error of the sample mean.

Vol 1, pg 572–575

The standard deviation of the distribution of sample means is known as the standard error of the statistic.

When the population variance, σ^2, is known, the standard error of sample mean is calculated as:

$$\sigma_{\bar{x}} = \sigma / \sqrt{n}$$

where:
$\sigma_{\bar{x}}$ = the standard error of the sample mean
σ = the population standard deviation
n = the sample size

© 2015 Wiley

Example 1-2: Calculation of Standard Error when Population Variance is Known

A manufacturer claims that the life of the batteries that it produces is normally distributed with an average life of 30 hours, and a standard deviation of 5 hours. For a random sample of 40 batteries calculate the standard error.

Solution

$$\sigma_{\bar{x}} = \sigma/\sqrt{n} = 5/\sqrt{40} = 0.79$$

Interpretation: If we were to take all the possible random samples of 40 batteries each from the entire population of batteries produced by this manufacturer, and prepare a distribution of sample means, the distribution would have an average life of 30 hours, and a standard error (standard deviation of the sampling distribution) of 0.79 hours.

Practically speaking, population variances are almost never known, so we estimate the standard error of the sample mean using the sample's standard deviation:

$$s_{\bar{x}} = \frac{s}{\sqrt{n}}$$

where:
$s_{\bar{x}}$ = standard error of sample mean
s = sample standard deviation.

Example 1-3: Calculating Standard Error with Sample Standard Deviation

A sample containing the monthly returns for 50 U.S. stocks has a mean of 5% and a standard deviation of 10%. Calculate the standard error of the sample mean.

Solution

Since the population standard deviation (the standard deviation of monthly returns of *all* stocks listed in the U.S.) is not provided, we have to work with the 50-stock sample's standard deviation to calculate the standard error of sample mean.

$$s_{\bar{x}} = \frac{s}{\sqrt{n}} = 10\%/\sqrt{50} = 1.41\%$$

Interpretation: If we were to take all possible samples of 50 stocks' monthly returns from the population of all stocks listed in the U.S., the sampling distribution would have a mean of 5% and a standard error of 1.41%.

If we were to use the same values for sample mean (5%) and sample standard deviation (10%) and only increase the size of the sample, the calculated standard error of the sampling distribution would *fall.* Standard error *decreases* as sample size *increases.*

© 2015 Wiley

LESSON 2: POINT AND INTERVAL ESTIMATES OF THE POPULATION MEAN, STUDENT'S T-DISTRIBUTION, SAMPLE SIZE AND BIASES

LOS 10h: Distinguish between a point estimate and a confidence interval estimate of a population parameter. Vol 1, pg 575

A point estimate involves the use of sample data to calculate a single value (a statistic) that serves as an approximation for an unknown population parameter. For example, the sample mean, $\bar{x}$, is a point estimate of the population mean, μ. The formula used to calculate a point estimate is known as an estimator. The estimator for the sample mean is given as:

$$\bar{x} = \frac{\sum x}{n}$$

A confidence interval uses sample data to calculate a range of possible (or probable) values that an unknown population parameter can take, with a given of probability of $(1 - \alpha)$. α is called the *level of significance*, and $(1 - \alpha)$ refers to the degree of confidence that the relevant parameter will lie in the computed interval. For example, a calculated interval between 100 and 150 at the 5% significance level implies that we can be 95% confident that the population parameter will lie between 100 and 150.

A $(1 - \alpha)\%$ confidence interval has the following structure:

Point estimate $\pm$ (reliability factor $\times$ standard error)

where:
Point estimate = value of the sample statistic that is used to estimate the population parameter.

Reliability factor = a number based on the assumed distribution of the point estimate and the level of confidence for the interval $(1 - \alpha)$.

Standard error = the standard error of the sample statistic (point estimate).

LOS 10g: Identify and describe desirable properties of an estimator. Vol 1, pg 575–577

When choosing between a number of possible estimators for a particular population parameter, we make use of the desirable statistical properties of an estimator to make the best possible selection. The desirable properties of an estimator are:

- Unbiasedness: An unbiased estimator is one whose expected value is equal to the parameter being estimated. The expected value of the sample mean equals the population mean $[E(\bar{x}) = \mu]$. Therefore, the sample mean, $\bar{x}$, is an unbiased estimator of the population mean, μ.

- Efficiency: An efficient unbiased estimator is the one that has the *lowest* variance among all unbiased estimators of the same parameter.

© 2015 Wiley

- Consistency: A consistent estimator is one for which the probability of estimates close to the value of the population parameter increases as sample size increases. We have already seen that the standard error of the sampling distribution falls as sample size increases, which implies a higher probability of estimates close to the population mean.

LOS 10i: Describe the properties of Student's t-distribution and calculate and interpret its degrees of freedom. **Vol 1, pg 578–580**

Student's t-distribution is a bell-shaped probability distribution that has the following properties:

- It is symmetrical.
- It is defined by a single parameter, the degrees of freedom (df), where degrees of freedom equal sample size minus one (n-1).
- It has a lower peak than the normal curve, but fatter tails.
- As the degrees of freedom increase, the shape of the t-distribution approaches the shape of the standard normal curve.

A random sample of size, n, is said to have n-1 degrees of freedom. Basically, there are n-1 independent deviations from the mean on which the estimate can be based.

As the degrees of freedom increase, the t-distribution curve becomes more peaked and its tails become thinner (bringing it closer to a normal curve). As a result, for a given significance level, the confidence interval for a random variable that follows the t-distribution will become narrower when the degrees of freedom increase. We will be *more* confident that the population mean will lie within the calculated interval as more data is concentrated towards the middle (as demonstrated by the higher peak) and less data is in the tails (thinner tails).

Figure 2-1: Student's t-Distribution

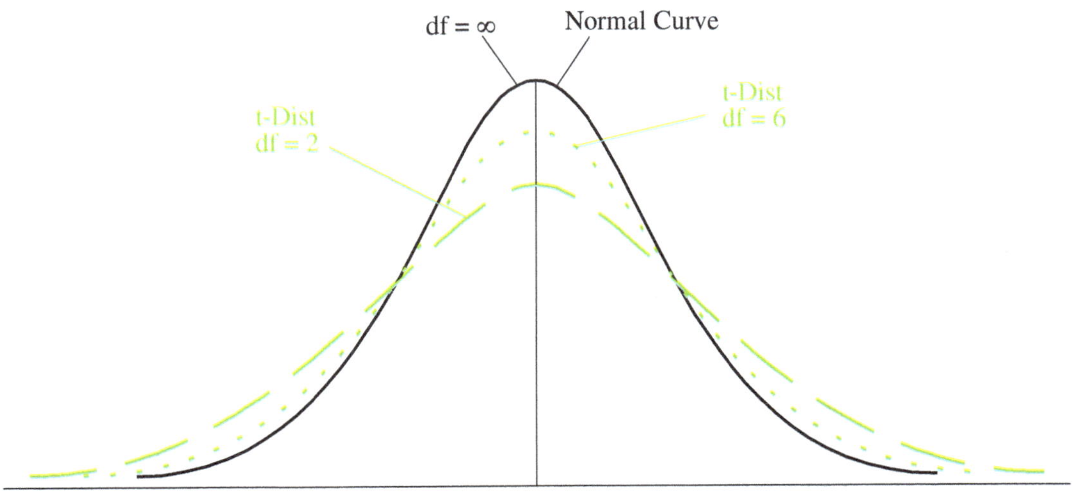

© 2015 Wiley

Table 2-1: Student's t-Distribution Table Extract

Level of Significance for One-Tailed Test						
df	**0.1**	**0.05**	**0.025**	**0.01**	**0.005**	**0.0005**

Level of Significance for Two-Tailed Test						
df	**0.2**	**0.1**	**0.05**	**0.02**	**0.01**	**0.001**
27	1.314	1.703	2.052	2.473	2.771	3.690
28	1.313	1.701	2.048	2.467	2.763	3.674
29	1.311	1.699	2.045	2.462	2.756	3.659
30	1.310	1.697	2.042	2.457	2.750	3.646
31	1.303	1.684	2.021	2.423	2.704	3.551

The t-distribution is used in the following scenarios:

- It is used to construct confidence intervals for a *normally* (or approximately normally) distributed population whose variance is *unknown* when the sample size is small ($n < 30$).
- It may also be used for a *non-normally* distributed population whose variance is *unknown* if the sample size is *large* ($n \geq 30$). In this case, the central limit theorem is used to assume that the sampling distribution of the sample mean is approximately normal.

LOS 10j: Calculate and interpret a confidence interval for a population mean, given a normal distribution with 1) a known population variance, 2) an unknown population/variance, or 3) an unknown variance and a large sample size **Vol 1, pg 578–582**

The confidence interval for the population mean when the population follows a *normal* distribution and its variance is *known* is calculated as follows:

$$\bar{x} \pm z_{\alpha/2} \frac{\sigma}{\sqrt{n}}$$

where:

$\bar{x}$ = The sample mean (point estimate of population mean).

$z_{\alpha/2}$ = The standard normal random variable for which the probability of an observation lying in either tail is $\alpha / 2$ (reliability factor).

$\frac{\sigma}{\sqrt{n}}$ = The standard error of the sample mean.

The following reliability factors are used frequently when constructing confidence intervals based on the standard normal distribution:

- For a 90% confidence interval we use $z_{0.05} = 1.65$
- For a 95% confidence interval we use $z_{0.025} = 1.96$
- For a 99% confidence interval we use $z_{0.005} = 2.58$

© 2015 Wiley

The area under the normal curve encompasses the entire range of data available for a population. For a 90% confidence interval we need to calculate the range of values within which 90% of the data lies. Since the curve is symmetrical, we need 5% in either tail, so for a 90% confidence interval the relevant z-score is 1.65. 5% of the data lies beyond 1.65 standard deviations *above* the mean and another 5% lies below 1.65 standard deviations *below* the mean.

Example 2-1: Confidence Intervals with the z-Distribution

36 students are taking a mock SAT exam to evaluate their level of preparedness for the actual test. The average score of these students is 1750. The standard deviation of scores of all students (population) who take the actual test is 200 points. Construct and interpret a 99% confidence interval for the average score of all students who take the SAT given the average score of these 36 students.

Solution

For a 99% confidence interval we use $z_{0.005} = 2.58$

$$\bar{x} \pm z_{\alpha/2}\frac{\sigma}{\sqrt{n}} = 1750 \pm 2.58\frac{200}{\sqrt{36}} = 1750 \pm (2.58 \times 33.33) = 1664 \leq \mu \leq 1836$$

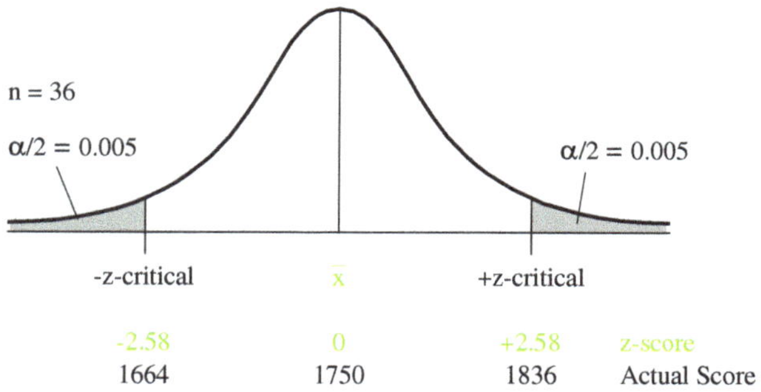

The 99% confidence interval ranges from 1664 to 1836.

This confidence interval can be interpreted in two ways:

- *Probabilistic interpretation*: After repeatedly taking samples of 36 SAT candidates' scores on the mock exam, and then constructing confidence intervals based on each sample's mean, 99% of the confidence intervals will include the population mean over the long run.

- *Practical interpretation*: We can be 99% confident that the average population score for the actual SAT exam is between 1663 and 1836.

When the variance of a *normally* distributed population is *not known*, we use the t-distribution to construct confidence intervals:

$$\text{Confidence interval} = \bar{x} \pm t_{\frac{\alpha}{2}} \frac{s}{\sqrt{n}}$$

Where:
$\bar{x}$ = sample mean (the point estimate of the population mean)
$t_{\frac{\alpha}{2}}$ = the t-reliability factor
$\frac{s}{\sqrt{n}}$ = standard error of the sample mean
s = sample standard deviation

Recall that the critical t-values or the reliability factor for constructing the confidence interval depends on the level of confidence desired, and on the sample size. Also recall that the t-distribution has fatter or thicker tails relative to the normal distribution. Since more observations essentially lie in the tails of the distribution, a confidence interval for a given significance level will be *broader* for the t-distribution compared to the z-distribution.

Example 2-2: Confidence Intervals with the t-Distribution

A sample of the monthly returns of Treptash Ltd. stock over the last two and a half years has a mean return of 3% and a standard deviation of 15%. Compute the 95% confidence interval for the average monthly returns on Treptash stock.

Solution

The population variance (variance of monthly returns on Treptash stock for its entire history) is unknown. Therefore, we calculate the standard error using the standard deviation of the sample.

$$s_{\bar{x}} = \frac{s}{\sqrt{n}} = \frac{15}{\sqrt{30}} = 2.74\%$$

© 2015 Wiley

Degrees of freedom = 30 - 1 = 29

For a 95% confidence interval we need 2.5% in either tail. The relevant t-score with 29 degrees of freedom is 2.045. 2.5% of the data lies beyond 2.045 standard deviations *above* the mean and another 2.5% lies below 2.045 standard deviations *below* the mean.

t-value = $t_{29,2.5}$ = 2.045

Confidence interval = 3% ± 2.045(2.74) = 3% ± 5.6%

The calculated confidence interval ranges from -2.6% to 8.6%.

Interpretation: We can be 95% confident that the monthly return on Treptash stock for its entire existence (population mean) lies between -2.6% and 8.6%

When the population is *normally* distributed we:

- Use the z-statistic when the population variance is known.
- Use the t-statistic when the population variance is not known.

When the distribution of the population is *nonnormal,* the construction of an appropriate confidence interval depends on the size of the sample.

- If the population variance is *known* and the sample size is large (n ≥ 30) we use the z-statistic. This is because the central limit theorem tells us that the distribution of the sample mean is approximately normal when sample size is large.
- If the population variance is *not known* and sample size is large, we can use the z-statistic or the t-statistic. However, in this scenario the use of the t-statistic is encouraged because it results in a more conservative measure.

This implies that we cannot construct confidence intervals for nonnormal distributions if sample size is less than 30.

When the variance of a *normally* distributed population is *not known*, and the sample size is large we use the z-distribution to construct confidence intervals:

$$\bar{x} \pm z_{\alpha/2} \frac{s}{\sqrt{n}}$$

© 2015 Wiley

Table 2-2: Criteria for Selecting Appropriate Test Statistic

When Sampling from a:	Small Sample n < 30	Large Sample n > 30
Normal distribution with known variance	z-statistic	z-statistic
Normal distribution with unknown variance	t-statistic	t-statistic*
Nonnormal distribution with known variance	not available	z-statistic
Nonnormal distribution with unknown variance	not available	t-statistic*
** Use of z-statistic also acceptable*		

LOS 10k: Describe the issues regarding selection of the appropriate sample size, data-mining bias, sample selection bias, survivorship bias, look-ahead bias, and time-period bias. **Vol 1, pg 583–590**

From our discussion so far, we have understood that there are various factors that affect the width of a confidence interval:

- The choice of test statistic: A t-statistic gives a wider confidence interval.
- The degree of confidence: A higher desired level of confidence increases the size of the confidence interval.

From our formula for the confidence interval, it is easy to see that the width of the interval is also a function of the standard error. The *larger* the standard error, the *wider* the confidence interval. The standard error, in turn, is a function of sample size. More specifically, a *larger* sample size results in a *smaller* standard error and *reduces* the width of the confidence interval. Therefore, large sample sizes are desirable as they increase the precision with which we can estimate a population parameter. However, in practice two considerations may work against increasing the sample size:

- Increasing the size of the sample may result in drawing observations from a different population.
- Increasing the sample size may involve additional expenses that outweigh the benefit of increased accuracy of estimates.

Other than the risk of sampling from more than one population, there are a variety of challenges to valid sampling. If the sample is biased in any way, estimates and conclusions drawn from sample data will be erroneous.

Types of Biases

Data mining is the practice of developing a model by extensively searching through a data set for statistically significant relationships until a pattern "that works" is discovered. In the process of data mining, large numbers of hypotheses about a single data set are tested in a very short time by searching for combinations of variables that might show a correlation.

Given that enough hypotheses are tested, it is virtually certain that some of them will appear to be highly statistically significant, even on a data set with no real correlations at all. Researchers who use data mining techniques can be easily misled by these apparently significant results even though they are merely coincidences.

© 2015 Wiley

Data-mining bias most commonly occurs when:

- Researchers have not formed a hypothesis in advance, and are therefore open to any hypothesis suggested by the data.
- When researchers narrow the data used in order to reduce the probability of the sample refuting a specific hypothesis.

Intergenerational data mining involves using information developed by previous researchers to guide current research using the same or a related data set.

Warning signs that data mining bias might exist are:

- *Too much digging warning sign*, which involves testing numerous variables until one that appears to be significant is discovered.
- *No story/ no future warning sign*, which is indicated by a lack of an economic theory that can explain empirical results.

The best way to avoid the data-mining bias is to test the "apparently statistically significant relationships" on "out-of-sample" data to check whether they continue to hold.

Sample-Selection Bias

Sample-selection bias results from the exclusion of certain assets (such as bonds, stocks, or portfolios) from a study due to the unavailability of data.

Some databases use historical information and may suffer from a type of sample selection bias known as survivorship bias. This bias is present in databases that only list companies or funds currently in existence, which means that those that have failed are not included in the database. As a result, the results obtained from the study may not accurately reflect the true picture.

Sample selection bias is even more severe in studies of hedge fund returns. This is because hedge funds are not required to publicly disclose their performance data. Only funds that performed well choose to disclose their performance, which leads to an overstatement of hedge fund returns.

Look-Ahead Bias

Look-ahead bias arises when a study uses information that was not available on the test date. For example, consider a test on a trading rule based on the price-to-book value ratio of stocks. Stock prices are usually easily available, but year-end book values are not available till the first quarter of the next year (when financial statements are released).

Time-Period Bias

Time-period bias arises if a test is based on a certain time period, which may make the results obtained from the study time-period specific. If the selected time period is relatively short, results will reflect relationships that held only during that particular period. On the other hand, if the time period is too long, the study might fail to uncover any structural changes that occurred during the period.

© 2015 Wiley

READING 11: HYPOTHESIS TESTING

LESSON 1: INTRODUCTION TO HYPOTHESIS TESTING

LOS 11a: Define a hypothesis, describe the steps of hypothesis testing, and describe and interpret the choice of the null and alternative hypotheses.
Vol 1, pp 607–611

LOS 11b: Distinguish between one-tailed and two-tailed tests of hypotheses.
Vol 1, pp 607–611

LOS 11c: Explain a test statistic, Type I and Type II errors, a significance level, and how significance levels are used in hypothesis testing.
Vol 1, pp 607–611

LOS 11d: Explain a decision rule, the power of a test, and the relation between confidence intervals and hypothesis tests.
Vol 1, pp 611–616

Hypothesis testing is the process of evaluating the accuracy of a statement regarding a population parameter (e.g., the population mean) given sample information (e.g., the sample mean). A **hypothesis** is a statement about the value of a population parameter developed for the purpose of testing a theory. Let's assume that we think (hypothesize) that the average points scored in each game by a basketball player throughout his career is *greater* than 30. First, we would need to get some sample information. Then we would conduct a hypothesis test on the *sample information* (average of his scores in, let's say, 49 randomly selected games) in order to be able to comment on the accuracy of the statement pertaining to the *population parameter* (his average score across all the games that he played in his entire career).

The null hypothesis will always include an "=" sign.

1. The **null hypothesis (H_0)** generally represents the status quo, and is the hypothesis that we are *interested in rejecting*. This hypothesis will not be rejected unless the sample data provides sufficient evidence to reject it. Null hypotheses regarding the mean of the population can be stated in the following ways:

$$H_0 : \mu \leq \mu_0$$
$$H_0 : \mu \geq \mu_0$$
$$H_0 : \mu = \mu_0$$

Where:
μ = population mean
μ_0 = hypothesized value of the population mean

In the basketball player's example that we just described, the null hypotheses would be that the player's average score is less than or equal to 30 points. Confirmation of our belief (that his average score is greater than 30) requires rejection of the null hypothesis.

2. The **alternate hypothesis (H_a)** is essentially the statement whose *validity we are trying to evaluate*. The alternate hypothesis is the statement that will only be accepted if the sample

© 2015 Wiley

data provides convincing evidence of its truth. It is the conclusion of the test if the null hypothesis is rejected. Alternate hypotheses can be stated as:

$$H_a : \mu > \mu_0$$
$$H_a : \mu < \mu_0$$
$$H_a : \mu \neq \mu_0$$

In our example, the alternate hypothesis is that the player's scoring average is greater than 30 points. Recall that we are trying to evaluate the validity of the statement that his scoring average is *greater* than 30 points.

A hypothesis test is always conducted at a particular level of significance (α). The level of significance represents the chance that we are willing to take that the conclusion from the test might be wrong.

Essentially, a hypothesis test involves the comparison of a sample's test statistic to a critical value.

- The test statistic is calculated as:

$$\text{Test statistic} = \frac{\text{Sample statistic} - \text{Hypothesized value}}{\text{Standard error of sample statistic}}$$

- The critical value depends on the relevant distribution, sample size, and level of significance used to test the hypothesis.

One-Tailed versus Two-Tailed Tests

Hypothesis tests can be either one-tailed or two-tailed. Under one-tailed tests, we assess whether the value of a population parameter is either *greater than* or *less than* a given hypothesized value. Hypotheses for one-tailed tests can be stated as:

1. $H_0 : \mu \leq \mu_0$ versus $H_a : \mu > \mu_0$ — When we are testing whether the population mean is greater than a given hypothesized value.

2. $H_0 : \mu \geq \mu_0$ versus $H_a : \mu < \mu_0$ — When we are testing whether the population mean is less than a given hypothesized value.

Example 1-1: One-Tailed Hypothesis Test

Suppose that the basketball player's average score in a sample of 49 games is 36 points with a standard deviation of 9 points. Determine the accuracy of the statement that his career scoring average is greater than 30 points. Use the 5% level of significance.

Solution

The null hypothesis is the statement that we want to reject (that his average score is less than or equal to 30), and the alternate hypothesis is the belief whose validity we are trying to ascertain (that his average is greater than 30).

© 2015 Wiley

Therefore:

$H_0 : \mu \leq 30 \rightarrow$ The theory that we want to reject
$H_a : \mu > 30 \rightarrow$ The theory that we want to validate

The observed sample's test statistic (z-score) represents the number of standard deviations away from the hypothesized mean the sample's mean lies.

$$\text{Test statistic} = \frac{\text{Sample statistic - Hypothesized value}}{\text{Standard error of sample statistic}}$$

$$\text{Test statistic} = \frac{\bar{x} - \mu_0}{s / \sqrt{n}} = \frac{36 - 30}{\left(9 / \sqrt{49}\right)} = 4.67$$

The critical value at the 5% significance level tells us the number of standard deviations away from the hypothesized mean, only 5% of observed sample means lie.

$$\text{Critical value} = z_\alpha = 1.645$$

The test statistic indicates that the sample mean (36) lies 4.67 standard errors, or standard deviations of the sampling distribution, away from the hypothesized mean (30). Therefore, it lies in the region where less than 5% of observed sample means lie. There is a less than 5% chance of observing a sample mean as high as 36 (given the sample size of 49 and a sample standard deviation of 9), if the population mean is 30. Therefore, at the 5% significance level, we can *reject* the null hypothesis, and conclude that the player's scoring average across his entire career is greater than 30.

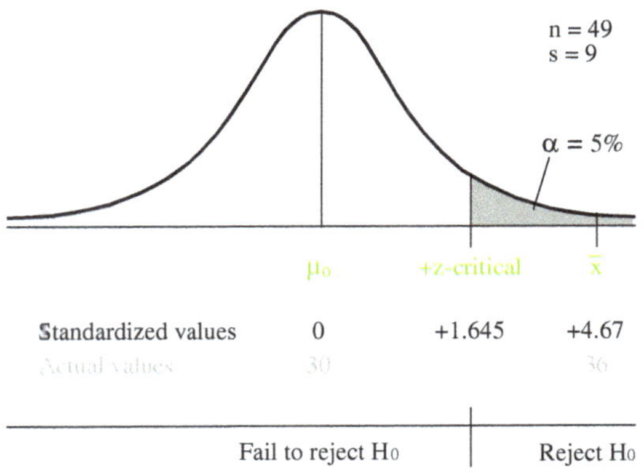

5% of observed sample means lie more than 1.645 standard deviations above the mean.

The test-statistic lies 4.67 standard deviations above the mean.

The chance of a sample having a mean of 36 (given the sample size of 49 and sample standard deviation of 9), when the population mean equals 30 is less than 5%. Therefore we **reject the null hypothesis.**

IMPORTANT:

The standard error of the sampling distribution equals the standard deviation of the sample divided by the square root of n. This standard error is also known as the standard deviation of the sampling distribution. Going forward we shall use the term standard deviation to stand for the standard error.

In this example, we want to ascertain whether the player's scoring average is *more* than 30. Therefore, we compare the test statistic to the *positive* critical value.

The following rejection rules apply when trying to determine whether a population mean is *greater* than the hypothesized value.

- Reject H_0 when:
  Test statistic > positive critical value

- Fail to reject H_0 when:
  Test statistic ≤ positive critical value

© 2015 Wiley

Example 1-2: One-Tailed Hypothesis Test

For the same data that we used in the previous example, assume that the sample has a mean of 28.5. Evaluate the validity of the statement that the player's scoring average over his career is less than 30 points at the 5% level of significance.

Solution

In this case, we want to reject the theory that his average score is greater than or equal to 30 and test the validity of the claim that his average score is less than 30.

Therefore,

$H_0 : \mu \geq 30 \rightarrow$ The theory that we want to reject
$H_a : \mu < 30 \rightarrow$ The theory that we want to validate

$$\text{Critical value} = -z_\alpha = -1.645$$

In this example, we want to ascertain whether the player's scoring average is *less* than 30. Therefore, we compare the test statistic to the *negative* critical value.

The sample's test statistic (z-score) represents the number of standard deviations that the observed sample mean lies away from the hypothesized mean. For the information we are given, the observed sample mean (28.5) lies 1.167 standard deviations *below* the hypothesized mean of 30.

$$\text{Test statistic} = \frac{\bar{x} - \mu_0}{s/\sqrt{n}} = \frac{28.5 - 30}{(9/\sqrt{49})} = -1.167$$

The critical value (-1.645) tells us the number of standard deviations *below* the mean, only 5% of observed sample means lie. The test statistic (1.167) lies *less* than 1.645 standard deviations *below* the mean. The sample mean lies close enough to the hypothesized mean for us not to be able to reject the null hypothesis. Therefore, at the 5% significance level, we fail to reject the null hypothesis.

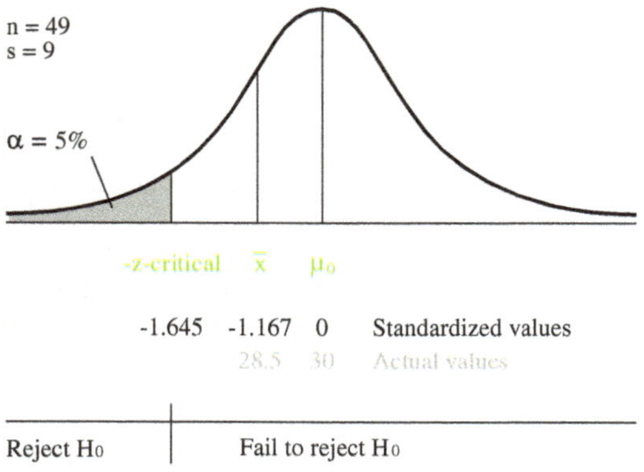

5% of observed sample means lie more than 1.645 standard deviations *below* the mean.

The test-statistic only lies 1.167 standard deviations *below* the mean.

The chance of a sample (given the sample size of49 and sample standard deviation of 9) having a mean of 28.5 when the population mean equals 30 is more than 5%. Therefore we **fail to reject the null hypothesis** at the 5% significance level.

© 2015 Wiley

The following rejection rules apply when trying to determine whether a population mean is *less* than the hypothesized value.

- Reject H_0 when:
  Test statistic < negative critical value

- Fail to reject H_0 when:
  Test statistic ≥ negative critical value

Under two-tailed tests, we assess whether the value of the population parameter is simply *different from* a given hypothesized value. The hypotheses for two-tailed tests are stated as:

$H_0 : \mu = \mu_0$
$H_a : \mu \neq \mu_0$

Two-tailed hypotheses tests have 2 rejection regions. Example 1-3 will illustrate how two-tailed hypotheses tests are performed.

Example 1-3: Two-Tailed Hypothesis Test

A **two-tailed test** will be used to determine if the player's scoring average is simply different from, or not equal to 30. His scores can differ from 30 in two ways—by being *less* than 30 or by being *more* than 30; hence the two-tailed test. Given that over a sample of 49 games, the player averaged 33 points with a standard deviation of 9 points, test whether his career scoring average is different from 30 at the 5% significance level.

$H_0 : \mu = 30$ The theory that we want to reject.
$H_a \;\; \mu \neq 30$ The theory that we want to validate.

$$\text{Test statistic } = \frac{\bar{x} - \mu_0}{s / \sqrt{n}} = \frac{33 - 30}{\left(9 / \sqrt{49}\right)} = 2.33$$

At the α level of significance, we want to determine whether the sample mean lies within $z_{\alpha/2}$ standard deviations from the hypothesized population mean. This leaves a combined probability of α in the tails.

$$\text{Critical value} = \pm\, z_{\alpha/2} = -1.96 \text{ and } +1.96$$

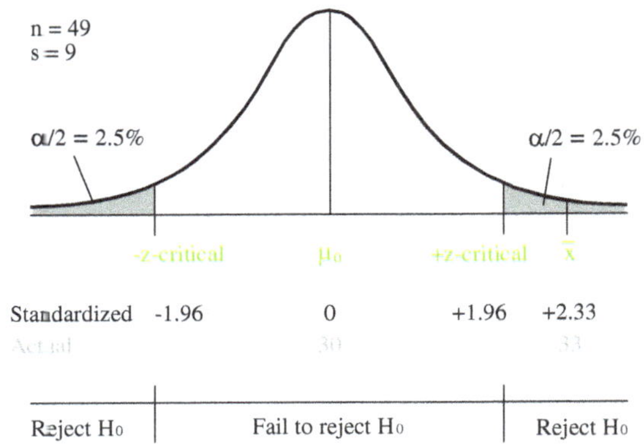

5% of observed sample means lie more than 1.96 standard deviations away from the mean, i.e. 2.5% in each tail.

The test-statistic lies 2.33 standard deviations *above* the mean.

The chance of a sample having a mean of 33 (given the sample size of 49 and sample standard deviation of 9) when the population mean equals 30 is less than 2.5%. Therefore **we reject the null hypothesis.**

© 2015 Wiley

At the 5% level of significance, the sample mean must lie within 1.96 standard deviations of the hypothesized population mean for the null hypothesis to not be rejected. If the sample mean lies beyond either 1.96 standard deviations *above* the mean or 1.96 standard deviations *below* the mean, we cannot conclude that the population mean equals the hypothesized value, and have to reject the null hypothesis. In this example, our test statistic (2.33) lies more than 1.96 standard deviations above the mean. The chances of a sample mean actually representing the population mean while lying so far away from the population mean (2.33 standard deviations) are extremely slim (less than 5%). Therefore, we reject the null hypothesis, and conclude that the player's career scoring average is not equal to 30 at the 5% significance level.

Rejection Rules for Two-Tailed Hypothesis Test

- Reject H_0 when:
  Test statistic < Lower critical value
  Test statistic > Upper critical value

- Fail to reject H_0 when:
  Lower critical value ≤ test statistic ≤ Upper critical value

Notice that in all the examples above we have been very careful to word the conclusions that we have drawn from the hypothesis tests. The conclusion of any hypothesis test is either the rejection of the null, or failure to reject the null. For example, we cannot make a statement like "the null hypothesis is accepted" because it is statistically incorrect to do so.

Type I and Type II Errors

Hypothesis tests are used to make inferences about population parameters using sample statistics. There is always a possibility that the sample may not be perfectly representative of the population, and that the conclusions drawn from the test may be wrong. There are two types of errors that can be made when conducting a hypothesis test:

- **Type I error:** Rejecting the null hypothesis when it is actually true.
- **Type II error:** Failing to reject the null hypothesis when it is actually false.

The significance level (α) represents the probability of making a Type I error. A significance level of 5% means that there is a 5% chance of rejecting the null when it is actually true. A significance level is required in any hypothesis test to compute critical values against which the test statistic is compared.

If we were to fail to reject the null hypothesis given the lack of overwhelming evidence in favor of the alternate, we risk a Type II error – *failing to reject the null hypothesis when it is false*.

Sample size and the choice of significance level (probability of Type I error) together determine the probability of a Type II error. Measuring the risk of Type II errors is very difficult, but to accommodate for the possibility of a Type II error, instead of concluding that

© 2015 Wiley

the null hypothesis is true, we simply state that the sample evidence is not enough to reject the null hypothesis at the particular significance level. Since the null is the status quo hypothesis, not rejecting the null maintains the status quo.

The power of a test is the probability of *correctly* rejecting the null hypothesis when it is false.

Power of a test = 1 – P(Type II error)

Decision	H_0 is True	H_0 is False
Do not reject H_0	Correct decision	Incorrect decision **Type II error**
Reject H_0	Incorrect decision **Type I error** Significance level = P(Type I error)	Correct decision Power of the test = 1 - P(Type II error)

- The *higher* the power of the test, the *better* it is for purposes of hypothesis testing. Given a choice of tests, the one with the highest power should be preferred. This statement is fairly straightforward—the test with the highest probability of rejecting the null hypothesis when it is false should be preferred.
- Decreasing the significance level reduces the probability of Type I error. However, reducing the significance level means shrinking the rejection region, and inflating the "fail to reject the null region." This increases the probability of failing to reject a false null hypothesis (Type II error) and reduces the power of the test.
- The power of the test can only be increased by reducing the probability of a Type II error. This can only be accomplished by reducing the "fail to reject the null region," which is equivalent to increasing the size of the rejection region and increasing the probability of a Type I error. Basically, an *increase* in the power of a test comes at the cost of *increasing* the probability of a Type I error.
- The only way to *decrease* the probability of a Type II error given the significance level (probability of Type I error) is to *increase* the sample size.

Relation Between Confidence Intervals and Hypothesis Tests

A confidence interval states the range of values within which a population parameter is estimated to lie. It is calculated as:

$$\left[\begin{pmatrix}\text{sample}\\\text{statistic}\end{pmatrix} - \begin{pmatrix}\text{critical}\\\text{value}\end{pmatrix}\begin{pmatrix}\text{standard}\\\text{error}\end{pmatrix}\right] \le \begin{pmatrix}\text{population}\\\text{parameter}\end{pmatrix} \le \left[\begin{pmatrix}\text{sample}\\\text{statistic}\end{pmatrix} + \begin{pmatrix}\text{critical}\\\text{value}\end{pmatrix}\begin{pmatrix}\text{standard}\\\text{error}\end{pmatrix}\right]$$

$$\overline{x} - (z_{\alpha/2})\ (s/\sqrt{n}) \le \mu_0 \le \overline{x} + (z_{\alpha/2})\ (s/\sqrt{n})$$

© 2015 Wiley

As you can see, we reach the same conclusion regarding our hypothesis using a hypothesis test or using confidence intervals. Confidence intervals and hypothesis test are linked by critical values.

- In a confidence interval, we aim to determine whether the hypothesized value of the population mean (μ_0), lies within a computed interval with a particular degree of confidence ($1-\alpha$). Here the interval represents the "fail-to-reject-the-null region" and is based around, or centered on the sample mean, $\bar{x}$.
- In a hypothesis test, we examine whether the sample mean, $\bar{x}$ lies in the rejection region (i.e., outside the interval) or in the fail-to-reject-the-null region (i.e., within the interval) at a particular level of significance (α). Here the interval is based around, or centered on the hypothesized value of the population mean (μ_0).

Figure 1-1: A 95% Confidence Interval for a Two-Tailed Test

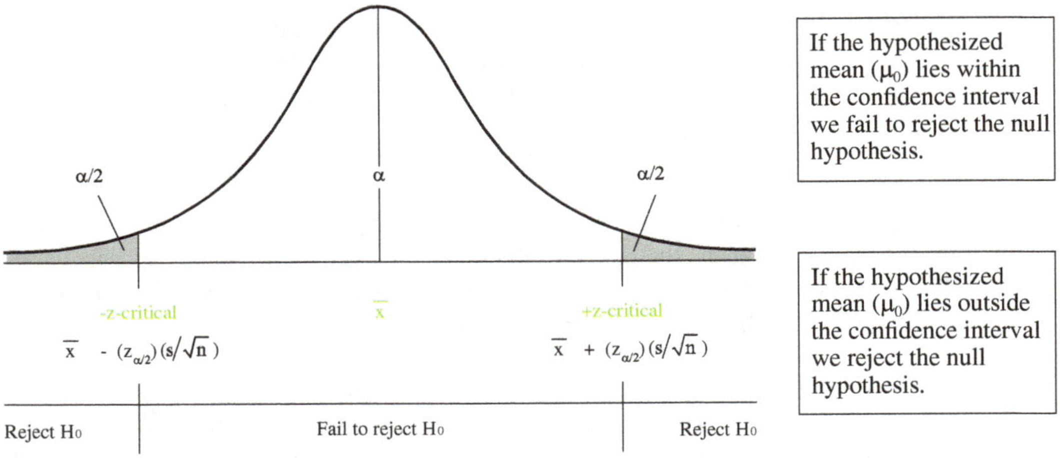

Example 1-4: Confidence Intervals

Construct a 95% confidence interval for the basketball player's career scoring average if, over a sample of 49 games, he averaged 31 points with a standard deviation of 9 points. Use this confidence interval to determine whether the player's career average is different from 33 points.

Solution

$$\bar{x} - (z_{\alpha/2})(s/\sqrt{n}) \leq \mu_0 \leq \bar{x} + (z_{\alpha/2})(s/\sqrt{n})$$

Critical value = $z_{\alpha/2} = z_{0.025} = 1.96$

Sample mean = $\bar{x} = 31$

$$31 - 1.96 \times (9/\sqrt{49}) \leq \text{career scoring average} \leq 31 + 1.96 \times (9/\sqrt{49})$$

$28.48 \leq$ career scoring average (hypothesized population mean, μ_0) ≤ 33.52

© 2015 Wiley

There is a 95% probability that the population mean lies within this interval given the sample mean of 31 points. The hypothesized population mean (33) lies within this range. Therefore, we fail to reject the null hypothesis at the 5% level of significance.

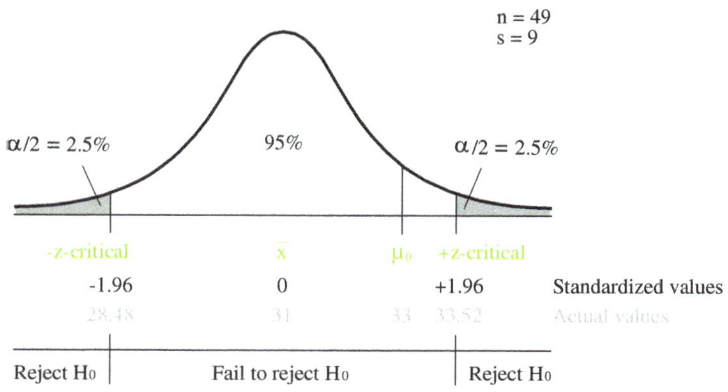

Conducting a hypothesis test would also lead us to the same conclusion:

$H_0 : \mu = 33$
$H_a : \mu \neq 33$

$$\text{Test statistic} = \frac{\bar{x} - \mu_0}{s/\sqrt{n}} = \frac{31 - 33}{(9/\sqrt{49})} = -1.556$$

The critical z-values at the 5% level of significance are –1.96 and +1.96. The test statistic (1.556) falls in the range between these two values. Therefore, we fail to reject the null hypothesis at the 5% level of significance. Note that both the confidence interval and the hypothesis test offer the same conclusion.

LOS 11f: Explain and interpret the p-value as it relates to hypothesis testing. Vol 1, pp 615–616

The p-value is the smallest level of significance at which the null hypothesis can be rejected. It represents the probability of obtaining a critical value that would lead to rejection of the null hypothesis.

For example, consider a two-tailed test where the test statistic is 2.5 and the critical values are –1.96 and +1.96. From the z-table, we find that the probability of attaining a value greater than 2.5 standard deviations above the mean is 0.0062. Since this is a two-tailed test, the p-value equals 2 × 0.0062 = 0.0124. This value tells us that we would reject the null hypothesis at the 5% level of significance, but not at the 1% level. 1.24 is the lowest level of significance at which the null hypothesis can be rejected.

- If the p-value is *lower* than the required level of significance, we reject the null hypothesis.
- If the p-value is *greater* than the required level of significance, we fail to reject the null hypothesis.

The table below summarizes everything we have learned about hypothesis testing so far.

Type of Test	Null Hypothesis	Alternate Hypothesis	Reject Null if	Fail to Reject Null if	p-Value Represents
One tailed (upper tail) test	$H_0 : \mu \leq \mu_0$	$H_a : \mu > \mu_0$	Test statistic > critical value	Test statistic ≤ critical value	Probability that lies above the computed test statistic.
One tailed (lower tail) test	$H_0 : \mu \geq \mu_0$	$H_a : \mu < \mu_0$	Test statistic < critical value	Test statistic ≥ critical value	Probability that lies below the computed test statistic.
Two-tailed test	$H_0 : \mu = \mu_0$	$H_a : \mu \neq \mu_0$	Test statistic < Lower critical value Test statistic > Upper critical value	Lower critical value ≤ test statistic ≤ Upper critical value	Probability that lies above the positive value of the computed test statistic *plus* the probability that lies below the negative value of the computed test statistic

LOS 11e: Distinguish between a statistical result and an economically meaningful result. **Vol 1, pp 613–615**

A larger sample size reduces size of the fail-to-reject-the-null region. It reduces the probability of a Type II error and increases the power of the test.

Sometimes differences between a variable and its hypothesized value are statistically significant but not practically or economically meaningful. Suppose we are testing a hypothesis that the returns from a technical trading strategy are greater than zero. If we use a large sample (n) when conducting the test, our standard error will be small, the "fail-to-reject region" narrower, and the greater the chance that the null will be rejected. The sample error decreases as sample size increases, and as sample size increases we can have situations where the null is rejected even when the sample mean deviates only slightly from the hypothesized value. Even though a trading strategy might provide a statistically significant return of greater than zero (based on a hypothesis test) it does not mean that we can guarantee that trading on this strategy would result in economically meaningful positive returns. The returns may not be economically significant after accounting for taxes, transaction costs and risks inherent in the strategy.

Even if we conclude that a strategy's results are economically significant, we should examine whether there is a logical reason to explain the apparently-significant returns offered by the strategy before actually implementing it.

© 2015 Wiley

LESSON 2: HYPOTHESIS TESTS CONCERNING THE MEAN

LOS 11g: Identify the appropriate test statistic and interpret the results for a hypothesis test concerning the population mean of both large and small samples when the population is normally or approximately distributed and the variance is 1) known or 2) unknown. Vol 1, pp 607–635

Hypothesis Tests Concerning the Mean

Tests Concerning a Single Mean

In the process of hypothesis testing, the decision whether to use critical values based on the z-distribution or the t-distribution depends on sample size, the distribution of the population and whether the variance of the population is known.

The t-test is used when the variance of the population is unknown *and* either of the conditions below holds:

- The sample size is large.
- The sample size is small, but the underlying population is normally distributed or approximately normally distributed.

The test statistic (t-statistic) for hypothesis tests concerning the mean of a single population is:

$$\text{t-stat} = \frac{\overline{x} - \mu_0}{s / \sqrt{n}}$$

Where:
x = sample mean
μ_0 = hypothesized population mean
s = standard deviation of the sample
n = sample size

In a t-test, the sample's t-statistic is compared to the critical t-value with n-1 degrees of freedom, at the desired level of significance. Practically speaking, the variance of the population is rarely ever known, so the t-test is very popular.

The z-test can be used to conduct hypothesis tests of the population mean when the population is normally distributed and its variance is known.

$$\text{z-stat} = \frac{\overline{x} - \mu_0}{\sigma / \sqrt{n}}$$

Where:
x = sample mean
μ_0 = hypothesized population mean
σ = standard deviation of the population
n = sample size

© 2015 Wiley

Notice the use of the sample standard deviation (s) when the population standard deviation (σ) is unknown. This is acceptable when sample size is large. However, note that use of the t-statistic in this scenario will be more appropriate as it is a more conservative measure.

The z-test can also be used when the population's variance is unknown, but the sample size is large.

$$\text{z-stat} = \frac{\overline{x} - \mu_0}{s / \sqrt{n}}$$

Where:
x = sample mean
μ_0 = hypothesized population mean
s = standard deviation of the sample
n = sample size

In a z-test, the z-statistic is compared to the critical z-value at the given level of significance. Going back to our examples about the basketball player's career scoring average, the population variance was unknown. However, because the sample size (49) was large ($n \geq 30$) the use of either test- the t-test or the z-test is appropriate. We know that as the sample size increases, the t-distribution converges towards the z-distribution. Since the sample size is large in our examples, the critical values for either test were very similar, and there was almost an identical chance of rejecting the null hypothesis using either distribution.

Example 2-1: Hypothesis Test

A manufacturer claims that the life of its batteries is normally distributed with a mean of 30 hours. For a random sample of 81 batteries it is observed that the average life of the batteries in the sample is 29 hours with a standard deviation of 5 hours. Using a 5% significance level, determine whether the manufacturer's claims are *inaccurate*.

Solution

Step 1: State the hypotheses

The null hypothesis is the position that is the status quo (the average battery life of all batteries produced is 30 hours).

$H_0 : \mu = 30$

The alternative hypothesis is the statement whose validity we are testing. (Manufacturer's claims are inaccurate)

$H_a : \mu \neq 30$

This is a two-tailed test.

Step 2: State the appropriate test statistic

The population variance is unknown. However, the sample size is large so both the z-test and the t-test can be applied here. We will work with the z-test in this example.

© 2015 Wiley

Step 3: Specify the level of significance

We are working with a 5% level of significance so we are accepting that there is a 5% chance of rejecting a true null hypothesis.

Step 4: State the decision rules

This is a two tailed test so we:

Reject H_0 when:
Test statistic < Lower critical value
Test statistic > Upper critical value

Fail to reject H_0 when:
Lower critical value ≤ test statistic ≤ Upper critical value

The critical values for this two tailed z-test at the 5% significance level are $\pm z_{\alpha/2}$. which equals ±1.96. Therefore we:

Reject H_0 when:
Test statistic < –1.96
Test statistic > 1.96

Fail to reject H_0 when:
–1.96 ≤ test statistic ≤ 1.96

Step 5: Calculate the test statistic

$$\text{Test statistic} = \frac{\overline{x} - \mu_0}{s/\sqrt{n}} = (29 - 30)/\left(5/\sqrt{81}\right) = -1.8$$

Step 6: Make a decision regarding the hypothesis

The z-stat of –1.8 lies in the region where we fail to reject the null hypothesis. At the 5% significance level, we fail to reject the claim made by the manufacturer that the average life of its batteries equals 30 hours. The average battery life of the sample is close enough to the advertised battery life.

We could also have used the t-test for this test as the sample size is greater than 30 and the population variance is unknown. If we were to use the t-test the test statistic would be the same and the critical values would be only slightly different. Therefore, the conclusion of the t-test would be the same as that of the z-test.

© 2015 Wiley

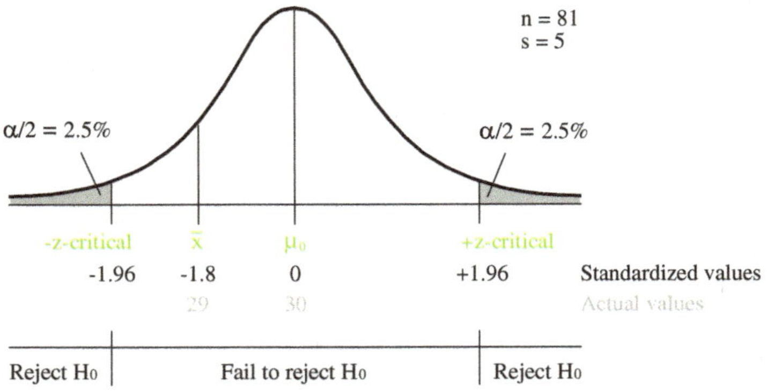

So far, we have been testing hypotheses relating to the mean of a single population. In practice however, we might want to test if there is a difference between the means of two populations.

LOS 11h: Identify the appropriate test statistic and interpret the results for a hypothesis test concerning the equality of the population means of two at least approximately normally distributed populations, based on independent random samples with 1) equal or 2) unequal assumed variances. Vol 1, pp 625–631

Pay careful attention to the wording of the LOS. You are only required to identify the appropriate test-statistic (z-stat, t-stat, chi-square stat or the F-stat) and interpret the results for all the hypothesis tests that follow. Don't be intimidated by the complicated formulas for the t-tests. You do NOT have to know them. Just know which test to apply in each case. Our summary tables should help you identify the appropriate test statistic, and the examples will provide you with an understanding of how to interpret the results of the tests.

Tests Relating to the Mean of Two Populations

- In one type of test we assume that the variance of the two populations is *equal.*
- In the other type of test we assume that the population variances are *unequal.*

Note: Both tests require that the populations are normally distributed and that samples are independent.

Hypotheses describing the tests of means of two populations can be structured as:

- H_0: $\mu_1 - \mu_2 = 0$ versus H_a: $\mu_1 - \mu_2 \neq 0$ when we want to test if the two populations' means are not equal.
- H_0: $\mu_1 - \mu_2 \geq 0$ versus H_a: $\mu_1 - \mu_2 < 0$ when we want to test if the mean of Population 1 is less than the mean of Population 2.
- H_0: $\mu_1 - \mu_2 \leq 0$ versus H_a: $\mu_1 - \mu_2 > 0$ when we want to test if the mean of Population 1 is greater than the mean of Population 2.

© 2015 Wiley

Tests for Means when Population Variances are Assumed Equal

In tests where it is assumed that the variances of the two populations are *equal*, we use the pooled variance (s_p^2) in the calculation of the t-stat. The test statistic, the pooled variance, and the degrees of freedom for the t-test are calculated as follows:

$$t = \frac{(\bar{x}_1 - \bar{x}_2) - (\mu_1 - \mu_2)}{\left(\frac{s_p^2}{n_1} + \frac{s_p^2}{n_2}\right)^{1/2}}$$

Where:

$$s_p^2 = \frac{(n_1 - 1)s_1^2 + (n_2 - 1)s_2^2}{n_1 + n_2 - 2}$$

s_1^2 = variance of the first sample

s_2^2 = variance of the second sample

n_1 = number of observations in first sample

n_2 = number of observations in second sample

degrees of freedom = $n_1 + n_2 - 2$

Both the tests for equality of means of two populations have the difference in sample means in the numerator.

Both are t-tests.

Example 2-2: Tests for Means when Population Variances are Assumed Equal

In this example, we test for the equality of returns on the FTSE across two decades. While there appears to be a substantially higher return during the 1960s, we want to determine if the difference was statistically significant at the 10% level of significance. We will assume that the variances for returns in the two decades are equal.

Decade	Number of Months	Mean Monthly Return (%)	Standard Deviation (%)
1950s	110	0.680	5.598
1960s	110	1.570	5.738

Solution

H_0: $\mu_1 - \mu_2 = 0$ The mean returns across the decades are equal.

H_a: $\mu_1 - \mu_2 \neq 0$ The mean returns across the decades are unequal.

Where:
μ_1 = mean return in the 1950s
μ_2 = mean return in the 1960s

© 2015 Wiley

Since we are testing whether the difference between the means is different from zero, this is a two-tailed test. The critical t-values at the 10% level of significance with 218 (110 + 110 – 2) degrees of freedom are –1.653 and +1.653.

Level of Significance for One-Tailed Test						
df	**0.1**	**0.05**	**0.025**	**0.01**	**0.005**	**0.0005**

Level of Significance for Two-Tailed Test						
df	**0.2**	**0.1**	**0.05**	**0.02**	**0.01**	**0.001**
120	1.289	1.658	1.980	2.358	2.617	3.373
200	1.286	1.653	1.972	2.345	2.601	3.340
∞	1.282	1.645	1.960	2.326	2.576	3.291

- We would fail to reject the null hypothesis if the test statistic falls between –1.653 and +1.653. (–1.653 ≤ t-stat ≤ +1.653)
- We would reject the null if the test statistic lies more 1.653 standard deviations *below* the mean or more than 1.653 standard deviations *above* the mean. Reject if t-stat < –1.653 or t-stat > +1.653.

Since we are assuming that the variances of the two populations are the same, we use the pooled variance to calculate the t-stat.

$$s_p^2 = \frac{(n_1 - 1)s_1^2 + (n_2 - 1)s_2^2}{n_1 + n_2 - 2}$$

$$= \frac{(110-1)(5.598)^2 + (110-1)(5.738)^2}{110+110-2}$$

$$\frac{3415.8 + 3588.79}{218} = \frac{7004.59}{218} = 32.1311$$

$$t = \frac{(\bar{x}_1 - \bar{x}_2) - (\mu_1 - \mu_2)}{\left(\frac{s_p^2}{n_1} + \frac{s_p^2}{n_2}\right)^{1/2}}$$

$$t = \frac{(0.68 - 1.57) - 0}{\left(\frac{32.1311}{110} + \frac{32.1311}{110}\right)^{1/2}}$$

$$t = \frac{-0.89}{0.764} \Rightarrow t = -1.165$$

The t-statistic of –1.165 falls within the range between –1.653 and +1.653. Therefore, we fail to reject the null hypothesis. At the 10% level of significance, we fail to reject the null hypothesis that the mean return on the FTSE was equal during the 1950s and the 1960s.

© 2015 Wiley

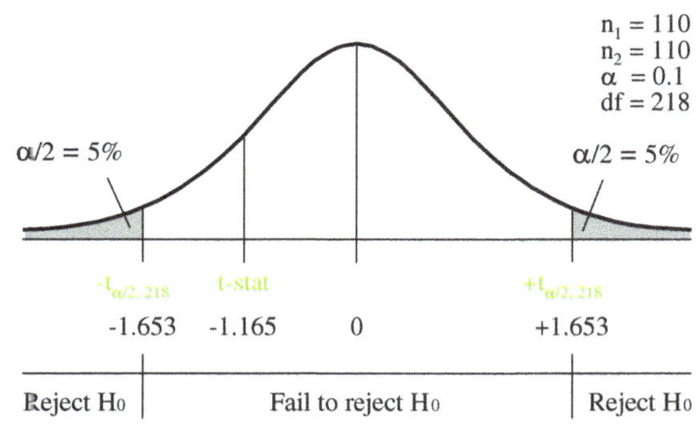

Tests for Means when Population Variances are Assumed Unequal

In hypothesis tests where it is assumed that the variances of the two populations are *unequal*, the test statistic and the degrees of freedom for the t-test are calculated as follows:

$$\text{t-stat} = \frac{(\bar{x}_1 - \bar{x}_2) - (\mu_1 - \mu_2)}{\left(\dfrac{s_1^2}{n_1} + \dfrac{s_2^2}{n_2}\right)^{1/2}}$$

$$df = \frac{\left(\dfrac{s_1^2}{n_1} + \dfrac{s_2^2}{n_2}\right)^2}{\dfrac{(s_1^2/n_1)^2}{n_1} + \dfrac{(s_2^2/n_2)^2}{n_2}}$$

Where:

s_1^2 = variance of the first sample

s_2^2 = variance of the second sample

n_1 = number of observations in first sample

n_2 = number of observations in second sample

Example 2-3: Tests for Means when Population Variances are Assumed Unequal

The table below details the average recovery rates for senior debt holders in financial and pharmaceutical companies in bankruptcy over the last 2 years. We want to know whether there was a difference between the recovery rates for investors in financial sector and pharmaceutical sector debt at the 10% level of significance.

Financial Sector			**Pharmaceutical Sector**		
Number of Observations	Average Price	Standard Deviation	Number of Observations	Average Price	Standard Deviation
31	$74.42	$24.03	74	$65.75	$35.17

© 2015 Wiley

Solution

We assume that the variances of the recovery rates for investors in financial sector and pharmaceutical sector debt are not equal. The data also suggests that the variances are unequal.

H_0: $\mu_1 - \mu_2 = 0$ There were no differences in recovery rates across the two sectors.
H_a: $\mu_1 - \mu_2 \neq 0$ There were differences in recovery rates across the two sectors.

$$\text{t-stat} = \frac{(\bar{x}_1 - \bar{x}_2) - (\mu_1 - \mu_2)}{\left(\frac{s_1^2}{n_1} + \frac{s_2^2}{n_2}\right)^{1/2}}$$

$$s_1^2 = 24.03^2 = 577.44$$
$$s_2^2 = 35.17^2 = 1236.92$$
$$n_1 = 31$$
$$n_2 = 74$$
$$\bar{x}_1 = 74.42$$
$$\bar{x}_2 = 65.75$$

$$t = \frac{(74.42 - 65.75) - (0)}{\left(\frac{577.44}{31} + \frac{1236.92}{74}\right)^{1/2}} = \frac{8.67}{35.3422^{\frac{1}{2}}} = 1.4584$$

$$df = \frac{\left(\frac{s_1^2}{n_1} + \frac{s_2^2}{n_2}\right)^2}{\frac{(s_1^2/n_1)^2}{n_1} + \frac{(s_2^2/n_2)^2}{n_2}}$$

$$df = \frac{\left(\frac{577.44}{31} + \frac{1236.92}{74}\right)^2}{\frac{(577.4/31)^2}{31} + \frac{(1236.92/74)^2}{74}} = \frac{1249.07}{14.9665} = 83.4$$

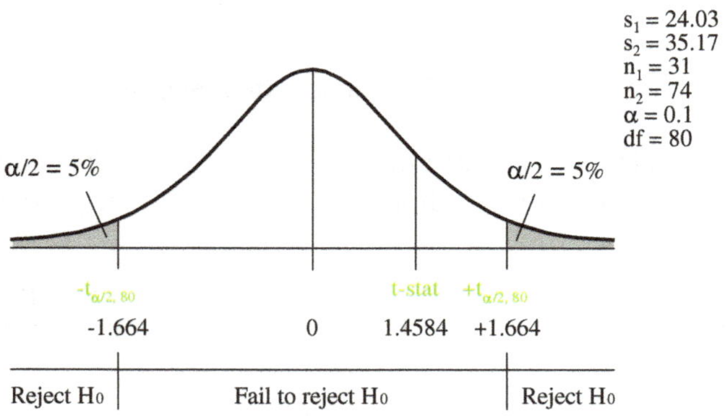

© 2015 Wiley

The closet figure to 83.4 that we find in the t-table is 80. For $\alpha = 0.10$, we find $t_{\alpha/2} = \pm 1.664$ (this is a two-tailed test).

The test statistic (1.4584) is less than the upper critical t-value of +1.664. At the 10% level of significance, we fail to reject the null hypothesis that the mean recovery rates on investments in financial and pharmaceutical sector bonds were equal.

LOS 11i: Identify the appropriate test statistic and interpret the results for a hypothesis test concerning the mean difference of two normally distributed populations. **Vol 1, pp 625–634**

When the samples of the two populations whose means we are comparing are dependent, the paired comparisons test is used. Dependence can result from events that affect both populations. For example, observed returns on two stocks over time are influenced by market and economic conditions. Remember that in order to conduct a paired comparisons test, the populations must be normally distributed. The hypotheses are structured as follows:

$H_0 : \mu_d = \mu_{dz}$
$H_a : \mu_d \neq \mu_{dz}$

Where:
μ_d = mean of the population of paired differences.
μ_{dz} = hypothesized mean of paired differences, which is usually zero.

For the paired comparisons test, the t-stat with n-1 degrees of freedom is computed as:

$$t = \frac{\bar{d} - \mu_{dz}}{s_{\bar{d}}}$$

Where:
$\bar{d}$ = sample mean difference = $\frac{1}{n}\sum_{i=1}^{n} d_i$

d_i = difference between the *i*th pair of observations

$s_{\bar{d}}$ = standard error of the sample mean difference = $\frac{s_d}{\sqrt{n}}$

$$s_d = \text{sample standard deviation} = \left[\frac{\sum_{i=1}^{n}(d_i - \bar{d})^2}{n-1}\right]^{1/2}$$

n = the number of paired observations

Example 2-4: Paired Comparisons Test

A researcher is trying to ascertain whether there is a difference in the annual returns on two investment strategies. Specifically, he is analyzing the return on a buy-and-hold strategy on the FTSE versus the return on the top ten dividend yielding stocks on the FTSE over the last 40 years. Determine whether the returns on the two strategies are different at the 1% level of significance.

Strategy	Mean Return	Standard Deviation
Buy and hold entire FTSE	17.66%	19.50%
Top 10 dividend yielding stocks on FTSE	14.71%	15.54%
Difference	2.95%	6.71% (sample standard deviation of differences)

Solution

The paired comparisons test must be used because both the populations that we are studying (various stocks listed on the FTSE) are influenced by economic conditions in the UK, and are therefore, not independent.

$H_0 : \mu_d = 0$
$H_a : \mu_d \neq 0$

The test-statistic is calculated as follows:

$$t = \frac{\bar{d} - \mu_{dz}}{s_{\bar{d}}}$$

$$t = \frac{2.95}{6.71 / \sqrt{40}}$$

$$t = 2.78054$$

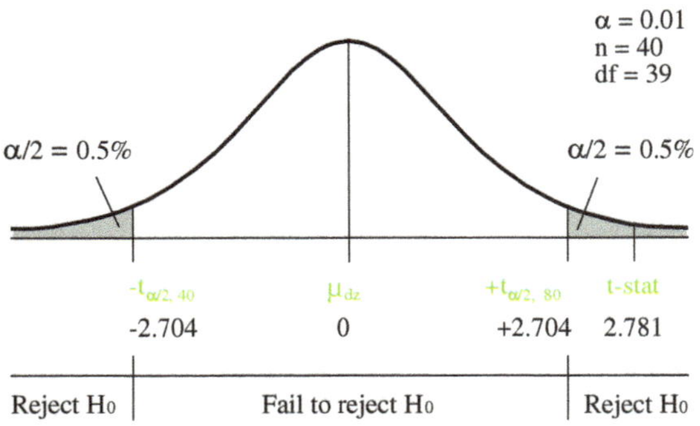

This is a two-tailed test. The critical t-values with 39 degrees of freedom at a 1% significance level are –2.704 and +2.704. Our calculated test statistic (2.78) lies above the upper critical value. Therefore, at the 1% level of significance we reject the null hypothesis of no difference, and conclude that there is a statistically significant difference in the returns on the two strategies over the last 40 years.

© 2015 Wiley

The table given below summarizes the important concepts that you should bear in mind from the examination perspective. We highly doubt that any question testing the ability of financial analysts would entail memorizing the complicated formulas above and performing tedious calculations. However, questions related to recognizing the test appropriate to verify the hypotheses, the test statistic, and drawing conclusions given the critical values and the test statistic are fair game.

Hypothesis tests concerning the mean of two populations.

Population Distribution	Relationship Between Samples	Assumption Regarding Variance	Type of Test
Normal	Independent	Equal	t-test pooled variance
Normal	Independent	Unequal	t-test with variance not pooled
Normal	Dependent	N/A	t-test with paired comparisons

LESSON 3: HYPOTHESIS TESTS CONCERNING THE VARIANCE AND NONPARAMETRIC INFERENCE

LOS 11j: Identify the appropriate test statistic and interpret the results for a hypothesis test concerning 1) the variance of a normally distributed population. Vol 1, pp 634–636

So far in this reading we have been testing hypotheses relating to means. Sometimes we may need to perform tests on the variance of normally distributed populations. We use σ^2 to represent the population variance and σ_0^2 to denote the hypothesized value of the population variance.

Tests relating to the variance of normally distributed populations can be one-tailed or two-tailed:

One-tailed tests:

$H_0 : \sigma^2 \leq \sigma_0^2$ versus $H_a : \sigma^2 > \sigma_0^2$	When testing whether the population variance is greater than the hypothesized variance
$H_0 : \sigma^2 \geq \sigma_0^2$ versus $H_a : \sigma^2 < \sigma_0^2$	When testing whether the population variance is lower than the hypothesized variance

Two-tailed tests:

$H_0 : \sigma^2 = \sigma_0^2$ versus $H_a : \sigma^2 \neq \sigma_0^2$	When testing whether the population variance is different from the hypothesized variance

Hypothesis tests for testing the variance of a normally distributed population involve the use of the chi-square distribution, where the test statistic is denoted as χ^2. Three important features of the chi-square distribution are:

- It is asymmetrical.
- It is bounded by zero. Chi-square values cannot be negative.
- It approaches the normal distribution in shape as the degrees of freedom increase.

To understand how to read the chi-square table, consider a two-tailed chi-square test with 20 degrees of freedom at the 5% significance level. As shown in Table 3-1, the critical chi-square values are 9.591 (lower bound) and 34.170 (upper bound). Chi-square values correspond to the probabilities in the right tail of the distribution. A two-tailed chi-square test at the 5% significance level requires a 2.5% probability in each tail. The upper tail of 34.17 is calculated as the critical value (assuming 20 degrees of freedom) that has 2.5% probability to its right. The lower bound of 9.591 is calculated as the critical value that has a 97.5% probability to its right (which effectively means 2.5% to its left).

Table 3-1: Chi-Square Table Extract

df	0.99	0.975	0.95	0.9	0.1	0.05	0.025	0.01	0.005
19	7.633	8.907	10.117	11.651	27.204	30.144	32.852	36.191	38.582
20	8.260	9.591	10.851	12.443	28.412	31.410	34.170	37.566	39.997
21	8.897	10.283	11.591	13.240	29.615	32.671	35.479	38.932	41.401
22	9.542	10.982	12.338	14.041	30.813	33.924	36.781	40.289	42.796
23	10.196	11.689	13.091	14.848	32.007	35.172	38.076	41.638	44.181
24	10.856	12.401	13.848	15.659	33.196	36.415	39.364	42.980	45.559
25	11.524	13.120	14.611	16.473	34.382	37.652	40.646	44.314	46.928

Figure 2-2: Example Chi-Square Test

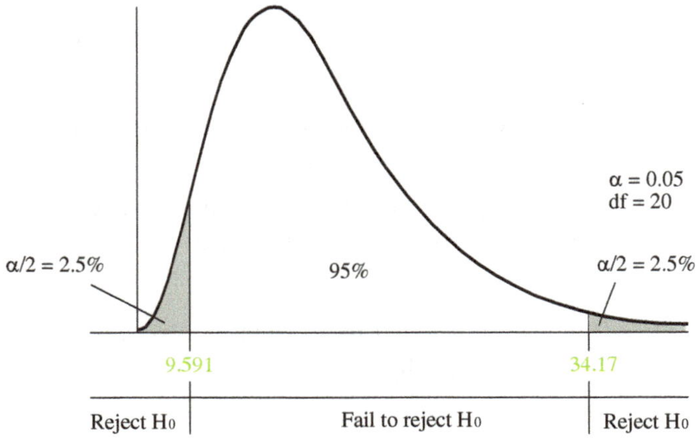

© 2015 Wiley

The chi-square test statistic is calculated as:

$$\chi^2 = \frac{(n-1)s^2}{\sigma_0^2}$$

Where:
n = sample size
s^2 = sample variance
σ_0^2 = hypothesized value for population variance

A chi-square test simply involves comparing the test statistic to the critical chi-square values given the level of significance and the degrees of freedom.

Example 3-1: Hypothesis Test Concerning the Variance of a Normally Distributed Population

Test the accuracy of a claim made by ZX Associates that the investment strategies they follow result in standard deviation of monthly returns of 5%. Use the 5% level of significance. ZX performance data for the last 25 months has a standard deviation of 5.2%.

Solution

We are testing whether the variance of returns is different from 0.0025, the hypothesized variance.

$H_0 : \sigma^2 = 0.0025$
$H_a : \sigma^2 \neq 0.0025$

Degrees of freedom = 25 – 1 = 24

The critical chi-square values at the 5% significance level with 24 degrees of freedom for a two-tailed test are 12.401 and 39.364.

The chi-square test statistic is calculated as:

$$\chi^2 = \frac{(n-1)s^2}{\sigma_0^2}$$

$$\chi^2 = \frac{(25-1)(0.052^2)}{0.05^2} = \chi^2 = 25.96$$

Conclusion: The chi-square test statistic (25.96) falls within the range between the critical values (12.401 to 39.364). Therefore, we fail to reject the null hypothesis that the standard deviation of returns on ZX's strategy equals 5%. The 25-month sample's standard deviation is close enough to the advertised standard deviation of 5% at the 5% level of significance.

© 2015 Wiley

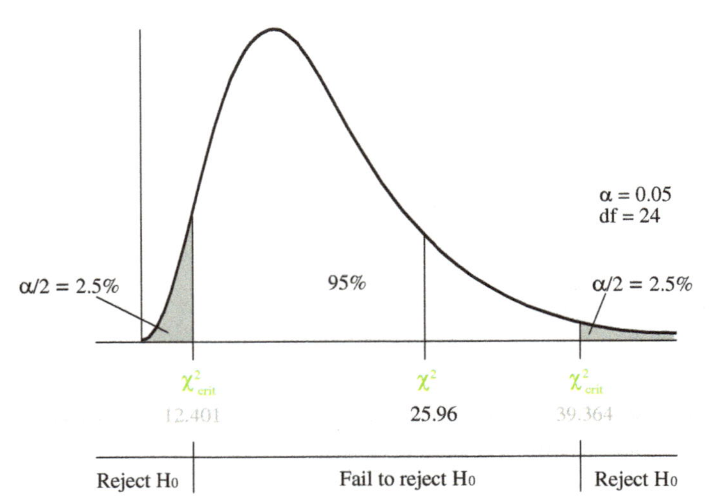

LOS 11j: Identify the appropriate test statistic and interpret the results for a hypothesis test concerning 2) the equality of the variances of two normally distributed populations, based on two independent random samples.
Vol 1, pp 636–637

Hypotheses related to the equality of the variance of two populations are tested with an F-test. This test is used under the assumptions that:

- The populations from which samples are drawn are normally distributed.
- The samples are independent.

Hypothesis tests concerning the variance of two populations can be structured as one-tailed or two-tailed tests:

One-tailed tests:

$$H_0 : \sigma_1^2 \leq \sigma_2^2 \text{ versus } H_a : \sigma_1^2 > \sigma_2^2$$
$$H_0 : \sigma_1^2 \geq \sigma_2^2 \text{ versus } H_a : \sigma_1^2 < \sigma_2^2$$

Two-tailed tests:

$$H_0 : \sigma_1^2 = \sigma_2^2 \text{ versus } H_a : \sigma_1^2 \neq \sigma_2^2$$

Where:

σ_1^2 = variance of Population 1

σ_2^2 = variance of Population 2

© 2015 Wiley

The test statistic for the F-test is given by:

$$F = \frac{s_1^2}{s_2^2}$$

Where:
s_1^2 = Variance of sample drawn from Population 1
s_2^2 = Variance of sample drawn from Population 2

Note: Always put the larger variance in the numerator when calculating the F-test statistic. Also note that the F-stat is simply the ratio of the two samples' variances.

Features of the F-distribution:

- It is skewed to the right.
- It is bounded by zero on the left.
- It is defined by two separate degrees of freedom.

The rejection region for an F-test, whether it be one-tailed or two-tailed, always lies in the right tail. This unique feature makes the F-test different from all the other hypothesis tests that we have performed.

Example 3-2: Hypothesis Test for Equality of Variances

Susan is examining the earnings of two companies. She is of the opinion that the earnings of Company A are more volatile than those of Company B. She obtains earnings data for the past 31 years for Company A, and for the past 41 years for Company B. She finds that the sample standard deviation of Company A's earnings is $4.40 and that of Company B's earnings is $3.90. Determine whether the earnings of Company A have a greater standard deviation than those of Company B at the 5% level of significance.

Solution

$H_0 : \sigma_A^2 \le \sigma_B^2$ = The statement that we are trying to reject.
$H_a : \sigma_A^2 > \sigma_B^2$ = The statement that we are trying to validate (i.e., the variance of Company A's earnings is greater).

σ_A^2 = variance of Company A's earnings.
σ_B^2 = variance of Company B's earnings.

Note: $\sigma_A^2 > \sigma_B^2$. In calculating the F-test statistic, we always put the greater variance in the numerator.

$$df_A = 31 - 1 = 30$$
$$df_B = 41 - 1 = 40$$

The critical value from F-table equals 1.74. We will reject the null hypothesis if the F-stat is greater than 1.74.

© 2015 Wiley

Table 2-2: F-Table Extract

	24	**30**	**40**
30	1.89	1.84	1.79
40	1.79	1.74	1.69
60	1.70	1.65	1.59

Degrees of freedom for the numerator are along the top row in bold, and degrees of freedom for the denominator are along the left most column in bold

Calculation of F-test statistic

$$F = \frac{s_A^2}{s_B^2} = \frac{4.40^2}{3.90^2}$$

$$F = 1.273$$

The F-statistic (1.273) is not greater than the critical value (1.74). Therefore, at the 5% significance level we fail to reject the null hypothesis.

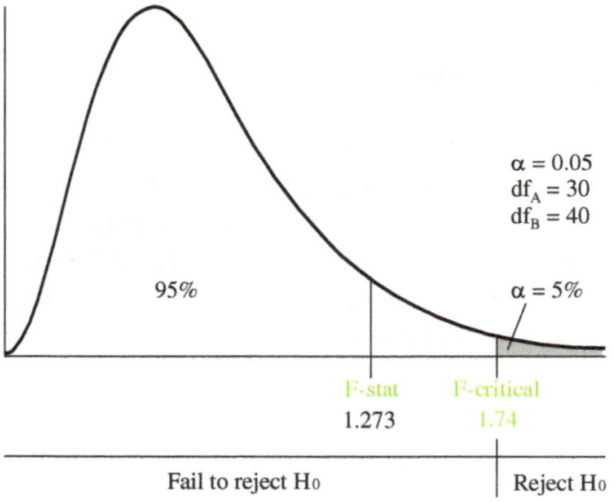

Hypothesis tests concerning the variance.

Hypothesis Test Concerning	Appropriate Test Statistic
Variance of a single, normally distributed population	Chi-square stat
Equality of variance of two independent, normally distributed populations	F-stat

© 2015 Wiley

LOS 11k: Distinguish between parametric and nonparametric tests and describe the situations in which the use of nonparametric tests may be appropriate. Vol 1, pp 637–642

A parametric test has at least one of the following two characteristics:

- It is concerned with parameters, or defining features of a distribution.
- It makes a definite set of assumptions.

The hypothesis tests that we have conducted in this reading were all parametric tests because we used the mean and variance (population parameters) to define the normal distribution. Further, we also assumed that the populations followed a normal distribution.

A non-parametric test is not concerned with a parameter, and makes only a minimal set of assumptions regarding the population. Non-parametric tests are used when:

- The researcher is concerned about quantities other than the parameters of the distribution.
- The assumptions made by parametric tests cannot be supported.
- When the data available is ranked (ordinal measurement scale). For example, non-parametric methods are widely used for studying populations such as movie reviews, which receive one to five stars based on people's preferences.

The Spearman rank correlation coefficient is a non-parametric test that is calculated based on the ranks of two variables within their respective data sets. It lies between –1 and +1 where –1 (+1) denotes a perfectly inverse (positive) relationship between the ranks of the two variables, and 0 represents no correlation.

Often the results of parametric and non-parametric tests are both presented. This allows the reader to gauge how sensitive the conclusions are to the assumptions underlying the parametric tests. If the assumptions made under the parametric test are met, the use of parametric tests is preferred because they usually offer more crisp and reliable conclusions.

Table 3-3 lists examples of non-parametric alternatives to the parametric tests we have discussed earlier.

Table 3-3: Nonparametric Alternatives to Parametric Tests[1]

	Parametric	Nonparametric
Tests concerning a single mean	*t*-test *z*-test	Wilcoxon signed-rank test
Tests concerning differences between means	*t*-test Approximate *t*-test	Mann-Whitney U test
Tests concerning mean differences (paired comparisons tests)	*t*-test	Wilcoxon signed-rank test Sign test

1 - Table 9, p 610, Vol 1, CFA Program Curriculum 2014

© 2015 Wiley

Reading 12: Technical Analysis

LESSON 1: TECHNICAL ANALYSIS: DEFINITION AND SCOPE

LOS 12a: Explain principles of technical analysis, its applications, and its underlying assumptions. Vol 1, pp 660–664

Technical analysis is a security analysis technique that involves the examination of past market trends (using data such as prices and trading volumes) to predict the future behavior of the overall market and of individual securities. It can be thought of as the study of collective investor sentiment. Technical analysis can be used in any global freely traded market (i.e., a market where buyers and sellers can trade without any external interference).

Technical analysis does not require an in depth knowledge of the security being analyzed, and can therefore be performed relatively quickly, while fundamental analysis usually takes longer. Further, technical analysis can be applied to identify short-term and long-term trends. Fundamental analysis is more time consuming so most investors with short time horizons focus on technical analysis.

Technical analysis is based on the following:

- Supply and demand determine prices in real time.
- Changes in supply and demand cause changes in prices.
- Prices can be projected with charts and other technical tools.

Principles and Assumptions

Fundamental analysts assert that markets are efficient and rational, but technicians believe that people often behave in an irrational and emotional manner, and tend to behave similarly in similar circumstances. Technicians suggest that market trends and patterns reflect irrational human behavior. Therefore, technicians study trends in the market, which they believe repeat themselves, to predict the future direction of security prices.

> Fundamental analysts with long time frames often perform technical analysis to time the purchase and sale of the securities they have analyzed.

Technicians believe that the market reflects collective investor knowledge and sentiment. They rely on price and volume information from the market itself to understand investor sentiment and to make investment decisions.

While some financial instruments (e.g., stocks and bonds) have associated income streams (e.g., dividends and coupon payments), which can be used to determine their intrinsic values, others (including commodities and currencies) do not have underlying financial statements or associated income streams. Technical analysis is the only tool available to investors to forecast future prices for these asset classes.

Technicians believe that security price movements occur before fundamental developments occur or are reported. An important tenet of technical analysis is that the equity market moves roughly six months ahead of crucial turning points in the broader economy.

Technical Versus Fundamental Analysis

Technical analysis uses only trading data, which includes market price and volume information. Fundamental analysis uses external information (e.g., financial reports, industry and macroeconomic analysis) and also incorporates social and political variables.

© 2015 Wiley

The data used by technical analysts is more concrete and reliable. The financial statements used by fundamental analysts are subject to manipulation by management.

Fundamental analysis is more conceptual as it aims to determine the theoretical long-term (intrinsic) value of a security. Technical analysis is more practical as it studies actual trading patterns to evaluate the market price of a security. Stated differently, fundamental analysts aim to forecast where a security *should* trade, while technicians focus on predicting the level at which it *will* trade.

Technical analysis has been in use for a longer period in investment decision-making. Fundamental analysis is a relatively new field.

Drawbacks of Technical Analysis

Technicians only study market movements and trends, which can change without warning. Further, it may take some time for a clear, identifiable trend to emerge. Technicians can therefore make incorrect investing decisions and can be late in identifying changes in trends.

Fundamental analysts demand an understanding of factors that will drive a company's performance going forward. Technicians expect trends to repeat themselves so a change in investor psychology may be missed by them.

Application of technical analysis is limited in markets that are subject to significant outside manipulation (markets that are not freely traded) and in illiquid markets (where even a modest trade may have a relatively significant price impact).

LESSON 2: TECHNICAL ANALYSIS TOOLS: CHARTS, TREND AND CHART PATTERNS

LOS 12b: Describe the construction of different types of technical analysis charts and interpret them. **Vol 1, pp 664–673**

Charts and indicators are the primary tools used in technical analysis.

Charts

Charts are used to illustrate historical price information, which is used by technicians to infer future price behavior. A wide variety of charts are used in technical analysis. The choice of charts is governed by the purpose of the analysis.

Line Charts

A line chart (see Figure 2-1) is a simple graphical display of prices over time. Usually the chart plots closing prices as data points, and has a line connecting these points. Time is plotted on the horizontal axis and prices are plotted on the vertical axis. Line charts provide a broad overview of investor sentiment, and the information they provide can be analyzed quickly.

© 2015 Wiley

Figure 2-1: Line Chart

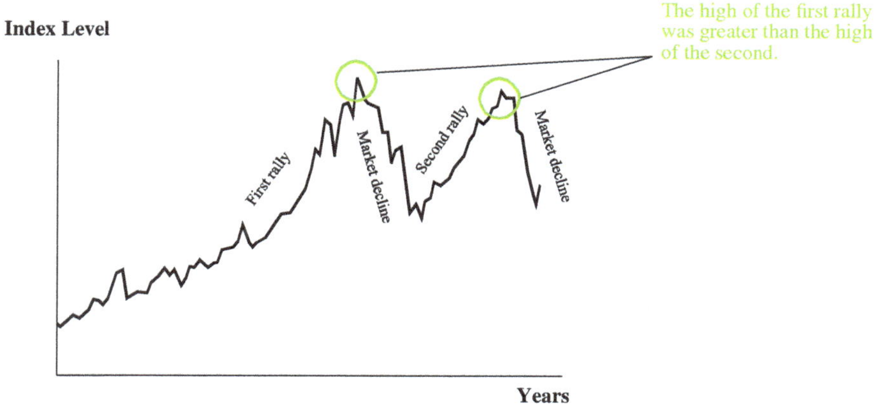

Bar Charts

While a line chart has one data point for each value of the horizontal axis (time), a bar chart presents four pieces of information—opening price, highest and lowest prices, and the closing price for each time interval (see Figure 2-2). Bar charts enable an analyst to get a better sense of the nature of trading during the period. A short bar indicates low price volatility, while a longer bar indicates high price volatility.

For each time interval, the top of the line shows the highest price, while the bottom of the line shows the lowest price. The cross-hatch to the left indicates the opening price, while the cross-hatch to the right indicates the closing price. (See Figure 2-3.)

Figure 2-2: Bar Chart Notation

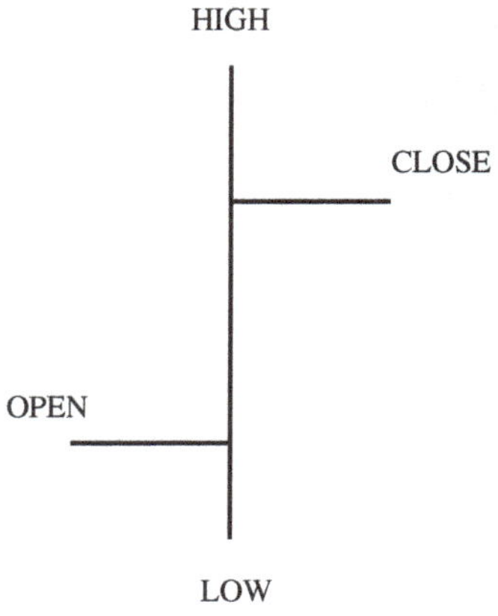

Figure 2-3: Bar Chart

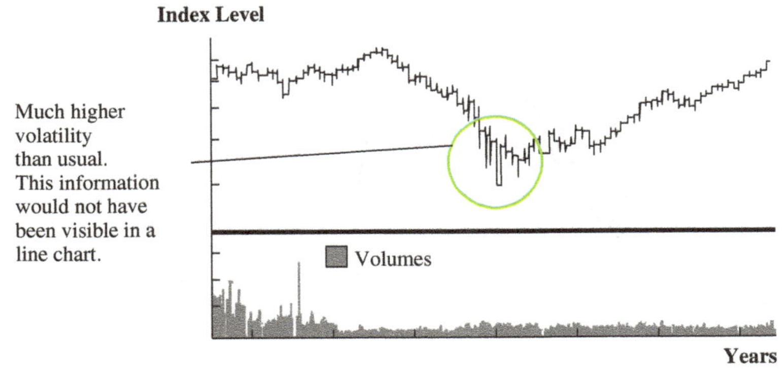

Candlestick Charts

A candlestick chart provides the same information as a bar chart (i.e., opening and closing prices, and highs and lows during the period). Further, it also clearly illustrates whether the market closed up or down. The body of the candle is shaded if the closing price was lower than the opening price, and the body is clear if the closing price was higher than the opening price. (See Figures 2-4 and 2-5.)

Figure 2-4: Construction of a Candlestick Chart

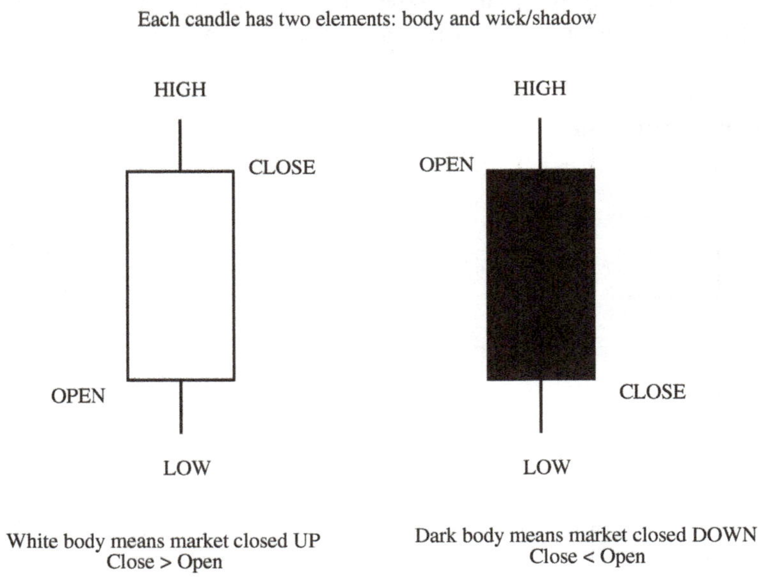

© 2015 Wiley

Figure 2-5: Candlestick Chart

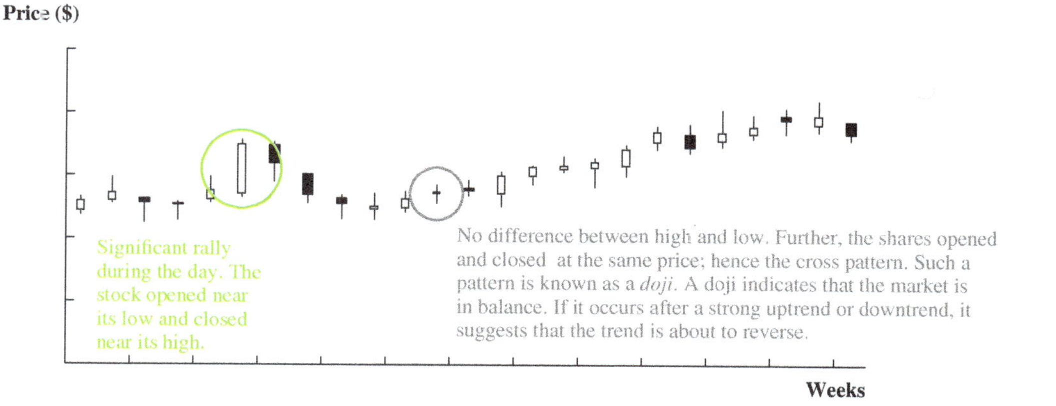

Point and Figure Chart

To construct a point and figure chart, a box size and a reversal size must first be determined. The box size refers to the minimum change in price that will be represented by a box on the chart, while the reversal size determines when a new column will be created on the chart. The reversal size is typically a multiple of the box size. A reversal size of three means that an analyst will move to the next column when the price reverses, or changes direction by three or more boxes. The vertical axis measures discrete movements in price.

To construct the chart, an "X" is plotted for an increase in price, while an "O" is plotted for a decrease in price. For example, assume that the box size is $1 and the reversal size is $3. If the price rises by $1 on the first day, the analyst puts an X. On the next day, if the price increases by $2 the analyst plots 2 further Xs on top of the X already plotted. On the third day, if the price rises by $0.50, nothing is plotted on the chart (as the price change is lower than the box size). The analyst will continue to mark Xs in the same column whenever the price increases by more than $1 on a given trading day until a reversal occurs. A reversal would occur in this case when the price falls by $3 or more. When a reversal occurs the analyst would move over to the next column and start marking Os. The first box to be filled with an O would be the one to the right and below the highest X in the previous column. (See Figure 2-6.)

The point of having a multi-box reversal size is to ignore the short-term price volatility or noise that does not alter the long-term price trend.

Box and figure charts are useful as they highlight the prices at which trends change (when the columns change), as well as price levels at which the security most frequently trades (congestion areas). Long, sustained price movements are represented by long columns of Xs and Os.

Figure 2-6: Point and Figure Chart

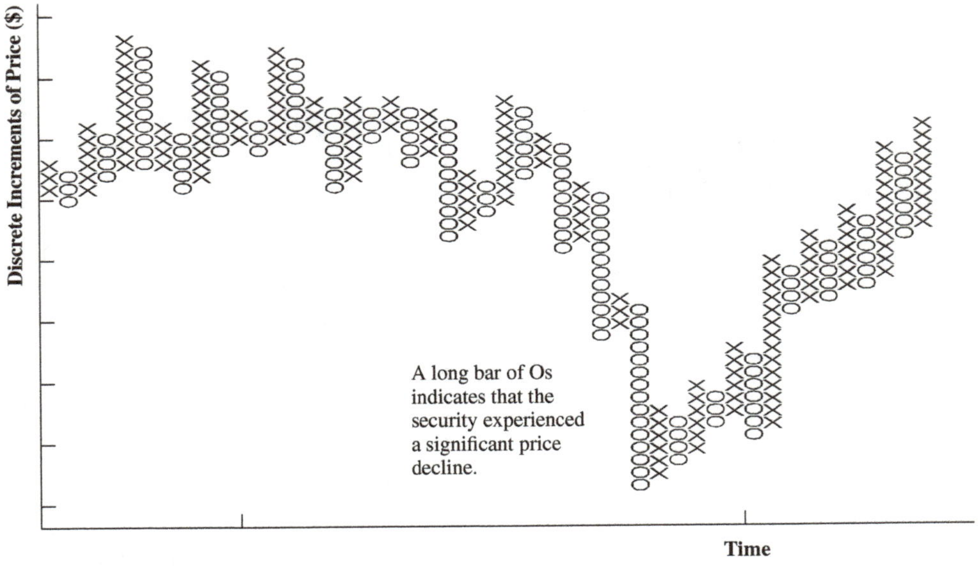

Scale

The vertical axis on any of the charts that we have already discussed can be constructed with a linear (arithmetic) scale or a logarithmic scale. A linear scale is more appropriate when the data fluctuate within a narrow range (see Figure 2-7). In a logarithmic scale, percentage changes are plotted on the vertical axis. They are more appropriate when the range of data is larger (see Figure 2-8). Time is plotted on the horizontal axis. The length of the time period depends on the underlying data and the purpose of the chart. Active traders typically prefer shorter time intervals.

Figure 2-7: Linear Scale[1]

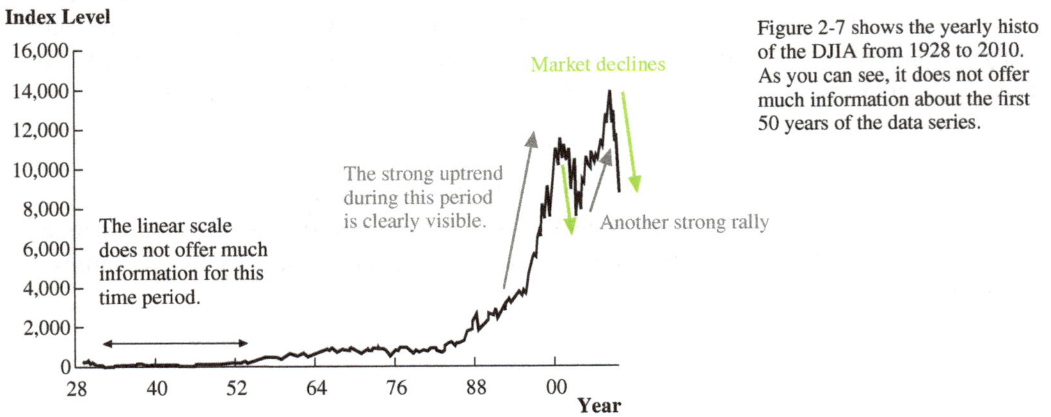

1 - Exhibit 7, Volume 1, CFA Program Curriculum 2014

© 2015 Wiley

Figure 2-8: Logarithmic Scale[2]

Figure 2-8 shows the yearly history of the DJIA over the same period shown in Figure 2-7. In this figure the Great Depression of the 1930's clearly stands out, but over the next 75 years the data follow a relatively stable upward trend.

Volume

Volume is used by technicians as a barometer of the strength of a trend. Volume-related information is typically included at the bottom of most charts (see Figure 2-9).

If a security's price is increasing with increasing volumes, it shows that more and more investors are purchasing the stock at higher prices. This indicates that the trend is expected to continue as the two indicators "confirm" each other.

If a security's price is rising with declining volumes (the two indicators are diverging), it suggests that the trend is losing momentum as fewer investors are willing to buy at higher prices.

Figure 2-9: Daily Price Chart and Volume Bar Chart

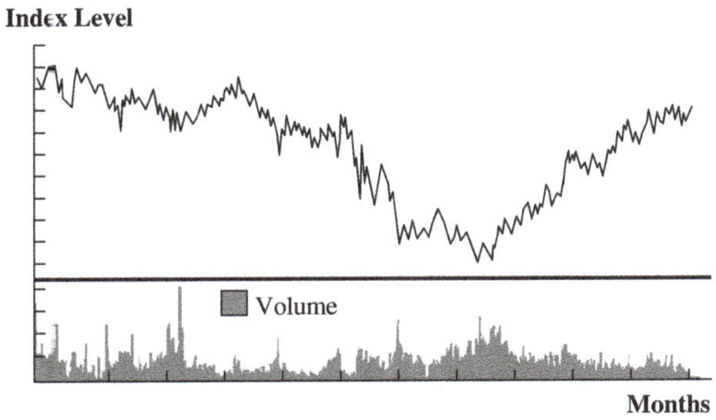

2 - Exhibit 8, Volume 1, CFA Program Curriculum 2014

© 2015 Wiley

Time Intervals

Charts can be constructed using any time interval. The decision regarding which interval to use varies across the nature of trading—short-term investors may create charts with intervals less than a minute long, while longer-term investors may use charts with intervals as long as one year.

Relative Strength Analysis

Relative strength analysis is used to evaluate the relative performance of a security compared to a stated benchmark by plotting the ratio of the security's price to the benchmark index over time. An upward-sloping line indicates outperformance, while a downward-sloping line suggests underperformance. (See Figure 2-10.)

Figure 2-10: Relative Strength Analysis: Stock X and Y vs. Benchmark Index

The units on the vertical axis are not significant; the ratio is a function of the relative prices of the assets under consideration. The important information is how the ratio has changed.

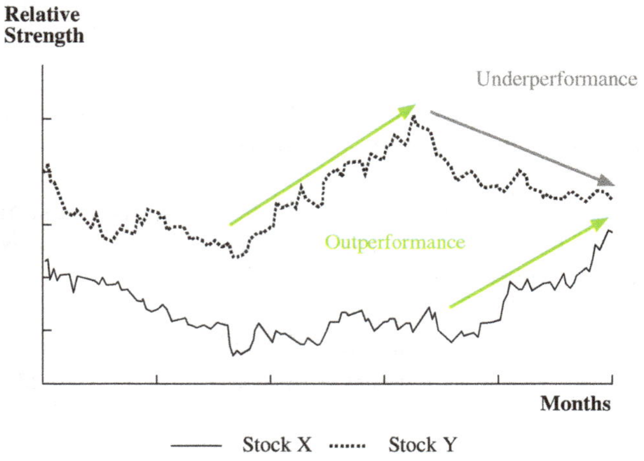

LOS 12c: Explain uses of trend, support, resistance lines, and change in polarity. Vol 1, pp 673–675

Trend analysis assumes that investors tend to behave in herds and that trends usually continue for an extended period of time. Stock price data may show an uptrend, a downtrend, a sideways trend, or in some cases no trend at all.

An uptrend occurs when a security's price makes higher highs and higher lows. Higher highs occur when each high lies above the previous high, and when the price declines (there is a retracement) each subsequent low is higher than the prior low. To illustrate an uptrend, the technician connects all the lows on the price chart with a straight line. Major retracements (that drag the security's price significantly below the trend line) indicate that the uptrend is over and that the price may decline further.

In terms of demand and supply, during an uptrend, there are more ready buyers for a security than there are sellers and traders are willing to pay a higher price for the security over time.

A downtrend is indicated by lower highs and lower lows on the price chart. A technician connects all the highs on the chart to illustrate the downtrend. Major breakouts above the trend line may indicate that the downtrend is over and that the security's price could rise further.

© 2015 Wiley

In a downtrend, sellers are willing to accept lower and lower prices for the security, which indicates negative investor sentiment regarding the asset. (See Figure 2-11.)

In some cases, a security may trade within a narrow range. During such a sideways trend, there is a relative balance between demand and supply. Typically, options positions are more profitable than long or short positions on the security itself during a sideways trend.

Figure 2-11: Trend Analysis

Trend analysis involves the use of support and resistance levels. A support level is defined as the price at which there is sufficient buying interest in the stock to arrest the price decline. At this level, investors believe that the security is an attractive investment despite the recent price decline. (See Figure 2-12.) On the other hand, a resistance level is the price at which enough selling activity is generated to prevent any further increase in price. At the resistance level, investors believe that the security is overpriced. Support and resistance levels may be horizontal or sloped lines.

> The psychology behind the concepts of support and resistance is that investors have come to a collective consensus about the price of a security.

The change in polarity principle (a key tenet of trend analysis) asserts that once the price rises above the resistance level, it becomes the new support level. Similarly, once the price falls below a support level, it becomes the new resistance level.

Figure 2-12: Support Level

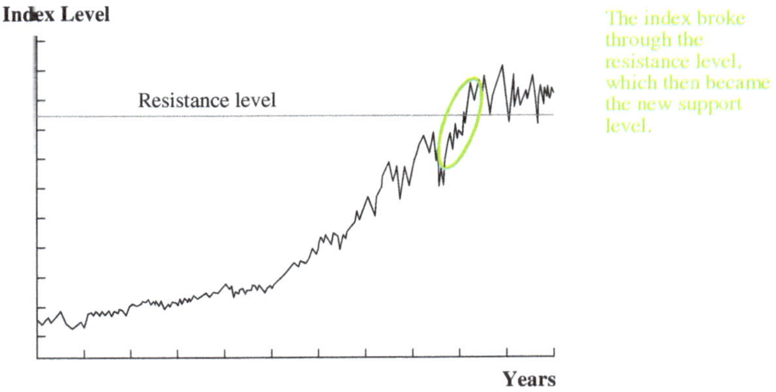

LOS 12d: Identify and interpret common chart patterns. Vol 1, pp 676–687

Chart patterns are formations on price charts that look like recognizable shapes. Recurring chart patterns can be used to predict future prices because these patterns essentially represent collective investor sentiment over a given time period. Chart patterns may be categorized as reversal patterns or continuation patterns.

Reversal Patterns

As the name suggests, reversal patterns indicate the end of a prevailing trend.

> The most important concept to understand in using chart patterns is that without a clear trend in place prior to the pattern, the pattern has no predictive value. This aspect is frequently forgotten by investors who are so eager to identify and use patterns that they forget the proper application of charts.

Head and Shoulders

A head and shoulders pattern, see Figure 2-13, follows an uptrend in the price of a security. It is composed of three parts:

Left shoulder: The left shoulder consists of a strong rally with high volumes, with an upward trend that has a slope that is steeper than that of the preceding uptrend. The rally then reverts to the same price that it started from, creating an inverted "V."

Head: The price starts to rise again, and this time records a higher high than the one reached in the left shoulder. However, volumes in this rally are lower. The price then again falls to the level that the head started from (the same level at which the left shoulder began and ended). This price level is called the **neckline**.

Right shoulder: The right shoulder is similar to the left shoulder, but with lower volumes. The price rises almost to the same level as the high of the "left shoulder," but remains lower than the high reached during the "head."

While the formation on the price chart may not always be perfect, the head should clearly be above the two shoulders, both of which should be similar. Note that the neckline may not always be a perfectly horizontal line.

Volume is very important in analyzing head and shoulders patterns. The fact that the high of the "head" is higher than the "high" of the left shoulder, but has lower volumes, indicates that investor interest is waning. When one indicator is bullish (rising price) while another is bearish (lower volumes) it is known as a **divergence**.

Once a head and shoulders pattern has formed, prices are expected to decline (the uptrend that preceded the head and shoulders pattern is expected to reverse). Technicians use filtering rules to ensure that the neckline has been breached. An example of such a filter is the price declining to a level 3–5% below the neckline. Once the price falls below the neckline (which previously acted as a support level), it becomes the new resistance level (change in polarity principle).

© 2015 Wiley

Figure 2-13: Head and Shoulders Pattern

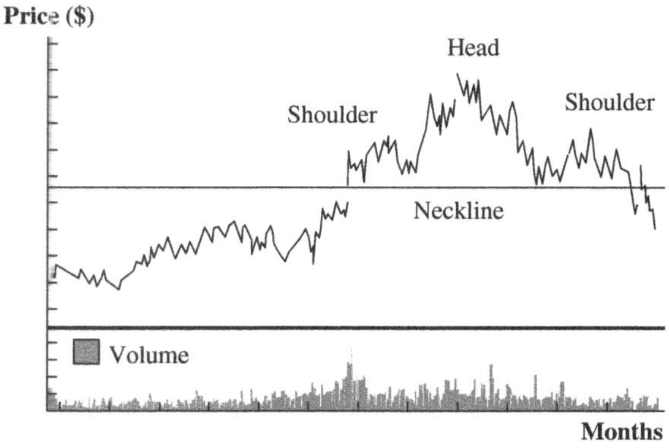

Inverse Head and Shoulders

A downtrend in prices precedes an inverse head and shoulders pattern. The price characteristics of each of the three segments of the head and shoulders pattern are reversed in an inverse head and shoulders pattern, but the volume characteristics are the same. For example, in the left shoulder, the slope of the price decline is greater (more negative) than that of the preceding downtrend, but volumes are heavier. Then the rally reverses (with lower volumes) toward where it originated, and forms a "V."

Setting Price Targets with Head and Shoulders Patterns

Once the neckline has been breached in the head and shoulders pattern, the price is expected to decline by an amount equal to the distance between the top of the head and the neckline. An investor can benefit from this expected reversal by shorting the security once the price falls below the neckline and then repurchasing it (closing the position) at the (lower) target price. As shown in Figure 2-14, the price target is calculated as:

$$\text{Price target} = \text{Neckline} - (\text{Head} - \text{Neckline})$$

Typically, the stronger the rally preceding the head and shoulders pattern, the more pronounced the expected reversal.

Figure 2-14: Calculating Price Target

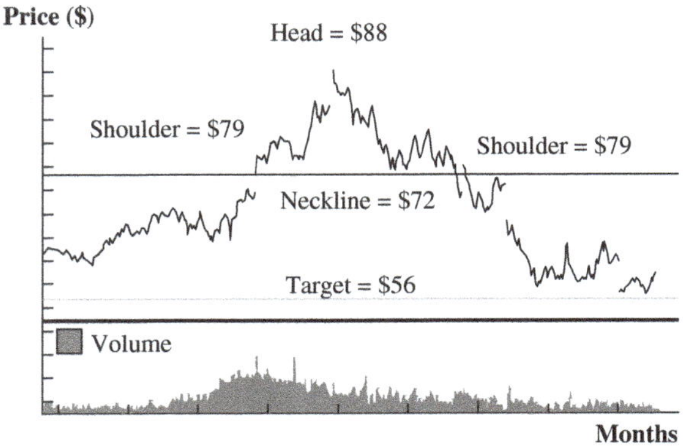

© 2015 Wiley

Setting Price Targets for Inverse Head and Shoulders Patterns

Inverse head and shoulders patterns are preceded by a downtrend. Therefore, prices are expected to rise or break out above the neckline after the right shoulder has been formed. (See Figure 2-15.)

Price target = Neckline + (Neckline – Head)

Figure 2-15: Calculating Price Target for Inverse Head and Shoulders Pattern

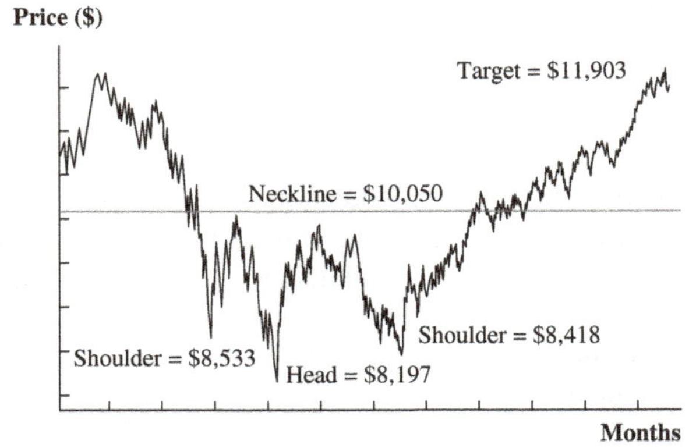

Double Tops and Bottoms

A double top occurs when an uptrend in prices reverses twice at approximately the same price level (two highs are recorded at roughly the same level). Usually, the first top has a higher volume.

For a double top, the price target (where the reversal will end) is established at a level that is lower than the valley (the low recorded between the two tops) by an amount that equals the distance between the tops and the valley.

The more significant the sell-off after the first top (deeper the valley) and the longer the time period between the two tops, the more significant the formation is considered to be.

A double bottom indicates the reversal of a downtrend. It occurs when, following a recent downtrend, prices fall to a certain level, rise for a bit, then fall back to the same level and rise again. (See Figure 2-16.)

For double bottoms, the price is expected to rise above the peak between the two bottoms by approximately an amount equal to the distance between the bottoms and the peak.

© 2015 Wiley

Figure 2-16: Double-Bottom Pattern

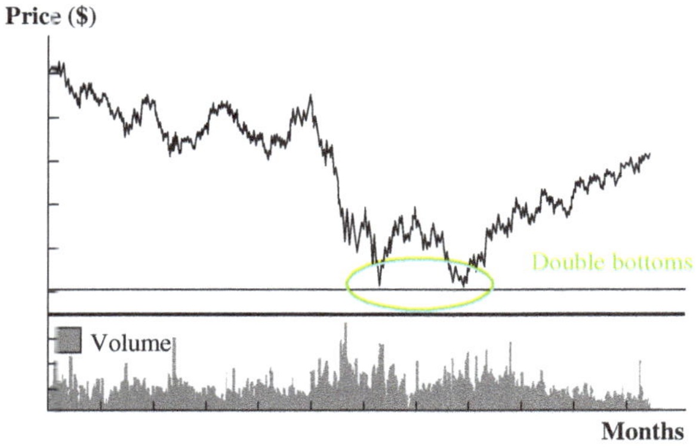

Double tops and bottoms are significant because they indicate that at a particular price level, investors are ready to step up and reverse the prevailing trend. For example, with a double bottom, the suggestion is that price declines have been arrested at a similar level on two different occasions, indicating that market consensus is that the price is low enough for the security to be an attractive investment.

Triple Tops and Bottoms

A triple top consists of three peaks at roughly the same level (see Figure 2-17), while a triple bottom occurs when three troughs are formed at roughly the same price level. Triple tops and bottoms are rare, but when they occur, they indicate more significant reversals than double tops and double bottoms. Generally speaking, the greater the number of times the price reverses at a given price level, and the longer the period over which the pattern is formed, the more significant the expected reversal.

Figure 2-17: Triple-Top Pattern

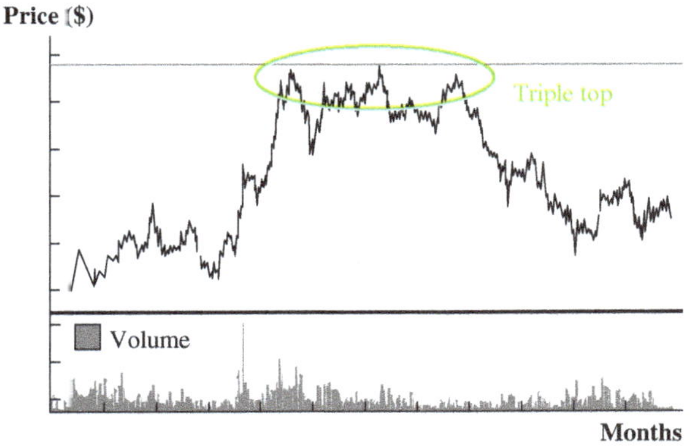

© 2015 Wiley

Continuation Patterns

A continuation pattern is used to confirm the resumption of the current market trend. Also known as "healthy market corrections," these patterns suggest that the current price trend will continue as ownership of securities changes from one group of investors to another. In an uptrend for example, while one group of investors is looking to exit, another stands ready to take a long position on the asset at approximately the same price level.

Triangle Patterns

A triangle pattern is formed when the range between highs and lows over a period narrows down on the price chart. The line connecting the highs over the period eventually meets the line connecting the lows, forming a triangle.

An ascending triangle is formed when the trend line connecting the highs is horizontal while the trend line connecting the lows is upward sloping (see Figure 2-18). Ascending triangles formed during an uptrend indicate that investors are selling the stock at a particular price level, but buyers are willing to purchase the stock at higher and higher prices following any sign of a sell-off. Eventually the share price is expected to rise.

Figure 2-18: Ascending Triangle

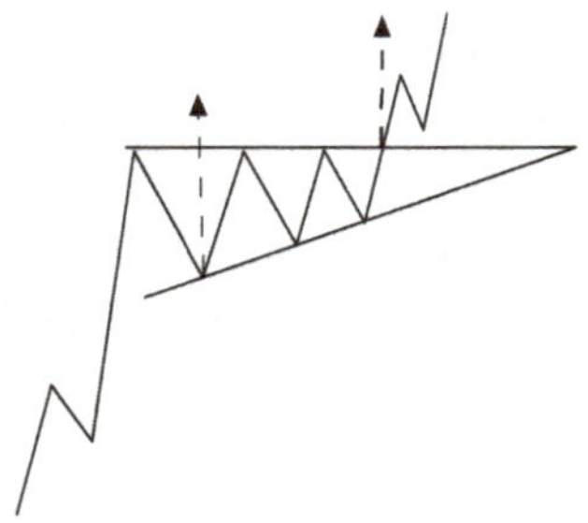

A descending triangle on the other hand, suggests that the stock price will continue to decline. The line connecting the highs is downward-sloping, while the line connecting the lows is horizontal. (See Figure 2-19.)

Figure 2-19: Descending Triangle

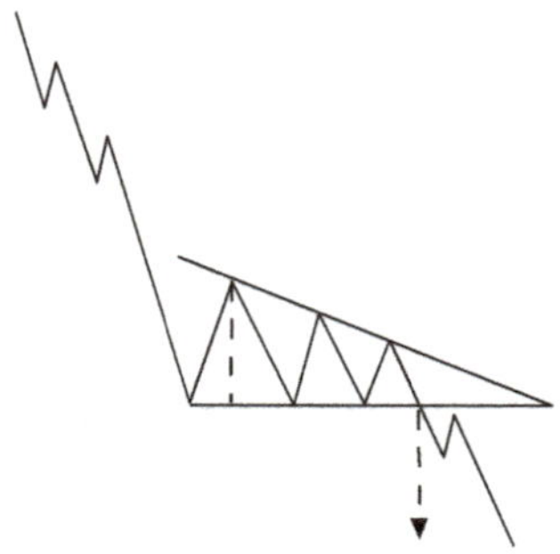

© 2015 Wiley

In a symmetrical triangle, the line connecting the highs is downward-sloping, while the line connecting the lows is upward sloping. The resulting triangle is somewhat symmetrical. (See Figure 2-20.) Such a formation suggests that buyers are becoming more bullish as they continue to buy at higher prices than before, but sellers are becoming increasingly bearish as they sell at successively lower prices. After these little skirmishes between buyers and sellers are over, the trend ends up in the same direction as the trend that preceded the triangle formation.

Figure 2-20: Symmetrical Triangle

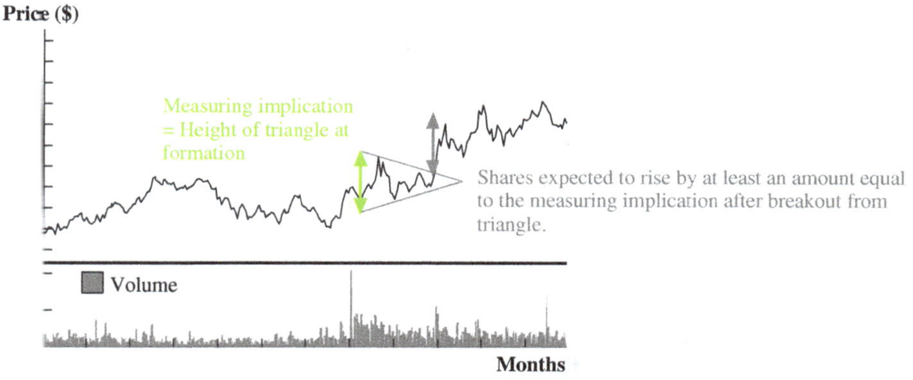

The height of the triangle (also known as **measuring implication**) equals the distance between the two trend lines at the start of the formation. Once the price breaks through one of the trend lines, analysts expect the price to move further by roughly the measuring implication. Usually, the breakout from the triangle occurs between halfway and three-fourths of the way into the pattern; not at the end of the pattern. The longer the triangle pattern, the more significant and volatile the subsequent price movement is expected to be.

Rectangle Patterns

When the two trend lines (one that connects the highs and the other that connects the lows) are both horizontal, a rectangle pattern is formed (see Figure 2-21). Once a breakout occurs, the trend in prices is the same as the trend that preceded the rectangle formation.

For example, in a bullish market, the rectangle pattern shows that investors are booking profits at the resistance level, but re-entering the stock at the support level. Once the price breaks out above the rectangle, it will continue to rise.

Figure 2-21: Rectangle Patterns

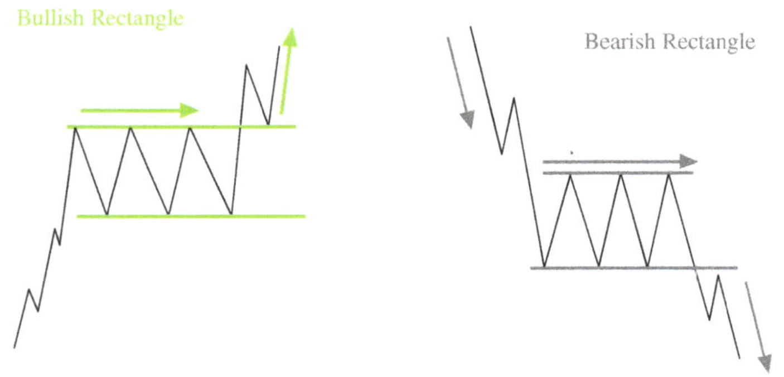

© 2015 Wiley

Flags and Pennants

Flags and pennants form over a much shorter time interval (usually on a daily price chart over a week) compared to triangles and rectangle patterns. A flag is formed when two trend lines are parallel to each other (similar to country flags or parallelograms). Typically, the slope of the trend lines is opposite to that of the prevailing trend. For example, in an uptrend, the trend lines comprising the flag slope down.

A pennant (see Figure 2-22) is basically a triangle that is formed over a relatively short span of time (typically over a week).

For both flags and pennants, the expectation is that the trend that preceded the formation will continue after the pattern. The breakout beyond the trend line is expected to roughly equal the distance between the start of the trend and the flag or the pennant.

Figure 2-22: Pennant Formation

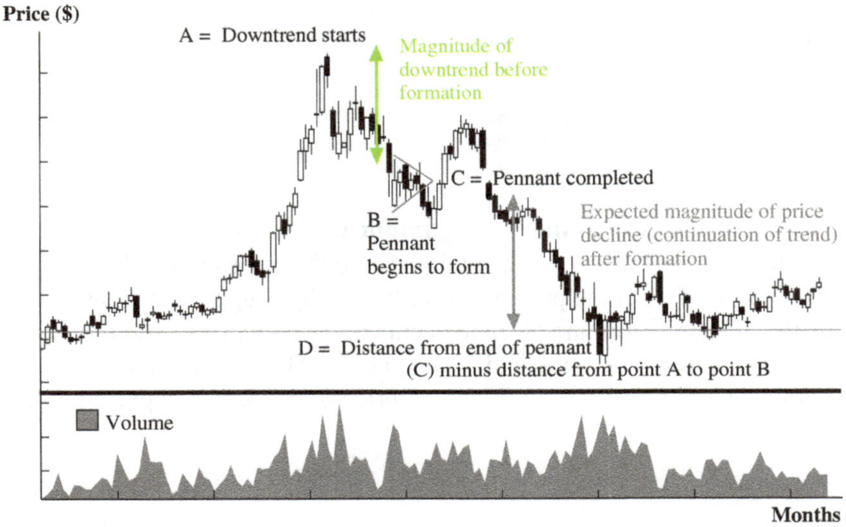

LESSON 3: TECHNICAL ANALYSIS TOOLS: TECHNICAL INDICATORS AND CYCLES

LOS 12e: Describe common technical analysis indicators: price-based, momentum oscillators, sentiment, and flow of funds. Vol 1, pp 687–704

Price-Based Indicators

Price-based technical indicators incorporate current and historical market price information.

Moving Average

A moving average is the average of the closing price over a given number of periods. Moving averages smooth out short-term price fluctuations and therefore, give a clearer picture of a market trend.

- A simple moving average uses the arithmetic mean, weighing each price equally in computing the average.

© 2015 Wiley

- An exponential moving average attaches a greater weight to recent prices in computing the average.

Applications of Moving Averages

- Generally, a stock that is in a downtrend tends to trade below its moving average, while one in an upward trend will typically trade above its moving average.
- Moving average trend lines can also act as support or resistance levels. When the stock price starts falling toward its moving average, investors might purchase the stock believing that it is approaching its support level.
- When the short-term moving average intersects the long-term moving average from below, the formation is referred to as a *golden cross* and is a bullish sign. On the other hand, when the short-term moving average intersects the long-term moving average from above, it forms a *dead cross* which is a bearish signal. (See Figure 3-1.)

Figure 3-1: Moving Averages

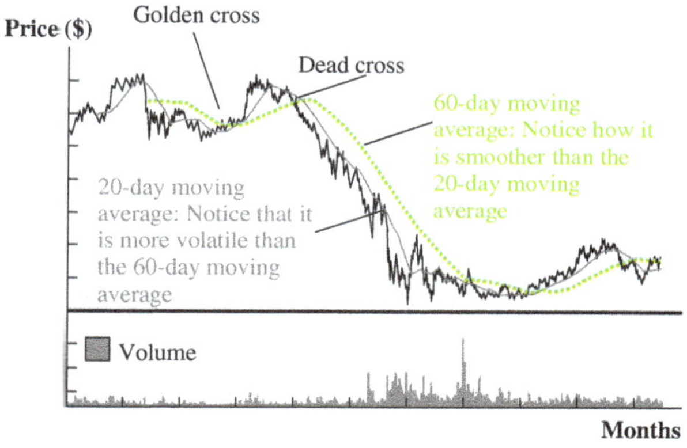

Bollinger Bands

Bollinger bands consist of a simple moving average plus upper and lower bands that are calculated by adding and subtracting a specific number of standard deviations from the moving average.

Applications of Bollinger Bands

- A contrarian technical strategy based on Bollinger bands aims to sell the security when it reaches the upper band and purchase the security when it touches the lower band. The assumption here is that the security will continue to trade within the bands.
- A long-term investor may purchase the security once it has broken out significantly above the upper band, or short the security once it has fallen significantly below the lower band.

© 2015 Wiley

Figure 3-2: Bollinger Bands

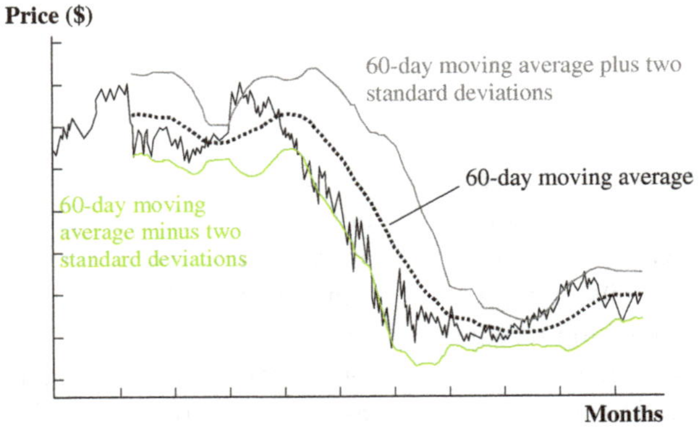

Momentum Oscillators

Momentum oscillators are used to identify changes in market sentiment. They are calculated in such a manner that they either fluctuate within a range (usually between 0 and 100) or hover around a number (such as 0 or 100). It is easy to identify extreme highs and lows on oscillators, and these extremes indicate that market buying/selling activity is more aggressive than historical levels.

Technicians focus on whether oscillators and price data are moving in the same direction (convergence) or in different directions (divergence). For example, when the price forms a new low, but the momentum oscillator is not at its lowest, the formation is a divergence. It implies that the downtrend is weakening and is expected to end soon.

Applications of Momentum Oscillators

- The oscillator range for a security can be used to determine the strength of a trend. Oversold conditions suggest that bearish market sentiment will end soon, while overbought conditions signal that the bullish market sentiment may soon change.
- They may signal a trend reversal when they reach historical highs or lows.
- They can be used to make short-term trading decisions in nontrending markets.

Momentum or Rate of Change Oscillator

A momentum oscillator [rate of change (ROC) oscillator] is calculated as follows:

$$M = (V - Vx) \times 100$$

where:
M = momentum oscillator value
V = last closing price
Vx = closing price x days ago, typically 10 days

© 2015 Wiley

When the momentum oscillator value crosses zero into positive territory in an uptrend (when prices are also rising), it is a bullish signal. When it crosses zero into negative territory in a downtrend (when prices are falling), it is a bearish signal. Crossovers that occur in the opposite direction of the trend are ignored because technicians who use oscillators first consider the general trend when making trading decisions.

The base value for an oscillator can also be set at 100. In this case, the oscillator is calculated as:

$$M = \frac{V}{Vx} \times 100$$

Relative Strength Index

A relative strength index (RSI) compares a security's gains with its losses over a given time period (see Figure 3-3). The 14-day RSI is the most popular one, but longer-term investors will usually use a longer time period.

The RSI is calculated using the following formula:

$$RSI = 100 - \frac{100}{1 + RS}$$

$$\text{where } RS = \frac{\Sigma(\text{Up changes for the period under consideration})}{\Sigma(|\text{ Down changes for the period under consideration }|)}$$

The RSI lies between the 0 and 100. A value above 70 typically represents an overbought situation, while a value below 30 usually indicates an oversold situation. However, bear in mind that less volatile stocks may trade in a narrower range. Further, the RSI range for any stock does not need to be symmetrical around 50.

Figure 3-3: Relative Strength Index (RSI)[3]

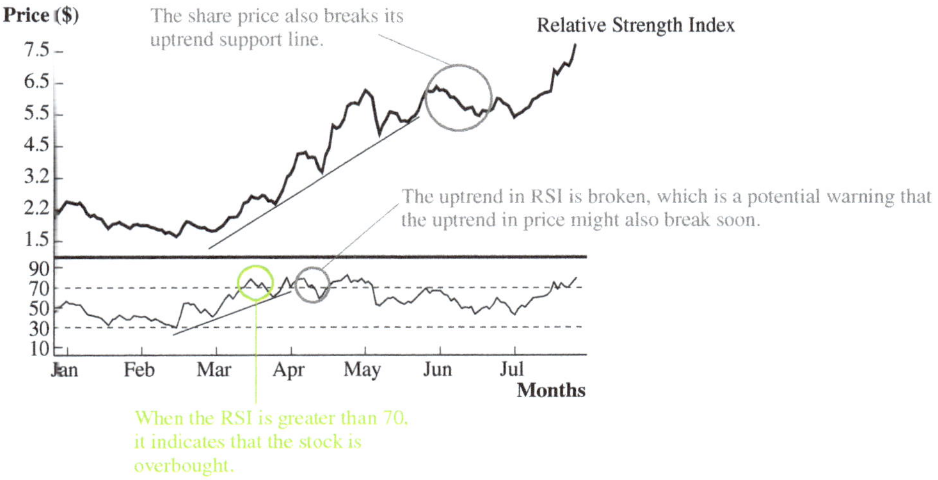

3 - Exhibit 27, Volume 1, CFA Program Curriculum 2014

© 2015 Wiley

Stochastic Oscillator

A stochastic oscillator is based on the assumption that in an uptrend, the stock price tends to close near the high of its recent range, while in a downtrend it tends to close around its recent low (see Figure 3-4). The underlying logic is that if the stock price rises during the day, but loses value near the close, the rally is not very strong, as selling pressure eventually negates the buying interest. On the other hand, if the stock price rises during the day and manages to hold on to most of its gains at the close, the signal is bullish.

The stochastic oscillator lies between 0 and 100 and is usually calculated using 14-day price data. It is composed of two lines, %K and %D, which are calculated as:

$$\%K = 100\left(\frac{C - L14}{H14 - L14}\right)$$

where:
C = last closing price
L14 = lowest price in last 14 days
H14 = highest price in last 14 days

%D (signal line) = Average of the last three %K values calculated daily.

The stochastic oscillator should be used with other technical tools, such as trend analysis or pattern analysis. If both methods suggest the same conclusion, the trader has convergence (or confirmation), but if they give conflicting signals, the trader has divergence, which is a warning signal suggesting that further analysis is necessary.

Applications of Stochastic Oscillators

- Generally speaking, when the stochastic oscillator is greater than 80, it usually indicates that the security is overbought and should be sold. A value lower than 20 indicates that the security is oversold and should be purchased. However, analysts should consider the absolute level of the two lines in light of their historical range.
- Crossovers between the two lines can also give trading signals similar to crossovers of moving average lines. When the %K (smoothed line) crosses %D from below, it is a short-term bullish signal, and if it crosses %D from above, it is a bearish signal.

Figure 3-4: Stochastic Oscillator[4]

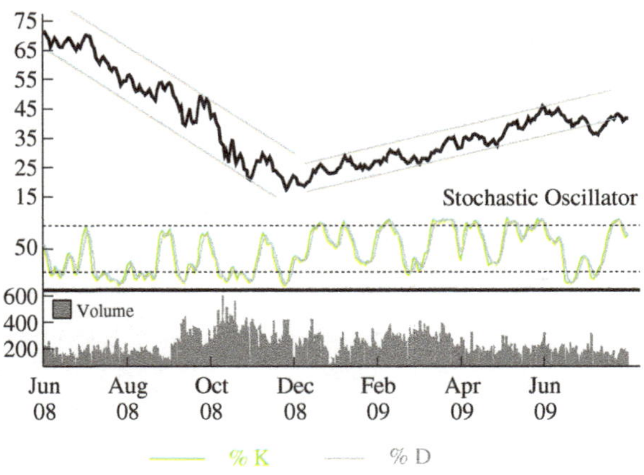

This figure provides a weekly price chart and a stochastic oscillator. Note that during the downtrend on the left side of the chart the stochastic oscillator often moved below 20. Each time it reached 80, however, it provided a valid sell signal. When the downtrend ended and an uptrend began, the stochastic oscillator was regularly above 80, but each time the %K line moved above %D, a valid buy signal was given.

4 - Exhibit 28, Volume 1, CFA Program Curriculum 2014

© 2015 Wiley

Moving Average Convergence/Divergence Oscillator

The moving average convergence/divergence oscillator (MACD) is the difference between the short-term and long-term moving average of a security's price. The MACD is composed of two lines:

- The MACD line, which is the difference between two exponentially smoothed moving average lines (typically over 12 and 26 days).
- The signal line, which is the exponentially smoothed moving average of the MACD line, (typically over 9 days).

The MACD is compared with its historical levels to determine whether market sentiment regarding the security is different from what it usually is. The indicator itself moves around 0 and has no limits. (See Figure 3-5.)

Applications of the MACD Oscillator

- Crossovers of the MACD line and the signal line may indicate a change in trend (similar to crossovers of moving averages and the stochastic oscillator).
- When MACD line moves outside its historical range, it indicates a weakening in the current trend.
- Convergence (which suggests that the trend will continue) occurs when the MACD and price move in the same direction, while divergence (which suggests that the trend will reverse) occurs when the MACD and price move in opposite directions.

Figure 3-5: MACD[5]

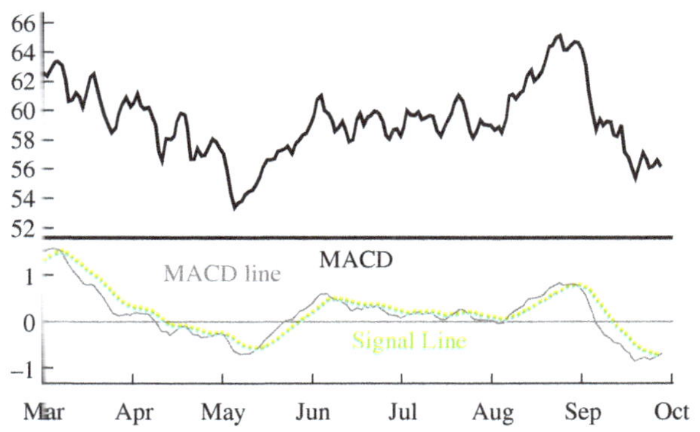

This figure shows a daily price chart with the MACD oscillator.

Notice the convergence in May when both the price and oscillator bottomed out, which provided confirmation of a change in trend. This change was further confirmed with the MACD line crossing the signal line.

A bearish signal was given in September with the change in trend of both price and oscillator and the crossover of the signal line by the MACD line. The fact that the MACD oscillator was moving up to a level that was unusually high for this stock would have been an early warning signal in September.

Sentiment Indicators

Sentiment indicators evaluate investor activity looking for signs of bullishness or bearishness.

Opinion Polls

A number of companies conduct regular polls of investors and investment professionals to gauge market sentiment. Technicians compare the data (which is also presented graphically) with recent market highs, lows, and inflection points to establish relationships that might be useful in predicting future market direction.

5 - Exhibit 29, Volume 1, CFA Program Curriculum 2014

© 2015 Wiley

Calculated Statistical Indices

- Investors who purchase put options are bearish, while those who buy call options are bullish. The **put/call ratio** is calculated as the volume of put options traded divided by the volume of call options traded. A high put-call ratio indicates that the market is bearish, while a low ratio suggests that the market is bullish.
- The **CBOE Volatility Index (VIX)** measures short-term market volatility and is calculated from the prices of options on stocks in the S&P 500. The VIX rises when the market fears a market decline.
- Studies have shown that **margin debt levels** (loans taken by individual investors to fund stock purchases) are very strongly correlated with the movement in the market. For example, margin debt reached its peak in the summer of 2007 (when the market recorded a recent high as well). Margin debt declined sharply in the second half of 2008 when the subprime crisis hit the market.
- Short interest refers to the number of shares sold short for a particular security. The **short interest ratio** is calculated as:

$$\text{Short interest ratio} = \frac{\text{Short interest}}{\text{Average daily trading volume}}$$

This indicator may be interpreted in two ways. A high ratio may suggest that:

- There is overall a negative outlook on the security and one should expect the price to decline.
- The effect of short sales has already been factored into the current market price. When these short sellers cover their positions, the price of the stock will rise.

Flow of Funds Indicators

Technicians also look at the potential demand and supply for securities in making trading decisions.

Arms Index

Also called the short-term trading index (TRIN), the Arms index is a common flow of funds indicator that looks at how much money is flowing into, and out of leading stocks.

$$\text{Arms Index} = \frac{\text{Number of advancing issues / Number of declining issues}}{\text{Volume of advancing issues / Volume of declining issues}}$$

When the market is in balance, the Arms index is close to 1. Values above 1 indicate that there is more activity in declining stocks, and that the market is in a selling mood. Values below 1 indicate that there is more activity in advancing stocks and that market sentiment is currently bullish.

© 2015 Wiley

Margin Debt

Margin loans may increase stock purchases, while declining margin balances may force the selling of stocks.

Mutual Fund Cash Positions

Mutual funds typically hold a proportion of their portfolios in the form of cash to fund redemptions and to pay for miscellaneous expenses. Contrarian technicians believe that low mutual funds cash positions mean that mutual funds have already invested in the market, while high cash positions show that mutual funds are relatively liquid, and security prices will rise once they enter the market. Therefore, contrarians buy when mutual funds' cash positions are high and sell when their cash positions are low. The average cash percentage of mutual funds has historically hovered around 6.8%.

New Equity Issuance

Issuers of new securities try to time the offer such that it coincides with a period during which investor appetite for new issues is high and when the market is bullish so that they can obtain premium prices. Premium prices occur near market peaks. Therefore, when the new equity issuance indicator is high, the market is usually near its peak and is likely to decline in the future.

Secondary Offerings

Technicians also observe secondary offerings of shares. While these offerings do not increase the number of shares outstanding, they do increase the number of shares available for trading (the free float). Therefore, secondary offerings affect the supply of shares just like IPOs.

LOS 12f: Explain how technical analysts use cycles. **Vol 1, pp 704–705**

Cycles

Over time, technicians have observed recurring cycles in the markets, only some of which can be logically explained. By identifying different cycles, technicians look to predict the market's future direction.

Kondratieff Waves

Nikolai Kondratieff suggested that economies went through a 54-year economic cycle. His theory was mainly derived from economic cycles and commodity prices, but similar cycles have also been seen in equity prices during the time of his work.

18-Year Cycle

The 18-year cycle is usually mentioned in real estate markets though it can also be observed in equities and other markets.

© 2015 Wiley

Decennial Pattern

The decennial pattern traces the average annual stock returns (based on the DJIA) according to the last digit of the year. The DJIA has historically performed poorly in years ending with a 0, while the best ones have been years that end with a 5.

Presidential Cycle

Historically, it has been observed that the third year (of the four-year U.S. Presidential term) boasts the best stock market performance. The stock market has done reasonably well in the fourth year as well. One explanation for this is that politicians up for re-election inject stimuli into the economy to increase their popularity.

LESSON 4: ELLIOT WAVE THEORY AND INTERMARKET ANALYSIS

LOS 12g: Describe the key tenets of Elliott Wave Theory and the importance of Fibonacci numbers. Vol 1, pp 705–708

Elliott Wave Theory

In 1938, R. N. Elliott proposed that the market moves in regular cycles or waves. In a bull market, the market moves up in five waves (called **impulse waves**) in the following pattern: 1 = up, 2 = down, 3 = up, 4 = down, and 5 = up. The impulse wave is followed by a corrective wave that has three components: a = down, b = up, and c = down. The same pattern is reversed in a bear market. (See Figure 4-1.)

The Fibonacci Sequence starts with the numbers 0, 1, 1, and then each subsequent number in the sequence is the sum of the two preceding numbers: 0, 1, 1, 2, 3, 5, 8, 13, ...

Elliott also proposed that each wave can be broken into smaller waves. Starting with the largest "grand supercycle," which takes place over centuries, waves can be broken down into supercycles, cycles, and subcycles which take place over shorter and shorter intervals.

Elliott discovered that market waves followed patterns that were ratios of numbers in a **Fibonacci Sequence**. Positive price movements would take prices up by a factor equal to the ratio of a Fibonacci number to its preceding number, while negative price movements would reverse prices by a factor of a Fibonacci number to the next number. He also described the characteristics of each wave.

Figure 4-1: Impulse Waves and Corrective Waves

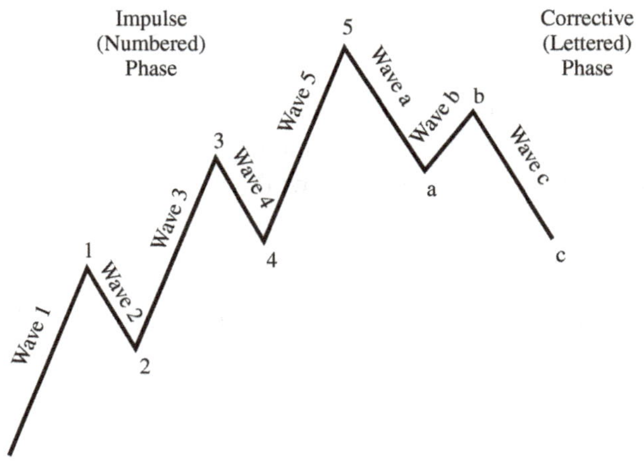

© 2015 Wiley

Elliott Wave Theory is used along with Dow Theory, trend analysis, pattern analysis, and oscillator analysis to forecast market movements. Its biggest advantage is that it can be applied in short-term trading as well as long-term economic analysis.

LOS 12h: Describe intermarket analysis as it relates to technical analysis and asset allocation. Vol 1, pp 708–710

Intermarket Analysis

Intermarket analysis refers to the technique of combining analysis of different markets to identify trends and reversals of trends. It is based on the principle that markets for different categories of securities (stocks, bonds, currencies, commodities, etc.) are interrelated and influence each other, and asserts that these relationships are strengthening with increasing globalization. Some of the relationships that have been observed between different asset classes are:

- Stock prices and bond prices tend to move in the same direction. Therefore, rising bond prices are a positive for stocks.
- Declining bond prices are a signal of commodity prices possibly rising.
- A strong dollar usually results in lower commodity prices. (See Figure 4-2.)

Technicians often use relative strength analysis to identify **inflection points** in a particular market and then look for a change in trend in a related market.

Figure 4-2: Relative Strength of 10-Year T-Bonds vs. S&P 500[6]

6 - Exhibit 35, Volume 1, CFA Program Curriculum 2014

© 2015 Wiley

Figure 4-3: S&P 500 Index vs. Commodity Prices

Given technical observations regarding the business cycle at any time, relative strength analysis can be used to identify potentially lucrative investments from within the equity market. For example, sectors like utilities and financials tend to perform well during the beginning of an economic cycle, while retailers and consumer durables do well once an economic recovery is well underway.

Intermarket analysis can also be used to identify which countries one should invest in. Countries like Australia, Canada, and South Africa are driven by commodity markets, while others like India and China are primarily reliant on exports, which are driven by GDP growth in the rest of the world.

© 2015 Wiley